WOMEN, PEACE AND WELFARE

A suppressed history of social reform,
1880–1920

Ann Oakley

First published in Great Britain in 2018 by

Policy Press
University of Bristol
1-9 Old Park Hill
Bristol
BS2 8BB
UK
t: +44 (0)117 954 5940
pp-info@bristol.ac.uk
www.policypress.co.uk

North America office:
Policy Press
c/o The University of Chicago Press
1427 East 60th Street
Chicago, IL 60637, USA
t: +1 773 702 7700
f: +1 773 702 9756
sales@press.uchicago.edu
www.press.uchicago.edu

© Policy Press 2018

British Library Cataloguing in Publication Data
A catalogue record for this book is available from the British Library.

Library of Congress Cataloging-in-Publication Data
A catalog record for this book has been requested.

ISBN 978-1-4473-3256-5 hardcover
ISBN 978-1-4473-3260-2 ePub
ISBN 978-1-4473-3261-9 Mobi
ISBN 978-1-4473-3259-6 ePdf

The right of Ann Oakley to be identified as the author of this work has been asserted by her in accordance with the Copyright, Designs and Patents Act 1988.

Cover design by River Design
Front cover image: The Hague Women's Peace Congress, 1915, courtesy of London School of Economics Library
Printed and bound in Great Britain by TJ International, Padstow
Policy Press uses environmentally responsible print partners

MIX
Paper from
responsible sources
FSC
www.fsc.org   FSC® C013056

I do not desire so greatly a world in which we shall all, somehow or other, checkmate one another's desires to make war as I desire a world in which we stand shoulder to shoulder, all peoples working for those great ends which interest all people alike, and to which the native differences of different peoples are the greatest possible contribution.

Emily Greene Balch (1917) 'The war in relation to democracy and world order', *Annals of the American Academy of Political and Social Science*, 72 (28–31): 30

We move through a world filled with labels, and we are most of us content to accept the mere name on the label for that which it represents, without seeking to know anything further ... Commerce, Prosperity, Industry, the Iron Trade, War, Peace – what do all these mean? I confess that as I try to grasp them I can represent them to myself, always and ever, in terms only of human beings.

Florence Bell (1907) *At the works: A study of a manufacturing town*, London: Edward Arnold, pp viii–ix

Contents

Sources for illustrations

Note: other illustrations used in the book are in the public domain. Dates, where available, are given for images where they appear in the text. The sizing of some individual images has been constrained by their resolution and other technical considerations.

Sources for illustrations

List of abbreviations

BfM	Bund für Mutterschutz und Sexualreform
DAR	Daughters of the American Revolution
IAW	International Alliance of Women
ICW	International Council of Women
IFUW	International Federation of University Women
IPL	Immigrants' Protective League
IRI	International Industrial Relations Institute
IWSA	International Women's Suffrage Association
KCHSS	King's College of Household and Social Science
LHPA	Ladies' Health Protective Association
LSE	London School of Economics
LSMW	London School of Medicine for Women
MIT	Massachusetts Institute of Technology
MWIA	Medical Women's International Association
NAACP	National Association for the Advancement of Colored People
NCL	National Consumers' League
NPS	National Progressive Service
NUWSS	National Union of Women's Suffrage Societies
RCL	Royal Commission on Labour
TRL	Tax Resistance League
UN	United Nations
WFL	Women's Freedom League
WIC	Women's Industrial Council
WILPF	Women's International League for Peace and Freedom
WOWO	Women's Organisation for World Order
WSPU	Women's Social and Political Union

Acknowledgements

The research for this book involved many libraries and archives, and I am indebted to the help of many staff who diligently searched for the treasures I was after. The list includes: the British Library; Carlisle Archive Centre, Cumbria; Collection IAV at Atria, Institute on Gender Equality and Women's History, Amsterdam; Division of Rare and Manuscript Collections, Cornell University Library; ETZ Zurich University Archives; the Franklin D. Roosevelt Library; Imperial War Museum; The Keep, Brighton, Sussex; King's College, London; Library of Congress; Lady Margaret Hall, Oxford; MIT Museum; London Metropolitan University Archives; Modern Records Centre, University of Warwick; Museum of London; Schlesinger Library, Radcliffe Institute, Harvard University; Special Collections Research Center, University of Chicago; Somerville College, Oxford; Sophia Smith Collection, Smith College; the Truman Library; the Women's Library at the London School of Economics.

A number of people read the manuscript of *Women, peace and welfare* for me, and I am enormously grateful to them for the trouble they took to do this and to provide me with detailed and thoughtful comments. Many, many thanks to: Cynthia Cockburn, Graham Crow, Sue Fyvel, Anne Ingold, Robin Oakley, Penrose Robertson, Joy Schaverien and John Stewart. The book has benefitted hugely from their input, but I, of course, am solely responsible for the final version. Thanks also to Tom Rivers, who helped me to understand the complexities of copyright law; to Penrose Robertson, who provided help with technical aspects of the illustrations; and to Robin Oakley and Cynthia Cockburn, whose invaluable work on the list of women reformers in the Appendix made order out of chaos. As always, I am grateful to the dedicated team at Policy Press, who approached with unwavering commitment, persistence and respect the mammoth task of turning the manuscript of *Women, peace and welfare* into a book.

My first and last thanks must go to my family, for (yet again) understanding the importance of the fascination with research and writing that has dogged me all my life, and for forgiving the derelictions of duty that inevitably go with this. Without their support and love none of this would have been accomplished.

Ann Oakley
July 2017

ONE

Legacies of difficult women: the story of this book

This book tells the stories of some of the many thousands of women who in the late 19th and early 20th centuries took the reform of society as a serious intellectual and political goal. They were active and practical reformers, and they thought deeply about the forms of social organization and values that give rise to the problems calling for reformers' attention. They were also among the first to develop the tools of social science that brought such problems firmly within the remit of public policy. Women's exclusion at the time from many areas of public life, their development of international networks and their convictions about peace also called into question dominant ideas about the supremacy of nation-states and about the place of nationality in identity and citizenship. Most of these women were seen as 'difficult' in one way or another by the communities within which they lived and worked. They broke or challenged an uncomfortable number of laws and customs; they dug out facts politicians and policy makers would rather not have had to confront; they created new groupings, platforms and forms of organization; they queried long-accepted notions of heterosexual family living; and they placed exceptional demands on government agendas at local, national and international levels. But most of all they wove a rich tapestry of ideas about how human beings might live more harmoniously and altruistically together. Conceptions of social welfare and gender equality were yoked inexorably to the idea of a society in which warfare, militarism and aggression could no longer play any part. Masculinity could be stripped of its damaging apparel, and so, too, could and should the nation-state. The citizenship women claimed – and which they had been denied for so long – was a new form of *human* citizenship, embedded in a transnational solidarity and community in which everyone would share.

Almost as extraordinary as these radical blueprints for a better society is the fact that they are virtually unknown today. Remnants may survive in our reminiscences of individual women, for instance the visionary American writer and reformer Charlotte Perkins Gilman, who appears in Chapter Two, or the British Emily Hobhouse, whose government-affronting protests against war at home and abroad are charted in Chapter Seven. Histories of social science and philanthropy also remind us of women's importance in the social settlements that multiplied in late 19th-century Europe and America (Chapter Three), and in spearheading early philosophies of the welfare state. Women are visible in accounts of protest against the dehumanizing impact of industrialization on the urban poor (Chapters 3 and 9), and in histories of sanitation and cleanliness in and outside the home – always feminine specialities (Chapters 4 and 5). But, until recently, most histories of the period between 1880 and 1920 have reduced women's activism and social analysis to the pursuit of the vote, as though they were only selfishly after one thing. The suffrage campaign was, for many women, not simply a key to entering the male world of politics – 'an isolated political pantomime' – but a methodology for proposing new understandings of what it means to be a woman and how the inclusion of women in politics could effect a much-needed reordering of society.[1] Feminism and the development of state welfare policies were closely linked through women's representation of state welfare as a universal social right; and the struggle for equality joined the invention of an empirical social science as methodologies in the cause of social welfare.[2]

When the study of the past is fractured into 'women's history' and mainstream history (which is about men but not so labelled), and when the history of women is divided up into chunks – the suffrage campaign, feminism, social reform, entry into the professions, domestic labour and family relations, feminism, socialism and trade unionism, pacifism and so forth – it becomes impossible to see the connections between these different areas.

There *were* connections that operated both on the level of practice – the ways in which individual women moved between the different areas of activity – and as they imaginatively sought to understand how private and public lives work symbiotically together, and how conventional divisions between policy domains, for instance, between education, health and welfare, obstruct the connected thinking needed to solve social problems. Histories which treat women's involvement in peace movements separately from their work in social reform and welfare may wrongly persuade us that promoting welfare and working for peace were two entirely disconnected ventures. They were not.

In the years between about 1880 and about 1920 in Europe, North America and other Western countries there was a general awakening to the urgency of social reform and the need for systematic social investigation. The legitimacy of women's claims for an equal share in public life was increasingly coming to the fore; and the importance of developing methods to avoid destructive internecine conflicts both nationally and globally was acknowledged in a growing peace movement. These years contain what is known as the 'Progressive Era' in the US and the beginnings of the modern welfare state in many countries including Britain, France, Germany, Scandinavia and Australia and New Zealand. The connections between the rise of welfarism in state policies and women's philanthropic and political work are much debated in the academic literature on the welfare state, which began by paying very little attention to matters of gender.[3] Large-scale welfare programmes did emerge at the same time as women's social action movements in countries such as France, Germany, Britain and the US, but historians, studying these separately, have missed their 'deep and intricate connections'.[4] Female-led modes of action and policy not dependent on the usual channels of political parties, trade unions and official bureaucracies have been especially likely to evade attention.[5]

When the American sociologist Mary Jo Deegan was looking for a woman to write about in a column of *MS Magazine* in the early 1970s, she discovered a buried treasure in the basement of the Regenstein Library at the University of Chicago.[6] These neglected books and archives contained the stories of many 'lost' scholars, all of whom were candidates for her column. Deegan's sense of amazement at so much hidden history has been shared by other researchers. The British social historian Jane Martin was impressed by the ways in which the professional identities and activities of women historians, economists, educationalists and labour activists have been suppressed or ignored, in part through the hegemony of the suffrage story.[7] Others have taken as case studies British women such as Annie Besant, Octavia Hill and Mary Ward (Chapter Three) to expose the contrast between their public images today and the nature of their work then.[8] In the US, the historian Linda Gordon has traced the biographies of many women 'welfare-state builders', and has attempted to restore their neglected contributions to welfare thinking and systems;[9] Patricia Lengermann, Gillian Niebrugge and Mary Jo Deegan have given us valuable sourcebooks of forgotten women social scientists.[10] We now have compendia of women economists, women social reformers, women scientists, women in political life, women in the suffrage movement, women humanitarians, women in the peace movement, women writers and so forth, all of which give us a different lens through which to view this period of history.[11] But multiple lenses don't offer the unified vision that brings all these domains together, which is why the methodology of case studies – as in the portraits of women which appear in this book – is so important.

Choices in life are often a matter of serendipity. One can see how, in the narratives of the women who move in and out of the chapters that follow, being in a certain place at a certain time with certain people was consequential in terms of how they chose to act, think and declare their positions. The British historian Sybil Oldfield became a women's historian by accident, when she bought a novel by Flora Mayor in a university bookshop in the early 1950s. Finding no trace of Mayor in any relevant dictionary or biography, she set out on a journey to discover her, in the process identifying many other significant women and finding her life's work: 'the resurrection of our most humane female dead'. 'Why have we never heard of her?' her students asked, when she introduced them to Harriet Martineau, Josephine Butler, Barbara Bodichon and others.[12] Oldfield wrote a book about Mayor, and her friend the pacifist Mary Sheepshanks (see

Chapter Six),[13] and then she turned to researching the hundreds of thousands of German anti-Nazi resistance women, for whom Hitler built special prisons and concentration camps before the Second World War.[14] Oldfield's later dictionary of British women humanitarians takes as its starting point the names of the 275 women who supported the momentous women's peace congress held at The Hague in 1915 (see Chapter Six). She asks why 20th-century biography focuses on crazed political dictators, military generals and others of their kind – what another scholar called 'the catastrophic and great-man myth of history':[15] 'Why should exemplary cruelty be of more historical interest than exemplary kindness?' inquires Oldfield. 'Why do we write histories of conflict, but not of conflict resolution, of persecution, but not what brings it to an end, of power as domination rather than as empowerment?'[16] The answer that can't be avoided here is that 'masculinism and patriarchy'[17] have limited the kinds of history that have been written, just as they have constrained the possibilities of our social relations. Thus 'empirical retrieval work' is needed as a corrective to historical amnesia.

Sybil Oldfield comments that, not only were the women she discovered life-savers in their own time, they were life-savers for *her*. They strengthened her faith in human kindness and sometimes she would 'laugh out loud with joy and incredulity at the sheer inexhaustible energy of "my" women'.[18] This is a feeling I've shared in the writing of this book. I've been constantly amazed by the women's stories, by their diversity as well as their commonality, and by what they managed to achieve against the odds of being seen as a class that rightly belonged in the private sphere of the home. Each day of the research for this book has been a discovery, of 'new' women and of remarkable connections between them and their theories and practices. I came, like Oldfield, to think of them, possessively and unreasonably, as 'my' women.

Subjects and stories pass through the heads and lives of people who make a habit of ferreting out taboo topics and forgotten histories. They occupy us, obsess us, for a time, and then we let them go, hoping that our small correctives to historical amnesia will inform and engage people's views of what happened in the past. Although the origins of *Women, peace and welfare* reflect my long-term interests in gender and in evidence-based public policy,[19] the project of the book and the research that went into it were unplanned. A few years ago, when I was writing an intellectual/social history of my own and my father's work on welfare and social policy,[20] I stumbled across women attached to the tail end of one of *Women, peace and welfare*'s sub-themes: the divorce of social work from social science and public policy. Eileen Younghusband, the most influential social worker in the first three decades of the British welfare state,[21] and Charlotte Towle, an American social worker renowned for her defence of socialized public welfare,[22] were both associated with the academic department at the London School of Economics (LSE), which my father, Richard Titmuss, took over in 1950. Its original legacy of philanthropic work and empirical social investigation had migrated by then into a female-staffed training centre for professional social workers. Titmuss reshaped the department and changed its gender character: by 1960 it had a clear focus on social policy and was staffed mainly by men. In orchestrating these changes, Titmuss had problems with some of the women social work staff, whom he found 'difficult'. Towle and Younghusband were the most difficult of all, although they give none of this difficulty away in the gentle personae of their photographs. As a child (I was six years old in 1950), I heard my father's complaints about these difficult women and stored up a question or two for the future about what might really have been going on.

1.1: Charlotte Towle, 1960s

1.2: Eileen Younghusband, 1970s

In the Modern Records Centre at Warwick University, and in the archives of the University of Chicago, where Mary Jo Deegan found her buried treasure, I learnt that Towle and Younghusband were not just difficult women at the LSE but part of an international network of women social workers, reformers, activists and thinkers who shared 'a social democratic vision of a welfare state'.[23] This was a network which combined a passion for social justice, civil rights and the professionalization of public services.[24] Younghusband was an 'extraordinary leader' in the social work world, akin in stature to Alice Salomon in Germany (see Chapter Seven) and Edith Abbott in the US (see Chapter Three).[25] Towle worked at the University of Chicago for 30 years from 1932. She knew many of the women there who were connected with settlement and social reform movements and who feature in this book, including Jane Addams, Sophonisba Breckinridge, Edith and Grace Abbott, Julia Lathrop and Florence Kelley. She shared with these women the distinction of being publicly branded 'dangerous' as well as 'difficult' in the McCarthy era. Helping to sponsor a world peace conference in 1949, Towle was listed as a subversive communist sympathizer by the Committee on Un-American Activities, in the company of such celebrities as Leonard Bernstein, Marlon Brando, Charlie Chaplin, Aaron Copeland and Albert Einstein.[26] The plates of the book she wrote about public welfare clients, *Common human needs*, were destroyed by government order.[27] When arrangements had been made for her to be seconded to the LSE for a year in the early 1950s, my father had to intervene in the political struggle to get her a passport.

I met Towle through my father, although I don't remember this. I learnt it from reading her diary in the University of Chicago library. She came to our house in January 1955 for a dinner party in her honour, at which she met Barbara Wootton, a noted social scientist.[28] I do remember Eileen Younghusband in the period before she stopped being invited to our home when hostilities at the LSE intensified. There are personal connections with other women who feature in *Women, peace and welfare*. Eleanor Rathbone, famed for her promotion of family allowances, thanked my father for his help in providing 'facts and figures' that she cited in her *The case for family allowances*.[29] The

Titmuss family photograph album holds a small, square. black-and-white photo of me as a small child being blown about in a gale in front of the house in Cornwall where Rathbone wrote *The disinherited family*, the founding document for the family allowance movement, regarded by William Beveridge and other leading economists of the period as one of the most important modern treatises on distributive economics.[30] Around the same time, there was the quiet figure of Edith Eckhard, the de facto head of the social administration department at the LSE before my father got there. It was Eckhard who persuaded William Beveridge, then Director of the LSE, to start the first mental health course for social workers in the country in 1929. Eckhard had been inspired by her observations of social service in the US on one of the many transatlantic trips made by social workers in the early decades of the 20th century.[31] The copy of housing reformer Octavia Hill's biography I inherited from my father has Edith Eckhard's name in it – did she perhaps lend it to him in order to educate him about what social workers before her had really been up to? Eckhard was a close friend of Kathleen Courtney, a suffragist, peace campaigner and internationalist. Eckhard and Courtney lived together in London, some of the time with the pacifist doctor Hilda Clark, and Clark's partner, the midwife and Quaker pacifist Edith Pye; all these co-residents were part of a network which took in many of the women who appear in this book.

Among the ghosts of childhood, I remember another one, 'Charlie' (Charlotte) Marsh, whom I knew as a social worker friend of my mother's, and whose long, once-golden hair I much admired. But Charlie had a much more gripping history that wasn't mentioned in my childhood home. She had been a leading militant suffragette, imprisoned on three occasions, and one of the first to be forcibly fed. Her statuesque bearing made her a premium choice to lead demonstrations and processions; she headed the funeral procession for Emily Wilding Davison, killed by the King's horse at the Derby in 1913.[32] The photograph on page 9 shows her as the colour bearer for a Women's Social and Political Union (WSPU) demonstration in Hyde Park a few years earlier. She wears her hunger-striker's medal proudly and seems altogether a creature from a different planet compared to the serious, hatted crowd behind her. The sociologist Liz Stanley, who came across Marsh when researching Emily Wilding Davison's life, talks about the feminism of these women as blending socialism, animal rights, vegetarianism, pacifism, opposition to colonialism: 'a feminism of practice and of action in the public sphere ... expressed through a growing and widespread women's community, embedded in a myriad of local groups, organizations and friendship networks'.[33]

Why didn't I know any of this? Why did I emerge from 20 years of formal education believing that history was made by great men, with women watching, aproned, from the sidelines, occasionally murmuring a complaint about the doors that were closed to them? The urge – both intellectual and emotional – to

1.3: Charlotte Marsh leading a WSPU demonstration, 1910

bring lost history back to life was an important motive in the writings of second-wave feminism, yet this feminism itself seems to have forgotten much of what went before. In our haste to protest and theorize, we (I include myself in this mistake) thought we were doing this act of retrieval for the first time, but we weren't. Like Deegan and Oldfield and many others, I'm quite shocked that the women I discovered through this roundabout route of childhood memories and questions about how social science and social policy were shaped was a matter of stumbling unawares, in the dark, over buried treasures. We – or some of us – call our Western democracies egalitarian and consider that the main barriers to gender equality have disappeared; but what is egalitarian about a culture in which the work and perspectives of more than half the population (as well as those of other social minority groups) are systematically marginalized by what we teach and learn about the past? And how does it help us to solve pressing social problems *not* to understand how welfare requires that we live in peace with one another?

Mary Ritter Beard, a woman whose name is unfairly noted in history chiefly for her being the wife of another historian,[34] wrote *On understanding women* in 1931. The photograph of Beard opposite was taken two decades later (it's inscribed 'grandmother Beard' at the bottom) and shows her appropriately dwarfed by the pile of books and papers on her desk. The 'prefatory note' in her *On understanding women* might well be appended to *Women, peace and welfare* too: 'There is sure to be an over-emphasis in places but my apology is that, when contentions have long been weighted too much on one side, it is necessary to bear down heavily on the other.'[35] In order to understand women (a task not many people in the 1930s, when she wrote her book, were trying to do), Beard argued that 'the narrative of history must be reopened, must be widened to take in the whole course of civilisation as well as war, politics, gossip and economics'.[36] Her book takes a wide sweep through all this, from 'primitive' man and woman, and their respective roles in warfare and welfare (men either fighting or day-dreaming, women doing most of the care and health work), up to the present day. Beard's project was to demonstrate that women have always played a much more important role in human culture than most people believe they

1.4: Mary Ritter Beard at her desk, 1954

have. Like other scholars who've taken this kind of journey, she uncovered a plethora of unnoticed heroines.[37]

But history isn't made by heroines on their own, and it wasn't an objective of Beard's book, just as it isn't of this one, to rehabilitate exceptional women. It's the context that counts. When, at another point in her distinguished historical career, Beard complained about the defects of the *Encyclopaedia Britannica* with respect to women's history, its editor invited her to produce a report on how to correct these. After 18 months' work the report was done. Why not an entry on 'Queen' to counterbalance 'King'? Why were women not mentioned in the entry on 'medical education'? Some entries, for example those on 'matriarchy', 'wealth' and 'land', were so bad that they ought to be jettisoned altogether, while others were seriously deficient: 'reform movement' omitted the suffrage movement in Britain; where settlements were mentioned, the most famous American one, Hull-House, was missing; and from the article on cookery one would suppose that no woman ever entered a kitchen.[38] The editor promised to take all the report's recommendations on board, but he never did. When a keen researcher applied to the *Encyclopaedia Britannica* in 1976 for copies of the report and correspondence related to Mary Beard's work, the answer was that no trace of either could be found.[39]

Other women's efforts to improve the historical record with respect to their sex have been occluded by the clouds of masculinist history. Who today has heard of Lina Eckenstein's *Women under monasticism*, published in 1896, or Annie Abram's work on *Social England in the fifteenth century* (1909), or Alice Clark's *Working life of women in the seventeenth century* (1919), or Ivy Pinchbeck on *Women workers and the Industrial Revolution* (1930) – all texts that show how women's agency predated, and frequently triumphed over, their oppression?[40] As Lina Eckenstein's friend Dr Ethel Williams wrote of her: 'It is easy for the feminist movement to appraise what it owes to its executive and political leaders; it is more difficult to realize what it owes to its scholars and philosophers.'[41] It is, indeed, quite hard to tell from much 'women's history' what a significant part women have played as social theorists and philosophers. The American settlement founder, Jane Addams, for example, produced a remarkable body of theoretical work analysing the relationship between militarist ideology and weaknesses in democratic institutions.[42] Virginia Woolf, known more for her fiction than for her social theory, published in 1938 a still unparalleled dissection of how the structures of militarism and patriarchy interlock and fertilize one another.[43] Abram, Clark and Pinchbeck's texts were written originally as PhD theses at the LSE, which housed a stellar collection of women scholars decades before the conflicts over social work training broke out. 'It seems surprising that so little is remembered of what these women did,' observes Maxine Berg, who has studied the first female economic historians with the same attention to documentary detail as they themselves displayed.[44] These earlier LSE women made up a kind of mini-network meshed together by a devotion to gender-equal history, social reform and the peace movement. The questions they asked of the past were informed by their own experiences.[45] Alice Clark, a member of the Quaker shoemaking Clark family, was, along with her sister Hilda, deeply committed to the causes of pacifism and humanitarian aid. Eileen Power, a later member of the LSE network, wrote books on the medieval period which provided a new form of social history intended to spread a message of humanitarian internationalism. She demonstrated her pacifism in her writing and speaking as a public intellectual who believed that academics should not shy away from political causes.[46]

The reductionist prism of the vote has been influential in other ways: 'Since women did not vote ... historians considered them irrelevant and wrote nothing about them,' observes Elisabeth Perry in her study of the Progressive Era in the US.[47] Definitional categories filter and seriously limit what we know about the past. The same is true of the historical focus on the nation-state. Eileen Power argued that international peace would be achieved only through a repository of common historical ideas shared *between* nations.[48] History must stress what nations have in common, not how they differ and jostle aggressively for their own places in the world. Many of the women in this book rejected nationalism and the patriotism that went with it, identifying with a transnational identity. Many would have signed up to Virginia Woolf's famous statement in her *Three guineas*, 'As a woman I have no country. As a woman I want no country. As a woman, my country is the whole world.'[49] Transnational history examines the interactions of people and ideas that cross and question the borders of nation-states.[50] In the late 19th and early 20th centuries, women's limited rights of citizenship and nationality drew them naturally to other women in other countries who were similarly determined to address these exclusions and their consequences for public policy. Their networks of reform and anti-militarism built on older ones: temperance, abolitionism, moral reform, the very beginnings of the women's rights movement. Disenfranchisement bred what the American feminist writer Katharine Anthony called in 1935 an 'unconscious internationalism', which in turn produced in women a new and much broader view of citizenship.[51]

After the intense activities of the years which are this book's main focus, women's work in social reform and welfare, social science, and the peace movement carried on, but it had to struggle with a post-First World War denial of women's opportunities, the effects of widespread economic depression and the disastrous peace of the Versailles Treaty, which mired the contributing nations in continued belligerence. It was evident that, if the right steps weren't taken, the documentary record of women's achievement might easily disappear. In 1935 the Hungarian pacifist Rosika Schwimmer, a woman of great determination, huge conviction and a beguiling tendency to annoy even her best friends (see Chapter Six), proposed to her American friend Mary Ritter Beard the founding of a World Center for Women's Archives. The idea was that it would serve as a repository for documents, and also as an educational centre 'in which the culture represented by the archives will receive the attention at present given in "seats of higher learning" to the culture of men alone'.[52] This was a visionary enterprise which predated by some 35 years the women's studies centres and programmes of second-wave feminism. But the 1930s weren't propitious years to get such a project off the ground. Overwhelmed by world events and lack of funding, the Center closed in 1940. During its short life it acquired various journals, papers and letters from the history of the suffrage movement in the US: a copy of the memoirs of Gluckel von Hamelin (1646–1724), a businesswoman whose diaries allow us to see what it was like to live in a German Jewish ghetto in the Rhine valley in the 17th century; and the original records, maps and charts of American aviation pioneer (and feminist) Amelia Earhart's last flight.[53] Such ill-assorted records remind us that the range and format of women's contributions has often been spectacularly diverse. Had the World Center for Women's Archives succeeded as a project, researchers attempting their own reconstructions of the past might have had an easier time. *Women, peace and welfare* reflects, as any such account must do, the incomplete, scattered and fugitive nature of archival records, and the legacy of many bonfires and other wilful destructions. Any biographer or writer of collective biography – the heavyweight academic term is 'prosopography' – wrestles with the legacy of silences and absences and gaps that people leave behind.

Ever since I first realized I was writing a book about all this I've struggled with how to contain it, both in terms of time and geography and with respect to its leading characters, whose stories can be hard to find. When Kirstin Downey embarked on a biography of New Deal reformer Frances Perkins, for example, she found she had let herself in for a 10-year detective project: Perkins' papers lay in more than a dozen archives, with revealing documents housed, unrecognized, in obscure corners of other collections. One crucial story, about the genesis of the New Deal in an appalling factory fire, 'was written up in pencil on a pad of yellow paper, jotted down by an obscure New Yorker, and stored almost forgotten in a warehouse in the Maryland suburbs'.[54] What, of all this hidden and forgotten history, deserves to resurface? The British researcher and writer Olive Malvery, whose exploits appear later in Chapter Three, put the problem most succinctly at the beginning of her book *The soul market* (1906), which is about her travels among the poor and the homeless: 'Sitting here confronted with the burden of a contract which binds me to deliver a book I have promised to make into the publisher's hands by a specified time,' she complained. 'Which of all the events shall I choose, and which leave out? How will it be possible to make anything like a consecutive narrative of things that have befallen, where there are thousands of miles to bring within a narrow compass?'[55]

Faced with an indomitable cast of characters, I wanted to include as many as I could in my book: this was a very sizeable network and its quantity as much as its quality clamours to be represented. One of the dedicated people who read the manuscript of *Women, peace and welfare* for me told me there are 351 women in the book (I hadn't dared to count them myself). I apologize if this overcrowding produces headaches; I've tried to make the reader's task a little easier by inserting visual images and appending a list of women (see Appendix: list of women reformers). Another problem that needs to be acknowledged is that researching an international network demands an expert linguist, which I am not. Many texts, biographies and archive materials relating to key non-English-speaking women have simply not (yet) been translated. Thus the geographical spread of the book is, regrettably, skewed by the English language. The main focus, on white middle-class women in Europe and North America, mustn't be taken as suggesting that there weren't many equally committed women elsewhere (some of whose records may be even harder to find). All the women in the book were active in either one or more areas: social reform, social science, the suffrage, feminist and peace movements; many are to be found in more than one or in all of these. I've declined to get involved in the business of labelling them as feminists or socialists or social workers or social scientists and so forth, since a focus on what they did and said is a good deal more revealing. Most of *Women, peace and welfare* concentrates on the four decades between 1880 and 1920, but sometimes the women urged me to extend it backwards (to take in the mid-19th-century work of Fredrika Bremer in Sweden, for example) or forwards (to cover the New Deal and women such as Frances Perkins and Eleanor Roosevelt in the US). I decided to follow stories rather than strict boundaries of time and place. Stories, personal and public, are what engage people the most, especially when they encapsulate new and interesting ideas, and I wanted to make this book as accessible and engaging as possible.

Readers looking for comprehensive academic accounts of how social work, social science and social reform became differentiated pursuits won't find such accounts here – although there are certainly clues embedded in the women's stories. Due to limitations of space, there is more detail about some endeavours (for example, healthcare) than others (for example, the rise of state education). As to the women whose stories the book depends on, I've avoided detailed accounts of the most well-known (Jane Addams, Ellen Key, the Pankhursts, Rosa Luxemburg and Beatrice Webb, for instance) and focused on some of those with whose lives and work we are less familiar. I make no claim for comprehensiveness; this is a partial account, a limited excavation of just some of the points of entry into a whole mound of archaeological treasures, the legacies of difficult and dangerous women whose programme for a more just and caring society opposed the dominant ideological currents of their time. I'm also not pretending that the positions of the women whose lives and work do form the stories included in this book were homogeneous: different women took differing stands, sometimes arguing these tenaciously with one another – indeed, conflict was sometimes as much a hallmark of their communication as consensus, although both were contained within a framework of deep attachment to each other and a set of core ideas about the welfare obligations of citizenship.[56] This was no idealized, universal, unproblematic sisterhood of transnationalism, but a world of hard work and long drawn-out debates and conversations, all miraculously conducted at a time before air travel or telephones and other kinds of modern electronic communication.

The next chapter introduces us to the project of imagining the kind of social system that would nourish both universal welfare and peaceful coexistence. Chapter Three is about the invention of social science in the form of the investigative work carried out in and around social settlements in Europe and North America. Women reformers' concern with cleaning up the cities and the home (Chapters Four and Five), often portrayed as a typically feminine role, hides what they actually *did*, which was to apply a much more assertive ('masculine') approach informed by science and the economics of public and private housekeeping. In Chapters Six and Seven the book focuses on pacifism as both practical activity and political philosophy, together with its outreach into modern ideas of cultural diversity and community. Chapters Eight and Nine follow women's involvement in the institutions of healthcare and their ideas about bodily rights; and illustrate the enormous contributions they made to charting and reducing the hazards of industrial work. A powerful strand of many women reformers' arguments took apart as anti-democratic the prevailing conventions of marriage and family life, a way of living that they themselves often tried to avoid: these domestic relations are the subject of Chapter Ten. Chapter Eleven takes the story a little further by looking at some of the ways in which the women's reform agendas expanded and bore fruit in the 1920s and 1930s. A final chapter attempts to pull the overall case together and consider why there are so many women on the 'missing persons' list when it comes to histories of welfare, social science and peace movements.

The women in *Women, peace and welfare* whose stories I felt I temporarily owned often referred to the choices they made to take part in political work as no sort of choice at all. There was no alternative; they just had to do it. I have felt similarly, particularly when I've become aware of the threads that bind my own history to theirs. One moment in the writing of this book stands out. I was in my rural retreat, reading about the wonderful theologian, suffragist and pacifist Maude Royden (see Chapter Six) and the vicissitudes of her unconventional life. For a time in the early 1900s she lived with a vicar and his wife in a small village in the middle of England. I looked out of my window, and there was the spire of the church Royden and her vicar had worked in, and in which she had (unsuccessfully) tried to instil a sense of Christian discipline into the unruly children and young girls of the village. This village shares with many other places the misfortune of having lost sight of the likes of Royden, bred in the interstices of the Victorian and 20th-century worlds, alive to the distressing dislocations of those worlds and determined to engineer a 'substitution of nurture for warfare' in an effort to create a better society.[57]

TWO

Imagining the good society: from economic facts to utopian fictions

Sunday, 26 July 1896 was a day of inclement weather in London. In the early afternoon the skies opened on the big peace demonstration that preceded the week-long International Socialist Workers and Trade Union Congress. The Congress itself was dominated by well-known male names in labour politics, and turned out to be a chaotic event given over more to arguments about who among the 768 delegates from 20 countries was really entitled to attend and to vote than to the matter at hand, namely the abolition of the capitalist state.[1] Seven of the delegates were from the US; they included the social economist and novelist Charlotte Perkins Gilman, whose work on economics, domestic labour and the design of feminist utopias is the focus of this chapter. Gilman's work touches on many of the themes which run through this book. Other delegates were a city planner called Mary Kingsbury (later Simkhovitch) and a distinguished economist and winner of the Nobel Peace Prize, Emily Balch. A fourth American woman, the writer and suffragist Harriot Stanton Blatch, was married to an English businessman and living in Surrey at the time. Gilman (then known as Stetson) was there as a delegate of the Alameda County Federation of Trades, having read the membership card for the Congress and discovered that she couldn't pretend to be an international socialist since she disagreed with the theory and method advanced by the followers of Marx. At the peace demonstration she found herself sharing a speakers' wagon with August Bebel and George Bernard Shaw. Shaw, as a Fabian, was much more to Gilman's political liking, although she observed his curious dress: he and other male

Fabians sported knee-breeches, soft shirts, woollen hose and home-made sandals.[2] She was herself a keen analyst of clothing as a social issue, later producing a text on dress reform in which she reasonably contended that the liberation of women required their release from the uncomfortable bonds of feminine fashion.[3]

During her stay in England, Gilman met various other English Fabians, including Beatrice and Sidney Webb. Beatrice had enjoyed Gilman's poetry – a volume called *In this our world* had been published three years earlier. Gilman's international reputation was originally made through her poetry: an Australian suffragist had discovered it on her travels in the US and brought it to the attention of a London publisher, an act which amply demonstrates a major theme of *Women, peace and welfare*: the power of women's networks.[4] Beatrice Webb asked Gilman to read some of her poetry to a Fabian meeting; the Fabian Society in London would later make her an honorary member.[5] Gilman was invited to spend a few days in a Surrey rectory rented by the Webbs, Shaw and a wealthy woman called Charlotte Payne-Townshend, whom the Webbs were cultivating because of her financial generosity to their infant prodigy, the London School of Economics. This rural stay was marred by Beatrice's cold, which made her more irritable than usual, by the food, which, due to Beatrice's anorexia, was never luxurious, and by arguments with Shaw about his play *Candida*, which offered its heroine a choice of men, not in some people's eyes much of a choice at all. On the rectory lawn were a tent and a summer house; Gilman got on with her writing in one, while Shaw worked on his play *The devil's disciple* in the other. A diversion was her introduction to the new fashion for bicycle riding, a tricky art that it took her five years to acquire.

The rain that day in 1896 had a dampening effect on the delegates when they reached the reception at the Horse Shoe Hotel in Tottenham Court Road. Many had to go to bed while their suits dried out. What Charlotte Perkins Gilman did about her drenched costume is not known. The conversation, though, must have been fascinating. Gilman's compatriot Harriot Stanton Blatch was the daughter of the pioneering women's rights activist Elizabeth Cady Stanton, she who had been instrumental in initiating the women's movement in the US at Seneca Falls in

1848. Other female notables at the 1896 Congress were Marx's daughter Eleanor; the formidable German Marxist-feminist Clara Zetkin, who organized the world's first International Women's Day in 1911; and her friend the equally redoubtable revolutionary socialist Rosa Luxemburg, whose anti-war protests were to land her in Polish and German prisons for several years. The Anglo-Irish suffragist Charlotte Despard also attended early in her post-widowhood career of radically philanthropic works. What did all these enterprising women talk about together? The official report on 'Women at the International Congress' wasn't particularly revealing, noting disparagingly that 'The bourgeois woman's movement makes a great deal of noise … They do not, as a rule, know what Socialism means, but think it spells bloodshed and violence.'[6]

The rejection of bloodshed and violence was intimately entangled with the development of feminism in those days of multiple congresses, conferences, declarations and petitions. The period from the mid-19th century through the first decades of the 20th century saw an astonishingly fertile burgeoning of organizations devoted to rights, reform and the general removal of oppression. 'In my youth the world was full of "Movements", of an eager massing together to work for "causes"', reminisced Charlotte Perkins Gilman in her autobiography. 'There was the Labor Movement, the Temperance Movement, the Woman's Suffrage Movement, the Dress Reform Movement, a general movement towards better methods in education, from the Kindergarten to University Extension, and a broad, deep, liberalizing of religion. There was the Society for The Prevention of Cruelty to Animals, and another to protect children – the state reaching out at last to recognize the child as a citizen, not the property of the parents. There was the Organization of Charities, steps in Prison Reform and in the Care of the Insane; a demand for right teaching of children as to sex, and for an equal standard of chastity, equalized up, not down.'[7]

Gilman was one of many women who analysed what was wrong with the social system and proposed strategies for putting it right. A photograph on the next page taken of her in 1900 shows a rather severe, dark-haired profile and an intent gaze fixed somewhere on the horizon. 'If I had been sex-conscious and

2.1: Charlotte Perkins Gilman, 1900

dressed the part, she commented sardonically, 'I think I would have been called beautiful. But one does not call a philosophic steam-engine beautiful.'[8] The sociologist Lester Ward described her as 'direct, abrupt, blunt, devastating, as the need arises' when she wrote or spoke about her favourite subjects of the home, economics, women and nationalism.[9] She was a charismatic and enlivening speaker, with a 'light penetrating voice', who treated her audiences to a mix of grand theory and illustrative anecdote from her own experience.[10] Gilman wrapped up her ideas sometimes as fiction, and sometimes not: aside from the poetry, she published eleven major non-fiction books and a great mass of shorter non-fiction works, eight novels, seven dramas, nearly 200 short stories and an autobiography. Her life was a dramatic synopsis of the themes which occupied her as a writer and economist/sociologist: the immorality of marriage;

the inefficiency of the home; the oppression of women by housework and of children by adults; the systematic distortion of human sociality by the politics of a gender-segregated culture; the devastating consequences of masculine violence. Neglected as the major social theorist she was – 'the Marx and Veblen of the women's movement'[11] – people today remember her best for her short story 'The yellow wallpaper', a powerful rendition of what would later be (mis)named as postnatal depression.[12]

In 1884 at the age of 24, Gilman had married, with some misgivings, a handsome patriarchal artist, Walter Stetson, who had a fondness for painting water colours of female nudes. What else, apart from marry, was a young woman living on the east coast of the US to do then, given that most of the public world of politics and work was formally closed off as an option? A week after the wedding Gilman wrote in her diary that she had suggested her husband should pay her for the housekeeping services marriage evidently entailed, but 'he much dislikes the idea. I am grieved at offending him.'[13] She was trying hard to be a good wife. Their daughter, Katharine, was born a year later. When Katharine was two, and Charlotte had become housebound and depressed, she was dispatched by her husband and her mother to experience something called 'a rest cure' developed by the neurologist Dr Silas Weir Mitchell, the most famous and successful women's doctor of his generation.[14] Gilman prepared for Dr Mitchell a long letter outlining 'the history of the case', which he considered proved self-conceit. 'I've had two women of your blood here already,' he complained to her scornfully.[15] This was a reference to Gilman's two famous great-aunts, Catharine Beecher and Harriet Beecher Stowe, who had each campaigned in their own way against social injustice.

The Weir Mitchell story is part of a larger long-standing medical ploy to treat women's invasion of the public sphere as a sign of disease. The rest cure that Mitchell prescribed was hailed at the time as 'the greatest advance of ... practical medicine', although it was subsequently shown actually to make people worse rather than better[16] – as well as, of course, being a really astounding example of medical misogyny. Gilman, like other women before and after her, was instructed to lie still in bed without books, conversation or family and friends, given

23

massages and electrical stimulation, and fed enormous quantities of food. Refusing these might mean being whipped to enforce obedience or forced feeding through the nose or rectum. Bladder and bowels were emptied by medical intervention; the only action the patient was allowed to perform unaided was to brush her teeth. Men with nervous problems due to overwork (whereas women's were caused by too much education) were more likely to be sent on the 'west cure' – episodes of cattle-roping, hunting and male bonding in rugged frontier locations.[17] The scope of Weir Mitchell's influence was considerable, involving the treatment of other notable women such as Jane Addams, Edith Wharton and Virginia Woolf – the latter via an interesting transfer of ideas from the US to Britain, whereby Mitchell's approach was enthusiastically adopted by a well-known gynaecologist who added a prescription for foreign travel to Mitchell's regime, thus, unintentionally probably, doing wonders for women's networking experiences.[18]

Gilman's 'The yellow wallpaper' is a persuasive allegorical statement about the psychological confinement and oppression experienced by women in the decades before and after the start of the 20th century. It describes the descent of a woman subjected to a postnatal rest cure by her well-meaning physician husband; the patient becomes obsessed with the yellow wallpaper in her room and convinced that there are other women hiding behind it. Gilman herself gave up on the rest cure and, after a few hesitations, left her husband and moved west, eventually sending Katharine to live with Walter and his new wife and freeing herself for a life of political activity, research and writing. For this unconventional approach to motherhood she was much criticized in some circles, while others understood. Dr Alice Hamilton, an expert in occupational health and a leading pacifist campaigner, met Charlotte in Chicago in the winter of 1898, noting in a letter to her sister that 'Mrs. Stetson ... is very attractive. She is the woman ... who couldn't stand being married ... and now is on excellent terms with her former husband and his present wife, who takes care of Mrs. Stetson's little girl, an arrangement which I fancy I should approve of.'[19]

One of Gilman's many enterprises was to set up a social reform magazine aimed at attracting 'ordinary' women to the cause of women's rights. *The Forerunner* was published from 1909 to 1916. Gilman wrote every word of it herself, including the few advertisements she tolerated for a while – Moore's Fountain Pen and Fels-Naphtha Soap (endorsed because the first didn't leak when one bent over to wash floors or change diapers, and the second was 'artistically and antiseptically' clean).[20] One remarkable feature of Gilman's writing is the way in which public issues and private concerns are constantly connected. This is the essence of her theoretical framework: homes are the world's business, and public politics must embrace the home. Her orientation in *The home: Its work and influence*, published in 1903, is principally that of an economist who looks at the way homes are organized and sees a huge waste of human resources: 'The little industrial group of the home ... is very near the bottom of the line of economic progress. It costs men more money, women more work, both more time and strength than need be by more than half. A method of living that wastes half the time and strength of the world is not economical.'[21] Her book was read as a 'full-scale, full battle-dress assault'[22] on an ancient and cherished institution, a reaction that annoyed her greatly: she wasn't trying to destroy the home but, on the contrary, was doing all she could to *preserve* it by removing its inefficiencies and inequalities. Her argument about women was that gaining the ballot would not be enough to give them freedom and equality or to gain for children the proper care and respect they needed. Those goals demanded the redefinition of what we now call gender, and a reshaping of ideas about individualism and community.

Gilman also tried out her fiction in *The Forerunner*, including her utopian trilogy, *Moving the mountain* (1911), *Herland* (1915) and *With her in Ourland* (1916). The first two are utopias; the third is a utopian encounter with the dystopia of contemporary society. Gilman's view of a fictional utopia was that it represents the awakening of people, especially women, 'to existing possibilities. It indicates what people might do, real people, now living.'[23] In *Moving the mountain*, the male protagonist, John Robertson, is found by his sister Nellie in a remote area of Tibet, having spent the past 30 years with amnesia there following an accident. When he recovers his memory it is 1940.

Nellie takes him back to the US on a ship powered by electricity. Their country, she explains, has been through socialism and out the other side to something much better. John fears the worst: 'Are the men doing all the housework?' he enquires. 'You call that the worst?' replies Nellie.[24] The hallmarks of the new order are rationality, efficiency, prosperity, equality and cooperation. As they approach New York, Nellie points out to him 'an experimental station in applied sociology'. A Commission on Human Efficiency had been set up in 1913 to apply new methods of scientific management to the problems of human living. The result is a society without poverty, disease, disability, accidents, fear, unemployment, crime, alcoholism, smoking, gender or ethnic inequalities, name-changing on marriage, deforestation, pollution, domestic animals or (much) meat-eating. Energy comes from windmills, water mills, tide mills, solar engines and domestic exercise machines for the lazy, with hand or foot attachments, useful for heating houses. Freight is carried underneath cities on silent monorails or on the waterways. Housework has been socialized rather than masculinized, as John feared. It, and childcare, has become the domain of well-paid professional experts. Religion and ethics are no longer necessary: 'We show the child the patent facts of social relation, how all our daily life … rests on common action, on what people do together.'[25]

But it's all very carefully calculated: before she inscribed the imagined geography of her utopias, Gilman had published in 1898 her *Women and economics*, 'the bible' of feminism for many women.[26] The book argued that the economic dependence of women in the home is the key to their subordination. Gilman's text advocated kitchenless houses and apartments and communal dining and day care, helping to fertilize a whole ideological movement devoted to collective housekeeping.[27] Written in 39 days, the book had gone through nine printings by 1920, had been translated into seven languages and had brought her international fame. Gilman's position as the intellectual leader of the women's movement during this period was acknowledged by many, including Mary Ritter Beard (see Chapter One) in the text Beard wrote with her husband, Charles, *The rise of American civilization*.[28] When Gilman spoke about *Women and economics* at an International Woman Suffrage Alliance meeting in Berlin in 1904 so many people came to hear her that she had to give the address twice over. Audiences were divided, half the women saying they would never give up cooking for their husbands and hand their children over to professional carers, and the other half agreeing with Gilman that women had spent far too much time on unproductive domestic labour. Gilman the economist is specific about the financing of her utopia: the entirely non-military nation sketched in *Moving the mountain* is paid for out of the 70% of the national income that used to be spent on war. The big industries are nationalized, but there is room for private initiative; indeed, the de-privatization of housework, with food and clean laundry delivered through underground tunnels and homes planned to be dust- and housework-free, stemmed originally from the business acumen of a group of women who started an outfit called the Home Service Company. Individual housekeeping is criminally wasteful, so much so that there is a good deal of profit to be made from turning it into a business. *Moving the mountain*'s utopia is also all about science: good nutrition and food production are matters of science, so every town has its Food Bureau, as well as its own power plant, its Child Garden for growing children, its workshops and its communal socializing facilities.

The exact private–public mix of welfare in this first of Gilman's utopias is somewhat hazy. Likewise, her dependence on eugenics for reducing criminality, disease and disability and her references to racial purity have been much criticized. They appear again in the more fully fledged utopia of *Herland*, which maps a country about the size of Holland with a population of around three million – all women. Gilman is vague about how this came about, but it had to do with war, the decimation of the male population, a volcanic eruption which cut the land off from the rest of 'civilization' about 2,000 years ago, and the energies of the women who survived and determined to create a healthy culture. They started miraculously to give birth to girls, establishing a routine whereby women who chose motherhood would each have five daughters. This parthenogenetic all-female world is discovered by three men on a scientific expedition: a playboy explorer, a doctor and a sociologist, who naturally find it hard to believe that any civilized society is possible without men. Gilman enjoys their surprise, depicting their reactions humorously to expose the strange customs of her/their own culture. For example, on learning that there are no animals in Herland because the land is needed to feed the people instead, one of the men asks what the women do for milk. 'We have our own in abundance', he is told (his reaction isn't recorded). The sociologist, the most thoughtful of the three male visitors, becomes less and less proud of what manhood has done. He understands that the women of Herland, 'had had no wars. They had had no kings, and no priests, and no aristocracies. They were sisters, and as they grew, they grew together – not by competition but by united action.'[29]

The most important aspect of Herland from Gilman's programmatic point of view is that it's built on, and by, motherhood, which is counted the 'highest social service'. Because motherhood stands at the centre of everything, concepts such as 'home' and 'family' have no place in Herland. 'They loved one another with a practically universal affection, rising to exquisite and unbroken friendships', notes the sociologist, over-romantically, of Herland's women, 'and broadening to a devotion to their country and people for which our word PATRIOTISM is no definition at all. Patriotism, red hot, is compatible with the existence of a neglect of national interests, a dishonesty, a cold indifference to the suffering of millions.'[30] This, of course, is Gilman speaking. *Herland* was written in the early days of the First World War, when many millions of women across the globe were connecting their own pursuit of social reform with an opposition to violence, war and nationalism.

The third story in the trilogy, *With her in Ourland*, begins at this point. The sociologist has married a Herland woman and he takes her back to the Europe and America of 1915, eager to show her the benefits of his own civilization. Instead he finds a world war: war is human nature, she is told. But if it's human nature, why don't women do it? she enquires. What strikes this inquisitive visitor most of all about America is its 'unmotherliness': nothing is really taken care of. Overcome by the social atmosphere of suspicion, hatred and ruthless self-aggrandisement, she locks herself up in her room and sobs her heart out. Her husband confesses that he now realizes that what he considered civilized isn't so at all. Her response is to study this uncivilized world: she becomes 'more and more the sociologist, the investigator', hiring a young historian to explain to her why history is about the recitation of wars, kings and conquests; she takes apart popular economic theories about wages and supply and demand, showing them to be merely statements of capitalist opinion; she looks carefully at child-rearing, attributing the tremendous differences in the behaviour of men and women to their cultural conditioning as infants in different forms of dress and training; she asks why some of America's important men and women can't work out 'an experimental station in methods of living – an economic and social unit, you know – to have for reference, to establish facts'. Above all, she can't understand why so many women in America spend so much time doing housework. 'We isolated Herlanders', she declares 'never heard of Socialism ... We had no German-Jewish economist to explain to us in interminable, and, to most people, uncomprehensible prolixity, the reasons why it was better to work together for common good. Perhaps "the feminine mind" did not need so much explanation of so obvious a fact'[31] At the end of all her investigating and observing she tells her husband she will never have children in a place like this. They return to Herland, where she gives birth to a son – a surprising, perhaps intentionally sardonic, denouement.

Gilman's utopian trilogy nestled in its own historical tradition of utopia making. H. G. Wells, an argumentative fellow Fabian with Shaw and the Webbs, had imagined gender equality in his *A modern utopia*, published in 1905.[32] In *Angel Island*, published in 1914 by the American writer Inez Haynes Gillmore, a group of men find themselves stranded on a Pacific island which is occupied by winged women; the men catch the women, clip their wings and domesticate them, but the women learn to walk and eventually have their revenge.[33] Gilman would have read this delightful and disturbing fantasy, since she and Gillmore were both members of the creatively named Heterodoxy Club, a dining club for 'unorthodox' women founded in Greenwich Village in 1912, about whose operations rather little is known, since its very unorthodoxy meant that no formal notes were ever kept of its meetings in order to protect its members.[34] Clubs and organizations for women of various political hues on both sides of the Atlantic in this period played a crucial role in extending and cementing their connections and interests.

Utopian fiction is a technology for experimenting with radical ideas. Since a utopia's mission is to provide a speculative vision of the desired goals of human existence, it's not surprising that we find utopias most at times of social change, when customary ideas and practices are being challenged, especially by those whose lives are constrained by them. In the early 20th century, when Gilman was writing hers, the difficulties of living in crowded, dirty urban centres, doing unprotected, unorganized work outside the home and childcare and housework under impossible conditions inside it, became a focus of political attention for many theorists, social investigators, writers and activists. The American socialist writer Edward Bellamy's nationalist movement, which advocated government ownership of industry and the abandonment in social life of the competitive principle, was launched in 1888 with the publication of his own famous utopian novel *Looking backward 2000–1887*.[35] This has echoes of Mary Griffith's *Three hundred years hence* (1836) – the first utopian novel to use the device of projection into the future of the writer's own society, and a book which by 1900 had sold more copies than any other American book, apart from Gilman's great-aunt Harriet Beecher Stowe's anti-slavery novel, *Uncle Tom's cabin*.[36] Bellamy's novel spurned a nationalist (for which read 'socialist') movement and carried Gilman along with it. His utopian construction of women made them economically independent and named the state as the proper provider of domestic services, but women were still emotional appendages of men. Gilman's *Herland*, with its one-sex/gender society, took the collectivist principle in quite another direction. Her fundamental thesis was that the ethic of individualism is the most severe obstacle to social change. Healthy social solidarity is born of cooperation and collective social reform.

A manless society is a rhetorical device for revealing the ideology and injustices of gender. Women, stripped of their artificial femininity, become human beings. Gilman called herself a humanist, rather than a feminist, and she might have been the first to observe that the opposite of feminism is masculinism, namely the ordinary state of affairs, albeit one not normally known by this title.[37] The distinction between sex (biology) and gender (culture) would have served Gilman's thinking well, but it wasn't around at the time; the focus of her attention was on those aspects of what she called 'sex-distinction' that could and couldn't be changed. She was heavily influenced by the gynaecocentric theory of the panoramic American scientist Lester Ward, another contact she made at the London Congress in 1896. Ward worked for the federal government as a geologist and a paleontologist, but turned his science to the wider service of society in proposing that human interventions based on scientific principles are the best method for enhancing social welfare. These were early days for sociology, and the notion that the social sciences were evolving from a base in the natural sciences very much reflected the Darwinist mood of the times. Gilman liked Ward's science, but what endeared him to her most were his observations of the animal world which caused him to argue that 'the female sex is primary in point both of origin and of importance in the history and economy of organic life … the grandest fact in nature is woman'.[38] Thus, Ward went on, the only sure method for social advance is to place the future in women's hands. His theory of gynaecocentrism, which ensured his success as 'a women's movement celebrity and ladies' man',[39] was first expounded at a meeting on 'Sex Equality' in a Washington hotel in the spring of 1888. Harriot Stanton Blatch's mother, Elizabeth Cady Stanton, was one of those who listened to Ward's paper on 'Women: our better halves'.

Ward and Gilman had a complex relationship, with him persistently seeing her as a poet, and her continually reminding him she was a sociologist. This kind of cultural exchange marked many conversations between women intellectuals and significant male figures at the time. Gilman's non-fiction exposé of patriarchal cultural customs in *The man-made world* (1911) was dedicated to Ward: the book gallops through the institutions of 'the man-made family'; health and beauty; men and art; masculine literature, games and sports; ethics and religion; education, society and fashion; law and government; crime and punishment; politics and warfare; and industry and economics, taking conventional masculinist thinking and practice apart and exposing examples of how gendered men and women are produced by, and in turn sustain, an androcentric culture. For instance, politics as 'the science of government' might just as well apply to the home, since family life entails the preservation of family members' safety, peace and prosperity, the defence of their rights and their moral and educational improvement. This is what women do all the time. But it isn't counted as politics. Our androcentric culture has particularly misled us with respect to the ultra-masculine habit of warfare. We speak of 'civilized warfare': we might just as well speak of 'civilized cannibalism'. Peace congresses compete with toy soldiers and with books celebrating adventurers and destroyers rather than benefactors of human culture. Life, to the male mind, is a fight, so party politics can be redefined as merely 'the technical arrangement to carry on a fight'.[40]

Human work, Gilman's most ambitious text, is a sustained critique of the mistaken economic thinking underlying capitalism and its defenders. Wrong ideas about work underlie much of our distress, she argues. What we need instead is 'the patient, scientific study of the social body, its structure and functions, anatomy, physiology, and pathology, as we have had it for the physical body; we need careful recorded observation of the results of previous remedies, and of new ones as well, and all this in a new field of science'. She uses the analogy of a watch that has gone wrong; the watch must be examined in order to be mended: we must know what a watch is, what it is for, how it is made and how it works. 'So if Society goes wrong we must examine its works, and we cannot tell if they are wrong, nor set them right, unless we have some knowledge of what Society is, what it is for, how it was made, and, above all, how it works.'[41] She wasn't modest about her task in this book, which, unlike her earlier speed-writing for *Women and economics*, went through four drafts: '*Human Work* ... was not to be reeled off like my usual stuff. Here was an enormous change of thought, altering the relationships of all sociological knowledge. As in astronomy we had to change from the geo-centric to the solar-centric theory of our planetary system, with complete revision of our earlier ideas, so here was a change from the ego-centric to the socio-centric system of sociology, with wide resultant alterations in prior concepts.'[42]

'There is nothing of the formal saint in Charlotte Perkins Gilman,' reflected Lester Ward in his Foreword to her autobiography, 'But, essentially, what is a saint? One, perhaps now as always, who would save the world.'[43] Gilman's ideas embraced landscapes far beyond the simple granting of the suffrage; they drew in women from diverse interest groups who found meaning in her texts about the oppressions of domestic life, the misuse of the environment, dress reform, children's rights and/or the dangerous ideologies of patriotism. She dissolved the borders between the family and the home, between the private and the public, turning the entire human world into a policy issue. Her favourite opening gambit in many of the lectures she gave (to mainly female audiences) was a rhetorical question: 'Shall the home be our world? Or the world our home?'[44] Her ideas were radical and exciting, but most of all they made sense at a time of a general 'awakening' among women. This was the title of a special supplement to the (then) new journal the *New Statesman* in 1913. The contribution by Gilman reflected the influence of her work in Britain, and her panoptic idea of the women's movement transforming both national and international relations was echoed in Beatrice Webb's introduction. 'We shall never understand the Awakening of Women until we realize that it is not mere *feminism*,' wrote Webb. 'It is one of three simultaneous world-movements towards a more equal partnership among human beings in human affairs.'[45] (The other two were the labour movement and unrest among 'subject peoples' struggling to develop their own national identities.)

The awakening of women received many organizational prods in these years. Three years after the wet 1896 Congress, an International Congress of Women convened in London by the International Council of Women provided another opportunity for transatlantic interaction.[46] On this occasion, Gilman stayed in a boarding house in Hammersmith recommended by Ellen Starr, the co-founder of the world-famous American Settlement, Hull-House, and she attended a reception in Fulham Palace held by the bishop of London, Mandall Creighton, and his wife, Louise, who wrote historical books and would later lecture on household economy and the theory of the state at the LSE. Tea with Queen Victoria was on offer for the international delegates, but Gilman declined, noting later that her decision had been the right one, because after a long wait the Queen turned up in a coach for only a bit, and tea was served by flunkies. During this stay in England, Gilman renewed some of her previous British contacts. They included someone with wide-ranging interests akin to her own, Jane Hume Clapperton, whose book *Scientific meliorism and the evolution of happiness*, published a decade earlier, promoted science, cooperation, communal living and municipal socialism as keys to social reform.[47] Alice Ravenhill, an educationalist and specialist in household economics and hygiene, who would later help to set up a course on Household and Social Science at the University of London, was representing the National Health Society at the Congress and she also came to call on Gilman. In the formal sessions, Gilman spoke about equal pay for equal work and about her *Women and economics*. Seated next to the Dutch doctor Aletta Jacobs at one of the conference dinners, Gilman took the opportunity to ask her to translate the book into Dutch. Jacobs agreed. A decade further on, Jacobs would also accomplish the translation into Dutch of the book many regarded as the successor to Gilman's: Olive Schreiner's *Woman and labour*.[48]

The focus of the 1899 International Conference of Women was on the economics of women's lives; education, the professions, labour legislation for women and children, the home as a workshop, trade unionism. The gargantuan task of editing the seven volumes of the Conference Proceedings was taken on by Ishbel Hamilton-Gordon, Marchioness of Aberdeen and Temair, the *grande dame* of the International Council of Women. Very tall, with a regally erect carriage, she floated around these gatherings wearing silver and lace, jewels and a tiara.[49] Her aristocratic philanthropy may have annoyed some, but its networking potential was enormously important. Ishbel Aberdeen herself appears under her husband's name in the *Oxford Dictionary of National Biography*, where she is noted to have secured equal access for women to secretariat posts in the League of Nations and to have been an early campaigner for the ordination of women, as well as having accomplished many other beneficent

2.2: Ishbel Hamilton-Gordon, 1899

acts. The 1899 meeting of the International Council of Women was particularly focused, under Aberdeen's direction, on work for peace and international arbitration. She tried to persuade the Austrian peace propagandist and writer Bertha von Suttner to speak, but von Suttner declined, due to illness; she had in any case already made a pivotal contribution to the peace movement with her anti-war novel *Lay down your arms*, which is credited with converting the Tsar of Russia to the peace cause.[50] Von Suttner was the first woman to be awarded the Nobel Peace Prize in 1905, a prestigious institution that she had herself suggested to Alfred Nobel: 'Inform me, convince me, and then I will do something great for the movement,' he told her.[51] Among her litany of achievements was joining Aletta Jacobs as a translator of Gilman's *Women and economics* into German.

One participant who reviewed the Congress for *The Economic Journal* observed that its deliberations provoked two particular questions – questions which are central themes of this book. The first question was, 'What will be the effect on our economic theories and practices if a body of thinkers start with the home and its needs ... and work out into the organisation of the State?' The second was, 'Will the exclusion of women from public life tend to make it easier for them to be pioneers in the interchange of international sympathy and consequent international relations?'[52] The Congress agenda included Clementina Black, a British political activist, suffragist and writer, who talked about the feudal nature of domestic service, and Lina Morgenstern, from Germany, who described the establishment of 'People's Kitchens' in Berlin. This 'prandial prodigy', the brainchild of a wealthy industrialist's 'dreamy' daughter, fed two million people a year on the principle that human welfare depends on the satisfaction of primal needs, of which food, scientifically prepared, is one.[53] Morgenstern may have been considered dreamy, but she was practical enough to set up the Housekeepers' Union, a cooperative store with four thousand members; to have organized an international congress about women's work in Berlin in 1896; and to be an active member of the executive committee of the German Peace Society. Her Berlin kitchen, which spawned an outcrop of many People's Kitchens in many places, was philanthropy, of course, but it also participated in the very important practical project of outsourcing the wasteful domestic labour Gilman and others complained about. Utopian ideas about socialized housework and cooperative housekeeping (as Gilman insisted, these are not the same) were everywhere in this period. Although she is perceived today as something of an extremist with her kitchenless houses and professionalized childcare, Gilman's vision was actually central to a much broader material feminist movement for the redesign of homes. In turn, the socializing of domestic work that could be facilitated only with new architectural formats was ideologically central to important strands of the feminist movement in many countries.

Gilman had her own special mentor in household economics, a woman, 21 years older than she was, to whom she referred in her diaries and correspondence as 'mother', and with whom she lived for some years in a close domestic partnership. Helen Stuart Campbell was born Helen Campbell Stuart but put her mother's maiden name last in her *nom de plume* and then kept it. She was a pioneering social economist who made advanced use of multiple research methods (official reports, government documents, family budgets, individual case-studies). Like many feminists of the period, her interest in creating a better future stemmed from her analysis of present, uncomfortable realities: in *Prisoners of poverty: Women wage-workers, their trades and their lives* (1887), she documented how impossible it was for women and their children to survive on the low wages paid by employers in an unregulated labour market.[54] When she travelled to England, France and Italy to research its sequel, *Prisoners of poverty abroad* (1889), Engels was one of those to whom Campbell took her searching questions about women's work. The book deployed Campbell's characteristic mix of methods, including what official data could be found and case studies ('Among the Dressmakers', 'Nelly, a West-End Milliner's Apprentice', and so on) to show how the conditions of women's labour in the big European cities condemned them and their families to ill-health and poverty. Here she is writing of Covent Garden Market in London, a place luxuriant in class distinctions: 'So, though Covent Garden has in winter "flowers at guineas apiece, pineapples at guineas a pound, and peas at guineas a quart", – these for the rich only, – it has also its possibilities for the poor. They throng about it at all times, for there is always a chance of some stray orange or apple or rejected vegetable that will help out a meal ... Gaunt forms barely covered with rags, hollow eyes fierce with hunger, meet one at every turn in this early morning ... Food for all the world, it would seem, and yet London is not fed ... Men and women huddle here, and under the arches children skulk away like young rats, feeding on offal, lying close to dark corners for warmth, and hunted about also like rats. It is a poverty desperate and horrible beyond that that any other civilized city can show; and who shall say who is responsible, or what the end will be?'[55] Campbell's conclusion from observing this dystopia was, like Gilman's, but considerably before hers, a utopian one: industrial cooperation and organization, land nationalization, state responsibility in the form of a 'co-operative commonwealth'.[56]

Gilman and Campbell set up and ran the Chicago Household Economics Society. Its prospectus contained training classes for household workers, employment registers and detailed proposals for the design of homes. The redesign of housework according to scientific principles was a central part of the reform agenda. Transforming the conditions of domestic life was seen as a matter of political urgency. Utopia might be one name for such a programme; another was welfare. The welfare society one glimpses in these women's texts was driven by the anti-capitalist values of cooperation, altruism and democratic ownership of both power and opportunities, certainly, but it also, very importantly, breathed the ethic of science. *How* society is governed – how its moral aims are best accomplished – must be determined, above all, by *facts*. The spirit of scientific enquiry was spawning *social science*, which was a very different animal from *social work*, the domain to which many women were used to being confined by the masculinist terminology of the times. And it was the tools of social science that promised the best route for turning reform agendas into political reality.

Some of the women who appear in this book were recognized in their lifetimes, others were not. The economist Emily Greene Balch, who attended the 1896 Congress along with Gilman and other notables, was sacked from her professorship in economics and sociology by her university in the US in 1918 for engaging in the international peace movement, and she wasn't even acknowledged by it or by the United States government when she was awarded the Nobel Peace Prize in 1946. She is 80 in the press photograph which was taken for the occasion, and she wears a suitably grave expression under an uncharacteristically floral hat. As a young woman, Balch had studied economics in Berlin and sat in the Tiergarten there alongside the 'beautiful golden-haired' Mary Kingsbury (later Simkhovitch), with whom she read Kant and tried to hear the nightingales reputed to inhabit the garden. She and Kingsbury had to get permission from the Rector of the University and from all the professors individually with whom they wanted to study, as women were barred from the University of Berlin; it helped this process, noted Balch wryly, that Kingsbury was so beautiful.[57] In a long life of extraordinary (and extraordinarily forgotten) accomplishments,

Balch's understanding of the meanings of national and cultural identity, a subject embedded in the move from a warfare to a welfare society, marked her out from other scholars and activists. She wrote once about her own personal sense of being a global citizen: 'Every night before I go upstairs to bed I step out of doors and look up at the sky ... The stars are remote, innumerable, incomprehensible ... My mind returns as a bird to its nest to

2.3: Emily Balch in 1946, receiving the Nobel Peace Prize

the familiar earth. The stars are alien to me but no spot on earth is alien to me – the earth is my home ... I cannot be expatriated or exiled, alive or dead.'[58] On her 75th birthday, the Women's International League for Peace and Freedom, the organization with which Balch was most associated, gave a lunch in her honour; her speech was called 'Towards a planetary civilization':

> When war came in 1914 I felt this at first mainly as a senseless interruption of social-economic progress. I felt that war must be got rid of so that the threat of war might not interrupt and distort the course of this progress. Only gradually I came to understand at least partly how deeply war is intertwined with our whole economic and social system, our scale of values, our ideas of what is right and of supreme importance.
>
> I see no chance of social progress apart from fundamental changes on both the economic and political side, replacing national anarchy by organized cooperation of all peoples to further their common interest, and replacing economic anarchy, based on the search for personal profit, by a great development of the cooperative spirit. Peace is too small a word for all this, too negative in its connotations.
>
> I have a very considerable distrust of government as such, and see no reason to be sure that a world government would be run by men very different in capacity and moral quality from those who govern national states.
>
> My thoughts run rather to international administration of those matters which are of common interest – to the setting up of international authorities to take charge of interests which concern all peoples. They must act as trustees, in fact. The psychology of a trustee is very different from that of a politician ...

When Balch had finished her speech there was no applause: people were shocked into silence, thinking it might be her last. No, she said, this isn't my swan song, I intend to live a while longer: my grandfather used to say an old woman is as tough as a boiled owl.[59]

THREE

Settlement sociology: discovering social science

This was the first generation of women to have the experience of university education, and no one knew quite what to do with them. So they had to invent their own project. For many, this was the Social Science Movement, a heroic determination to combine an understanding of how society works with efforts to make it work better. From a seamless joining of science, imagination and radical reform, they proposed a world that dissolved the traditional bifurcation of the public and the private, the domestic and the social, which has always handicapped attempts to establish effective welfare services. Because the women's project seemed so different, it has been eclipsed by the way in which the histories of social science and reform have been written. These have shone the spotlight instead on men's efforts to build a theory-based social science, removed from practical realities and safely ensconced in the detached haven of universities.

This chapter is about the development of social science and voluntary welfare services outside universities in social settlements which were established in Europe and the US in the late 19th century. Although Settlements weren't uniquely female innovations, the women who set many of them up and worked in them did help to generate a particular kind of knowledge about social conditions. 'Settlement sociology' describes a mix of empirical research, pioneering methodology, social theory and socio-political activism that typified the work of reformers living in these places.[1] Women organizing as women wasn't itself a new idea. Before the First World War, it was the rule rather than the exception in many countries for women to organize separately from men; they weren't, on the whole, welcome in the men's organizations. In Britain, for example, membership conditions for the Labour Party kept most women out (members had to be male heads of household or belong to a trade union).[2]

Women's education had also, of course, mostly been on special terms: women's colleges, women teachers, women's subjects, a blanket prohibition on admission to the spaces of masculine academia. In London, the British Museum Reading Room furnished a physical and metaphorical illustration of the problem. 'The swing doors swung open,' wrote Virginia Woolf in *A room of one's own* in 1929, 'and there one stood under the vast dome, as if one were a thought in the huge bald forehead which is so splendidly encircled by a band of famous names.'[3] The masculine panopticon of the Reading Room was under constant surveillance by a superintendent, who wore a top hat and was seated on a raised central platform. By the 1870s, when the room had become distinctly overcrowded, complaints were made about the pressure caused by the presence of ladies, whose silk and muslin skirts disturbed with their rustling, who ate strawberries and talked and who, most significantly, refused to keep to the two tables set aside specifically for their use.[4] This demonization of women readers was repeated on the other side of the Atlantic, where public libraries sported feminine reading rooms with fireplaces, potted plants and small tables designed for letter writing rather than serious reading.[5]

In the 1880s and 1890s in the British Museum Reading Room, British Fabian socialist, researcher and cofounder of the LSE Beatrice Webb was there, researching trade unions, encouraged by Sidney, who thought she should do more of this kind of sensible documentary research rather than spending her time interviewing or observing. Beatrice talked to Marx's fiery daughter Eleanor in the refreshment room, thinking her slovenly in appearance and peculiar in her views about love: Marx herself was outraged to discover the Library's copy of the Kama Sutra locked up and unavailable to women. Other women who used the Reading Room as what one of them called a 'workshop' and a 'refuge' included the social investigator Clementina Black and the writers Margaret Harkness, Amy Levy, Vernon Lee and Olive

Schreiner, whose reputation for both fact and fiction weaves its way through any story about what women did and thought during these transformative years. The office of the Women's Trade Union League, which Black helped to found, was round the corner from the British Museum, and she, Levy and Marx all lived in Bloomsbury, within walking distance. The three of them went together to the first London performance of Ibsen's infamous *The doll's house*; Levy wrote some scathing satires about the misogyny of Reading Room customs, and about the arrogance of male professors who grumble about women; and Marx co-authored a forgotten new version of the third act of Ibsen's play, *A doll's house repaired*, which parodies public views about the independence of 'the new woman'.[6]

While all this, and a good deal more, was going on in London, a group of keen young college-educated 'new women' had conceived a grand plan for university outposts in some of the most disadvantaged urban neighbourhoods in the US. The driving force was a professor of English literature, prolific writer and religious radical, Vida Dutton Scudder, a serious young woman in the photograph taken around the time the developments described in this chapter got off the ground. Born in India in 1861, Scudder was the daughter of a congregational missionary; she spent much of her early life in European art museums and galleries, and much of her adult life trying to engineer a fit between Christianity and Marxist socialism: her friends joked that her real home was either the Middle Ages or the utopian future.[7] She had attended the liberal arts faculty for women in Massachusetts, Smith College, five years after it was founded, and then on graduation became one of the first American women to study at Oxford. There she heard John Ruskin's last series of lectures on 'The pleasures of England'; it was Ruskin who converted her to socialism. Ruskin may have been the first

3.1: Vida Scudder, c. 1890

to float the idea of the 'settlement' to his students in his grand house in London's Denmark Hill at a meeting in 1868. The idea was that 'colonies of settlers' should be formed in working-class neighbourhoods as a strategy for bridging the growing chasm between rich and poor.[8] The immediate result was Toynbee Hall in Whitechapel, opened by Canon Samuel Barnett and his wife, Henrietta, on Christmas Eve 1884, in a gothic Victorian vicarage next to Canon Barnett's church, St Jude's. Henrietta had more to do with this venture than is usually acknowledged, including coming up with the name.[9] The political economist Arnold Toynbee, another of Ruskin's disciples, had nothing to do with the Settlement named after him, having done only two weeks' vacation work in the East End, and having died prematurely from meningitis at the age of 30 the year before. But Toynbee *was* a man brave enough to teach Oxford women political economy in a room above a baker's shop at a time when they were prevented from attending college lectures.[10]

As capitalist industrialization and urbanization gained pace in both Europe and America from the mid-19th century on, so the exploitation of male workers and of women and children increased and became literally more visible. Social consciences were aroused, but facts were needed. Who were the poor, and how many of them were there? Why were they poor? What was the answer: private charity or state welfare? The story of Settlement sociology takes us into a landscape of interconnected histories: of people's attempts to understand and ameliorate the rampant damages of 19th- and early 20th-century capitalism; of women's emancipation; of their largely unvalorized stamp on the policy-making process; of the wonderful forms that social investigation can take; of class and ethnic conflict and their meanings in everyday life; of how political and social networks are formed and operate; of how, out of all this, something we ultimately called 'the welfare state' came to be woven. Among the welfare achievements accredited to the Settlement movement are the following: the first public baths; the first distribution system of safe milk for children; well-baby clinics; supervised public playgrounds; pre-school care and education; industrial trade schools; the school nursing and public health nursing services; model housing developments and laws to regulate low-income housing; minimum wage legislation and legislation restricting working hours and women and children's labour; the first probation system and juvenile courts; public libraries; and schools for disabled children. Among the roll-call of the famous who passed through the doors of one Settlement or another in Britain or the US and were influenced by Settlement sociology are Britain's LSE director and architect of the welfare state, William Beveridge; Clement Attlee, another reformer who taught at the LSE and was later prime minister; two other prime ministers to be, of Canada and Britain, Mackenzie King and Ramsay Macdonald; and a number of architects of the New Deal legislation of the 1930s in the US, Eleanor Roosevelt, Frances Perkins and Henry Morgenthau among them.

The American English literature specialist Vida Scudder had met the Barnetts, and she'd heard about Toynbee Hall. She was excited by the potentially revolutionary programme of undertaking social reform by living among the poor. It happened like this: she was walking and talking at a reunion with her Smith College friends in meadows by the wide Connecticut river in the autumn sunshine of 1887 when, 'Suddenly, a Thought flew among us, like a bird coming out of the air; flashing above and around, seen, vanished: Why could not we young women start something of the same kind in our own country?'[11] It took them two years, held back by the lack of funds and by parental opposition, but they – the prime movers were Scudder and two other university women friends, Katharine Lee Bates and Katharine Coman – managed to open the first women's Settlement in the United States at 95 Rivington Street on New York's Lower East Side in September 1889.

Scudder's Settlement was in an old, run-down aristocratic mansion at the centre of a highly congested tenement-house district. When the College Settlement, as it was named, first opened its silver-hinged mahogany doors, there were seven residents, representing three women's colleges. They painted floors and sewed carpets, washed windows and shovelled snow. Their first visitor was the local policeman, perplexed by the presence of such women in the midst of the slums, and suspecting it to be a house for ladies of a different kind. Many women were attracted to the idea of thus living in the slums:

there were 80 applications for residency in the first year. The College Settlement's first offering to the neighbourhood was a facility for bathing at five cents a time in gas-lighted bathrooms. Following huge demand, this activity was soon taken over by other charitable organizations. In 1911, 95 Rivington Street boasted multiple clubs and classes, a library, a savings bank, a kindergarten, music and cooking schools, medical aid, and work in connection with the courts, schools, churches and other philanthropic organizations. Social science classes had been started in 1894 to generate social awareness among residents and the community about subjects such as tenement housing, public schools and the history of factory legislation; social reform was a key Settlement aim.[12]

The opening of Scudder's College Settlement predated by two weeks the much more famous Hull-House Settlement in Chicago (a fact which she is at pains to point out twice in her autobiography, *On journey*). Hull-House, the most renowned of all the women's Settlements, was also prompted by the model of Toynbee Hall. It was initiated by another young woman in search of a vocation, Jane Addams, whom Samuel Barnett once called 'the greatest man in America'.[13] Founded five years after Toynbee Hall in 1889, Hull-House was a phenomenal achievement; and if there is one woman whose life and philosophy run like an iron seam throughout this book, it is Jane Addams. The story of how she and her accomplice, Ellen Starr, collaborated in the setting up of

3.2: Jane Addams, 1914

Hull-House is well known: two young, educated women, searching for a satisfying occupation in a world of narrow opportunities, finally deciding to set up a 'Toynbee Hall experiment' in a poor district of Chicago.[14] Addams described her new neighbourhood thus: 'The streets are inexpressibly dirty, the number of schools inadequate, factory legislation unenforced, the street-lighting bad, the paving miserable and altogether lacking in the alleys and smaller streets, and the stables defy all laws of sanitation. Hundreds of houses are unconnected with the street sewer.'[15] In 1889 Addams and Starr took over part of a house built by a wealthy philanthropist, Charles Hull, then the whole house, and eventually it expanded into no fewer than 13 buildings. Hull-House stood on South Halsted Street, one of Chicago's great thoroughfares, at the corner of Polk Street, between the stockyards to the south and the ship-building yards on the north branch of the Chicago river. Addams lived in Hull-House for the rest of her life; it's one of two affiliations she asked to have inscribed on her gravestone.[16] Under her leadership, Hull-House became a research, community and professional training centre, all at the same time. Her reputation as 'the lady abbess of Chicago' concealed an 'expert executive' with formidable talents in initiating and organizing activities and people; someone whose ability to finance Settlement sociology was a matter both of shrewd business acumen and of knowing the right people.[17] Samuel Barnett was right, although he got the gender wrong: Jane Addams was, during the early years of the 20th century, quite the most famous woman in America. When she seconded Theodore Roosevelt's nomination as the presidential candidate for the Progressive party in 1912, her ovation was as great as his.[18]

It is to Jane Addams that we must turn for the fullest articulation of Settlement house philosophy and sociology. Addams was born and died in the same years as Charlotte Perkins Gilman, sharing with her both the challenge of developing an intellectual and moral framework for a new orientation to knowledge and social action, and various life experiences, including a mental breakdown and the draconian Weir Mitchell method of repair. Both women recovered by locating themselves in female communities and a restorative vision of a social system that would not drive women mad, impoverish more than half the population and drive wedges between people of different genders, ethnicities and classes. Addams and Gilman met for the first time in 1894, and the following year Gilman lectured at Hull-House and stayed there, returning in 1896 and then repeatedly. It was said that many of the practical reform suggestions outlined in Gilman's utopian novels and non-fiction works had originally been designed and tested in Ward Nineteen (where Hull-House was located). It was there that Gilman personally witnessed the imaginative projects she advocated: the public kitchen, where professionals prepared healthy family meals; the professionally run day-care centres which freed women for outside work; the resource of community-based recreation with music, art, a library, a theatre and a gymnasium. Addams actually asked Gilman to head another Settlement, Unity House, on the North Side of Chicago, in an area of decrepit housing and lawlessness otherwise known as 'Little Hell': 'The loathly river flowed sluggishly by, thick and ill-smelling ... low, dark brick factories and gloomy wooden dwellings often below the level of the street; foul plank sidewalks, rotten and full of holes; black mud underfoot, damp soot drifting steadily down over everything.'[19] Gilman's description of the district reflected her feelings about it, and she declined Addams' offer, handing on the job instead to her friend Helen Stuart Campbell.

Addams' view of the contribution Settlements could make to knowledge involved the redefinition of knowledge itself. 'Just as we do not know a fact until we can play with it,' she wrote in a paper on 'A function of the social settlement' in 1899, 'so we do not possess knowledge until we have an impulse to bring it into use; not the didactic impulse, not the propagandist impulse, but that which would throw [it] into the stream of common human experience.' Addams argued that the work of the Hull-House women and other like-minded reformers represented the coalescence of two disparate traditions: the Charitable and the Radicals. Both came to recognize that the social causes of poverty and injustice had to be addressed in a programme of 'Vital Welfare' which could be mounted only on a basis of 'verified knowledge' and social legislation. Rejecting conventional philanthropy, she stressed the need not to impose knowledge from above but to create it together: social science knowledge must come from civic participation across class and ethnic divisions. We must, she said, recognize the 'social disorders arising from conscienceless citizenship'. Above all, she saw the work of Settlements as about socializing democracy and extending it beyond its simple political expression. The vote itself is no guarantee of democratic participation; people may have the vote but nonetheless be condemned to lives of ostracism and exclusion.[20]

The women researchers and reformers who gathered around Jane Addams and her vision effectively made up 'a Hull-House School of Sociology'.[21] There were the Abbott sisters, Edith and Grace, the one a more theoretical version of the other. Edith had a PhD in economics, studied at the LSE with the Webbs, and took back to Wellesley College, where she taught, the outline of the Webbs' course on methods of investigation. Edith Abbott's prolific publications and policy inputs included work on immigrants, women in industry, the penal system, and a direct role in the 1935 Social Security Act. The focus of much of her sister Grace's attention was on child labour. Their co-

3.3: Hull-House sociologists: Edith Abbott and Grace Abbott, Julia Lathrop (top), Sophonisba Breckinridge, Florence Kelley (bottom)

resident Julia Lathrop headed the first United States Children's Bureau between 1912 and 1921, before Grace took it over; in her early years at Hull-House, Lathrop had personally inspected all 102 poorhouses for which the state of Illinois was responsible, and had described and campaigned against a system which put mentally ill people alongside the physically ill and destitute, depriving them of light, proper food, employment, trained care and the possibility of cure.[22] She also undertook research on infant mortality, using the results to argue successfully for federal aid to protect mothers and children, and she worked with Sophonisba Breckinridge, one of the first American women lawyers, to create the Chicago School of Civics and Philanthropy, which later became part of the University of Chicago. Breckinridge's own mark was on almost every area of Hull-House's expertise: housing; immigration; women's work; child labour; juvenile delinquency; the family and the state; social welfare policy. Another Hull-House resident, Florence Kelley, was also legally trained. In addition Hull-House was home to Dr Alice Hamilton, who invented toxicology and the study of occupational health through painstaking research on the links between dangerous trades and their impact on the human body. When British social investigator Beatrice Webb visited Hull-House in 1898, she found all these personages highly confusing – 'a stream of persons, queer, well-intentioned, cranky, moving restlessly from room to room'; combined with the unappetizing food and the unspeakable garbage outside, Webb's visit was like a bad dream lightened only by Jane Addams' 'charming grey eyes and gentle voice and graphic power of expression'.[23]

The socialist lawyer and Settlement resident Florence Kelley, 'the woman who had probably the largest single share in shaping the social history of the United States' in the first 30 years of the 20th century,[24] first showed up at Hull-House just before breakfast time on a snowy morning between Christmas 1891 and New Year 1892. She came with a distinguished pedigree in law, economics, sociology and socialism, and during her time at Hull-House she established a fiery reputation as a social analyst, researcher and campaigner. Born in 1859 in a comfortable home in Philadelphia, Kelley was one of eight children, only three of whom survived into adulthood. Her five sisters died young of preventable infections. And, 'All this grief', she noted in her autobiography, 'occurred, not on the plains as a hardship of pioneer life, not in the Great American Desert where physicians were out of reach, but within four miles of Independence Hall, in one of the great and famous cities of the Nineteenth Century.'[25] She herself rarely went to school, because of the danger that she too would become ill and die. The other powerful influence of Kelley's early life was her father's conviction that well-off children must know how poor children live. He taught her to read with a text carrying woodcuts of deformed children labouring in factories, and told her about the evils of industrialization and slavery. William Kelley, a friend of Abraham Lincoln, an abolitionist and a principled opponent of free trade, took Florence as a child in 1883 to see child labour in glass and steel factories, and later to England. 'Never to be forgotten,' she wrote later in her autobiography of this visit, 'was the first of our visits in the Black Country. A poor woman working in a lean-to at the back of her two-room cottage, was hammering chains on an anvil. The raw material was brought to her by a man driving a wagon-load to be distributed throughout the neighbourhood, and the chains were collected and paid for by him when finished for the owner. Her tears fell on her anvil as she told us, without pausing to look up, how she had been arrested and taken before the Justice of the Peace, who sent her to jail for her third failure to send her children to school under the compulsory education law which had then been in force thirteen years ... Father asked why a justice sent a mother of three children to jail instead of the father. She replied: "But Sir, that was an act of mercy, because he earns more than I do, and the loss to the family was less when I was sent away."'[26]

There were thoughtful and radical women in Kelley's background too, especially great-aunt Sarah Pugh born in 1800, who never wore cotton or ate sugar because both of these were produced by slaves. On Sundays Sarah would sit on the porch, knitting, to protest against the rigid Sabbatarianism of Philadelphia, together with her friend Lucretia Mott, co-organizer with Elizabeth Cady Stanton of the famous 1848 Seneca Falls Women's Rights Convention, the first public women's rights meeting in the United States. A concern for the plight of women was unsurprisingly central to Kelley's adult work. After her unconventional childhood education, she took a first degree in history and social science at Cornell University, and then, rejected because of her sex by the University of Pennsylvania, she moved for graduate study in government and law to the University of Zürich, which had quietly opened its doors to women in 1867, the first European university to do so. Zürich was full of women studying law and medicine, and there was a good sprinkling of revolutionary socialism among many students. Added to Kelley's feminism, this produced a highly combustible mixture. People knew her as explosive and hot-tempered, as frighteningly vital and demanding, with the voice and the presence of a great actress. She was described in her Cornell days as a tall, erect young woman of graceful carriage with an abundance of chestnut hair. Later, and like many women activists of the period, she had no time for clothes or fashion and so was regarded as dowdy.[27]

The socialism Kelley met at the University of Zürich wasn't the watered-down Anglo-American variety, but the full-blooded Marxist kind. Wondering what she might do to help the movement, and having read all the Marxist literature she could lay her hands on, she discovered that, although *Das Kapital* was in the process of appearing in English, no one had yet taken Engels' *The condition of the working class in England* out of its original German. Engels' book, written in his early twenties about industrial life in Manchester, appealed to her for its methodological mixture of keen observation and systematic statistics, an approach she would follow in her own work. Tentatively, she wrote to the great man. Thus began a memorable correspondence that lasted, with one slightly acrimonious break, until Engels' death in 1895. They met briefly only twice.[28] Kelley's translation appeared in 1887 in the US and in 1891 in the UK and was the only one available in English until 1958. She accomplished it while giving birth to three children and dealing with the consequences of her marriage to an unstable Russian doctor, Lazare Wischnewetzky. Kelley decided to leave the marriage and relocate in Illinois, where a legal divorce might be possible. The account of the hearing at which she sought custody of her children records what we know today to be a sadly ordinary account of domestic violence to which Kelley never referred in any of her autobiographical writings or extant correspondence: Dr Wischnewetzky hit his wife, disfiguring her, spat in her face and used abusive language to her in front of the children, for no apparent reason. As Kelley told the judge, on one such occasion, 'the mantel-piece had not been dusted, the Doctor came down before the dusting was done and the Doctor was very much outraged over it'.[29]

Nicholas Kelley was six when his mother took him and his siblings to Hull-House. On that snowy winter's day when they arrived on the doorstep of Hull-House they found there 'Henry Standing Bear, a Kickapoo Indian, waiting for the front door to be opened. It was Miss Addams who opened it, holding on her left arm a … fat, pudgy baby belonging to the cook, who was behindhand with breakfast. Miss Addams was a little hindered in her movements by a super-energetic kindergarten child, left by its mother while she went to a sweatshop for a bundle of cloaks to be finished.' Florence Kelley stayed seven years as a resident at Hull-House (she later moved to the Henry Street Settlement in New York), and Henry Standing Bear stayed some months, as a Hull-House janitor, before rejoining his tribe.[30] It was the best bringing-up and educating of anyone he knew, reported Nicholas Kelley decades later: 'Nothing else is like a good settlement, and Hull House in those early days was the settlement of settlements. Every day held an adventure of some kind.'[31] At the beginning, Florence Kelley's children were boarded temporarily with a family nearby, and she shared a room with Dr Harriet Rice, a young African-American doctor who couldn't get work in Chicago because of the double jeopardy of being Black and female: instead she provided free medical services for the Hull-House neighbourhood. Kelley herself began by teaching English in the evenings to 600 eager immigrants a week – Austrians, Bohemians, French, Germans, Poles and Russians. As she would later show in her research, the square mile around Hull-House was home to no fewer than 18 different nationalities. Her daytime task was to run a small experimental employment office for working girls and women set up in a corner of the undertaking establishment next to the main Hull-House building on Halsted Street. 'I am … learning more in a week, of the actual conditions of proletarian life in America, than in any previous year,' she wrote enthusiastically to Engels. 'We have a colony of efficient and intelligent women living in a workingmen's quarter, with the house used for all sorts of purposes by about a thousand persons a week. The last form of its activity is the formation of unions of which we have three, the cloakmakers, the shirtmakers and the bookbinders. Next week we are to take the initiative in the systematic endeavor to clear out the sweating dens. There is a fever heat of interest in that phase of the movement just at present.'[32]

The 'sweating system' was a well-developed but virtually unregulated method of exploiting the labour of families making or finishing goods at home. It was widespread in the later 19th and early 20th centuries in Europe and the US. Because women and children predominated among the workers, sweating was a key focus of many women reformers' and researchers' attention. The work was often done under dangerous and insanitary conditions, for long hours and at very low rates of pay. It was highly profitable for the manufacturers, who could thereby cut the employment of men in the factories. Kelley had started to work on child labour before she went to Hull-House, interrogating official data, which were horribly inadequate, but they did show that in 1880 there were 1,118,000 American children aged 10 to 15 working in every conceivable industry. State records showed textile workers as young as five and tenement workers as young as four vulnerable to appalling casualties: fires, scalding, drowning in vats of acid, maiming of limbs by unguarded machinery.[33] Kelley's work attracted the attention of Carroll D. Wright, the United States Commissioner of Commerce and Labor. Kelley proposed that the State Bureau of Labor should make a formal investigation of the sweating system; the spring after her arrival at Hull-House, she was taken on by the Bureau as a Special Agent. Her investigations included 10,000 'schedules' to be filled in by sweaters' victims in the clothing trades: the work, she explained to Engels, 'consists in shop visitation, followed by house-to-house visitation'. This must have been laborious work, and it certainly called on her linguistic skills, since her interviewees included 'Poles, Bohemians, Neapolitans, Sicilians and Russian Hebrews'.[34]

Kelley defined social science as 'the science of social relations'. 'These must be studied as they exist,' she insisted, 'with patient care; but exact tabulation of facts is the beginning only; afterward comes the work of interpretation.'[35] Her work was the driving force behind the best-known of Hull-House's social science products, *Hull-House maps and papers: A presentation of nationalities and wages in a congested district of Chicago, together with comments and essays on problems growing out of the social conditions*, published in 1895. The Hull-House volume's 10 chapters included two by men, the first by a local leader of the Italian community, Alessandro Mastro-Valerio, and the second by Charles Zeublin, ex-Hull-House resident, founder of the Northwestern University Settlement and a sociologist at the University of Chicago. Ten Hull-House residents contributed to the venture, which was modelled on Charles Booth's 17-volume *Life and labour of the people in London*, published six years earlier. Booth's own attempt to inject facts into the debate about the extent and nature of industrial poverty was actually the result of a 20-strong team, including six women, who contributed to the collection of statistics, the interviewing and the writing. The women included Beatrice Webb (then Potter); Mary Booth, Charles's wife (and Beatrice's cousin); the housing reformer Octavia Hill; and the statistician and economist (and friend of Eleanor Marx) Clara Collet.[36] It was Beatrice Webb who recognized, when she looked back at her life in *My apprenticeship*, just how pioneering Booth's work had been in using a team to develop methods for joining qualitative with quantitative information about social structure – a discovery claimed much later by social scientists in the 1980s.[37] In an incisive page in her autobiography, Webb also drew attention to the issue of gender and interviewing, noting that she was a much more sensitive interviewer than Charles Booth, and would, for example, have got much more out of 'Mr. L.', a defensive factory inspector at the Home Office, a 'square-built man, with general impression of checked suit', than Charles did.[38]

Florence Kelley's son Nicholas remembers as a child seeing the residents of Hull-House sitting in Jane Addams' study, colouring in the maps which are a central feature of *Hull-House maps and papers*. One showed the distribution of different ethnic communities, another their incomes: gold meant 20 dollars or more total weekly income for a family; black, five dollars or less. As Kelley noted, the Hull-House maps bore much more black than gold. Florence Kelley wrote a chapter on the sweating system, and another with Alzina Stephens on wage-earning children. By the time the book was published, she had been appointed Chief State Factory Inspector, and Stephens was her Assistant Inspector, a post for which she was, sadly, well-fitted, having lost a finger to an unguarded loom as a child labourer in a New Hampshire cotton mill. Kelley, Stephens and their staff of 12 spent the first three months finding out where women and children were employed, and weighing, measuring and photographing children in order to demonstrate the adverse physical effects of particular types of work. Boys working in the cutlery trade, for example, all showed the same deformity of their right shoulders. Kelley's Factory Inspector reports were full of comprehensive maps and tables, plus insights and analytical discussion: 'She regarded each one not as routine duty, but rather in the nature of a sociological study.'[39]

This was a social science that was being invented hand-in-hand with the passion for welfare reform. A defining characteristic of Kelley's own mix of philanthropy and social science was its theoretical framework. This she outlined most notably in a paper written 'in the intervals of daily drudgery' when her children were little, partly in response to Engels' call that the American middle classes might benefit from a series of pamphlets introducing them to Marxist socialism. Kelley's 'The need of theoretical preparation for philanthropic work' was essentially an elementary lesson in Marxism.[40] A socialist analysis of philanthropic work, she argued, highlights the existence of two kinds of philanthropy, 'bourgeois' and 'working class'. Bourgeois philanthropy is one of palliatives and restitution. But working-class philanthropy is reciprocal and mutual. Through such activities as trade unions and sick-benefit societies, workers help each other, simultaneously striking heavy blows at the production of surplus value. The point about surplus value may have escaped the average reader, but Kelley's attack on bourgeois philanthropy was enormously powerful, and offensive to many. Her paper was read to the May 1887 meeting of the New York chapter of the Association of Collegiate Alumnae and, when published in the Christian Union a month later, provoked over 80 letters of enquiry and remonstrance. One protesting article was signed by Vida Scudder, who took issue with the 'bitter tone' of Kelley's essay and decried 'intense radicals who foster class hatred'. Kelley's calm reply observed that such comments totally lost sight of the *economic basis of the argument*.[41]

Women Settlement researchers, living, as many did, in the midst of immigrant communities, were early sensitive to ethnic divisions. Economist Emily Balch, a Settlement researcher and regular visitor to Hull-House, carried out research on immigrants from Eastern Europe both in America and in their origin countries; her *Our Slavic fellow citizens* (1910) was a magnum opus of 536 pages based on meticulous statistical and participant observation research, and a scholarly defence of the cultural and economic benefits of free immigration from diverse places.[42] The economist and first woman professor of statistics in the United States, Katharine Coman – she who helped Vida Scudder set up the College Settlement Association – researched the lives of Black freehold farmers in the South (as well as economic history in Britain and the US, the sweating system, the market and water supply, and contract labour in Hawaii – an encyclopaedic spread of subjects characteristic of much female Settlement sociology).[43] Grace Abbott, the political scientist who lived at Hull-House, published on the Greeks in Chicago in the *American Journal of Sociology* in 1909, and had a lifelong interest in immigrant culture and living conditions.[44] The African-American academic and activist W. E. B. DuBois's much-acclaimed study of *The Philadelphia Negro* in 1898 happened only because the sociologist Katharine Bement Davis, who headed the College Settlement in Philadelphia, and Susan Parrish Wharton, a reformer with a long-term interest in the conditions of the Black population, persuaded the University of Pennsylvania to sponsor such a study.[45] DuBois followed the example of the Hull-House women in designing the questionnaires and maps for his project. Rarely remembered is the fact that almost a fifth of DuBois's landmark study was written by a resident of Hull-House, Isabel Eaton, who took on the forgotten subject of poor Black women's domestic work.[46]

Women substantially outnumbered men in Settlement work. At a time when they couldn't vote, or lead governments or churches, or practise as professionals, or exercise property rights and rights over their children, or do any number of things which men could do, Settlements enabled women to create independent, community-based democracies. They offered women the chance of independent living, of networking and friendship with other women, and a route into policy-relevant social research. The dominant metaphor for male Settlement-founders, on the other hand, was one of colonization: colonies of settlers bound for the distant lands of places not so far away which needed some civilizing influence.[47] The British Labour politician George Lansbury remarked, rather unkindly, that 'men who went in training under the Barnetts … could always be sure of government and municipal appointments … [They] discovered the advancement of their own interests and the interests of the poor were best served by leaving East London to stew in its own juice.'[48] Toynbee Hall resembled a cross between an Oxbridge college and a gentleman's club, but the interiors of the women's Settlements looked like ordinary homes.

Robert Woods, an American theologian and apostle of the Settlement movement, who spent six months at Toynbee Hall in 1890, listed in the *Handbook of settlements* that he co-authored in 1911 a total of 479 then in existence, including 413 in the US and 46 in the UK.[49] By 1900, the Settlement movement had spread throughout the British Empire, to Western Europe, Japan, China, India and Canada. The first Nordic settlements (known as 'hemgårdar') started in Stockholm and Copenhagen in 1912, with a strong emphasis on practical research.[50] The first Austrian settlement, in Vienna, was the brainchild of two feminists, Else Federn and Marie Lang, both of whom had been exposed to Settlement life in London.[51] Settlements were part of a 'transatlantic network of reform movements', accentuated, in the case of women, by their shared commitment to enlarging the sphere of women's public work.[52] This cross-cultural exchange of ideas about Settlement sociology and reform was fertilized by the explosion of print culture and the growth in international communication which happened between about 1880 and 1920. Women's reform networks developed their own routes for exchanging ideas and information; for example, key periodicals such as the Boston-based *Woman's Journal* and London's *Votes for Women* shared a reprint arrangement, publishing letters from readers in each other's countries and offering as prizes subscriptions to the other journal.[53] Some reformers such as Alice Salomon in Germany (see Chapter Seven) were especially dedicated to spreading information about developments in other countries. Salomon took the trouble to publicize in Germany the work of Settlements and of women factory inspectors in the US and Britain, and she was enthusiastic about the invaluable British work being done on survey and other social research methodology.[54]

The Settlement scene is inhabited by many major and minor characters, some more remembered than others. There was, for example, the Victoria Women's Settlement in Liverpool, founded eight years after Hull-House, the centre of much original work into the conditions of labouring families and the breeding ground for some of British social reformer/politician Eleanor Rathbone's pioneering ideas about the need to break the cycle of women and children's economic dependence on the fluctuating fortunes and attitudes of men. It was from the Victoria Women's Settlement that Rathbone undertook her modest enquiry in 1907–8 into the conditions of dock labourers' families: 41 households completing 429 weeks of detailed budget and menu diaries, requiring 629 visits from the investigative team, in an enterprise intended to do for Liverpool what Mr Seebohm Rowntree had done for York. In one of these Liverpool households, a father and mother and four children – an 18-year-old girl in the tobacco works, a 15-year-old errand boy and two younger children – lived in three sparsely furnished dirty rooms. Out of 80 food items entered for one week, 57 consisted of bread, margarine and tea.[55]

The Fern Street Settlement in London's East End confronted many of the same social problems. Clara Ellen Grant, who opened it, was the rebellious daughter of a rural family, a head teacher of a 'little tin' school on Bow Common in one of London's most deprived districts (where all the schools were built of tin). Grant observed that exhausted, malnourished children are unlikely to learn. So she started providing school breakfasts of bread and butter and warm milk, sleep time for the smallest children and a school nurse – the first in London. The school nurse also visited at home every baby born to a family in the school community throughout its first year of life, attempting to lower what Grant recorded as the unacceptably high rate of infant mortality in the area. In her application for the job, she had written that she had studied 'sociology in its simpler and more practical aspects'; at the interview, when asked in wrathful tones what she knew about it, she had replied, 'I follow Mr and Mrs Sidney

3.4: Clara Grant, 'the Bundle Lady of Bow'

Webb's advice. I study the little bit of social structure to which I belong.'[56] Having spent some time at Toynbee Hall and having met Jane Addams, Grant started a small, informal Settlement in her own home in Fern Street. There people could find cheap clothes, a food cooperative, a library, classes in practical subjects, information about any jobs going, a medical club, a boot club, a fireguard club and emergency help for any kind of problem. Grant's informal title, 'the farthing bundle woman of Bow', was derived from the parcels of toys she made up for children, who queued outside the school from early in the morning to get them, sometimes as many as five hundred by 6 am. The children paid a farthing for their toys, since Grant believed that paying a notional amount would encourage self-respect.[57] In all these ventures, Grant was encouraged by Jane Addams' remark to her, that in the field of altruism and social action there was a place for both small and large Settlements.[58]

A decade before Grant's venture, on the other side of the Atlantic, the daughter of a slave, Janie Porter Barrett, founded the first Settlement for African-Americans in Virginia, from similarly small domestic beginnings. Her work began when she watched a group of girls playing outside her home on Locust Street in a black area in Hampton, Virginia. Barrett thought that children and young people deserved more resources for leading constructive lives. The Locust Street Settlement, founded in 1890, started with a sewing club and then attracted parents and young people alike to a range of 'Departments' or clubs that encouraged habits of efficiency, productivity and good citizenship. You could

3.5: Janie Porter Barrett

learn how to keep chickens or grow vegetables all year round, but there were also night classes in academic subjects intended to raise the status and employability of the Black community.[59] These endeavours produced Barrett's other big achievement, the Virginia Industrial School for Colored Girls, which began life as a more humane alternative for the large numbers of young African-American girls (some as young as eight) who were being sent to jail for minor misdemeanours. The School was so successful that by 1920 it had been taken over by the State government and incorporated into the Virginian welfare system.[60] The career of many Settlement reforms was just like this: the women did it, it seemed to work, the policy makers took it over. Welfare systems were built piecemeal, their landmark legislation often only the final recognition of what had been put in place through such local and impassioned efforts.

Settlement workers provided services, and they studied the communities with whom they worked, using the tools of an emerging social science. Individual Settlements became associated with specific areas of work. In the US, Mary McDowell headed another settlement in Chicago, in the stockyards district, where her research into sanitary conditions and waste disposal cleaned up Chicago and turned her into an international expert on refuse disposal and municipal housekeeping (see Chapter Four). The year before, in Manhattan, New York, nurse Lillian Wald set up the Henry Street Settlement, which became the base for the world's first public health nursing service (see Chapter Eight). Housing reformer Mary Kingsbury Simkhovitch, who had been to the 1896 Socialist Workers' Congress with Charlotte Perkins Gilman in 1896, started a Settlement called Greenwich House in New York in 1902. Greenwich House had a Social Investigation Committee whose members undertook studies of family budgets, sanitary conditions, education, employment and housing, and produced what was probably the first handbook on tenants' rights in the world.[61] Simkhovitch herself became a prominent housing reformer, helping to establish the Committee on the Congestion of the Population in 1907, which in turn led to the first National Conference on City Planning in 1909. Its emphasis, on the role of planning in solving social problems, met with enormous resistance from the male establishment.[62]

The investigative and reforming anger of women settlers about the conditions of working-class labour and family life, and their imaginative efforts to outline alternatives, held within it different approaches to the position of women. In a sense all could be called 'radical', but some were closer to a paradigm of a 'radical femininity' which dressed women's public works in a domestic guise.[63] This was true of Henrietta Barnett, co-founder of Toynbee Hall, who didn't think suffrage for women a good idea, and who held to the view that homemaking was at the heart of

3.6: Henrietta Barnett and Samuel Barnett

women's mission. The photograph shows her husband leaning comfortably on her. The iconography of feminist history has tended to dismiss Henrietta Barnett, despite her pioneering work in housing reform, her achievements in reforming educational institutions for girls and young women, and her careful and sympathetic documentation of the conditions of working-class life. One of the examples Barnett gives in an article on 'The poverty of the poor' in 1886 is Mrs Marshall, whose husband is in an asylum: two of Mrs Marshall's four children have been taken by the poor law authorities into one of their district schools; she works 11 hours a day as a 'scrubber' in a public institution where she earns nine shillings a week and her dinner. When the rent, light, firing, boots and clothing have been paid for, there is 3s 4d left in Mrs Marshall's purse to provide food for herself and three meals daily for two children of 10 and 11. Barnett's calculations showed that a minimally adequate diet for this size family would cost 5s 11¼d a week.[64] Most working-class incomes were simply insufficient to feed families. Another example of Barnett's radical campaigning was her work on behalf of the children in industrial or 'barrack' schools, which were offshoots of workhouses catering for homeless children aged from 3 to 16. These were huge, austere, disciplinary institutions, providing rudimentary education and training for menial work, in which children weren't allowed any personal possessions, clothes, toys, recreational activity or even their own names, and were routinely beaten and strapped into 'restraining' chairs. Through Barnett's efforts all this was changed. She inspired her brother-in-law Ernest Hart, a doctor and editor of the *British Medical Journal*, to initiate an inquiry into barrack schools. This produced a departmental committee on Poor Law Schools. Barnett was the only woman on the committee and she wrote most of the report published in 1886, an angry and impassioned document which led to comprehensive reform.[65]

Henrietta Barnett's 'radical femininity' was shared by two other British women whose names pepper the history of social reform and social science: Mary Ward and Octavia Hill. Ward was more in favour of state welfare than Hill; both behaved like independent women, while articulating moral reservations about female independence. Mrs Humphry Ward,

3.7: Mary Ward

as she was known, came from a prominent intellectual family that included the famous headmaster of Rugby school, Thomas Arnold (her grandfather), the poet Matthew Arnold (her uncle) and Julian and Aldous Huxley (her nephews). Mary Ward was a flamboyant literary hostess and novelist, and also a fierce proponent of higher education for women, a co-founder of Somerville College, Oxford and originator of the Passmore Edwards Settlement

in London, where the first play-centres and after-school centres and the first centre for physically disabled children in Britain were set up in the 1890s. Her many social reform novels were based on the kind of fastidious research that went into other women's social investigation texts. Ward's novel *Sir George Tressady* (1896), for example, which was about the sweated trades, earned congratulatory comments from Beatrice Webb on the clarity of its case for the Factory Acts: the 'most useful bit of work that has been done for many a long day'.[66] (As a vehicle for contemporary ideas, Ward's novels do, however, also contain a host of unpleasant, cold, selfish and invariably ugly suffragist women.)

Octavia Hill made her reputation and is remembered today as an unusual kind of housing reformer who developed a commercially successful system of 'friendly visiting' for rented housing. Beatrice Webb called her 'a

3.8: Octavia Hill, portrait, 1898

small woman with a large head',[67] but in the portrait reproduced here, which was commissioned for Hill's 60th birthday, she looks quite proportionate and self-satisfied. Hill was the grand-daughter of the sanitary reformer Dr Southwood Smith. She learnt about the area of work to which her name is always attached, housing reform, from her grandfather, and about the work of the Settlements from her mother, who, when widowed, had started a small social centre in their home. Octavia ran a workshop there, and one evening she escorted home a woman who had fainted in a sewing class and saw, and was moved by, the damp and overcrowded housing conditions in which she lived. Octavia's early talent as an artist brought her into contact with John Ruskin (who seems to have a good deal to answer for as a background figure in the history of Settlement sociology). In a much speculated-on personal life, he was attracted to young girls, one of whom was Octavia Hill, whom Ruskin discovered when she was 15. In a somewhat clichéd act, he invited her to his Denmark Hill mansion to look at his art, then went on to offer her training as an artist, deploying her to this end as a copier for a good 10 years. In 1865 he gave her money to buy leases on her first three houses in London's Paradise Place, thus starting her career in housing reform. The houses were typical of the district: 'The plaster was dropping from the walls, on one staircase a pail was placed to catch the rain that fell through the roof. All the staircases were perfectly dark, all the banisters were gone, having been used as firewood by the tenants. The grates, with large holes in them, were falling forward into the rooms ... The dust-bin, standing in front of the houses, was accessible to the whole neighbourhood, and boys often dragged from it quantities of unseemly objects and spread them over the Court. The state of the drainage was in keeping with everything else.'[68] Hill's housing system, which brought her international renown, both satisfied capitalist interests with a sound 5% return on property investment and provided tenants with practical help in a collective approach to social improvement known as 'friendly visiting'. Hill described its principles in the following way: 'There would be no interference, no entering their rooms uninvited, no offer of money or the necessaries of life. But when occasion presented itself, I should give them any help I could, such as I might offer without insult to other friends – sympathy in their distresses; advice, help, and counsel in their difficulties; introductions that might be of use to them; means of education; visits to the country, a lent book when not able to work; a bunch of flowers brought on purpose; an invitation to any entertainment, in a room built at the back of my own house ... I am convinced that one of the evils of much that is done for the poor springs from the want of delicacy felt, and courtesy shown, towards them, and that we cannot beneficially help them in any spirit different to that in which we help those who are better off.'[69]

As Hill acquired more houses, she needed more and more volunteer rent-collectors/friendly visitors. The British equivalent of Vida Scudder's university Settlement house in New York was the Women's University Settlement established by Barnett and Hill in London's Southwark in 1887. The base in Southwark was chosen partly because Hill already supervised many properties there, and the Settlement became in effect a training ground for Hill's staff and the base for the first professional social work training in Britain. Many famous names feature on the list of Hill's volunteers: Henrietta Barnett, the young Beatrice Potter/Webb, and her sister Kate, later Kate Courtney, a leading figure in the peace movement, among them. One of Hill's methodological contributions to the evolving social science was a quantitative one: her insistence on sound business methods turned the tasks of bookkeeping, accounting and business administration into respectable female activities.[70] British policy makers called on her expertise: she gave evidence in 1882 to the Select Committee on Artisans' and Labourers' Dwellings, in 1884 to the Royal Commission on Housing for the Working Classes and in 1893 to the Royal Commission on Pensions for the Aged Poor. In 1905 she was a member, as were various others of her ex-rent collectors including Beatrice Webb and Helen Bosanquet, of the Royal Commission on the Poor Law.

Hill's radicalism, like Barnett's, has been ignored, and her philanthropic work much misunderstood, perhaps because it combined the two apparently contradictory principles of kindness and profit. Many overseas visitors came to witness her methods, which were transported to Philadelphia in 1887 and followed by an Octavia Hill Association in 1896. There were other, more exotic international connections, as well: Queen Victoria's third child, Princess Alice of Hesse-Darmstadt, took a particular interest in Hill's work. Finding life in a provincial German city stultifying and her husband, a minor German prince, incapable of intelligent conversation (although they did have seven children together), she developed a social conscience, organized meetings known locally as the 'Parliament of Women' to discuss poor women's education and employment, and took to visiting, incognito, working-class homes around Darmstadt. Hearing about Hill's work, she asked for a meeting, and in 1876 visited some of Hill's properties in London.[71] The two women became friends, corresponding about methods of housing management, and Princess Alice translated into German Hill's *Homes of the London poor*.

Visiting the poor was a way of finding out about them. Another was what later came to be named in academic social science as 'covert ethnography': this was an approach to generating knowledge practised by a number of reforming women.[72] In the autumn of 1883, when she was 25, Beatrice Potter/Webb had resolved to remedy her own ignorance of living conditions among

3.9: Four covert ethnographers: Beatrice Webb, Mary Higgs (top), Olive Malvery, Elizabeth Cochran Seaman ('Nellie Bly') (bottom)

the manual working class by going to live with a family in the Lancashire mill town of Bacup; because the family she lived with were relatives of her mother's, she presented herself as 'Miss Jones', a Welsh farmer's daughter. One 'shrewd old man smelt a rat' and interrogated her about farming methods, but she managed to pass the test.[73] Later, in 1888, when working with her cousin Charlie Booth on his mammoth *Life and labour of the poor in London*, she pretended to be a Jewish tailoress, a challenge complicated by her accent and her incompetence with the needle, but one which inspired dramatic writing, close, perhaps, to the fiction she always longed to write: 'Some thirty women and girls are crowding in. The first arrivals hang bonnets and shawls on the scanty supply of nails jotted here and there along the wooden partition separating the front shop from the workroom ... There is a general Babel of voices as each "hand" settles down in front of the bundle of work and the old tobacco or candle box that holds the cottons, twist, gimp, needles, thimble, and scissors belonging to her ... The forewoman calls for a pair of trousers, already machined, and hands them to me. I turn them over and over, puzzled to know where to begin.'[74] 'Pages from a work-girl's diary' was published in 1888, around the time Webb was putting in her first public appearance as an expert on poverty and industrial conditions by providing testimony to a House of Lords Committee on the Sweating System.

Beatrice Webb ultimately deserted the method of covert ethnography for the less exciting world of documentary facts, perhaps under the influence of Sidney, which is why we find her in the British Library talking to Eleanor Marx. Mary Higgs, a vicar's wife from Oldham, who in her early 50s dressed as a tramp and visited workhouses, casual wards and lodging-houses for days and nights at a time as a way of understanding the experience of homelessness, had none of Beatrice Webb's qualms about this covert approach. Such exploration, Higgs insisted, was the very 'method of science', a 'method of personal experiment, which is the nearest road to accurate knowledge' when it comes to probing 'the microbes of social disorder'.[75] Higgs' study of unemployment uses these metaphors of science to see unemployment as a disease with causes and symptoms that must be placed under a 'social microscope' in order to be mended.[76] She turned her Oldham home into a mini social-welfare centre, started a paper-sorting industry for poor women, and mother and infant centres, and personally befriended homeless women. In the early 1900s she helped to run yearly summer schools for the study of social questions; these were attended by experts from the Settlement movement and other fields of social reform. Higgs was a suffragist and an environmentalist. She founded the Beautiful Oldham Society in 1902, which encouraged the growing of flowers and trees in urban spaces, and led a few years later to the founding of Oldham Garden Suburb, a Higgs initiative which in turn was inspired by another of Henrietta Barnett's, Hampstead Garden Suburb (see Chapter Ten).[77]

But homelessness was Mary Higgs' main passion. In one of her publications on homeless women, *Where shall she live?* (1910), she called this 'not a work that can be done all at once. It needs patient investigation of local need, patient adaptation of means to ends, patient experiment.'[78] She studied homelessness through 'literary investigation', statistical analysis, comparisons of policies in different European countries (Denmark, Germany, Holland, Switzerland) and what some people might now call 'participatory research'. Mary Higgs' combination of methods was facilitated by her background: she was the first woman to take the natural science Tripos at Cambridge (at Girton College in 1874), and her leanings towards psychology and religion (she was the daughter and the wife of Congregational ministers) led her to place great value on personal experience. Higgs' account of her research into homelessness, *Glimpses into the abyss*, published in 1906, anticipated by 27 years George Orwell's much more famous *Down and out in London and Paris.* In it she plunders the (scanty) available facts and figures on homelessness and its causes; considers its history and current policy provision in England; reprints her correspondence with 'a working man' who, like so many of the homeless people she encountered, became a tramp through personal misfortune; and describes the days and nights she spent 'as a tramp among tramps'. She took a friend with her, Annie Lee, a cotton-worker: they dressed very shabbily, though cleanly, with ragged shawls and boots with holes: in the photograph (page 67) we see Higgs in her tramp headgear wearing a slightly mournful but determined look. The two women carried soap and a towel, a change of stockings, tea and sugar and, in case of starvation, a substance called plasmon, a powdered milk protein, very popular at the time (Ernest Shackleton took plasmon biscuits on his expeditions to the Antarctic). Higgs' narrative of their travels is much occupied with measuring the paltry food on offer, the awful sanitary arrangements and the prevalence of dirt and bugs. It has a strong vein of moralizing, especially about prostitution, but it does give us a detailed and vivid account of urban provision for the homeless and travelling working-class at the time. Higgs continued her investigations for years, sometimes fitting in a bit of covert ethnography before a public-speaking engagement, on these occasions shadowed not by Annie Lee but by a plain-clothed policeman or her son 'dressed as a working man'.[79] She became an acknowledged authority on vagrancy, giving evidence at government inquiries, producing practical manuals and founding the National Association for Women's Lodging-Homes in 1909. Her discovery that most of the tramps she met were made so 'by circumstances' was very like the understanding reached by Octavia Hill and other visitors to the poor, who realized that poverty is caused by social calamity, not individual fecklessness, and especially by the failure of society, whether in the form of voluntary or state effort, to make any kind of reasonable provision for the misfortunes of the industrial age. In the review section of *The Economic Journal*, William Beveridge admired Higgs' revelations, considered that they bore 'the stamp of truth', were completely in accord with other evidence, and couldn't fail to hasten the reform of vagrancy treatment (although he did also say there was far too much about dirt in her text, and she used far too many italics).[80]

The use by women of covert ethnography to collect policy-relevant data is a story that crops up in many places. Olive Malvery, an Anglo-Indian musician (see page 67), deployed her 'outsider' appearance to masquerade as a costermonger, street singer, factory girl, shop assistant, barmaid and flower-girl among the London poor around the same time as Higgs, in the early 1900s. Malvery had run a Girls' Club in Hoxton, London, the Girls' Guild of Good Life, and had co-authored with an ex-MP from Australia an early account of white slave traffic in Asia. She was an altogether colourful character, especially at her society wedding to the American consul to Muscat in 1905, for which she wore Indian dress, was given away by the bishop of Bombay, and attended by coster girls from Hoxton and an invited audience of a thousand East End young women.[81] To serve her somewhat more mundane ethnographic work, she rented a room in a poor district from which she could sally forth in any disguise. Here she stored a large quantity of disinfectant, wigs, theatrical paints and 12 different sets of clothes.[82] Her published articles and books focused mainly on the evils of child labour and the conditions of women's work. One of her trademarks was the liberal illustration of her texts with photographs of herself dressed up – a genre that might be regarded either as sociology or as early photo-journalism.[83] On one occasion she was befriended by a coster-woman in Hoxton, and slept in a shared tiny attic room in an airless house crammed with 37 lodgers, surreptitiously munching on her extra rations to supplement the meagre diet: 'It was a hard life enough. Up at four each morning, to bed never before eleven: the long walks to the market, and the endless standing by the barrow in rain and shine.'[84] Malvery practised her covert ethnography in a tremendous range of dangerous trades which were also the subject of the first women factory inspectors' investigations (see Chapter Nine): she was to be found in factories which made meat products out of mildewed offal; in jam factories where the raw material was unwashed fruit; in aerated bottle establishments where frequent explosions ejected broken glass into the women workers' faces; and what Malvery called the 'very worst form of home industry', fur-pulling, a nasty occupation which involved manually separating the coarse from the fine fur on the skins of hares and rabbits.[85] Malvery travelled widely in Europe and the US, giving musical performances or talking about temperance. Her travels took her to Hull-House, and to 'Miss Adams [sic] ... a well-known student of sociology'. She called her visit to Hull-House 'a liberal education in the making of citizens'.[86] Malvery's extraordinary life is another that has escaped much attention.

The writer, charity worker, industrialist and inventor Elizabeth Cochrane Seaman, alias Nellie Bly (see page 67), provides an example of early covert ethnography on the other side of the Atlantic.[87] Bly was the sparsely educated daughter of a Pennsylvania mill worker who launched herself on a journalistic career by complaining about a misogynistic column in the local paper when she was 16. Her complaint earned her a job on the paper. Not content to write for the 'women's pages', she took herself to Mexico as a foreign correspondent, but her most famous stunt involved feigning insanity in New York in 1887 as a strategy for finding out about conditions in a women's lunatic asylum. Bly practised deranged expressions in front of a mirror, checked into a boarding-house, behaved insanely, was taken by police to a courtroom and then to medical experts, all of whom declared her insane and had her committed to an asylum.[88] In this venture she was some 86 years ahead of the experiment famous in the sociology of health and illness which involved eight sane people successfully deceiving mental hospital psychiatrists.[89] Bly's book *Ten days in a mad house* (1887), a description of conditions which she alleged would drive anyone insane, caused a sensation. It resulted in a judicial inquiry and a large addition to the budget of the Department of Public Charities and Corrections. In 1888 she challenged her newspaper editor to sponsor an attempt to turn Jules Verne's *Around the world in eighty days* from fiction into fact (she did it in 72 days, visiting the real Jules Verne in Amiens on the way).[90] She went on to marry an ageing millionaire industrialist and become the president of an iron manufacturing company, in which position she patented new designs for milk containers, a stacking garbage can and the first leakproof metal oil drum.[91] When the company went bankrupt, she returned to reporting, covering the Woman's Suffrage Parade of 1913 and predicting (accurately) that American women would have to wait until 1920 for the vote.[92]

Bly was a multi-faceted woman, given to methodological explorations of the boundaries between fact and fiction. She was a member of a group of 'girl stunt reporters' who were mistresses of covert ethnographic disguises, infiltrated mainstream journalism and helped to raise the sales figures of newspapers in the early 20th-century US.[93] One of them, Elizabeth Banks, took stunt-reporting to Britain in the early 1890s, becoming one of London's best-known journalists. Through the medium of her inventive cross-class masquerades, Banks disclosed the underside of women's industrial labours; like Malvery, she published a photo gallery of her different investigative selves in her *Campaigns of curiosity: Journalistic adventures of an American girl in London* (1894).[94]

It can be quite hard to tell the difference between genres in the investigative lives of these women, many of whom wrote novels which relayed the conditions of working-class life, and theorized about class and gender inequalities, with quite as much painstaking care as they and their sisters took in analysing statistics, filling in 'schedules' or carrying out house-to-house enquiries. Margaret Harkness was one of the defiant band of female activists and reformers who disturbed the masculine peace of the British Museum Reading Room. She was another of Beatrice Webb's cousins, and a close friend of Eleanor Marx. Between 1887 and 1905, Harkness published six novels about life in the slums, along with other 'factual' pieces on women's employment, municipal reform and underfed children. She immersed herself in working-class life by living in one of Octavia Hill's tenement buildings, and by other devices such as visiting working-class districts in Manchester, along with Beatrice Webb and Mary Ward: it is tantalizing to imagine what these three women might have conversed about on the way.[95] Of all Harkness's writings, it was her novels that had the most impact. She sent *A city girl: A realistic story* (1887) to Engels, who did admire its realism – in fact he complained that it wasn't quite realistic enough: the working-class characters were too passive. 'I must own, in your defence,' he conceded at the end of his letter to her, 'that nowhere in the civilized world are the working people less actively resistant, more passively submitting to fate, more bewildered than in the East End of London. And how do I know whether you have not had very good reasons for contenting yourself, for once, with a picture of the passive side of working-class life, reserving the active side for another work?'[96]

Vida Scudder, the founder of the first American Settlement, wrote novels too. The main character in her *A listener in Babel* (1903), Hilda Lathrop, is, like Scudder, dissatisfied with her education and in favour of life rather than academic work or professional study. She works in the slums at a Settlement house, is initially exhilarated by the expanded horizons, but then yearns for a more immediate solution both for her own problems and for the economic and social distress of the poor. She goes to work in a factory and decides to set up a cooperative community.[97] Scudder herself, in her non-fiction mode, commented later that the ardent political bonds of Settlement life were akin to membership of the Communist Party in their strength – though not in their gender; for the ways in which women in Settlements were able to weave together ties of affection, activism, science and sisterhood − 'an astonishing enlargement of the power of affection' − were unique. As she pointed out, Settlement women did much to separate social science from what Kelley called 'bourgeois philanthropy'. The term 'social service' was obnoxious to them; '"Sharing" is a noble and democratic word, when it does not degenerate into cant; it was the key-note of our movement.'[98]

The principle behind the Settlements, expressed by Vida Scudder and her friends, by Samuel and Henrietta Barnett, by Jane Addams and her formidable sisters at Hull-House, and by many others elsewhere, was the principle of altruism: the idea that a good society is one in which people give to one another services of welfare, understanding, kindness and a commitment to constructive social change. The community, not the individual, is the fundamental social unit: community cohesion is vital, dissolving when social groups no longer associate with one another on a personal, everyday basis and giving rise to problems such as poverty, disease and social turmoil. The more unequal a society becomes, the more need there is for altruism.

The sociology of the Settlement houses played a role in virtually all the social reforms of the Progressive Era in the US and in shaping what emerged as Britain's welfare state. Settlement sociology in the US was, however, rather more reform- and research-minded than its equivalent in Britain. The confluence of the Social Settlement and Social Science Movements was more complete there, probably due to the greater proportion of American women who had access to higher education, and the more *laissez-faire* turn of government, which made the argument for state intervention a new and fundamental challenge. In Britain, some of the most active women reformers and social scientists chose to operate outside the Settlement movement. The bigger story here is one about the contexts within which evidence-based policy making is best enacted: in spheres independent of government and the introspective, often conservative-leaning, interstices of academia, as with the women social scientists of the American Settlements; or in circles with strong connections to establishment institutions, as in Britain. The demand for what is now called evidence-based policy was not heard within Settlement sociology in exactly those terms, but Frances Kellor, a Hull-House resident who worked on immigration issues, domestic service and criminology, put out a definitely modern call in 1914 for a government 'laboratory', 'a general clearinghouse for information', which would use social science expertise in order to design the kind of effective and efficient public administration that women such as Charlotte Perkins Gilman could only imagine.[99] Kellor's vision is returned to in Chapter Eleven.

FOUR

Municipal housekeeping: women clean up the cities

'Women explore stench "inferno"', proclaimed the headline in the *Chicago Daily Tribune* on 19 June 1910. Twenty members of the Chicago Women's City Club had gone on a sightseeing trip to the garbage-burning section of Chicago near the stockyards. They carried parasols to protect themselves from the sun, but left their automobiles behind in order to 'hike' from one garbage dump to another. One of them said after the trip, 'Now I know why I have to sprinkle cologne around the house when the wind blows from the west'. Beginning at the University of Chicago Settlement, they were led by its head resident, Mary McDowell, first to gaze at the foul waters of so-called Bubbly Creek, a long, dead arm of the Chicago river full of carbonic gas from years of untreated human sewage and the greasy detritus of the meat-packing industry, and from there to the vast open pits full of putrefying garbage where uncovered horse-drawn wagons daily dumped every kind of rubbish. The Chairman of the Club's Housing Committee, Mrs Henry Solomon (Hannah Greenebaum Solomon, founder of the National Council of Jewish Women), explained to the *Chicago Daily Tribune* reporter that the reason for the malodorous expedition was the Club's ambition to bring about municipal ownership of more scientific and effective methods of garbage collection and disposal. Mary McDowell, from the Settlement, pointed out the connection between Chicago's garbage problem and the high rate of infant mortality prevailing in the area – at least double that in the districts from which the parasol-carrying ladies came. Research McDowell had carried out with local doctors and nurses estimated that a third of the area's babies died before they were two, and the most important causes were the open sewer of Bubbly Creek and the garbage dumps – half of the babies who died lived within three blocks of the dumps.[1]

Dirt and cleanliness are recurring themes in women's history. They stand for the human struggle to impose cultural order on natural *dis*order, but they also signal one of the strategies that masculine power structures have used to keep women (and other subordinates) in their place. The place of women is in the home. But what if women redefine the home, so that it becomes all-embracing, holding within it all those discursive practices that happen in the public sphere and are traditionally uncontrolled by women's civilizing influence? This chapter is concerned with a movement for 'municipal housekeeping' that was mounted in the period from the 1880s through the first decades of the 20th century by a large contingent of women's organizations and by many creatively pugnacious individuals in different countries. They wrestled with indolent city governments and greedy, self-serving capitalists and politicians to ask unladylike questions about garbage, sewage and industrial and urban filth, driven by a vision of the city as a home that provided a powerful antidote to the prevailing masculine model of the city as a site for business: 'the city profitable' versus 'the city livable'.[2] 'What is the city but the larger house in which we dwell?' asked one of them in 1894. 'Good city government is good housekeeping, and that is the sum of the matter.'[3] The municipal housekeeping movement did what thinkers such as Charlotte Perkins Gilman had envisioned and articulated in recasting the traditional separation of private and public spheres as one holistic attempt to create the conditions for a healthful human life. Some municipal housekeepers were suffragists; others were not. Some rejected the language of militarism, while others saw themselves as fighting significant battles. Cleaning up the public world was for many a method of enlarging women's activities, important on its own, yet symbolic of the way in which barriers to public life wasted women's potential.

Mary Eliza McDowell was born in 1854 in a house, built by her grandfather, who made steamboats, overlooking the Ohio River. Her abolitionist father was a friend of Abraham Lincoln,

America's 16th President, and also of Rutherford Hayes, its 19th. Mary, the first of six children, didn't go to college, but trained as a kindergarten teacher. Her first experience of social service was at the age of 17 during the great Chicago fire of 1871, when she took the family's wagon and horses and helped bring people and their possessions out of burning homes. In 1890 she went to Chicago's Hull-House Settlement to run the kindergarten there; in 1892 she started the Hull-House Woman's Club. Around the same time, a group of Christian philanthropists at the new University of Chicago sent their sociology students out to survey living conditions, and they decided that another social centre was badly needed in the area known as 'back of the yards' given over to meat processing and packing. Aside from the service to the community such a centre would offer, it would also function as a 'laboratory' for university social science students.[4] On the advice of Jane Addams, Mary McDowell was given the position of head of the University of Chicago Settlement, which opened in 1894 in a small tenement apartment at the heart of the yards. 'Over this home there were often clouds of smoke so thick that they hid the sun,' reported Alice Masaryk, a Settlement resident in 1904–06, and later founder of social work in Czechoslovakia. 'This heavy smoke was from the stockyards, making the air so poisonous that we had to close the windows carefully in order not to choke.'[5] In these insalubrious surroundings, McDowell embarked on a singular career as an advocate for her neighbours in sanitary reform, unionization and labour legislation, and the rights of women, children and immigrants, gaining a national and international reputation as an activist and a fearless uncoverer of the facts about how America, the land of the free, imprisoned many of its citizens in degrading poverty and appalling living and working conditions. Her confrontations over garbage with the city authorities and the industrialists of Packingtown, as the meat-packing area was known, earned her a list of sobriquets: 'the Garbage Lady', 'the Duchess of Bubbly Creek', 'the Angel of the Stockyards', 'Mary the Magnificent', 'Fighting Mary', and so on; and led to her appointment by the mayor in 1923 as Chicago's first Commissioner of Public Welfare. When asked her occupation, however, McDowell answered 'citizen'.[6] Described as 'plump, jolly, blue-eyed and Scotch',[7] her determination to get all this done is evident in the photograph of her standing with Jane Addams and Julia Lathrop of Hull-House at a women's suffrage event in 1913.

It's hard to appreciate what garbage ladies like McDowell were fighting against without understanding what it was like to live and work in a big industrial city in the 1890s and early 1900s. First of all there was the phenomenal growth of population: in the US between 1840 and 1920, the urban population expanded from 1,845,000 to over 54 million: from

4.1: Mary McDowell (right) with Jane Addams (centre) and Julia Lathrop (left) at the Woman Suffrage Parade in Washington, DC, 1913

11% to 51% of the total population. Chicago, the US's second-largest city, doubled in population between 1880 and 1890.[8] Contrast with this London, which grew from 4.8 million in 1881 to 6.5 million in 1899.[9] Europe and the US confronted a set of huge, interrelated physical problems: overcrowding in poor housing; deficient or absent sanitation; and completely inadequate and perilous refuse collection and disposal practices. Private contractors controlling housing, water and refuse removal acted in their own and not the public's interest. It was not illegal to pollute, contaminate, poison or dump. In Britain, the 'municipalization' movement, which took these utilities out of the private market, had made considerable headway by the end of the 19th century, but the US, with its market ideology and addiction to private property rights, lagged a long way behind.

Chicago was particularly filthy, because it produced most of the meat Americans ate. The meat-production industry had started on swampland south of the city in 1865, and by 1890 it was processing nine million animals a year. In a series of 10 papers about Chicago's housing conditions, published in the *American Journal of Sociology*, Hull-House's Sophonisba Breckinridge and

Edith Abbott observed that 'No other neighborhood in this, or perhaps any other city, is dominated by a single industry of so offensive a character. Large numbers of live animals assembled from all sections of the country, processes of slaughtering and packing, the disposition of offensive animal waste, constitute an almost unparalleled nuisance … In the Stockyards … are the mingled cries of the animals awaiting slaughter, the presence of uncared-for-waste, the sight of blood, the carcasses naked of flesh and skin, the suggestion of death and disintegration – all of which must react in a demoralizing way, not only upon the character of the people, but the conditions under which they live.'[10] All the animals had to be driven through the streets (depositing their own refuse on the way) by cowboys on horses (more refuse) and killed before nightfall. In her early days at the University Settlement, Mary McDowell wondered why people came home from work at all hours of the day and in the evening. When she enquired, 'I was told that the killing had to go on until there were no cattle left to be cared for overnight; and when in my greenness I would ask why a packing industry could not keep cattle overnight when farmers did it very well, I was surprised to learn that because it cost something to feed and water them, men must butcher often sixteen hours at a stretch.'[11]

The meat factories deposited 131,000 pounds of matter a day in the gaseous waters of Bubbly Creek, and dumped other garbage in one of the four enormous pits owned by a notorious alderman, Tom Carey, who had clay dug out of the pits for his brickyards and then made a fortune by leasing the pits as garbage dumps, and charging scavengers $15 a week to sort through the decaying mounds (after which the women and children moved in to find rancid mattresses, bits of wood or even food): unsurprisingly, Carey was a major resister of McDowell's garbage campaign.[12] The meat-processing industry spawned others which made industrial commodities out of more than 40 of its by-products (glue, margarine, sausage casings, fertilizer, bristles, soap, buttons and so forth). One inhabitant of Packingtown recalled the (in)sanitary conditions of his childhood there: 'We had no pavements, no sewage system, outside toilets, and the sink drainage emptied into open ditches bordering the sides of the street. … Much open land near our homes was rented to the packers for hair fields. Hog hair was spread out until the flesh particles decayed and the hair was cleansed by the wind, rain, and sun. Sickening smells emanating from these fields permeated the air.'[13] Only a third of Chicago's streets and alleys were paved, compared with two-thirds of New York's.[14] Horses' hooves stirred the street dust into heavy clouds in the summer; the rest of the time it was converted into mud holes bordered with dirty pools of stagnant water. People threw rubbish into the alleys or put it in open cans and boxes where children played with it and it lay unemptied for weeks. There were no trees, no grass or shrubbery. The streets and houses were grey, and so was the air.

McDowell's philosophy was always that she worked not *for* the subjects of social enquiry as a missionary 'but *with* them as a neighbor and seeker after truth'.[15] She told the story of how she became a municipal housekeeper in a chapter of an unfinished autobiography written in 1927. A Bohemian woman living close to the Settlement who 'had become outraged by the conditions asked me if I would go to the City Hall with some of the woman householders. They complained not only of the dumps but of the uncovered wagons reeking with filth and flies.' McDowell went with the women to City Hall, where they saw the Commissioner of Health and were speedily sent on to the new Commissioner of Public Works, an 'intelligent, college-bred young man', who told them they wouldn't be able to do anything unless they first changed public opinion.[16] (The young man resigned a few weeks later, explaining that he was a socialist.) McDowell recognized that she was the only one of the group, mostly immigrant women, who could speak to the motley public of Chicago, although she was hardly qualified, not knowing anything about the science of rubbish and its effective disposal. Much could be learnt about garbage disposal, however, from books and monographs, which she studied assiduously. An enlightened judge came to hear one of her public talks on the subject and he told her afterwards that if they came to his court the next day he'd give them an injunction against the Health Department for garbage dumping. 'I never knew,' he said, 'where our refuse was taken; now I know and this injustice must be ended.'[17]

Thus began McDowell's 'sanitary journey'. A member of the Woman's City Club, Ethel Sturges Dummer, gave McDowell a cheque and suggested she go to Europe to study scientific systems of city waste collection and disposal. Dummer wasn't only a useful funder but also a significant sociologist of the period, acting as a 'research agency, a journal club, a public library and ... a "principal investigator"', for much of the University men's sociological business.[18] One of the most reputed sociological texts of the period, W. I. Thomas's *The unadjusted girl* (1923), was directly an outcome of Dummer's interest in the double standard of morality whereby women were targets of police attention for venereal disease but men were not.[19] With Dummer's support, McDowell went to Glasgow and interviewed the superintendent of the city's Cleansing Department, who urged her to go to Germany. He said that the Germans had been in Glasgow and taken all that they'd tried out and improved on it, so McDowell was bound to find the best methods anywhere in Hamburg and Frankfurt-am-Main. So she went to Germany and found he was right. In Frankfurt, the sewage and garbage plants on the edge of the city featured attractive buildings surrounded by landscaped gardens. McDowell's enthusiastic description is prescient of *Herland*: 'Roses were in bloom, vines covered the building, and nowhere were there bad odors or disorderliness about the place. A beautiful, high smoke stack carried odors into the air high above the city, leaving only the pleasant odors of roses and hay about us.'[20] Adjacent buildings housed the process of incinerating all combustible refuse and garbage, thus generating electric light for the city. In the Bavarian town of Fürth, the expense of both disposal and collection was met by the sale of steam for electric power and light, and refuse was collected in covered trucks by cleanly uniformed officials. McDowell asked the sanitary engineer in Frankfurt whether he would ever hope for a financial return on its refuse system (because, she said, that was the question she'd be asked when she got back to Chicago), and he replied that nobody but an American would ask such a question: the primary consideration must be sanitation, not economics.[21]

Armed with 'stereopticon slides and factual analyses' showing how other municipalities solved the garbage problem, and dreadful stories about how people lived in Packingtown, McDowell returned to her crusade to convince public opinion. She spoke to all kinds of clubs, societies and churches in Chicago.[22] Another prod to the public conscience had arrived a few years earlier when a young man appeared one day at the Settlement to see McDowell, handing over a letter of introduction and explaining that he had come to gather material for 'the Uncle Tom's Cabin of the Socialist movement'. Over the next few weeks, he asked lots of questions. The young man was Upton Sinclair, and the book he wrote was *The jungle*, published in 1906. The novel recounts the sad and difficult life of a Lithuanian immigrant, Jurgis Rudkus, to whom almost every conceivable awful event happens: members of his family die in factory accidents and of food poisoning; one child drowns on a muddy street, another is eaten by rats; his wife is raped and then dies in childbirth; Rudkus himself is driven to drink and then to socialism. Sinclair's intention was to focus on immigrants' working conditions, but the message the public and politicians took from the book was one about sanitation and health. McDowell, to whom Sinclair sent the book, found it 'filled with half-truths', but nonetheless a useful indictment of the industrial system.[23] It roused President Theodore Roosevelt to action and, with a little advice from McDowell, the President supported the introduction of the 1906 Meat Inspection and Pure Food and Drug Acts, the latter establishing what eventually became the Food and Drug Administration.

The city of Chicago also agreed to set up a committee to investigate the waste problem. This volte-face, after years of resistance and prevarication, happened because in July 1913 Illinois women gained the municipal franchise. At the first meeting of the newly constituted waste body, its members realized that they had no name, no place to meet and no money. McDowell said she was tired of being called the Garbage Lady and proposed the 'City Waste Commission' as a name; if the mayor wouldn't give them money for their work, she'd go out with a hat and raise it herself.[24] The city produced the money; the City Waste Commission brought in two engineers to help, and a report was submitted to the City Council. It recommended municipal ownership and operation of the city's waste disposal system, and the construction of a central reduction plant and a number of subsidiary incineration plants, following the model that McDowell had witnessed in Europe. The report was accepted and a small reduction plant was constructed in Packingtown, followed by the elimination of the dumps. The incineration plants took longer, and the campaign against Bubbly Creek was only partly successful. The legacy of Chicago's disreputable waste practices remains there today, with millions of gallons of raw sewage deposited in the stagnant (and still malodorous) waters of Bubbly Creek during heavy rain; serious contamination found in its sediment stalled a $15.4 million renovation plan in 2015.[25]

The years of McDowell's consciousness-raising about garbage were years which spawned an enormous amount of voluntary female activity on the municipal housekeeping front. Women's groups all over the country got involved in sanitary reform, cleaning up the streets, inspecting food markets, improving air and water quality and reforming waste disposal. Women's clubs appointed 'garbage committees'. The area where McDowell's University Settlement was located had an active anti-garbage association by 1896, which promoted many practical ideas. At one meeting, a Miss Harriet A. Shinn brought out a metallic garbage pail and demonstrated how it was hung, filled, emptied and cleaned. A committee had been set up to inspect the alleys. 'The inspector of our ward does not inspect,' Shinn reported tersely, 'or, if he does, he does it in secret ... I once wrote him a note suggesting an interview, but he neither called nor replied.'[26] The idea of having refuse containers on streets reputedly derives from a women's organization in Philadelphia which purchased and placed them, then inducing the city authority to take them over. In that city in 1913 a woman called Edith Pierce was formally taken on as a street inspector. She designed badges of good street-cleaning citizenship for schoolchildren.[27]

Municipal housekeeping protected public health, just as domestic housekeeping ensured health at home. The American historian and researcher Mary Ritter Beard carried out a survey of what she called 'women's work in municipalities' in 1915. For this she searched the records of hundreds of organizations and societies to uncover the extent of women's labours for civic improvement. 'The task has been difficult owing to the immense amount of material which months of research accumulated,' she complained.[28] Her book covered a vast landscape of pioneering but under-recognized effort, and a long list of topics including garbage, health, education, noise, housing, public safety, municipal art and tree planting. By 1910, for example, 546 women's clubs in the US had helped to set up hospitals and tuberculosis clinics and sanatoria, 452 had arranged open air meetings to discuss improvement of health conditions and 246 had placed wall cards in public places giving information about public health ordinances.[29]

Ada Celeste Sweet, the first US Government Pension Agent in 1874, and the architect of a programme of much-needed civil service reform, which politicians detested, also found the time to be an active member of the Chicago Women's Club and to found the Municipal Order League of Chicago, yet another society designed to improve sanitary conditions. In 1890 Sweet raised the money to buy and equip the city's first police ambulance.[30] The first of many Ladies' Health Protective Associations (LHPA) appeared in 1884 in New York City, where 11 women residents of the exclusive residential area Beekman Hill were unhappy about the foul smell of a nearby manure heap. Discovering that its owner had a brother-in-law in the city government who was protecting it and him, they secured a legal order for the removal of the nuisance.[31] The Philadelphia branch of the LHPA, founded in 1892, focused on dirty water; it hired and paid an expert to carry out an examination, and then persuaded the city to invest $3,000,000 in the new method of sand filtration recommended by the expert. In 1897, the Philadelphia LHPA turned its attention to 'the disgusting habit of expectoration in public places', determining that streetcar companies should make each individual conductor responsible for the clean condition of his car. In the process they also managed to ban smoking on streetcars.[32] The work of the LPHAs was pioneering in another fundamental way because they advocated that women – then barred from legal education and practice – learn about the law in order to use it. This they did very effectively, essentially functioning as 'cause lawyers', a practice that, according to standard legal history, was not developed until much later. 'Cause lawyering' is notably not about clients, or rights, or legal process but about 'a vision of the good society'.[33]

Women's labours in cleaning up the environment were a way for them to learn about how party politics worked. There seems little doubt that their political consciousness and self-confidence were well served by this study of political manoeuvring. And what they understood wasn't flattering to the men. Images of dirt in the streets were used to talk about 'dirty' politics.[34] As Jane Addams put it, politely but forcefully: 'A city is in many respects a great business corporation, but in other respects it is enlarged housekeeping. If American cities have failed in the first, partly because office holders have carried with them the predatory instinct learned in competitive business, and cannot help "working a good thing" when they have an opportunity, may we not say the city housekeeping has failed partly because women, the traditional housekeepers, have not been consulted as to its multiform activities? The men of the city have been carelessly indifferent to much of this civic housekeeping, as they have always been indifferent to the details of the household.'[35] As she pointed out in her *Democracy and social ethics*, the politics revealed by women's engagement in municipal reform were also the politics of social inequality: 'the positive evils of corrupt government are bound to fall heaviest upon the poorest and least capable. When the water of Chicago is foul, the prosperous buy water bottled at distant springs; the poor have no alternative but the typhoid fever which comes from using the city's supply. When the garbage contracts are not enforced, the well-to-do pay for private service; the poor suffer the discomfort and illness which are inevitable from a foul atmosphere.'[36]

Since Jane Addams did everything, one would expect her to be prominent on the municipal housekeeping front too, which indeed she was. Children around Hull-House played in the huge, uncovered wooden garbage boxes which were fastened to the street pavement and full of decaying and highly pungent matter. In 1893 the Hull-House Woman's Club discussed the high infant death rate in the area – everywhere municipal housekeepers made this connection between rubbish and infant deaths, between contamination of the city and of the home. In the Hull-House case, 12 of the neighbourhood women, aided by Hull–House residents, took on a careful investigation of the state of the alleys, reporting to the Health Department 1,037 legal violations of waste disposal ordinances in two months. Nothing much was done. In 'sheer desperation' – the phrase she used in her memoir *Twenty years at Hull-House*[37] – Addams put in a bid for the garbage removal contract for the Nineteenth Ward herself. She was told her application had been thrown out on a technicality, but actually it had been blocked by the notorious Chicago ward boss and alderman John Powers, a man who singlehandedly controlled the enforcement of public regulations and the provision of city services in that district and who had become Addams' particular adversary.[38] As a kind of consolation prize, the mayor appointed Addams as garbage inspector of the ward at a salary of $1,000 a year. She and other Hull–House residents got up at six o'clock every morning to make sure the ward's nine garbage wagons were doing their business, and they persuaded the contractor to add eight more. One constant problem was the dead animals that littered the streets, which the private contractor was paid liberally to remove; his attention was dilatory, and when he did get round to it he got the carcasses transported by police ambulances and sold to a soap factory in Indiana (which he owned).

During the 1902 typhoid epidemic in Chicago, cases clustered disproportionately in the Nineteenth Ward. The women of Hull–House launched another detailed social and scientific investigation. Again, this exposed institutionalized corruption among officials and slum landlords. The full story of the Nineteenth Ward typhoid investigation as told by Dr Alice Hamilton, a doctor and bacteriologist who moved into Hull–House in 1897, appears in Chapter Nine. But among all these 'extraordinary ordinary'[39] women, who weren't afraid to get down on their knees to clean up the nation, the one who most of all gained the title of 'America's Housekeeper' was a Unitarian minister and sociologist called Caroline Bartlett Crane. Crane's archives at Western Michigan University were discovered some years ago almost accidentally by a student, Linda Rynbrandt, who was looking for a dissertation topic on gender, sociology and the history of social movements.[40] Crane was born in Minnesota in 1858. She became a teacher and a journalist and then, in 1889, attended the Chicago Theological Seminary, was ordained as a minister and took up a position at the Unitarian Church in Kalamazoo, a town about 150 miles from Chicago – a trajectory that's reflected in the quiet authority of her photograph. Crane belonged to the social gospel movement, as did a number of Progressive Era reformers and sociologists. According

4.2: Caroline Bartlett Crane, 1912

to their philosophy, the kingdom of God is not in heaven, but it is, or rather should be, here on earth. A trip to England, to witness Toynbee Hall and the Salvation Army, was followed by Crane's transformation of the Kalamazoo church from a house of God to a house for God's people, much along the lines of a social Settlement, with a free kindergarten, a women's gymnasium, household science classes and a literary club. The church, also much like Settlements such as Hull-House, became the base for systematic investigation of local social conditions and services. Its 1897 Report noted that they had submitted their 'A study of the social conditions of Kalamazoo', with its accompanying tables, maps and diagrams, to the University of Chicago Department of Sociology, which was now using some of the material to illustrate methods for the scientific study of social conditions.[41] Crane, a suffragist, took graduate sociology classes at the University of Chicago in 1896 and married a doctor 10 years her junior – both life-changing events. Next came an interruption, a mysterious break of two years in which she retired from public work, emerging as a committed social reformer. She began with food. Unable to find an expert to speak to the local Women's Club on the topic of healthy food, she decided to research it herself.

Her methodology was the same as McDowell's: first a sightseeing trip, together with a number of prominent citizens, this time to the Kalamazoo slaughter-houses. Her description of what they found anticipates the trials of Upton Sinclair's Jurgis Rudkus, and was followed by pressure (on pain of boycott) on local butchers to provide more sanitary meat, the usual representations to a largely deaf city authority and the preparation by Crane of a federal Bill allowing cities to devise their own meat inspection ordinances. The Bill was passed in 1903.

Having acquired the reputation of being something of an expert on the subject of safe meat – somewhat paradoxically, since she herself was a vegetarian – Crane found herself much in demand by other cities, which wanted her to inspect their slaughter-houses and generally advise on public health. 'Mrs Robert M. La Follette' wrote about municipal housekeeping and Caroline Bartlett Crane in the *Washington Post* in 1911. Mrs La Follette went with her on one of her tours: 'No skilled scientist', she reported, 'could pursue an investigation with greater thoroughness: no skilled housekeeper could be more observant of dust and dirt in her own house than she of the good and bad conditions of a city … In one instance a large pan of delectable cream puffs sat on the floor in the neighborhood of a rat trap … In another the baker sat on the mixing table as he talked to us. Think of a woman sitting on a bread board!'[42] (This comparison of women's thoughtfulness and efficiency vis-à-vis men's neglect of housekeeping matters was a constant motif in the municipal housekeeping movement.) 'Mrs Robert M. La Follette' – Belle Case La Follette – was no ordinary journalist, but a lawyer, the first woman graduate of the University of Wisconsin Law School, a suffrage worker, a co-founder of the Woman's Peace Party, an activist in the post-war Women's Committee for World Disarmament, and a co-founder of the National Council for the Prevention of War in 1921. As befits such a record, at her marriage in 1881 to the man who would become the Governor of Wisconsin, a US Senator and presidential candidate, the word 'obey' was omitted from the marriage vows.[43]

In a newspaper article with the headline 'How women would sweep our streets', Crane complained about the inefficiency with which men did it.[44] In 1904 she formed the Women's

Civic Improvement League in Kalamazoo to prove her point. The League convinced the City Council to allow it to clean six blocks in the main business section of the city for three months as a demonstration project. The women used a combination sprinkler-and-sweeper machine invented by a Miss Emily Parpart, and the 'Waring' system, owned by the sanitary engineer responsible for New York's Central Park, which incorporated a bag-carrier for hand-sweepings patented by Mrs Waring.[45] The women were in charge of men street-cleaners, whom they coached for this purpose, and they also got the council to pass an anti-expectoration ordinance (spitting, related to the transmission of tuberculosis, was obviously a big problem). They took photographs and sent them to tenants, house-owners and the Health Officer. Boys from their Junior Street-cleaning League were equipped with thousands of leaflets asking people to put their litter in bins. After all this effort, the streets were a lot cleaner, and the street commissioner promised to keep them that way.

Crane was an extremely professional operator. She developed a kind of municipal/sanitary consultancy, whereby she would visit a city, undertake direct observations and interviews, administer a survey questionnaire, analyse local records and newspaper articles, then hold a public meeting in the town to reveal her results. She used, in other words, the full range of 'mixed methods', including 'consumer involvement', which are beloved of social scientists today. Crane finished each survey with a report detailing recommendations for change. Her sanitary surveys were comprehensive, covering street sanitation, water, sewage, waste disposal, milk and meat, markets and shops, food factories, schools, tenements, hospitals and prisons. While the invitations to undertake a survey usually came from women's clubs, she wouldn't accept them unless the women had first gained the approval of city officials; she advised the club women how to fund her surveys and how to promote and publicize her work. She carried out 62 such surveys in 14 states, including three with state-wide coverage.[46] Crane was a member of that remarkable network of women reformers who put their stamp on the Progressive Era. She knew and worked with other women whose names are key to this book: Jane Addams, Carrie Chapman

Catt, Charlotte Perkins Gilman, Florence Kelley. When visiting Chicago for work, Crane would stay at Hull-House; Gilman and other women were in turn housed by Crane in Kalamazoo.[47]

A catalogue of books and journal articles – most produced by feminist scholars in recent decades – tell us about the history of women's municipal housekeeping in the US, but the literature on municipal housekeeping in Europe is sparse. Structures, systems and traditions were different in Europe, with an earlier move to recognize the need for public control and provision. 'Municipal housekeeping' for George Bernard Shaw, who published a book with the title *Mind your own business: The case for municipal housekeeping* in 1905, was mostly about the argument for the state provision of public services, and the duty of every citizen to vote for these. As he noted, there had been, in Britain, considerable advances already by then: 'Yesterday I walked through miles of London streets. At the end my boots were as clean as when I started. Had I lived in the era before we began to mind some of our business I should have had to plough through mire and mud and slime, dodging the sweepings from butchers' stalls, the refuse of houses and shops, dead dogs and cats, and garbage of every kind.'[48] Shaw considered London cleaner than the big American cities. This was the view of many European visitors: Charles Booth's Chicago was a mass of wet mud and rubbish, old boilers and drainpipes; the Barnetts considered Boston more refuse-filled and packed with more insanitary houses than Whitechapel.[49] The facts supported them, with a study done in the year of Shaw's comments showing that American cities generated almost twice as much rubbish per capita as English ones, while German cities beat the English, with less than three-quarters of their totals.[50]

Ada Brown, later Ada Salter, was born in Northamptonshire, England, in 1866 to a Methodist farming family; she abandoned her comfortable home for the London slums in 1896. She moved into the recently founded Bermondsey Settlement the following year, taking charge of the girls' clubs. Rather like Caroline Bartlett Crane, she startled everyone by marrying in her mid-30s a doctor somewhat younger than she was. The Salters set up home in an unlovely area of Bermondsey, where Alfred saw astounding numbers of patients every day, often charging nothing, and Ada continued her work with girls' clubs, got involved in local Liberal politics, and gave birth to their only child, Joyce. Ada and Alfred struggled about where to send Joyce to school – a Quaker boarding school (Alfred's choice) or the local state school (Ada's). Ada won.[51] Had she read what Florence Kelley of Hull-House had written in 1898? 'You must suffer from the dirty streets, the universal ugliness, the lack of oxygen in the air

4.3: Ada Salter

you daily breathe, the endless struggle with soot and dust … you must send your children to the nearest wretchedly crowded school and see them suffer the consequences, if you are to speak as one having authority and not as the scribes in these matters of the common, daily life and experience.'[52] The Salters went to great lengths to protect Joyce from these dangers – they set aside a special room in their house for Joyce and her playmates which was thoroughly disinfected after every use. But despite these precautions their daughter caught scarlet fever three times, and the third time she died of it, aged eight.[53] Since these diseases were spread by insanitary slums, Ada Salter spent the rest of her life trying to eradicate them. Her commitment saw good housing as necessary to a good society, one that would also abolish warfare in favour of welfare – Salter's impassioned activities on behalf of the peace movement reappear in Chapter Six. In 1914 she was elected president of the Women's Labour League, an organization that campaigned for women's political representation, becoming the women's section of the Labour Party when women got the vote on limited terms in 1918. By 1913, the Women's Labour League's housing committee had developed a comprehensive plan for municipal reform which included building cottage-style houses and providing public baths and communal kitchens and laundries to reduce housework.

Ada Salter became London's first female mayor in 1922. She began as she intended to go on, by refusing to wear the mayoral robes and chain and removing the Union Jack from the Town Hall (and then returning unspent at the end of her term most of the generous personal expenses to which she was entitled as mayor).[54] One of her first actions was to set up a Beautification Committee with a very ambitious agenda. Major items were the identification of any waste ground, private or public, that could possibly be planted with trees and shrubs; turning churchyards into playgrounds; providing free window boxes to anyone who wanted them; and screening all the borough's public toilets with shrubs and foliage. Experts from Europe came to witness the results of Ada Salter's municipal beautification, which, in 1926, provided enough work for 44 Beautification Department staff.[55] Almost overnight, Bermondsey became a marvellous place where you would chance upon swathes of green and splashes of vivid colour – red dahlias, yellow daffodils amid the soot-grimed buildings: 'They were like vases of flowers in a dusty room.'[56] Seventy of Bermondsey's 80 miles of streets were lined with 10 thousand trees. Most of these came from the gardens of a house in Kent which the Salters bought and gave to the council as a convalescent home for nursing mothers.

Housekeeping the cities – although not their beautification – was made easier when the sanitary reform movement in Britain instituted Lady Sanitary Inspectors in 1893. A specimen examination paper on municipal hygiene set by the Sanitary Inspectors' Board does, however, make clear that their remit extended to the kinds of 'nuisances' American women embraced as their civic duties: 'Question 1, "How would you deal with the following nuisances, and what evidence would you require to take a case into court? (a) Dust trade nuisances; (b) Human remains near dwelling; (c) River polluted with sewage; (d) Smoke nuisance; (e) An offensive trade."'[57] Another transatlantic difference was British women's ability, from 1888, to vote in local elections, and from 1907 to stand for local election – although many had an earlier route into policy making by serving as Poor Law Guardians and on School Boards and other such bodies.[58] This local government work was an important element in women's journey into public life as 'noisy, central and core members of a local reform movement'. They made a substantial difference to local welfare services and to welfare spending, and in the process acquired a consciousness about women's exclusion from the world of male policy makers.[59]

Although the metaphor of municipal housekeeping translated differently into reform activities in Europe as compared to America, there were strong international connections. The story of Alice Masaryk, from what is now the Czech Republic, who lived in Mary McDowell's Settlement in Chicago, and who also spent time at Hull-House, is an example of transnational learning, and also of the way in which women's engagement in research, political analysis and reform stretched across oceans and national frontiers. Like Jane Addams, but somewhat later, Alice Masaryk began and abandoned medical training: this interest in medicine perhaps points to both women's concern with science as a strategy for reform, and to the inhospitable nature of medical education for women at the time. After she gave up medicine, Masaryk travelled with her father to England, where she encountered the original London Settlement, Toynbee Hall. She changed to historical/social research, writing a PhD at the University of Berlin on England's Magna Carta, informed by the clear perception of central issues that is evident in her photograph. The Masaryks were a famous family: Alice's father, Tomáš Garrigue Masaryk, was a philosopher and politician, the first president in 1918 of an independent Czechoslovakia. He took his middle name from his wife, Charlotte Garrigue, an American musician: as well as giving birth to five children, Charlotte worked in the Czech women's movement, researched and popularized the composer Bedřich Smetana, translated into Czech John Stuart Mill's *Subjection of women*, and wrote one of her husband's major statements on sex equality, *Polygamy and monogamy*.[60] The Masaryks' son, Jan, a diplomat and Czech foreign minister, was assassinated by the communists at the Czernin Palace in Prague in 1948.

The tortuous political events of her father's and brother's lives – which would involve her deeply – lay in the future when Alice Masaryk went to live in the University of Chicago Settlement in 1904, at the very same time as the young Upton Sinclair was there, asking questions about conditions in the slaughter-houses.

Her father, who was also in Chicago lecturing at the University on the problems of small nations, was often to be found in the Settlement playground, sitting on the corner sand-box, talking contentedly to children in Polish, Slovak, Bohemian, German or English. Alice Masaryk, whom people described as 'talented, attractive and well-educated', with 'gorgeous dark eyes' and always smiling,[61] had come to Chicago to learn about social conditions in America, about settlement work and reform, and to research the lives of the Bohemian people in the US. Chicago was the third-largest Bohemian city in the world; Masaryk also visited Bohemian settlements in Iowa, Nebraska, Cleveland and New York.[62] The Slovak woman who cleaned Hull-House became a particular friend. When Alice visited Czech women in their homes and heard about their brutalizing work in the stockyards, she would return to her room and weep over what America was doing to her people. Mary McDowell got her involved in the business of municipal street-cleaning, and Masaryk helped to organize a group of 12- and 13-year-old boys into the 'Cleaners' Club of Chicago', whose declaration of rights was: 'we young citizens of Chicago have a right to a city of clean streets, clean air, clean alleys, clean milk, and clean water'.[63] Most movingly, it was one of these boys, Dr Harold O. Rosenberg, who was responsible for inviting Alice Masaryk back to the University of Chicago Settlement during her exile from Czechoslovakia in the Second World War.

Alice Masaryk was the founder of modern welfare systems and of a training school for social workers in Czechoslovakia. She also initiated the 'Sociological Section' of Charles University in Prague, bringing in specialists to lecture to students about social problems: neglected children; nutrition; housing;

4.4: Alice Masaryk in Chicago, 1904

workers' conditions. Transatlantic networks helped Alice Masaryk during a particularly demanding period of her life. By the time of the First World War she was a declared pacifist, working with American and other European women in the peace movement, and helping to found its Czech branch. In October 1915 she was working as a nurse in a military hospital in a town near Prague when she was arrested, interrogated for two weeks and accused of high treason on the grounds of hiding her father's political papers.[64] She spent eight months in cell number 207 of Landesgericht prison in Vienna. In one of many letters from her prison cell to her mother, she bravely remarked that 'Every experience helps us in life, and this is truly better than the *Ladies' Home Journal* experience which many women have.' She asked her mother to send her books on 'practical sociology'.[65] Tomáš Masaryk, who was out of the country at the time campaigning for Czech independence, enlisted the help of his friend, the businessman Charles Crane, and he wrote to Mary McDowell in Chicago explaining that the government had struck at him through Alice, who was completely innocent.[66] As a result of McDowell's response, 40,000 letters and telegrams were sent to Vienna petitioning for Alice Masaryk's release. The case got a great deal of media publicity in the US. Signatories of the petition included McDowell, Jane Addams and Florence Kelley from Hull-House; Lillian Wald from the Henry Street Settlement in New York, the social reformer and leader of the National Consumers' League, Pauline Goldmark; and the reformer and suffragist Mary Mumford. Julia Lathrop, the head of the Children's Bureau in the Department of Labor, the highest-ranking woman in the federal government at the time, also intervened separately. A resolution was drawn up by Grace Abbott, Director of the Immigrants' Protective League, and then adopted by the Bohemian National Alliance, asking the US State Department to use all possible influence with the Austrian government.[67] Referring to Alice Masaryk's 'nobility of character, her fine sense of honor, her humanitarian interests, and her distinguished scholarship', her American friends argued that American women couldn't possibly keep still and allow 'this cruel act of injustice to a gentle young woman'.[68] Alice Masaryk was freed early in July 1916.

After her release from prison, Alice Masaryk's sociological work became an object of interest to the secret police, so she conducted it in secret, inviting young women interested in sociology to her home, discussing theory and practice with them and teaching them research methods. When her father became president of the new republic in 1918, she found herself with two jobs: since her mother was ill, she effectively became 'first lady of Czechoslovakia', entertaining her father's political colleagues, together with various kings, princes and lords, and famous personages such as Marie Curie, Thomas Mann, H. G. Wells and Mary Pickford in Lany Castle, a baroque establishment in the Křivoklát woods near Prague. In her day job, as a member of the National Assembly of Czechoslovakia and head of the Czech Red Cross, she was responsible for reforming the old Austrian welfare system and designing a new one for the new republic. The Czech Red Cross was the national welfare agency, and Masaryk spoke of it as a movement – much like the Settlements she had witnessed in the US – for promoting civic altruism.[69] Liberation from three hundred years of Austro-Hungarian rule, combined with the First World War, had left the Czechs with thousands of refugees and displaced persons, a shortage of everything and extremely patchy or non-existent welfare services. Deciding that what was needed was a thorough social survey on the American model, Masaryk turned to Mary McDowell for help. Three young American women were dispatched to Prague in 1919. Five areas were chosen for study: public health; social welfare; recreation; the social aspect of education; and the condition of women in industry. The work was done by Masaryk, nine American women and 35 Czech helpers. There was a pause while the Americans collected and had got translated a 'sociological library', helping their Czech colleagues with social research methods. Four volumes of the Prague Survey were completed in English, translated into Czech and published by the Czechoslovak Ministry of Social Welfare in the 1920s.[70] The McDowell–Masaryk connection continued for the rest of their lives. McDowell returned to Prague for six months in 1922 to live with the Masaryks and help with Alice's welfare work. Her contribution to modern Eastern European society was recognized in the award by Lithuania of the Order of the Grand Duke Gediminas, and by the Czech Republic of the Order of the White Lion.[71] Nonetheless, Alice Masaryk remains a marginalized historical figure, remembered chiefly as her father's daughter and First Lady of Lany Castle.[72]

Housekeeping, a term with seemingly limited application, became a transnational methodology. While women's representation of themselves as public housekeepers kept them safely within the 'separate spheres' ideology of men's and women's labour,[73] under cover of this veil they were able to get tangled up in all sorts of sanitary engineering and political adventures. The process of municipal housekeeping blurred the boundaries between personal and public health, stretching the concept of democratic rights to amenities previously regarded as comforts and conveniences rather than as necessities.[74] Municipal housekeepers can be seen as early environmental justice activists and founders of a particular model of 'citizen expert' skilled in bridging the communication gap between government and the people.[75] Both the effects of their work, and our historical memory of it, have lapsed with the passage of time. The story of how cities were cleaned and rendered more aesthetic has been fragmented into the history of women's organizations, of urban reform, of gender and class ideologies, of welfare legislation, of labour politics. These are not the same thing as municipal housekeeping, but they are all part of it. Strikingly as well, the story of municipal housekeeping doesn't appear in histories of housework, although the two were closely linked. Sanitary science – the application of scientific understandings to domestic work – the focus of the next chapter, is also missing from housework's academic study. My own books on housework written in the 1970s repeated this omission, much to my chagrin now.[76]

Emily Hobhouse, a prominent British welfare campaigner and international pacifist, led a life in which apparently different activities – investigating conditions for women and children in Boer War camps and setting up industrial schools in South Africa, working for the women's peace movement, carrying out social investigation for the Women's Industrial Council – can be understood only as aspects of an integrated vision. One of her 'careful and systematic' social investigations was called simply 'Dust-women'; it was published in *The Economic Journal* in 1900. 'The history of refuse is a veritable romance,' says Hobhouse, 'and women play no inconsiderable part in its changing fortunes.' Her paper reports statistics, observations and interviews related to the work of women who were hired by private contractors to sort through rubbish in London wharves and dust-yards. The dust-carts would empty their loads and the women would then descend upon these, throwing rags, bones, string, cork, boots, paper, coal, glass and hard core into different baskets. They were paid less than the men for this work, but many valued it for its open-air aspect, although they did all, of course, get very dusty themselves in the process. Hobhouse saw the trajectory of rubbish, its career, as a story for which we are all responsible, and of which we are all inevitably ignorant. 'We are glad to forget the waste of the house as soon as it leaves our door … Leaving the house in the decaying conglomerate of the dust-bin, this refuse matter dies temporarily to all use, then passes through the hands of women in the yards, and goes forth to fresh life and service unrecognized in resurrection clothes. Packets of best writing paper, glue, soap, bottles, wall-bricks and paving-stones spring from the dust-heap; even the glass … journeys to Sweden, returning as neat squares of emery paper … But the women who handle the refuse on the wharves see neither its beginning nor its end, they deal with it only at the worst and foulest moment of its history.'[77]

FIVE

Sanitary science: putting the science into housework

'Are you ready for the fresh alpine air to welcome you as you travel up the scenic mountain roads and into the quaint villages of the Adirondacks?' enquires the tourist website in 2017. 'Are you ready to settle into your home away from home ... to experience all that Lake Placid and the High Peaks Region has to offer?'[1] Lake Placid, a village in the Adirondack mountains region of New York State, has offered many recreations in its time, including a modestly successful film of that name starring a giant, man-eating crocodile, the 1932 Winter Olympics and a series of conferences held between 1899 and 1910 featuring the enormously important and equally undervalued subject of domestic economy or household science. These conferences laid the foundations of home economics as an educational science and produced both the American Home Economics Association and *The Journal of Home Economics*; the movement also took root in other countries, providing yet another, mostly female, international network for the exchange of ideas, work and friendship. This terrain of work had various names, and the topic of its naming occupied much intellectual energy among its proponents. What's in a name? A great deal, when what is at issue is the whole domain of work in and for the home, itself a topic that can never be discussed without tramping the treacherous landscape of women's identity, what they do and what they ought to do, and how all of this is tied into structures of production and reproduction in modern industrial societies.[2] Household science isn't the same thing as housework, although, according to the trailblazers who feature in this chapter, it ought

101

to be. The chapter complements the previous one in its focus on how women reformers extended the science of health and hygiene into the most intimate recesses of the home.

Telling women how to do housework has a long and sometimes not very salubrious history. Henrietta Barnett, co-founder of Toynbee Hall, wrote her own little treatise for elementary school children in 1885; she conceived of moral education in unselfishness as sitting quite happily side by side with a lesson on drains – although she did avoid 'speaking of the water-closet', fearing it might put her audience off.[3] No such timidity affected other women sanitary advisers. The wonderfully named *Women, plumbers and doctors*, published by the American reformer Harriette Plunkett in the same year as Barnett's text, invites women to familiarize themselves with every detail of how their homes are plumbed and drained and heated and lit: the results of advancing 'hygienic intelligence' are advertised as reducing the need for doctors, bringing healthier homes and advancing the cause of appropriate public health legislation.[4] Why had the subject been neglected for so long? 'The household has been treated by economists with curious negligence,' wrote British economist Mabel Atkinson in 1910. 'The founder of political economy,' she went on disparagingly, referring to Adam Smith and his *Wealth of nations*, 'showed so little insight into the real nature of the work carried on there as to class those whom he described as menial servants with unproductive labourers … the more modern school of economists, those who devote themselves to the history of economic development in the past or to the intensive study of special economic institutions in the present, have equally failed to discuss with any adequacy the organisation of the household.'[5] And all this despite the fact that housekeeping is, as Atkinson observed, the largest single industry in England. Or indeed anywhere.

Plunkett's and Atkinson's arguments, which were paralleled by many others, were emblematic of a new approach to the universal world of housework. This developed in the period from around 1870 through the first decades of the 20th century, and stirred scientific, creative and reforming imaginations alike. The simple proposition that housework is, or should be, a matter of *science* could be used to undermine its historical dismissal as a feature of women's biological character. This was a radically new frame of reference, connecting public and private confrontations with dirt and disorder by specifying the same solution (science) for both. While the municipal housekeeping movement had taken housework into the public world, sanitary science pressed the public world of science into the service of the home. 'Public welfare,' declared the American sanitary scientist Ellen Richards, 'demands that the home life shall be governed by the best knowledge which science has been able to gather with reference to health and efficiency.'[6] Physics, chemistry, bacteriology, physiology, biology – these, as well as ethics, economics and sociology, became indispensable tools for the well-run home, and the well-run home took its place as the mainstay of the nation's own health, welfare and well-being. In 'the world effort to promote human progress', pronounced Alice Ravenhill, one of the leading British exponents of the new approach, home economics must be one of the most important factors: its larger complex, hygiene, is 'the lens through which we should focus all learning upon the advancement of life'.[7] The reformulation of home economics from a means for teaching women domestic duties into an applied science was fostered by the growing cultural authority of science itself. It came into its own at a time when the new germ theory of disease fanned epidemics of microbial warfare, and when the analysis of vital statistics showed how much preventable disease and death, particularly among children, begins in the unsanitary conditions of the home. There was also, especially in Britain, concern about the quality of the population. The famous *Report of the Inter-departmental Committee on the Physical Deterioration of the Population*, published in 1904, and other public health literature of the time, pointed the finger at deficient domesticity in creating unhealthy bodies and producing untimely death.[8] Doctors bemoaned the inefficiencies of mothers (not fathers) in rearing healthy children. In these circumstances, prevention wasn't only better than cure, it was the sole strategy available. The sanitary science movement reflected the spirit of the times in its sexism, which was interlocked with imperialist and eugenicist agendas.[9] Scholarship on the topic has concentrated on these biases, rather than on the genuine efforts reformers made to improve the science of housework.

The American domestic scientist and Dean of Women at the University of Chicago, Marion Talbot, put forward another linch-pin argument of the sanitary reformers' case in an article called 'Sanitation and sociology' in one of the earliest issues of the *American Journal of Sociology*, in 1896. Vital statistics of life and death are all very well, she said, but sanitarians who restrict their aims to quantity of life are missing the importance of its quality; and in order to understand how sanitary science can improve the *way* people live, sanitation must ally itself with sociology, 'a weapon of great power' in demonstrating the impact of social context and conditions. Talbot's view was that home economics/sanitary science is concerned with the *relation* between household techniques and scientific principles, and between domestic activities and the wider society.[10] The new scientific housekeeping movement thus brought together two concerns of prime significance to women reformers: the status and life of the household, and the developing perspectives and methods of social science.

Britain's Alice Ravenhill visited Lake Placid in 1901 and enjoyed a 'wholly delightful week' of talk and plans about what the 'Lake Placid group' of household science reformers decided, after much debate, to call 'home economics'.[11] Ravenhill was then a 42-year-old County Council Hygiene Lecturer in Yorkshire, 'a busy, alert, shrewd, straight-backed Victorian ... keenly aware of the contemporary world', but also one 'virtually unknown in the historiography of the Edwardian era', despite being involved in many social welfare initiatives.[12] In the photograph, taken in her later years, her posture is straight-backed, serious and learned. Like many middle-class women

5.1: Alice Ravenhill, 1936

of the period, Ravenhill had been prevented by convention and an autocratic father from finding interesting work outside the home. Her early interest in science had to be conducted covertly; she read physiology and dissected snails and worms and, on one occasion, an ox's eye, in her bedroom. The tide turned when her father's investment in an Australian goldmine scheme failed and she was finally able to claim the right to earn her own living. She took a one-year diploma course in hygiene run by the National Health Society in 1893; the course, which included practical work in the Chelsea Poor Law Infirmary (much treating of bed sores, 'ghastly' ulcers and 'inhabited' heads[13]),was then the only such training open to women in Britain who wanted to work in public health. Ravenhill was one of the first four women to take the course: two of the others, Lucy Deane and Rose Squire, became the first Women Sanitary Inspectors in Britain. Ravenhill herself embarked on a peripatetic teaching career, beginning with lectures on hygiene and domestic science in rural villages in Bedfordshire and Lincolnshire with the aid of a home-made demonstration kit. This yielded much-needed concrete illustrations of domestic science lessons: small cardboard windows capable of being adjusted to show the importance of night-ventilation; dressed dolls and miniature furniture in a cardboard house to prove the dangers of overcrowding; Petri dishes with agar jelly into which dust from the floor could be sprinkled as evidence that dirt invariably multiplies. It was very brave work for a woman then; transport was difficult, in open gigs along dark roads, and sometimes she had to spend the night in a cold bed vacated by her village hosts. Ravenhill's career advanced considerably when the Co-operative Society and the Women's Co-operative Guild were looking for a lecturer on sanitary law. An air of mystery hangs over the offer she was made (and refused) in 1899 to become governess to the King of Siam's daughters in Bangkok; perhaps her refusal had something to do with the fact that the King's household contained no fewer than 44 of them.[14]

In the same year – and more significantly for the world of female networking in social reform – was Ravenhill's attendance, sponsored by the National Health Society, at the International Congress of Women in London, which was convened by the

International Council of Women. Here, as we know (from Chapter Two), Ravenhill met Charlotte Perkins Gilman and many other capable and fascinating women. Her international contacts were furthered by attendance at the annual conference in Paris in 1900 of the Royal Sanitary Institute, which would later elect her as its first woman fellow. Much of the Paris conference was occupied by presentations on developments in household science in the US – the first systematic educational efforts to teach in schools not just the *what* of household science, but the *why*; for instance, '*why* heat applied to foodstuffs in various forms effected familiar but hitherto unexplained changes in their appearance or digestibility; *why* certain substances cleaned fabrics or wood or metal without injury and *why* others were destructive'.[15] Ravenhill, highly enthused, came back and asked the Board of Education in Britain to fund an investigation which would find out more about these intriguing developments. And so it came about that she visited the US in the spring of 1901 for three months, investigating the teaching of domestic science in all grades of educational institutions in 17 different towns and attending the Lake Placid Conference. Since the Board of Education had offered only £30 for her expenses, she used her initiative (a substance she clearly wasn't short of), acquiring supplementary funds from both the West Riding of Yorkshire County Council and the Royal Sanitary Institute. She found many divergences in social habits between the US and Britain, including the 'excessive heat of the houses and public institutions', which meant she had to open her bedroom window at night when staying with the Dean of Women at a university in Philadelphia, thus setting off a burglar alarm and giving the Dean's elderly mother a near-fatal heart attack. In Philadelphia, Ravenhill witnessed the shocking sight of a 'Negro' shot when he tried to board a 'white' street car; in Chicago she encountered many novel educational methods and met many enthusiastic leaders in social reform, including Jane Addams. Crossing the river from Detroit into Canada, she was the guest of Adelaide Hoodless, the founder of Women's Institutes world-wide, from whom unfortunately she learnt little, as Hoodless was recumbent in bed with bronchitis at the time.[16]

5.2: Participants in the first Lake Placid meeting of sanitary scientists, 1899, Ellen Swallow Richards at the front

The organizer of Alice Ravenhill's North American travels, and her host at the Lake Placid Conference, was a woman many would consider Ravenhill's American counterpart in the household science field, Ellen Swallow Richards.[17] In the picture above Richard sits in front of a group of confident matrons at the first Lake Placid Conference in 1899. A trained chemist and the first woman to study and teach at the Massachusetts Institute of Technology (MIT), Richards was described by Ravenhill as 'Tiny in person but of great force of character and well-endowed with intellectual ability.'[18] Her struggles to get an education and professional work had, like Alice Ravenhill's a generation later, to overcome troublesome ideological and institutional obstacles. Richards was the only child of a rural Massachusetts family, and her parents, both teachers, did support her interest in becoming a scientist, but of course women didn't become scientists in those days. Eventually a newly opened women's college, Vassar, accepted her and she saved enough to go, and learnt how to do science from Maria Mitchell, Vassar's very own Professor of Astronomy and America's first professional woman astronomer. Mitchell had discovered her own comet, now known as 'Mitchell's comet', in 1847 at the age of 28, and held 'Dome Parties' for the Vassar students, which meant getting up in the middle of the night to gaze at stars, planets, comets and eclipses. Mitchell told her students that she believed in women even more than she did in astronomy, and she told Ellen Richards (then Ellen Swallow) to question everything, and to understand that science needs imagination as well as logic and mathematics.[19] Although Mitchell hoped that this talented student would take up astronomy, it was the classes in analytical chemistry that most grabbed Richards' attention. After Vassar, from which she graduated as the first American woman to gain a chemistry degree, she tried to get taken on by commercial chemical companies, but none would accept a woman. In 1870 she took the bold step of applying to MIT. It had never had a female student, but the maleness of the institution was so accepted that the rules didn't actually bar women. MIT eventually took her without charge as a 'special student'. Once there, Ellen Swallow had to work alone in the laboratory, her lessons left at a shut door, just as if she were 'a dangerous animal'.[20] She tactfully ingratiated herself with the men, bandaging cut fingers and mending professors' suspenders, so that they came to value her, and to ask her advice on scientific and mathematical problems. All this hard work paid off in 1872 when she was asked to help with a ground-breaking water survey undertaken by MIT for the Massachusetts Board of Health, which had become concerned about water pollution in the Boston area. She tested thousands of water samples for the presence of contaminants at a time when water analysis – 'limnology' – was a new science, and when protecting the environment hadn't yet entered the conceptual discourse of public health. By the time her report was published and the death rate from water-borne diseases in Boston had begun to decline, Ellen Swallow Richards' reputation as a water scientist had spread internationally.

Alice Ravenhill and Ellen Richards had corresponded before the Lake Placid event, but had not met. They shared many ideas about the centrality of a clean, rationally and efficiently run home in forming good citizens, and about the role of housework in the public and the national health. 'That the household is not run on economic principles is acknowledged by the neglect of it in the study of economics,'[21] Richards had said in 1899, anticipating Mabel Atkinson's later remarks about the failure of male economic theorists to entertain it as part of their subject.

Although their message was science, Richards and Ravenhill both published works called *The art of right living*. Ravenhill's, in 1913,[22] was decorated with drawings and photographs of windows, cesspits, teeth and beds, and was published by the Department of Agriculture in British Columbia for circulation to all local Women's Institutes. Richards' volume, published in 1904,[23] was the more scientific of the two, although much of the material (dirt, nutrition, exercise, air, water, sleep, recreation, the body) was common to both. From drains to teeth, the message was that science should be the mistress of the household. It mattered less what you called it (art or science) than that you accepted this basic tenet.

Dirt and dust were naturally major characters on the sanitary science stage. 'Dirt in any form means danger to health,' wrote Ravenhill. 'Imperfectly washed bodies are more liable to illness in its thousand forms, and offer much less resistance to its attacks than those braced by daily baths.'[24] Maria Elliott, a household economics instructor in Boston, composed a text on *Household Bacteriology* in 1907 which began with dust, 'a very important complex substance, which promises much of interest in its study'; within a few pages she had her audience doing experiments with yeast and Petri dishes, and perusing diagrams of horribly creepy bacteria.[25] The household as a business was a common metaphor. Heavy draperies, plush and velvet may look nice but are catch-alls for dust, instructed Richards: 'It is not business economy to put obstacles in the way for the sake of overcoming them.'[26] Alice Ravenhill's diagram headed 'The care and conduct of family life' shows an enterprise of frightening complexity, with 'mother' as the 'Chief Executive Officer' and both parents holding positions as 'Purchasing Agents', 'Conservers of Health', 'Controllers of Finance', 'Directors of Social Activities' and so forth.[27] From around 1912, the business analogy was enhanced when Christine Frederick in the US began propounding the idea that 'Taylorism' or scientific management techniques developed in industry should be applied to the home.[28]

Sanitary scientists advised not only on the best ways to do housework and why, but how to refashion homes so that they were more easily cleaned. In Richards' model home, for example, the kitchen floor would be 'lignolith', laid in one piece and creeping up the walls, thus eliminating the crevices of wainscoting which harbour insects and dust. Shelves would be made of antiseptic glass, as in hospitals. Windows must be dust-proof and fly-, mosquito- and moth-proof. 'Most certainly dirt will not be permitted to come in on shoes and long dresses.' A windmill on the roof could store power, or a 'solar motor' could save the sun's rays. For bedroom design, Richards turns to H. G. Wells' *A modern utopia*: no fireplace, a thermometer and six switches on the wall, one to warm the floor, one the mattress and the others the walls; a fan to circulate the air which enters by a device called a 'Tobin shaft'. In the bathroom, soap will fall hygienically out of a store-machine and after using it you drop it and soiled towels into a little box through which they enter a shaft and disappear.[29] These scientific plans for reforming households had much in common with the creative thinking of writers such as Charlotte Perkins Gilman in their attempts to divorce social customs from the searing effects of gender-divisive ideologies.

They tried to practise what they preached. Ellen Richards herself followed as many of these admonitions about sanitary living as she could in her own home, in Jamaica Plain on the outskirts of Boston. The house, bought in 1875 with her husband, Robert Richards, an MIT professor of mineralogy, became effectively 'a living laboratory'.[30] She tested the water that came into the house; they took all the old lead pipes out, replacing them with safer ones; they removed all the windows, putting in new ones that opened at the top; they cut holes in ceilings and walls for ventilation, installed fans to pull out stale air, stripped arsenic-contaminated wallpaper off the walls, took up dusty carpets and threw out all curtains, substituting oxygen-producing vines and flowering plants. The kitchen was converted from coal to gas, and meters were installed to monitor fuel usage. The Richards had no children, but they kept cats and parrots, which is perhaps a bit of a sanitary contradiction. The house in Jamaica Plain was also the first consumer products-testing laboratory in the country: Ellen Richards called it the 'Center for Right Living' and she brought her MIT students there to learn directly about the chemistry of cleaning and cooking, sanitation and nutrition.

MIT's response to 'the Swallow experiment',[31] as they called it, had not been to open the doors to more female students; they continued to see the remarkable Ellen Swallow Richards as an exception to a general rule. As indeed she was. She persuaded the governing board to let her use a gymnasium behind the Institute to set up the first chemistry laboratory for women. The Board agreed, on three punitive conditions: that she raise the money for it herself, assume total responsibility for its upkeep and teach its classes without pay. Rising to the challenge, she obtained the money from Boston's Women's Education Association, and took her new husband with her to Germany to purchase the very best equipment available, entering some laboratories dressed as a man because otherwise she would never have been allowed in (her fluency in German would have helped here). Robert complained about his wife's apparently limitless energy: she was a very organized and methodological person with a passion for detail: for example she noted in her diary the number of steps she climbed each day.[32] Richards' Women's Laboratory, opening in 1876, was the first institution of its kind in the world teaching science to women. It was a science, moreover, that she linked directly to social reform. For the young women to whom she taught basic biology and chemistry, fieldwork in factories was

5.3: Ellen Swallow Richards with MIT chemistry staff, 1900

compulsory, prompting them to ask awkward questions about the responsibilities of government and industry to protect workers' health. Eventually, in 1884, MIT hired Ellen Richards as a paid instructor to teach sanitary chemistry, sanitary engineering and air/water/food analysis to both male and female students. The posed photograph on page 111 shows her with the 25 mostly unsmiling, moustached, men who made up the rest of the MIT chemistry staff in 1900. Ellen Richards sits composed, her hands decorously arranged on her long silk dress, her hair grey but her eyebrows still dark, her direct gaze and the slightly lopsided tilt of her mouth inviting one to wonder what she might be plotting now.

The list of Ellen Richards' accomplishments is long: consulting chemist for the Massachusetts State Board of Health 1872–75; the Commonwealth's official water analyst 1887–97; nutrition expert for the US Department of Agriculture; the first woman member in 1879 of the American Institute of Mining and Metallurgical Engineers; co-founder of a Marine Biological Laboratory at Woods Hole, Massachusetts, which still exists today; author or co-author of at least 18 books; and a great deal more. As a result of her work, Massachusetts established the first water-quality standards in the US and the first modern sewage plant. In her Center for Right Living she tested foods for adulteration (common tricks at the time were packing sugar out with sand, cinnamon with sawdust, and tea with iron filings, and sprinkling ice-cream with streptococci). This work led to the first Pure Food and Drug Acts. In 1890 she opened the New England Kitchen, a community kitchen run on sanitary lines providing cheap nutritious meals; at the 1893 World's Fair in Chicago she designed another model kitchen, this time named after Count Rumford, an early physicist and nutritionist, where 20 pamphlets about diet and the human body were handed out and healthy lunches were available, accompanied by cards listing the calories, proteins, fats and carbohydrates in each. An early observer of the importance to child development of proper diet, Richards extended her model kitchen work to provide a school lunch programme for 4,000 students a day in 16 Boston high schools. The problem of nomenclature remained a worry. Richards ventured two new terms: 'oekology' and 'euthenics'. Oekology was the science of right living, an amalgam of applied sciences teaching the principles of normal, healthy, happy lives. Euthenics was the opposite of eugenics: the science of a controllable, rather than inherited, environment: 'The betterment of living conditions, through conscious endeavor, for the purpose of securing efficient human beings.'[33] Neither term really caught on, although 'oekology' is now considered to establish her as the founder of the modern ecology movement.[34]

Despite these impressive achievements, Ellen Richards' academic colleagues paid little attention to her household science work. They didn't consider it the work of a proper scientist, but an aspect of women's homemaking duty: the very canon, of course, against which she was fighting. Much the same attitude has prevented most modern historians from appreciating the drive and vigour of the sanitary science movement. It's been easier, and perhaps it's made a more straightforwardly feminist case, to assume continuity between the new approach to housework and women's traditional oppression in the home.[35] It *is* true, of course, that women like Ellen Richards and Alice Ravenhill often didn't actively contest women's responsibility for running households. Had they done so, they might have run the risk of being even less listened to than they were. But they did argue that there should be *less* housework (this being one of the goals of its rationalization), and many thought men as well as women should know more about household science.

The feminist case underlying sanitary science was generally proposed a little more subtly. For example, Ellen Richards headed a chapter on 'woman's responsibility' in one of her last books with quotations from the English novelist George Eliot about the importance of recognizing the great amount of socially *unproductive* labour women have to do, and from the sociologist W. I. Thomas who called opposition to women's full participation in life 'a romantic subterfuge, resting not so much on belief in the disability of woman as on the disposition of man to appropriate conspicuous and pleasurable objects for his sole use and ornamentation'.[36] Charlotte Perkins Gilman's point that housework and childcare aren't feminine instincts, but matters that must be learnt, was key to the women sanitary reformers' case. Richards' economic analysis of households drew out the argument, shared with other female economists such as Emily Balch and Clementina Black, that their transformation from centres of production to consumption enterprises makes householders and housekeepers all too easily the gullible victims of a voracious capitalism. 'Many really humane people are overawed by the authority of the pompous and powerful assertions of "successful" men of affairs,' Richards wrote declaratively, 'and they often sleep while such men are forming secret conspiracies against national health and morality with the aid of legal talent hired to kill. Only when the social mind and conscience is educated and the entire community becomes intelligent and alert can legislation be secured which places all competitors on a level where humanity is possible.'[37]

The Lake Placid Conference at which Alice Ravenhill and Ellen Richards met was the third home economics conference to be held in this pleasant spot, itself the location of yet another visionary project, a cooperative recreational retreat for teachers, writers and preachers started by two librarians, Dr Melvil Dewey and his wife, Annie Godfrey Dewey, a Vassar graduate interested in home economics, in 1895. (Annie is on the left in the Lake Placid photo, page 107.) Melvil Dewey was an eccentric, self-centred and rather prejudiced character and is best known as the originator of the Dewey Classification System (or Dewey Decimal System), a method of classifying library books by subject which is used today in more than 135 countries. His tidy and classificatory mind also yielded the Spelling Reform Association in 1886, whose principles he practised: for example, he said that the Lake Placid venture had begun with their 'mariaj' and very much included his 'wyf'.[38] Lake Placid was for the Deweys a model community, an example of how households should be run 'efficiently, inexpensively, and in accordance with the best principles of the domestic sciences'.[39] Given the difficulty sanitary reformers had with names and disciplinary boundaries, it is perhaps predictable that the Lake Placid Conference participants should have spent quite a lot of time arguing about how the Dewey Decimal System treated home economics. Melvil Dewey had put home economics as 'domestic economy' in category 640, at the same level as other applied technologies, but a sub-committee on classification led by Annie Dewey wanted its 'relational aspects' moved to 339 with sociology, which they felt would give the subject more prestige.[40]

All these moves to make domestic science a more important and respectable subject built on a long tradition of women's work in sanitary science education. It was increasingly felt that the subject was not taught in a sufficiently scientific way. Maude Lawrence, who wrote a report on cookery teaching for the British Board of Education in 1907, mentioned one teacher who told her class that scarlet fever and cholera could be eradicated by putting onions under the bed.[41] As Ravenhill showed in the reports to her funders, the teaching of domestic science in most countries concentrated on practical experience and was extremely short on science. The British Association of Teachers of Domestic Subjects, under its president, Mary Playne, launched a campaign to have domestic science – 'the science of home affairs', composed centrally of chemistry, physics and physiology – accepted as an examinable subject in secondary schools. Playne was one of Beatrice Webb's many sisters: there were nine altogether, with birth dates spread out over 20 years, a formidable sisterhood of variegated experiences and mutual support. (Two others, Catherine (Kate) Courtney and Rosalind (Rosie) Williams, also appear in this book.)[42] Mary Playne founded one of the foremost domestic science training colleges, in Gloucestershire. She took the argument about the importance of domestic science teaching to its logical conclusion, which was to propose that it should become a university-level subject.[43]

The whole case was helped by the movement of women into the sanitary science aspects of public health work. Margaret Pillow, Britain's first qualified sanitary science teacher, began her lectures in the 1890s with how to dig the foundations of a building, how to understand eight different varieties of subsoil, how to make a damp-proof course, and the best materials to use for walls, gutters and pipes. Like Ellen Richards, but perhaps less scientifically, she advised her students on how to test for the purity of water – one teaspoon of Condy's fluid (the crimson version) in one quart of water: five minutes later, if sediment has settled in the glass, the water is impure.[44] A procedure called 'the peppermint test', recommended by Pillow and other sanitary scientists for checking household plumbing, conjures up particularly entertaining images: the peppermint oil test required the pouring of peppermint oil into waste pipes at their highest point and then going round the house sniffing the air in every room to see if peppermint could be detected in it.[45] Asked how she prepared herself for such unladylike work, Pillow answered: 'I went ... into workshops and I learnt as much of plumbers' work as possible, to make joints, &c. I have spent hours over the practical laying of drains, water mains, and connections. I examined cisterns, learned to draw plans of houses, vertical section drainage of houses, &c. With regard to the actual inspection I examined and inspected wherever I could possibly go; I thoroughly studied the Acts of Parliament and ... bye-laws framed by the Local Government Board ... Among the places I visited were three dairies, one slaughter-house, two bake offices, sanitary arrangements of schools, several hospitals, disinfecting rooms and workshops, and one dust destructor.'[46]

The brief for the first women sanitary inspectors in Britain covered seven main categories of work: the inspection of laundries/workshops where women/girls worked and visiting outworkers' homes; inspection of lodging homes and tenement houses; notifiable infectious diseases and some non-notifiable childhood diseases; cases of tuberculosis; hotel and restaurant kitchens; public toilets for women; and deaths of infants under one year from diarrhoeal diseases.[47] Many women sanitary inspectors considered themselves different from their male colleagues in their orientation to social reform; they saw their role as embracing informing women, especially women working in 'sweated labour' in the home, to make more use of the legislation designed to protect them. Women inspectors joined the suffrage movement – a Women Sanitary Inspectors' and Health Visitors' Suffrage Group was formed in 1910, led by Theodore Fisher, Hampstead's woman inspector, who said that their knowledge of poor homes made women inspectors realize strongly the need for women to have a hand in framing laws which dealt with housing conditions, the feeding of children etc.[48] The whole evolution of public health sanitary work acted synergistically with the work of women who sought to reform the sanitary practices of homes, to generalize the message that science is the route to both public and private health.

After her first visit to Lake Placid, Alice Ravenhill was a regular contributor to the Lake Placid proceedings. In 1907 she reported a most exciting new development: the proposed introduction in the Women's Department of King's College in London, of a new scheme of studies which would give proper recognition to the subject of domestic science.[49] The idea turned into a new course – called initially 'home science' or 'home science and economics' – and then into a new university department with its own degree, diploma and other courses, and finally into a whole new institution, the first and only of its kind, a completely separate part of the University of London, the King's College of Household and Social Science (KCHSS). In 1928 KCHSS took its place with Westfield, Bedford and Royal Holloway Colleges as one of the constituent women's colleges of London University. KCHSS was an extraordinary development which lasted for 45 years but has been virtually banished from the history of British higher education – thereby driving home the point that nothing about housework is likely to be taken seriously for very long in a patriarchally structured world.

The origins and fate of KCHSS are a good illustration of the complex gender and disciplinary politics attendant on trying to enter the household into the domains of science and academia. Its story involves a variegated cast of characters. As one of them, Hilda Oakeley, put it in her memoirs, 'The chief aim may be described in one way as the elevation of Domestic Science, the "Cinderella of the Sciences," to a position beside her elder sisters within the citadel of orthodox university subjects. But this does little to convey the ideas which aroused so much enthusiasm, and appealed to people of many and varied interests.'[50] Oakeley was a philosopher, a suffragette, a friend of such notables as Eleanor Rathbone and Beatrice Webb, and she was Vice-Principal of

King's College Women's Department during the time when it transmigrated into KCHSS. A member of a liberal Anglican family, with strong colonial connections to India, Oakeley had resisted the claims of higher education until her late 20s, preferring self-education and work in a girls' club. The club habit continued at Somerville College, Oxford, where she

5.4: Hilda Oakeley

joined a discussion group called 'Associated Prigs' which met on Sunday evenings to talk about social subjects.[51] They debated factory legislation, conditions in the cotton mills, rural sanitation, co-education, the disestablishment of the church, and Plato on the position of women, probably with the great earnestness which is apparent in the photograph of Oakeley. Oakeley's enterprising career took her to Canada, where she ran the first residential women's college, the Royal Victoria College at McGill University, and to the US, where she visited all the American women's colleges and spent time (in 1904) in Chicago and was able to meet many of those associated there with social research and with Hull-House – particularly Edith Abbott and Sophonisba Breckinridge – and to see for herself the appalling conditions of life in the meat-packing district.[52] Not only did Hilda Oakeley do all that, but she was extremely active and much respected in the field of philosophical debate, the originator of a new theory of idealism in which minds contribute to experience through a process of 'creative memory'.[53]

Apart from Oakeley, and Ravenhill, the KCHSS group contained Lady Adele Meyer, wealthy society hostess, reformer, funder, social investigator (with Clementina Black) of women garment-makers' work[54] and founder/co-founder of the first rural health clinic and the first model infant welfare centre in Britain; Lady Thereza Rucker, educated at Bedford College for women, avid promoter of household science teaching, despite a rather poor understanding of its science (she kept electric plugs in every socket, in case electricity escaped onto the carpets) and married to the Principal of London University, Arthur Rucker (which came in handy during the negotiations for the new Household and Social Science degree); Lilian Faithfull, ex-Somerville College, Oxford and Vice-Principal of the King's College Women's Department before Oakeley; Mabel Atkinson, LSE researcher, philosopher, founder member of the Fabian Women's Group, lecturer in economics at King's College, pacifist and ardent suffragette – she boasted of having attended every suffragette demonstration (along with her mother). In Atkinson's much-read Fabian tract, *The economic foundations of the women's movement*, she took issue with 'that extraordinarily suggestive and interesting American, Charlotte Perkins Gilman', for being rather too optimistic about the chances of childbearing women being able to earn their own living, even with extensive help from the state.[55]

The women's section of King's College (the main men's section was in Central London, in the Strand) had started life in 1871, providing courses similar to university extension lectures for 'ladies' in Richmond and Twickenham, and then in Kensington, to where it moved in 1878. A popular 'household management' class was added at the request of students in 1897. The struggle to dignify the topic with mainstream university status took many years and reflected the interplay, as Oakeley suggested, of different kinds of ambitions. Conversations started around 1906 about a possible King's College course and were led by Lilian Faithfull and Thereza Rucker, fed with ample amounts of propaganda supplied by Alice Ravenhill. A Ladies' Committee was formed in 1907 to help generate enthusiasm and money. The critical turning point came when Adele Meyer happened to meet one of the doctors, Dr John Atkins of Guy's Hospital, who was concerned about the role in child health and development of unscientific home management. Most of the money for the King's College venture came from his friends and family, and from his wealthy Kensington patients; Meyer herself financed the residential student hostel. With these endowments, new architect-designed buildings were constructed on Campden Hill, an area of high ground adjacent to Kensington and Notting Hill in West London. The new buildings, of dark red brick with Portland stone accents, were modelled on Oxbridge, yet housed very modern and 'palatial' laboratories.

The home science courses in Campden Hill got off the ground in 1908, with the Diploma in Household and Social Science beginning in 1916, and a three-year BSc degree course in 1920.[56] The KCHSS syllabus was constructed around a solid core of sciences: chemistry, biology, physiology, bacteriology, hygiene, plus economic history, 'practical domestic arts' and business methods, and an elective element – divinity, physiology, logic, English literature or ethics. There were also a postgraduate diploma in dietetics, short courses in institutional and household management and a science course for State Registered Nurses. A sign of the degree course's emphasis on science was its very detailed teaching of applied chemistry: 'The constituents of the atmosphere and methods of estimation – water analysis with special reference to its use for drinking purposes, cooking, and in the laundry – the constituents of foods, adulterants, and preservatives, with a value to determining their wholesomeness – the chemistry of cooking and of the materials used in cooking – the chemical changes caused by organized and unorganized ferments, applied to the preparation, preservation, and deterioration of foods and to digestion – the chemistry of laundry work and other cleansing processes – the nature and quality of textile fabrics in common use; the physical and chemical properties of their constituent fibres – disinfectants and antiseptics – scientific principles underlying the care and preservation of the chief materials used in the structure and equipment of a house.'[57] Students worked most professionally in the laboratory and combined all the theory with useful everyday practice. One KCHSS student, Lucy Smart, said that on some days they were 'startled by flames of burning ether and explosions in treacle tins – during the so-called Chemistry lecture'. Then, 'After spending several hours staining our hands in trying to detect arsenic, we are allowed to go to the "Workhouse", where we learn how to remove the same stains and how to wash woollens.'[58] Students

5.5: Students in the laboratory, King's College of Household and Social Science, c. 1924

were drawn from all over the country, many from academically ambitious girls' secondary schools, and some from prominent families, including Ishbel MacDonald, who went there shortly before her father Ramsay MacDonald became the first Labour Prime Minister.[59] After he was installed in Number 10 Downing Street Ishbel lent its meeting rooms to various of her reform efforts, including the British Child Guidance Council.[60]

The King's College women argued that a university domestic science course would be of benefit to many groups of women, notably those who wanted to train as administrators of large establishments or estates or as teachers/leaders in social reform (the term used for the last of these was 'scientific philanthropy'). In the event, around half of KCHSS students took their first jobs in teaching; others worked in health visiting or childcare, dietetics or food science; some took jobs in hospitals or did laboratory work. A high proportion of later graduates worked in commercial laboratories for Lyons, the country's largest caterer, which in the 1920s churned out 26 miles of Swiss roll a day. It was less clear how a 'supervisor of factory output' at Selfridges department store, a 'peace negotiation committee rent collector' or an 'assistant to a stockbroker' were making use of their hard-won sanitary knowledge.[61] Although it had been planned for the whole college to move to the new site, the Household and Social Science Department was so successful in the inter-war period that it became the sole occupant of the purpose-built site, the other departments merging with the men's college and disappearing to the Strand. In 1928 the link between King's College and KCHSS was severed completely, and KCHSS students became separate internal students in the University of London's Faculty of Science.[62]

Alice Ravenhill's input to the KCHSS venture was heavily influenced by her contact with American models of domestic science. What her sanitary science colleague, Marion Talbot, had done in Chicago was a particularly relevant example. Talbot had been one of Ellen Richards' students: together Richards and Talbot had founded another significant network, the Association of Collegiate Alumnae (later the American Association of University Women), and one of its first actions was to form a Sanitary Science Club in 1883. The Club issued a manual co-authored by Talbot and Richards on *Home sanitation*, which prefigured many other such texts in its detailed advice about the creation of housework-reducing homes: 'Is the inside finish of the house as free as possible from horizontal projections, such as elaborate cornices and mantels ... Are useless ornaments and needle-work banished from the bedroom?'[63] At the University of Chicago, in what was called a Department of Household Administration, Talbot headed a scientific and research-based home economics programme. A journalist from the *Chicago Daily Tribune* who went to look at it in 1894 deemed it 'an interesting combination of theory and practice', and he much admired the 'quiet and low voiced' Talbot and the way she moved effortlessly between the silk-robed persona of a university professor to a woman in charge of teaching and practising such mundane matters as plumbing, water and food.[64] In the photograph we see her somewhere between the two, hatted and writing at her desk. Talbot had taught courses in sanitary science and food and dietetics in the Department of Sociology, an arrangement which produced an astounding moment in disciplinary naming when the sociology department became the 'Department of Social Science, Anthropology, and Sanitary Science'. 'This arrangement,' decreed Talbot, 'implies a recognition of the principle that a very close relationship exists between sanitary

5.6: Marion Talbot at her desk

conditions and social progress. Sanitation and sociology must go hand in hand in their effort to improve the race.'[65] In fact, Talbot had first tried to persuade the University to open a department of household technology, 'choosing the term on the analogy of departments in other fields', and then had argued for a department of public health which would teach courses on house sanitation, food analysis, municipal sanitation, 'sanitary jurisprudence' and domestic economy (scientific principles of the application of heat to food and the chemistry of cleaning).[66]

Talbot's visionary plan for a department of public health at the University of Chicago proved to be too much ahead of its time, but the Department of Household Administration which was set up in 1904 did cover a great deal: chemistry, bacteriology, physiology, house decoration, textiles and design; the state in relation to the household; the organization of the retail market; an introduction to the study of society; the social origins of the family. There was also a pioneering course on the legal and economic position of women taught by Sophonisba Breckinridge, with whom Talbot wrote a text *The modern household* in 1912. Each chapter of Talbot and Breckinridge's manual ended with questions, for example, 'What archaic methods and belated practices are retained in your household?' and a reading list, which included Gilman's *Women and economics*, Florence Kelley's *Some ethical gains through legislation*, the English sociologist Helen Bosanquet's books on the family and a work by a feminist anthropologist called Elsie Clews Parsons.[67] It did seem clear to many of these women, both in Britain and North America, that academia's neglect of sanitary science's claims was largely due to men's domination of the universities. Ravenhill observed in her memoirs that, 'The mere suggestion was also startling, that provision must be made in the course for practical tests on foods and cleansing agents; on household furnishings; or on clothing materials. The group of men to be convinced had never given a thought to these details of daily life.'[68] On the other hand, the men were more willing to let the women in when they could be tagged with the subject's traditional associations: in 1911, the male faculty at Cornell University rejected the general idea of women professors, but said they wouldn't object to their appointment in the Department of Home Economics.

5.7: Helen Stuart Campbell

Thus duly appointed, the new women professors were then referred to as 'cooks'.[69]

Helen Stuart Campbell, the close friend and live-in partner of Charlotte Perkins Gilman with whom Helen worked on household economics (see Chapter Two), did make it to the position of professor, albeit of home economics, at Kansas State Agricultural College in 1897. Her slightly untidy hair and sideways smile give her a homely appearance in the photograph. Having started out writing novels under a variety of male pseudonyms, Campbell came into her own with her work on wage-earning women and urban poverty in the 1880s and 1890s and quickly gained a reputation as a pioneering social economist. She married and divorced in 1871 (divorce being an unusual act at the time) an army surgeon whose name she then dropped. Campbell's *The problem of the poor. A record of quiet work in unquiet places* (1882), described the work of a city Settlement on the New York waterfront with which she was associated. She wrote about her main theme, the economic dependence on men that was forced on women through the low wages they were paid, in popular novels such as the domestically titled *Mrs Herndon's income* and *Miss Melinda's opportunity*.[70] Campbell spent 18 months travelling in Europe in order to learn about the problem of poverty outside the US; in England she met Engels in an encounter arranged by Florence Kelley. Her major contribution to household economics was a book of that name published in 1896, dedicated to Gilman and based on a series of lectures she had given at the University of Wisconsin on that paradigm-shifting combination, household *and* social science. In *Household economics* Campbell referred glowingly to Ellen Richards' work (the two women knew each other well), and complained about 'the weighty discourses of eminent men' who had liberally pronounced on their views about women, but had absolutely failed to notice the political economy of the home. 'The household' she announced, 'is the parent of the state', but it has escaped investigation by the methods of science applied to other areas of public life. Campbell optimistically called for a national commission to inquire into household economics, 'as important and useful as any bureau of inquiry yet instituted', but was not very hopeful.[71]

Like other aspects of women reformers' visions of welfare, and fostered by some of the same networks, the messages of sanitary science took root in other countries. An ex-KCHSS student, Helen Rawson, took its teaching with her to New Zealand, where she joined another British woman, Winifred Boys-Smith, the University of New Zealand's first woman professor, to set up courses in science, food and nutrition and practical courses in home and institutional management. Their school of home science opened in 1911 with five students in a tin shed which had belonged to the School of Mines. Professors from the Medical School taught the basic science courses as for the intermediate examination in medicine, including physics, inorganic chemistry, bacteriology, biology and physiology and public health. Boys-Smith and Rawson added household business affairs, applied chemistry, practical cookery, needlework and hygiene. A second professor, Ann Munroe Gilchrist Strong, a member of the original Lake Placid group, later joined them from the US.[72]

These were enterprising days, uniting in a common struggle coalitions of assorted interests: the women economists whose purview embraced what the male economists' did not; the women teachers and students eagerly spreading and learning the latest science of the home; the proponents of higher education and scientific and professional training for women; the imaginers of totally different ways of living and making homes. While some of their goals were won, others were lost, for a litany of reasons having to do with the inhospitality of public institutions and the longevity of old refrains about where women and housework rightly belong. A weighty counter-attack in Britain was launched by some academic women, fearful about where the new emphasis on scientific housework might lead: to a substitution for schoolgirls of domestic science for science proper; to a diminution of the energy going into opening scientific education and professional work for women?[73]

In the first volume of *The Journal of Home Economics*, Ellen Richards had talked about the new sanitary science 'sweeping back the ocean with a broom – an ocean of fashion, of commercial exploitation, or mercantile temptation'.[74] Brooms did, sadly, prove an insufficient deterrent to the tidal forces moving fashion and commercialism swiftly along. But this doesn't detract from the radical nature of sanitary science's educational project. It was a new way of conceiving disciplines and subjects. It was one of many historical attempts to revision and reposition housework as equal to other forms of work. It was another aid to dissolving that unhelpful, hard-and-fast distinction between private and public lives. And it was also about a very modern development, the demystification and democratization of specialized knowledge, the training of citizens in critical thinking skills. As Ellen Richards knowledgeably put it: 'Knowledge vital to the health of the people should be made as accessible as possible at as little expense and trouble to them as may be.'[75] She and her colleagues in the domestic sanitary science movement remained adamant that no educational institution worthy of its name would exclude it as a core subject. The decoupling of women from instinctive domesticity would introduce codes of rationality, efficiency and a revamped social economics that should bring the ethics of ecological justice right into the centre of the home. Welfare in the public sphere would get nowhere without this reconfiguration of housework as the scientific parent of public health.

SIX

'Peace is too small a word for all this': women peace makers

Between 1860 and the outbreak of the First World War in 1914, arguments across and within nations had already led to some 226 recorded armed conflicts killing around 15 million people.[1] 'All wars are men's wars. Peace has been made by women but war never,'[2] observed Carrie Chapman Catt, President of the International Woman Suffrage Alliance (IWSA), one of the many women's organizations which took part in an extraordinary peace campaign in the years leading up to the 'Great' War and during and after it. Since women are excluded from a political voice, demanded French feminists in 1915, are they not under an obligation to say that which the men cannot say?[3] The women's object was to try to prevent the war happening, then to block its escalation once it had begun, then to protest about and remedy the huge injustices of its consequences. Many women in the peace movement had a background in social reform, and the argument for peace derived directly from the case for human justice and equality. It was also about diverting the massive resources spent on war to the primary goal of promoting human welfare. By 'forcing war itself into outlaw status', women peace campaigners caused an interruption in the restricted vision of the reformist liberal male peace movement, from which, anyway, they were excluded. Their much more radical agenda attempted to change the nature of politics itself.[4] Historians of peace have, however, mostly not noticed this, or have projected images of 'the emotionalized woman pacifist' incapable of intellectual analysis. Of course, this may be partly because women's rejection of war has so often entailed extended (intellectual) critiques of masculinity.[5]

'The idea that these frail webspinners can affect the destiny of nations seems to me fantastic,' wrote Virginia Woolf, attending a peace rally at which, as Woolf unsympathetically put it, the economist Mabel Atkinson had 'drivelled at length about Peace'.[6] There's no doubt that the women's campaign for international peace did have an effect, although it was an effect that was much less than the one they hoped for. Their most impressive achievements lay as much in the outcome as in the process: in the formation of an extensive network of friendship and commitment that transcended national boundaries, and the creation of a vision of how the divergent peoples of the world might live peaceably together. The narrative in this chapter moves between biography, autobiography, history and political analysis as the only meaningful way to convey the force of Nobel Peace Prize winner Emily Balch's words, 'Peace is too small a word for all this'.[7]

Fredrika Bremer wasn't the beginning of the story, and her time was before most of the women in this book, but Bremer, born in 1801, the daughter of an affluent Swedish family, made a momentous contribution to the web of connections tying the demilitarization of society together with social reform and civil rights. She did this mostly through self-education, fiction and travel writing, thus illustrating the kaleidoscopic routes women have often taken to the promotion of a peaceful welfare society. Bremer's novel *Hertha, or, a soul's history: A sketch from real life* was published in English in 1855 and consumed by large quantities of readers in the English-speaking world who already knew Bremer as an inspiring writer of tales about the plight of women. The early life of *Hertha*'s main character is essentially a sketch

6.1: Fredrika Bremer, portrait, 1840s

of Bremer's own as the fifth daughter of a tyrannical father and a forceful mother whose only ambition for her daughters was a successful marriage. In the novel, Hertha manages to escape the clutches of domesticity after falling into a mystical sleep and imagining an internationalist feminist vision of free women with equal access to education who live together harmoniously in utopian communities. At every juncture, it seems, these women anticipate or return us to the vision of Gilman's *Herland*.[8]

Bremer's own emancipation encompassed charity work, women's rights, abolitionism and pacifism. At the same time as she started work on *Hertha*, in the middle of the Crimean War, Bremer published appeals in a number of newspapers for women across the world to come together in a global network of associations committed to the principle of peace, 'extending its healing, regenerating influence over the whole earth – an alliance in which diversities of language, of national character, of climate, of custom … may be regarded as of little import'. These associations, nationally and transnationally, would be based on women's existing philanthropic work and would provide care for the poor, the sick and the old, and prisoners and 'other fallen fellow-creatures'. Bremer's plans were very specific. The capital of every country should have a committee which would survey all the different female societies of that country and communicate the results, together with accounts of 'industrial efforts or good institutions' to similar committees in other countries. Her vision, like Hertha's, was of a chain of women around the world whose loving energies, motivated by a spirit of universal charity, would bring war to an end.[9] The London *Times*, which published Bremer's appeal in the summer of 1854, took a dim view of it, calling her ideas unrealistic and dangerous, and trotting out the old adages about women needing to stay at home and not meddle with relieving the world in general. Peace societies and other newspapers in Sweden and Britain agreed.[10]

Bremer's initiative has since been recognized as the most significant European reaction against the Crimean War.[11] When Civil War broke out in the US a few years later, she repeated her appeal in the *New York Daily Tribune*, advocating mediation and the abolition of slavery as civic rather than military projects. She knew about the US because she had been there, for two years in 1849 to 1851; this was itself a daringly unusual enterprise for the time – a single woman travelling huge distances on her own. Bremer considered herself a world citizen, not a patriot, so world-travelling was both a right and a duty. She went to see for herself the condition of women and slaves and the way men treated them in the New World. Her compendium of the letters she wrote on her American travels to her sister Agathe, *The homes of the new world: Impressions of America*, had to be reprinted five times in the first month after it was published in New York in 1853.[12] Bremer reached the US too late for the famous 1848 Seneca Falls Convention, but she did hear Lucretia Mott, co-author of the Seneca Falls' *Declaration of sentiments*, talk about slavery and the rights of women, and she met and admired a number of 'emancipated ladies' who delivered public lectures proficiently and with no loss of womanliness – a characteristic she valued and which seems over-emphasized in the stock images of her with a posed smile in a beribboned bonnet.[13]

Fredrika Bremer, the avant-garde pacifist, is also known for her influence in reforming the sexism of Swedish law. The Swedish edition of her novel *Hertha* mixes genres in carrying a 14-page appendix about the non-fictional insults of the Swedish legal system with respect to women, which treated all adult women, unless widowed or divorced, as incompetent wards of their male relatives. The result, in Sweden, was what was known as 'the *Hertha* debate', and it led to the law being changed and the creation of the first higher education institution for women in Sweden.[14] This trained many women who later worked in the peace movement, including Matilda Widegren, who helped to set up the peace initiative which is the main subject of this chapter.[15] Bremer herself missed most of the public debate inspired by her novel, since she was travelling again through Europe and to Malta and Palestine where, at the age of nearly 60, she traced the life of Christ by taking multiple ship, train, wagon and horseback journeys and wrote her six-volume *Life in the old world*.[16]

All this happened before most women in Western countries had begun to put pieces of the social reform and pacifist jigsaw together. The British pacifist and preacher Maude Royden played a vital role in the early 20th-century peace movement

and her story introduces those of
other women peace makers in this
chapter. Royden was born in 1876
to a wealthy ship-owning family
in Cheshire and was brought
up in a grand, turreted house
set in landscaped grounds. Her
education at Cheltenham Ladies'
College and Lady Margaret
Hall, Oxford, was followed
by a period 'slumming' (in the
Victoria Women's Settlement in
Liverpool), as was the custom
among young middle-class Anglo-
American women of her time.

6.2: Maude Royden

Then she turned to radical Anglican preaching and lecturing as
a career. Royden was the first woman to preach in an Anglican
church; the first to occupy Calvin's pulpit in the great cathedral
at Geneva; the first to become a Doctor of Divinity. Opposition
to all violence and militarism was central to her reworking of
the Christian theology. Jane Addams, whom Royden met on
one of her transatlantic journeys in 1911, called her 'the greatest
woman in England'; to others she was 'a modern Joan of Arc',
or simply 'the most famous woman preacher in the world'.[17]
Royden played an important role in the international feminist
peace movement. Her theology was critical in persuading many
women that feminism embraced pacifism and that both could
be settled comfortably alongside religious belief.

Royden's public life began in an unlikely place: a backwater of
rural England where she worked as 'a kind of unofficial curate'
in the early 1900s.[18] The village of South Luffenham in Rutland,
England's smallest county, was then an isolated parish, home to
around 300 souls who lived clustered around a rectory, a school
and a rather beautiful Norman church. Their vicar, George
William Hudson Shaw, told his parishioners that he wanted to
make the village a little 'city of God', but they turned out to
be 'as hard as nails religiously', so it was uphill work, and he
needed help.[19] Maude Royden met the Reverend Shaw in 1901
when she heard him lecture in Oxford. She was then 24; he

was 41 and married. They fell in love and the following year Maude went to live with him and his wife Effie, a mentally fragile semi-invalid, in the rectory in South Luffenham in order to help with parish work and with Effie's care. Royden visited the parishioners, took Sunday schools and mothers' meetings, and tried to teach the South Luffenhamers about Shakespeare. Her unusual three-way relationship with the vicar and his wife lasted 42 years. Royden's book about all this, *A threefold cord*, published in 1947, is both open and cagey about the exact nature of their relationships.[20] Hers was an intensely busy life, including the adoption (as a single woman) of two 'war' babies, one a starving, rickety, four-year-old boy from Vienna.[21] She talked about Freddie in her sermons. When she found him, he bore 'that terrible, anxious, harassed look that is pitiful on any human face, but is heartrending on a child's. He was only two years old when the war ended. He was not born when the war began. His fathers, you will say, made the war. Yes, perhaps. But we made the peace, and it was the war and the peace together that made Freddie look like that ... All the world has trespassed against that child ... *that is a political question.* Am I to be silent when the world treats children like that?'[22]

By the time Royden helped to found the Church League for Women's Suffrage in 1909, she had joined the National Union of Women's Suffrage Societies and become one of its main public speakers; later she took on the editorship of its newspaper *The Common Cause.* She used her controversial position in the Church to preach, talk and write openly about such topics as war, disarmament and peace; women's rights; the double standard of morality, venereal disease, birth control and maternal mortality; white slave trafficking, homosexuality, sex and Freud; capital punishment, unemployment, trade unionism and Irish independence. She wasn't afraid of shocking the establishment. Her remarks about the British government effectively acting as a procurer of prostitutes in its practice of recruiting women to service soldiers in '*maisons tolérées*' in France during the First World War provoked the Archbishop of Canterbury into raising the subject in the House of Lords. The Church didn't take kindly to Maude Royden's dismissive view of the virgin birth (there was no evidence for it, she said, and the doctrine 'has had a deplorable result in deepening men's feeling that sex is shameful'[23]), or her belief that sacramentality inheres in loving relationships rather than the institution of marriage, or her declaration that Christ approved of gender equality, including in his own Church. Addressing a large audience at the Queen's Hall in London in 1912 on 'The religious aspect of the women's movement', she described it as 'the most profoundly moral movement', since it affirmed the ideal of Christ for every human being. 'This is not, as it has been called, a *feminist* movement, but more rightly a humanist movement, because we ask for the whole human ideal for all, for purity and gentleness and self-sacrifice in men; for courage, judgment and wisdom in women ... The franchise that we ask is the franchise of the Kingdom of God.'[24]

The real problem wasn't God or Christ, but the Church establishment's attitude to women. The official view at the time was that, if women had to speak formally in churches, they should do so only to audiences of their own sex, and only from the foot of the chancel steps. When Maude Royden first stood in a pulpit to preach in the imposing City Temple church in London – almost the size of St Paul's cathedral – on Sunday 18 March 1917, the newspapers, predictably, were more interested in what she wore – a black cassock with a white net collar and a small biretta hat – than in what she said. This garb became her trademark, reproduced in the many photographs of her, a small, dark-haired woman with round glasses and a serious regard. Under the headline 'woman crank's sermon', the *Daily Express* reported long queues which had to be controlled by police;[25] large audiences, especially of women, were a feature of Maude Royden's sermons and talks everywhere. Her experience with the established Church drove her eventually, in 1921, to set up an alternative institution, the Guildhouse in London, an ecumenical place of workshop, a fellowship and a social and cultural centre. It provided 'Settlement' activities such as taking poor children to play in parks, and talks from prominent people: the scientists J. S. Haldane on the wider meaning of relativity and Julian Huxley on birth control; Alfred Hitchcock on sound film; Margery Fry on prison reform; Eleanor Rathbone (who had been a contemporary of Maude Royden's at Oxford) on family allowances. The politicians Lloyd George and Ramsay

MacDonald, and the peace makers Jane Addams, Mahatma Gandhi and Albert Schweitzer were other celebrity speakers. Royden was herself a celebrity speaker, relaying her radical messages all over the globe – in the US, New Zealand and Australia, Japan, China, India and Ceylon. On an American trip in 1928 she danced with Henry Ford and lunched at Hull-House in Chicago with Jane Addams.[26] Her travelling companion, Miss Dobson, observed, 'When we arrive at the station we are usually met … by a horde of reporters and photographers who … perpetrate flashlight atrocities in which Miss Royden almost invariably has half-closed eyes … Most of the reporters ask about the cigarette – what brand does Miss Royden smoke and how many per day, and does she inhale?'[27]

Women smoking was nearly as newsworthy as women preaching.[28] Both were signs that women could make up their own minds. In the years before the First World War, as international politics clouded over, Royden, like many other women, but unlike Millicent Fawcett and others in the British National Union of Women's Suffrage Societies, decided that women should do everything they could to protest about and stop the horrors of war. This was more important than the suffrage, although the two goals were connected, for surely, if women could vote, they would vote against war? The fear among male politicians of the time was very real that politics might be taken over by 'a monstrous regiment of women', with appalling consequences.[29] Hence such devious ideas as the 'lesser vote', whereby women's votes would be valued as half those of men. The rationale, constantly offered across the political spectrum, was that women don't understand 'imperial politics' and they don't share in the defence of the nation, so they can't expect the same vote. It was also, spectacularly, argued that women's support for peace actually *proved* their lack of intelligence and unfitness for the vote.[30]

Royden had an alternative slant on the gender difference: 'Women, whatever other claims may be made for them, are not equal to men in their capacity to use force or their willingness to believe in it. For them, therefore, to ask for equal rights with men in a world governed by such force is frivolous. Their claim would not be granted, and if granted would not be valid.'[31] In

1913 Royden joined the non-conformist/Quaker Fellowship of Reconciliation, later becoming its travelling secretary, and she went with her old Oxford friend Kathleen Courtney to the IWSA congress in Budapest. 'What is the great adventure?' she asked in one of her sermons: war, or peace? 'There is only one way to kill a wrong idea. It is to set forth a right idea … We peace people have made of peace a dull, drab, sordid, selfish thing. We have made it that ambiguous, dreary thing – "neutrality." But Peace is the great adventure, the glorious romance.'[32]

And so, for the women, it proved. Kathleen Courtney recalled how they all felt when the war began: a huge sense of shock, since most of them knew nothing about international affairs. 'They were considered the concern of the Foreign Office.'[33] But now women had to get involved. They had the basis of well-organized international suffrage associations to build on, with their established networks and common (though also varied) agendas. There was the International Council of Women (ICW), set up in 1888 and chaired for many years by the stately Lady Aberdeen. The ICW was a coalition of national women's rights groups; its entrée into the peace business came at its London meeting in 1899 when an International Standing Committee on International Arbitration was formed, with Aberdeen as chairman and another titled woman, Baroness Bertha von Suttner, the originator of, and the first woman to win, the Nobel Peace Prize, as secretary. Aberdeen's Congress address anticipated the challenge they all felt was on the horizon: 'whilst loving our own country we realise that a wider patriotism is needed, a patriotism which ignores all frontiers and raises us to a higher plane'.[34] Challenged by women who saw it as conservative and elitist, the ICW gave birth in 1904 to the IWSA, later the International Alliance of Women (IAW), a more broadly based women's rights organization. In turn the IWSA was the mother of the Women's International League of Peace and Freedom (WILPF), which arrived on the dramatic stage of a women's peace congress held at The Hague in 1915. Passing through many transformations, all three of these major organizations still exist today, although their role in creating the women's radical political vision of the early 20th century has been bleached from our historical memory.

It isn't really necessary to remember the exact names and dates: what matters is that women across the world came together with the twin goals of entering women into citizenship and removing citizenship from the battlefields of war and nationalism. In pursuit of these goals, there was much correspondence and deliberation, a great deal of shared commitment, some spectacular disagreements and points of conflict, countless meetings and conferences and many long drawn-out journeys by ship and train. It's impossible to read accounts of their adventures without marvelling at these women's capacity to execute complex journeys in an era reliant on slow train and sea travel. The travel was expensive; although many women reformers came from comfortably off families, many were also professional women who had to support themselves and other dependents, and/or they were activists who had to find the resources they needed for their political work. The financial aid of wealthy women, often through clubs and other women's organizations, was crucial, as also was the help of female and male partners and families, although, given the potent ban prevailing at the time against women entering the public sphere, many women found that they had to break from their families in order to do anything more than mild philanthropy. The funding of their travel and other network resources remains a bit of an unresearched mystery. The minutes of the ICW, for example, contain endless discussions about money, but few descriptions of what was actually done about it. The organization did pay travel grants after 1906, and the WILPF sometimes funded travel for women who couldn't afford it.[35]

However it was funded, the travelling helped to cement a serious and entertaining sisterhood. 'There are certain days which remain in our memories because we then seem to have broken through into that reality which ever lies beneath the outward appearance,' wrote Jane Addams of her journey with other women to the IWSA convention in Hungary in the summer of 1913. She travelled from Vienna by way of the Danube to the beautiful old city of Buda-Pest. 'These women from many nations sitting upon the deck of a river steamer felt that curious stimulus which comes from the discovery of like-mindedness between people of varied nationalities … that day was one of those moments described by Virginia Woolf, who tells us that reality "seems to be something very erratic and very undependable, sometimes it seems to dwell in shapes too far away from us to discern what their nature is …" Not a breath, not a tremor of the future, ruffled the polished surface of the Danube on that summer's day. There was no haunting apprehension that these bordering states within a year's time would be firing the opening shots of the most terrible war recorded in history.'[36] On the boat, the women had long discussions about the use of force, about military tactics versus constitutionalism. The day before the journey, the news had broken of Emily Wilding Davison's death – she who, in pursuit of the vote, had run into the path of the King's horse at the Epsom Derby, and whose funeral procession was fronted by the golden-haired Charlotte Marsh. Several women on the boat had known Davison well and had visited her in hospital after the accident. Maude Royden, who was on the boat too, was one of them.

The Budapest Congress of the ICW hosted 2,800 participants from 26 countries. Prolonged applause greeted the admission of the Chinese Women's Suffrage Society to the IWSA; their delegates reported that some Chinese women had even been decapitated 'for the truths they had told'.[37] The Congress's arrangements were all made by the 'very, very radical' Hungarian pacifist feminist Rosika Schwimmer, whose home town this was, and whose forceful dedication to pacifism spearheaded the women's campaign for many years and got her personally into a lot of trouble.[38] Schwimmer had met Carrie Chapman Catt, the IWSA president, in 1904 at an earlier women's congress; Catt, attracted to Schwimmer's commitment and charisma – and perhaps also by her fluency in nine languages – had recruited her to the international suffrage movement.

At the time of the Budapest Congress, Schwimmer was 37; she was known for her bright, loose-fitting dresses and abandonment of the usual structural feminine underwear (dress reform was another of her passions); with her cloud of black, frizzy hair, very dark eyes and brows and aristocratic gold pince-nez she was altogether striking. She was the eldest child of a middle-class Jewish family with a history of involvement in peace and reform movements. Her uncle, Leopold Katscher,

6.3: Rosika Schwimmer, 1890s

had been introduced to the peace movement by Bertha von Suttner and had helped her to find a publisher for her famous anti-war novel, *Die waffen Nieder!* (*Lay down your arms*). Schwimmer herself had started out as a bookkeeper, and as a journalist and campaigner for improved working conditions among Hungarian women. She had set up the Hungarian Feminist Association, which achieved many important reforms for women, culminating in the suffrage in 1920; together with Vilma Glücklich, her teacher friend (and the first woman admitted to a Hungarian university), she edited the feminist-pacifist paper *A Nő* (*The woman*) for 13 years. Schwimmer was known in Hungary as a prominent child welfare reformer; she was a member of the National Governing Board for child welfare, and she helped to draft legislation protecting underprivileged children and guaranteeing the child's right to care. She was multi-talented: an accomplished pianist and singer, a novelist and the author of books and pamphlets in both Hungarian and German on children and the state, marriage and rationalized housekeeping.[39] There were also children's books, including *Tisza tales*, a book of Hungarian folk stories illustrated by the Hungarian art nouveau artist Willy Pogány, who also illustrated suffrage material, including a famous IWSA poster about maternal mortality that depicted a naked baby and so offended London Transport that it was banned.[40]

Schwimmer did an excellent job of arranging the 1913 Budapest meeting. She organized English-speaking students to help with translation, and laid on many social functions, including specially composed music and poems, a Mozart opera and an open-air fête. Schwimmer, Jane Addams, Maude Royden and many others gave speeches, and Charlotte Perkins Gilman, whose *Women and economics* Schwimmer had translated into Hungarian, addressed the Congress on the topic of 'New mothers of a new world'. The IWSA decided to hold its next biennial meeting in Berlin in 1915. But the war intervened, and the Berlin meeting was cancelled.

In 1914 Schwimmer was in London, working as the IWSA press secretary, very pleased to have been accepted by the Foreign Correspondents' Club as its first woman member. That summer of 1914 was oppressively hot in London, and the international political scene offered no relief. When Archduke Franz Ferdinand, the heir to the Austro-Hungarian empire, was killed in Sarajevo in June, Schwimmer, with her background in Central European politics, knew what this could mean. On 9 July she arranged a breakfast meeting with Lloyd George, the Chancellor of the Exchequer, and later Prime Minister of the war-time coalition government, and she told him that the British government wasn't taking the assassination of the Archduke seriously enough. As Lloyd George later noted in his memoirs: 'I remember that sometime in July, an influential Hungarian lady, whose name I have forgotten, called upon me at 11, Downing Street, and told me that we were taking the assassination of the Grand Duke much too quietly; that it had provoked such a storm throughout the Austrian empire as she had never witnessed, and that unless something were done immediately to satisfy and appease resentment, it would certainly result in war with Serbia, with the incalculable consequences which such an operation might precipitate in Europe.'[41] Sadly, he discounted Schwimmer's warnings, saying that the reports he was receiving didn't suggest that any action was necessary. Later he admitted that Schwimmer knew more about European affairs than any of them.[42]

In London, Schwimmer lived and worked with two British suffragists, Catherine Marshall and Mary Sheepshanks. Marshall managed an active suffrage society in the Lake District, a branch of the National Union of Women's Suffrage Societies (NUWSS), and between 1911 and 1914 she worked full time as honorary parliamentary secretary at the NUWSS headquarters in London. Mary Sheepshanks had a background in Settlement work and educational administration: as Vice-Principal of Morley College for Working Men and Women, she had once recruited the young Virginia Woolf to teach history classes. Sheepshanks herself was recruited by Jane Addams in 1913 to become a member of the IWSA and editor of *Jus Suffragii* ('the right to vote'), an impressive production published monthly for 18 years in English and French and sold for either 4 pennies, 4 marks or 4 francs, dependent on the country.[43] The IWSA office in Adam Street was a short walk from Sheepshanks' narrow, ivy-covered house in Barton Street, Westminster, an excellent location for lobbying politicians – from its top window you could see the Houses of Parliament.

In that stiflingly hot summer of 1914, when war seemed increasingly likely, Schwimmer, Sheepshanks, Marshall and others discussed what they could do. They decided to produce an International Manifesto of Women: 'We, the women of the world, view with apprehension and dismay the present situation in Europe, which threatens to involve one continent, if not the whole world in the disasters and the horrors of war … We women of twenty-six countries, having banded ourselves together in the International Women's Suffrage Alliance with the object of obtaining the political means of sharing with men the power which shapes the fate of nations, appeal to you to leave untried no method of conciliation or arbitration for arranging international differences which may help to avert deluging half the civilised world in blood.'[44] They delivered the Manifesto by taxi to the Foreign Secretary and all the European ambassadors in London. A Women's Peace Meeting was organized for 4 August, attended by thousands, with many more turned away. The women took a resolution urging mediation by neutral countries to 10 Downing Street only minutes before Britain declared war on Germany late that evening.

In Mary Sheepshanks' Barton Street house, Schwimmer, distraught at the war news and unable to sleep, sat down and composed a plan for continuous mediation between countries in conflict with one another. Not wanting to be tied to the agenda of any organization, she resigned from her IWSA post. But her days in London were numbered. Following the declaration of war between Britain and Austria-Hungary on 10 August, she became an 'enemy alien' and was forced to register, be interrogated and have her footsteps followed. Because her plan for mediation involved an appeal to President Wilson, as head of the most powerful neutral country in the best position to take it up, she arranged to go to the US.

Many good ideas are born in more than one head at the same time. At the University of Wisconsin an English literature scholar, Julia Grace Wales (known as Grace), a serious young woman, was appalled at events abroad and determined, like Schwimmer and other women in the suffrage organizations, to do something about them. She used her Christmas break from teaching in 1914 to write a rough draft of her own plan

6.4: Julia Grace Wales, 1916

for 'continuous mediation without armistice'.[45] Her opening paragraph posed the question that the plan answered: 'Can a means be found by which a council of the neutral powers may bring the moral forces of the world to bear upon the present war situation and offer to the belligerents some opportunity involving neither committal to an arbitrary programme nor humiliation on the part of any one of them, to consider the possibility of peace?'[46] Wales proposed that the US should call a conference to which each of the 35 currently neutral nations of the world would send delegates. This international commission or 'world thinking organ' would mediate continuously with or without armistice, inviting suggestions from belligerent countries and submitting these for discussion. Wales' plan was based on a Wisconsin custom of calling on technical experts to help formulate public policy, but her idea of extending the practice to international relations was new. She presented her proposals to the Wisconsin Peace Society, which took them on and printed and distributed copies of the plan, which was thereafter known as the Wisconsin Plan. It was endorsed by the governors of six states, the Wisconsin State Legislature and some 20 US Congressmen. A copy was sent to the White House.

When Wales wrote her plan she had no idea that Rosika Schwimmer in London was thinking along similar lines. Meanwhile, Schwimmer had arrived in the US in September to present her petition to the President at a meeting arranged by Carrie Chapman Catt. Schwimmer handed over a petition signed by women from 13 belligerent and neutral nations asking Wilson to call a conference of neutral nations that 'would quietly transmit peace proposals to the belligerents until both sides through their confidential replies agreed on a basis for negotiations'.[47] Schwimmer, always persistent in her advice to important men, warned President Wilson that, unless he acted promptly, the US would be drawn into the war. She came out of the meeting saying that Wilson had declared he would lose no opportunity of taking steps to end the war. Wilson subsequently denied this, thereafter refusing to see any more pacifist representatives for some months.[48] Schwimmer then embarked on a speaking tour covering 22 states and more than 60 cities, calling for women to protest against war and put pressure on Wilson to act. She was, by all accounts, a most eloquent, fiery and witty lecturer, whose clever use of satire was reinforced with dramatic hand gestures. One newspaper called her 'the most brilliant European woman of today'.[49] The Dutch doctor Aletta Jacobs was of the opinion that she could have been another Charlotte Perkins Gilman, had she more time to work for the cause than for her bread.[50]

6.5: Emmeline Pethick-Lawrence

Rosika Schwimmer had trouble with money all her life.

Another woman from England with the same mission, Emmeline Pethick-Lawrence, joined Schwimmer in the US in October 1914. Bruised from a period of conflict with the Women's Social and Political Union, she arrived to talk at a public meeting in New York. She told her American audiences in no uncertain terms that it was time for the peace movement to become as militant (perhaps an unfortunate choice of word, given the parlous state of British suffrage politics) as the feminist one. European society, she said, had been brought to the brink of collapse by governments run by men: 'The failure of male statecraft in Europe is complete.'[51] Such radical sentiments were an odd contrast to Pethick-Lawrence's decorative middle-class persona, which was not to everyone's taste: as Emily Balch noted in her diary some months later: 'This evening Mrs. Pethick-Lawrence spoke, a friendly rather blousy lady in an ultra gown of the following materials swathed about her – brilliant green silk, with large rose pattern in two shades of orange, black fur round part of neck and hanging in a tail behind her shoulders, crimson silk right about the lower part … a lot of tarnished gold lace with crimson silk under it. I studied this as she talked – she told a series of stories about working girls, and slum children with the friendly unconscious patronage that hurts us in an English person of this type.'[52]

Pethick-Lawrence was another feminist pacifist with a Settlement background. She was also known for her unusual egalitarian marriage to Frederick Pethick-Lawrence (they had joined their surnames together when they married), a Liberal politician, Settlement house resident and lawyer, whose legal work aiding the militant suffragettes had landed him in prison. In the autumn of 1914 Emmeline Pethick-Lawrence and Schwimmer met up in Hull-House (all paths led there, and to Jane Addams, in those days), and decided to take the podium together. These two women from warring countries presented a persuasive image of sisterhood; at one meeting in Chicago, no fewer than a thousand people signed the petition to the President. At this same meeting Schwimmer met Lola Maverick Lloyd, a wealthy socialist reformer and ardent suffragist, who was a most useful source of lifelong social and financial support. Lloyd was the daughter-in-law of the socialist writer Henry Demarest Lloyd and his wife, Jessie Bross Lloyd, who were friends of Jane Addams, and who had taken in Florence Kelley's children when she fled her violent husband and turned up on the doorstep of Hull-House. Such are the never-ending connections of these networks.[53]

The Schwimmer–Pethick-Lawrence example was instrumental in convincing Jane Addams to help organize a national peace meeting. Although Addams considered it preferable for men and women to work together on public projects, she agreed that the war did pose unique questions calling for women's agency. The 'enlarged housekeeping' of women's public activism gave them a powerful interest and role in stopping war. And the *men's* peace societies were curiously inactive, and not without misogyny – for example, women had not been allowed to participate in the first international peace congress in 1899. As Carrie Chapman Catt complained to Addams, such organizations were 'very masculine in their point of view' and 'have as little use for women … as have the militarists'.[54] Addams was just as uncompromising in her *Peace and bread in time of war* (1922): 'The long established peace societies and their orthodox organs quickly fell into line expounding the doctrine that the world's greatest war was to make an end to all wars. It was hard for some of us to understand upon what experience this pathetic belief in the regenerative results of war could be founded.'[55]

The Woman's Peace Party, founded on 10 January 1915 at a gathering in the Hotel Willard in Washington, marked the formal beginning of a separate 20th-century women's peace movement. Around 3,000 women were there, representing a wide range of women's organizations; they elected Addams as chair and Schwimmer as secretary of the new organization. Sophonisba Breckinridge, from Hull-House and the University of Chicago, acted as treasurer. The purpose of the Women's Peace Party was ambitious: 'to enlist all American women in arousing the nations to respect the sacredness of human life and to abolish war'.[56] It would later become the American branch of the WILPF, while Margaret Bondfield, Margaret Llewelyn Davies, Mary MacArthur, Chrystal Macmillan, Catherine Marshall, Maude Royden, Ada Salter, Olive Schreiner, Helena Swanwick, Ethel Williams and their British colleagues would form the British branch. Grace Wales had attended the Woman's Peace Party meeting at the Hotel Willard to talk about her Wisconsin Plan. The immediate calling for a conference of neutrals was adopted as the first plank of the Woman's Peace Party platform.

In the Netherlands that difficult summer of 1914, Dr Aletta Jacobs had been seeing her great friend Olive Schreiner (who had been staying with her) off on the train from Amsterdam back

to England when the Dutch army was mobilized at the end of
July. The station, normally deserted in the early morning, was
full of men leaving their families to fight. Consoling some of the
women who stood there in tears, Jacobs realized that without the
men the women would have no money to support themselves
and their children. She helped to organize relief efforts – money,
soup kitchens, advice and support. But she began to wonder
whether, in relieving the consequences of war, she was not
at the same time supporting its continuation. The men who
brokered war and fought in it were responsible for the tragedy,
but 'we women could have quite possibly ended the slaughter
by collectively refusing to meet the needs caused by war and by
ignoring the pressure to keep society going. If women had *not*
agreed to take over wherever needed, if they had *not* been willing
to perform the work of men, then the governments would have
been forced to abandon the whole disastrous enterprise.' This
reasoning fuelled a desire 'to call on women from every nation
to protest together against the horrors of war'.[57] 'Day and night
I trouble my brains what we can do to stop this scandalous
bloodshed,' she wrote to other IWSA members. 'Ought not
the women of the whole world … send a strong and serious
protest to the different Emperors, Kings, and other responsible
men?'[58] As she recalled later, the task was to convince women
to feel that internationalism is higher than nationalism, so that
they would no longer stand by governments, but by humanity.[59]

When Jacobs heard that the meeting of the IWSA due in
Berlin in 1915 was to be cancelled, she argued for a meeting
in a neutral country. She suggested Holland, promising that
the Dutch branch would make all the necessary arrangements.
A preparatory meeting in Amsterdam was held in February,
attended by three Belgian, four German, five English and
several Dutch women. On 1 March 1915 *Jus Suffragii* published
an invitation to women of all nations to attend a meeting in
The Hague which would take place between 28 April and 3
May 1915. The British suffrage movement, already divided
over militancy and Millicent Fawcett's 'patriotic' decision to
suspend suffrage work for the duration of the war, ignited in
dissension once again. The National Executive of the NUWSS
crumbled a few months into the war when Kathleen Courtney,

Catherine Marshall, Maude Royden, Mary Sheepshanks and others resigned, thereafter working openly to support the international women's peace movement. It was the cause of pacifism that drove an immovable stake through the heart of the British suffrage movement.

Radical activism was one response to the war; another was to create different forms of polemical material. This story of women and the First World War can't be told without Vernon Lee, alias Violet Paget, and her bombastic and deeply satirical play *The ballet of the nations*, written in 1915 and reissued in a vastly extended format as *Satan the waster* in 1920. Violet Paget, who adopted the androgynous name Vernon Lee at the start of her publishing career (it being generally thought that women who wrote on weighty subjects should pretend to be men) was a secular humanist, a distinguished art historian, a travel writer, a novelist, a literary critic, a declared lesbian and an internationalist – English by nationality, French by birth, Italian by choice; a woman born too early, so she said, to be the free-thinking 20th-century woman she wanted to be.[60] Lee's portrait, painted by John Singer Sargent in 1881 when she was 25, exhibits a young woman whose vitality seems unwilling to be trapped by time and place. Her eyes were opened (like so many others) to the importance of 'the woman question' by Charlotte Perkins Gilman's *Women and economics*. Lee was active in the anti-war Union of Democratic Control and she wanted a democratic Europe governed by an intellectual élite with national borders drawn not by powerful states but by the self-determination of native populations. *The ballet of the nations* opens with Satan, the Lessee of the World, declaring that it's time to reopen the Theatre of the West: the Politicians and Armament Shareholders have got everything ready. Ballet-

6.6: Violet Paget ('Vernon Lee'), portrait by John Singer Sargent, 1881

Master Death promises to get the Dancers organized if Satan will find the orchestra, because the nations won't dance without the Music of the Passions. The first musician they ask, Self-Interest, has joined a Trade Union and declines to help. But Fear, Suspicion and Panic, Lust, Murder, Famine, Hatred and Self-Righteousness will. When all the dancers are assembled on the stage in theatrical costumes, a couple in modern clothes turn up: one looks like a city clerk ('Councillor Organisation') and the other is a lady 'in the spectacles and smock most commonly seen in laboratories' ('Madam Science'). Ballet-Master Death tries to kick these two out on the grounds that they're alien spies in the service of Life and Progress. All the Nations are instructed to look innocent while tearing off as much as possible of the clothes and limbs of their aggressors. But they can go on dancing provided their heads are unhurt – the 'Head which each Nation calls its Government' – and Ballet-Master Death ensures that they do, despite the blood and entrails and heaps of devastation on the stage. Thus, at the end of the ballet, the exhausted and depleted nations are still dancing.[61]

Vernon Lee wanted to go to what she called, in a letter to her German friend Irena Forbes-Mosse, the 'Grand Feminist Convention' in The Hague. In an endearingly loyal war-time correspondence between these two women of warring nations, Lee urged Forbes-Mosse to go to The Hague too: 'Dearest, do not call these people "dreamers of dreams." The dream, the infernal nightmare is the war, and peace is an inevitable natural awakening which sooner or later *must* come … it is your business and mine … to put all our effort and heart into preparing to let bygones be bygones and working for better realities. *That* is *not* a dream … Our only enemies are the base régimes we have allowed to grow up. But do not be sceptical … your part, your part of love for me, as much as mine of love for you, makes us into builders of the new world.'[62]

The trials and triumphs of the remarkable Hague meeting have been recounted in many histories. The Congress took place in the Dierentuin, a large meeting hall inside The Hague zoo. The giant ferns which decorated this pseudo-Moorish building feature in the iconic photograph on the cover of this book and opposite rise behind the 12 figures clustered around Jane Addams at the long table on the speakers' platform. The speakers are all moderately dressed, apart from the woman on the extreme left, a Swiss-born Armenian rights activist called Lucy Thoumaian, who was wearing traditional Armenian dress as a protest against the massacres that had just begun in the Turkish-Ottoman empire. The zoological location of The Hague Congress prompted many jokes about 'crankettes' or 'pro-Hun peacettes at the Dutch zoo'.[63] The British pacifist and writer Evelyn Sharp wrote a piece about the press's behaviour: 'There seems to be a certain set of adjectives specially reserved in newspaper offices for women who set out to try and make the world better. "Misguided" is one of the least offensive, perhaps; "babbling" is fairly common, so is "chattering;" "hysterical," of course, has become a byword in the mouth of any one who wants to fling a sneer at a woman. "Impossible" is very funny under the circumstances … That is exactly the one thing that events proved could not be said about them.'[64]

Much of the organization for the meeting was done by a core group of women led by Jacobs and including Anita Augspurg and Lida Heymann from Germany, and Chrystal Macmillan and Kathleen Courtney from Britain. Augspurg and Heymann, who were partners, were members of a network of radical German feminist-pacifist women. Augspurg was the first doctor of law in Germany, a severe and open critic of patriarchal marriage and of capitalism, a founder with Heymann of suffrage and feminist organizations; Heymann had co-founded the German movement to abolish prostitution and its state regulation, and had set up a women's centre and professional associations for female clerks and office workers. Like Rosika Schwimmer, Augspurg and Heymann weren't afraid of using their own initiative: when the war started, Heymann went to the Bavarian War Ministry, asking the minister to send a telegram to Czar Nicholas suggesting that he might act to stop the war. Frida Perlen, another member of the German network, had similarly cabled the German Kaiser.[65] The British Kathleen Courtney and Chrystal Macmillan weren't quite given to these dramatic gestures, but each made a solid contribution to the peace movement. Kathleen Courtney, confusingly, shared a name with Catherine Courtney, known

6.7a: The Hague Women's Peace Congress, 1915, speakers' platform

6.7b: The Hague Women's Peace Congress, 1915, participants in the hall

as Kate, who was also a peace campaigner. Kate, born in 1847, belonged to an earlier cohort of internationalists. She was another of Beatrice Webb's multi-faceted sisters, had worked with Octavia Hill and Henrietta Barnett in the Settlement movement, and became Lady Courtney of Penwith when her husband Leonard, a Liberal politician, acquired a peerage. Kathleen Courtney's own background was Anglo-Irish gentry; she was born in 1878, and her years studying languages at

Oxford had introduced her to a lifelong friendship with Maude Royden, with whom she shared an unwavering conviction that internationalism was the only secure route to peace.[66]

In a war-torn Europe, The Hague Congress called for superhuman organization. Mail was repeatedly lost, censored or confiscated. At the beginning of the war the British government had cut the cables linking North America and continental Europe, so that all telegraphic traffic had to be routed through Britain (where it could be suppressed). No French or Russian women made it to The Hague because of harassment, and sometimes actual imprisonment, by their governments, which suspected most feminist and/or pacifist tendencies. Some German women managed to get there, because in Germany passports were issued locally rather than nationally. From Italy came Rosa Genoni, a workers' rights advocate, seamstress and fashion designer, travelling with great difficulty because neither her pacifism nor her career as a fashion designer endeared her to Italian politics.

They were, both individually and collectively, dangerous women. The British government, too, would have been much happier had it been able to prevent any of its citizens from attending The Hague Congress, but three escaped its clutches – Emmeline Pethick-Lawrence because she was already in the US, and Kathleen Courtney and Chrystal Macmillan because they had gone to Holland earlier to help with arrangements. The other 180 British women who applied for travel permits were not so lucky.[67] The Defence of the Realm Act, passed four days after the war began, brought in censorship and restricted travel, allowing the government to decide that no meeting such as the one the women planned in The Hague was a good idea: 'His Majesty's Government,' Catherine Marshall was told by the Chief Permit Officer in Downing Street, 'is of the opinion that, at the present moment, there is much inconvenience in holding large meetings of a political character so close to the seat of war.'[68] At least, that was the officially stated view. When the decision was contended by the well-connected Kate Courtney it was partially reversed, allowing permits for a more limited list of 24 names plus four 'alternates'.[69] Among the names on the reduced list were Margaret Bondfield, Catherine Marshall,

Maude Royden, Ada Salter, Mary Sheepshanks, Lucy Deane Streatfeild and Helena Swanwick. Neither Kate Courtney nor Olive Schreiner nor Eleanor Rathbone made it from the longer list. Tremendous efforts were deployed to get the 24 successfully passported delegates to Tilbury for a boat that was due to leave at 7am on 20 April. Inevitably, there was a delay; then it was stated that a boat would certainly sail the next morning. But no boat materialized. A new Admiralty Order had just been issued, closing the North Sea to all shipping for an indefinite period.

A different (or perhaps supplementary, and certainly plausible) version of the government intervention is told by Maude Royden's biographer.[70] When newspaper reports of the planned Hague meeting had come to the attention of Lady Jersey, a conservative political hostess and stalwart opponent of women's suffrage, she wrote from her villa in Cannes to Sir Arthur Nicolson at the Foreign Office to point out how dangerous it would be for the English women, and especially Maude Royden, to be allowed to go to The Hague; she suggested that the women should be refused travel permits, but not until the last minute, so that it would be too late for them to make other arrangements. The loyalties of class intersect with those of gender, forming a picture that is never easy to decipher. Whatever the behind-the-scenes explanation of their fate, the disappointed women spent the days of the Congress in their hotel in Tilbury. 'All Tilbury is laughing at the Peacettes,' declared the *Daily Express* in its customary tone of ridicule: 'misguided Englishwomen who … are anxious to talk peace with German fraus over the teapot'.[71] Finally a telegram arrived to report that the Congress had been an enormous success and that Jane Addams, Aletta Jacobs and the Italian Rosa Genoni would shortly arrive in the UK as part of a mission appointed by the Congress to take its resolutions directly to the governments of both belligerent and neutral countries.

The American delegation to The Hague didn't have a smooth passage, either. As Carrie Chapman Catt put it (she declined to go): 'No one enjoys travelling in mine-strewn seas and under the uncomfortable arrangements which now exist for ocean travelling.'[72] Rosika Schwimmer and the entire Maverick Lloyd family (parents and four children) sailed from New York in early April; the other 42 delegates, plus the Pethick-Lawrences, and

Louis Lochner from the Chicago Peace Society, who acted as Jane Addams' private secretary, embarked on the Dutch steamship *The Noordam* on 13 April. The ship flew a fragile homemade banner, white with blue letters, spelling out the word 'peace'. It must have been an amazing adventure on all fronts: social, cultural, political and nautical. During the nine days of the voyage the women debated the resolutions they would put to the Congress, and in the evenings they talked about the peace question or foreign affairs more generally. Dr Alice Hamilton gave a lecture on medical aspects of war. She had been reluctant to join the expedition at first, but in the event she enjoyed the trip, describing it as 'like a perpetual meeting of the Woman's City Club, or the Federation of Settlements, or something like that'.[73] Others with Hull-House connections were also on the boat: Grace Abbott, Emily Balch, Sophonisba Breckinridge and, of course, Jane Addams. Grace Wales was there with her Plan, reading Addams' *Newer ideals of peace* in between all the other activities. 'We are a very jolly crowd,' wrote Wales in a letter home. 'The Pethick-Lawrences are tearing up and down the deck with a lot of others five abreast having the time of their lives. We are all having the time of our lives ... there is an undercurrent of absolutely united feeling.' It was an experience of sisterhood such as she had never had before: 'I am writing in Mrs Van Dusen's present of a looseleaf notebook, which is no end of a convenience. A bag Mrs Jastro gave me reposes beside me. The two steamer rugs that envelop me belong to Miss Eastman and Miss Webb. The two-inch card of needles, thread, etc. Miss Kellogg slipped into my bag at the last moment has already been useful ... the whole thing comes out like a symbol of the solidarity of the race, which is the one idea we are trying to stand for.'[74]

On the Thursday evening, about 10 o'clock, *The Noordam* was stopped by a British boat that came alongside and trained a machine gun on it; two German stowaways were removed, one shouting 'Hoch der Kaiser, Deutschland über Alles' from the gangplank. In the English Channel, off the cliffs of Dover, they were halted by an English cutter and held motionless for four days. Emily Balch, whose own travel reading comprised von Suttner's *Lay down your arms*, described how it felt: 'Around us were vessels not only of the English fleet, but of every sort, Norwegian, Greek, Spanish, and plain "United States", all with immense flags painted on their sides. Dispatch boats, torpedo boats, and torpedo destroyers rushed past … we find ourselves … suddenly caught and stopped in an invisible net of a power we do not understand and in a situation to which we have not the key. No one, certainly not the men either, know what it is sensible to attempt or to leave undone.'[75] Germany had proclaimed a war zone around the British Isles, within which not even neutral shipping was safe – earlier that month German U-boats had sunk six neutral steamships, including a Dutch one, without warning, and *The Noordam* itself had been damaged by a mine a few months earlier.

While *The Noordam* was unable to move, and the British women were confined to their hotel in Tilbury, Schwimmer and Lloyd fitted in a brief Scandinavian tour to drum up support for the Congress, then took a complicated train journey from Sweden to The Hague that involved being body-searched by the Germans and losing all their luggage. On the first evening of the Congress, Aletta Jacobs, as president of the Dutch Executive Committee, expressed her appreciation of the courage and determination all the women had shown in getting there. A total of 1,136 women from 12 countries made up the delegates who sat in the fern-decked Dierentuin inside The Hague zoo. The galleries accommodated another 2,000 visitors. All the neutral countries of Europe were represented; there were 43 women from Germany, Hungary and Austria, and 10 other more distant countries sent expressions of sympathy. Expecting hysteria, strife and disruption, the police and press reporters who came to the Congress hall in the zoo went away every evening disappointed. In Britain, the Congress was said to be pro-German, in Germany, pro-British; elsewhere it was said to be either virtually unattended or closing prematurely in a row.[76] Actually the women worked hard through three days of debates and discussions, with inspirational speeches given in English, French and German, and with a little time for sightseeing – the 'tulip fields near Haarlem, great stretches of solid color'.[77] There were often vigorous differences of opinion over details, and 'some energetic misunderstandings, for which the necessity of translating each speech into two other languages supplied many openings'.[78] Only women were eligible to vote at the Congress, and they had to agree to two principles: 'that international disputes should be settled by pacific means and that the parliamentary franchise should be extended to women'. The 20 resolutions adopted during the business sessions of the Congress combined radical feminism and imaginative public policy with judicious diplomacy, the latter well illustrated in Resolution 3, which leads in with the following proposition: 'Since the mass of the people in each of the countries now at war believe themselves to be fighting … in self-defence and for their national existence, there can be no irreconcilable differences between them, and their common ideals afford a basis upon which a magnanimous and honourable peace might be established.'[79]

The women at The Hague Congress decided that a permanent and just peace must rest on certain principles: autonomy and a democratic parliament in every nation; an agreement among all governments to refer all international disputes to arbitration or conciliation; the use of every kind of pressure against any countries that resort to arms; the democratic control of foreign policy; and equal political rights for women and men. Grace Wales' Wisconsin Plan for an immediate conference of neutral nations to offer continuous mediation was among their resolutions, as were the idea of a permanent International Court of Justice and a measured proposal for the (inter)nationalization of arms manufacture, removing it from the motive of private profit, which is 'a powerful hindrance to the abolition of war'. One resolution was specifically focused on the need for children's education to be reformed so that 'their thoughts and desires' are directed towards the ideal of constructive peace.[80] In order to preserve the momentum of the meeting and publicize its resolutions, an International Women's Committee for Permanent Peace was set up, with an office in Amsterdam, Addams as president and Schwimmer and Jacobs as vice-presidents. Rosa Manus from Holland, a friend of Jacobs, was made assistant secretary. The plan was for the Committee to meet at the same time and place as the official peace conference that was anticipated to mark the end of the war when it came.

The final resolution of the Congress was extraordinary, and it was added in a dramatic intervention by Rosika Schwimmer, who, with her customary passion, rose to her feet at the last minute to argue that women could do more to end the war than simply record their decisions on paper. Her idea was that a delegation of women from the Congress should personally carry its messages to the governments of both belligerent and neutral European nations and to the president of the United States. It seemed, to some of those who were listening, an outrageously melodramatic and probably personally hazardous idea. But, after a long and lively debate, and then a recount of the votes, the resolution for a deputation of envoys was carried. 'Only Madame Schwimmer could sweep the Congress off its feet,' noted Alice Hamilton.[81]

Thus began two more months of difficult journeying across Europe and the Atlantic, visiting 15 countries, 24 ministers, two presidents, one king and the pope, not to mention countless ambassadors and other more junior politicians. The women's methodology for their envoy mission was carefully thought out. Using their local contacts and working with diplomats and political leaders to set up meetings, they practised what they would say, took detailed notes and asked the men (they *were* all men) to confirm in written statements the initiatives that would be acceptable to them and their governments. The envoys were divided into two groups: women from countries involved in the war visited the neutral nations, with women from neutral countries going to the belligerent nations. The first group consisted of Jane Addams, Aletta Jacobs, Alice Hamilton and Mien Palthe (Frederika Wilhelmina van Wullften Palthe-Broese van Groenou, a friend of Jacobs from Amsterdam); they saw politicians in The Hague, London, Berlin, Vienna, Budapest, Bern, Rome, Paris and Le Havre. Alice Hamilton wrote to a friend before their visit to Germany: 'The party will consist of Dr. Jacobs, an elderly woman, very decided, fairly irritable and quite able to see that her own comfort is attended to; her friend Frau Palthe, the wife of a man who has a plantation in Java and is very rich but exceedingly careful about pennies, also elderly; and J. A. and myself.'[82] Although not an official envoy, Hamilton was needed for their interview with Pope Benedict XV, since he spoke only Latin languages and Hamilton could speak French. For this interview, the women's Italian friends, much excited, made sure that they were properly dressed in long-sleeved and high-necked dresses, with black Spanish lace on their heads.

The second group of envoys, made up of Rosika Schwimmer, Chrystal Macmillan, Emily Balch and Cor Ramondt-Hirschmann (from Holland), went to Copenhagen, Christiania (Oslo), Stockholm and Petrograd (as St Petersburg was renamed in 1914): Grace Wales accompanied them, as their secretary, to the Scandinavian countries. This group had a particularly cumbersome time travelling, since Macmillan and Wales, being British citizens, weren't allowed to cross Germany, so a boat had to be found, and when it was, it was a little freighter with only one cabin belonging to the captain, so Grace Wales went first, followed a week later by Chrystal Macmillan. Schwimmer, being technically an enemy, wasn't allowed into Russia, so Ellen Palmstierna from Sweden substituted for her there (Palmstierna later founded the Swedish branch of Save the Children). The surprise with which this whole difficult and courageous mission was greeted in many quarters is nicely illustrated by the story of Emily Balch, Cor Ramondt-Hirschmann, Rosika Schwimmer and Chrystal Macmillan's visit to the King of Norway: the taxi driver drove round and round the Royal Palace because he couldn't believe this group of women were really going to see the King.[83] They dressed up for the occasion, and in the photograph three of them are half-smiling in the perhaps unexpected Norwegian sun.

Everywhere the women went, political doors were opened to them and statesmen appeared to listen, and sometimes to agree with their arguments for peace. But not one of the statesmen was prepared to take the initiative in acting, for fear of being seen as weak. It was like a child's game where everybody is waiting for somebody else to make the first move. These repetitively non-committal postures were described in the envoys' report: 'We heard much the same words spoken in Downing Street as those spoken in Wilhelmstrasse, in Vienna as in Petrograd, in Budapest as in the Havre.'[84] Three of the five neutral nations visited appeared ready to join in a conference of continuous mediation, and two were deliberating calling such a conference.

6.8: Women's deputation to the King of Norway, in 1915: (left to right) Emily Balch, Cor Ramondt-Hirschmann, Rosika Schwimmer, Chrystal Macmillan

Jane Addams put it like this: 'Our first striking experience was to find that the same causes and reasons for the war were heard everywhere. Each belligerent nation solemnly assured us that it was fighting under the impulse of self-defence ... And in every capital we heard ... very much the same derogatory phrases in regard to the enemy whom they were fighting.'[85] A typical interview was the one the women had in Vienna with Count von Berchtold, the former Minister of Foreign Affairs, the man widely held to be mainly responsible for the war: 'the perfect type of diplomat, very high-bred, with easy, cordial manners, and an apparent frankness which covered absolute secretiveness'. He appeared eager to hear what they had to say, and he asked many questions, but 'when he had bowed us out and we looked back over the interview, we found he had said absolutely nothing'.[86] Nonetheless, it was the Austrian prime minister, Karl von Stürgkh, who banged his fist on the table when Addams diplomatically suggested he might consider it foolish for women to pursue peace in this way, telling her that what she had said was the first sensible thing he had heard for months.[87]

President Wilson appears to have vacillated in his attitude, first closing his mind to the mediation idea, then becoming more sympathetic, then in 1917 taking the decision to enter the US into the war. When Jane Addams saw him in the summer of 1915 to present The Hague resolutions, he told her this wasn't the right time to offer mediation. When Emily Balch saw him separately later that summer, he appeared interested in the detailed information she gave him about British moderates who supported mediation, but again would commit himself to nothing. When Aletta Jacobs tried in September, and Rosika Schwimmer in November, Wilson remained unmoved. Jacobs wrote to Jane Addams after her visit to Wilson to say that he had received her kindly – he had been 'man-like as well as gentleman-like' and 'very diplomatique'.[88] Wilson was by now used to peace crusaders – a special room had been set aside in the White House to contain all their letters and petitions.

President Wilson's refusal to call a neutral conference to mediate prompted an episode in the women's crusade for peace that gave the press even more material for patronizing jocularity. The industrialist Henry Ford, a publicity-hungry peace advocate, announced that if the president wouldn't call a mediation conference then he would do so without any governmental support. To this end he planned to charter a peace ship to convey participants to an international meeting and gain publicity for the peace venture which he was sure, he declared in a famous promise, would get the soldiers out of the trenches by Christmas. The peace ship was actually Rosika Schwimmer's idea, and it was she who mistress-minded the whole enterprise. All the first-class and second-class accommodation on a ship of the Scandinavian American line, *Oscar II*, was commissioned in extreme haste for the purpose, and redecorated at even more extreme expense with chintzes, soft pillows, lilies, begonias and multiple stuffed doves and olive branches. In addition to the Danish flag denoting neutrality, *Oscar II* carried a brilliant banner designed by Schwimmer's friend Willy Pogány depicting a ferocious knight on horseback over the words 'STOP THE WAR'.[89]

The Ford-Schwimmer Peace Ship left Hoboken in New Jersey on 4 December 1915, with 163 adults and three of the Lloyd children on board in varying degrees of comfort, illumination and consensus about the goals of the expedition.

The accounts of what happened on the transatlantic voyage and in the Scandinavian and other European capitals where the ship landed in the ensuing few months all paint a picture of melodramatic confusion and infighting, interlaced with much lavish expenditure on publicity and entertainment. This isn't the first point in the women's story where a bracingly entertaining film suggests itself. 'The Ship of Fools', as the press named it,[90] achieved only inconsequential meetings with officials in a few European governments. In Stockholm, which the ship reached at the end of February 1916, an unofficial neutral conference for continuous mediation was convened in the Grand Hotel with a flourish of publicity and an opaque agenda. Among those who had not been on *Oscar II*, but who attended the conference, was Emily Balch, who had prepared a position paper called 'International Colonial Administration'. In this she proposed a system of administration not unlike that of the mandate system later accepted by the League of Nations.[91] A similar process of barely acknowledged influence accounts for the clear imprint of the 1915 Hague Congress resolutions on President Wilson's renowned 'Fourteen Points' speech to the US Congress in January 1918. Wilson listed the requirements for world peace as entailing the abolition of secret treaties; armament reduction; decolonization; self-determination for national minorities; the removal of economic barriers between nations; and a world organization to keep all this in order – effectively a League of Nations, and actually almost a duplicate of the imaginative framework proposed by the women in 1915.

By the time the First World War ended, 20 nations were involved and 13 million people had been killed.[92] In Britain, the women who had supported The Hague Congress continued their work as the British section of the Women's International Committee for Permanent Peace. Helena Swanwick chaired the group. Swanwick, a writer and psychology lecturer, had been born in Germany to an originally Danish family; her father and one of her brothers were the painters Oswald and Walter Sickert. Swanwick came to the peace movement through reform work, and then the suffrage movement. She edited the suffragist newspaper *The Common Cause* for five years before Maude Royden took it over. Swanwick's particular contribution to

6.9: Helena Swanwick, 1917

the women's peace campaign was a theory of gender and international relations which has been largely ignored by historians of the subject. Swanwick saw militarism as intimately responsible for the degradation of women both in public and in private life: 'In militarist states,' she wrote, 'women must always, to a greater or less degree, be deprived of liberty, security, scope and initiative. For militarism is the enthronement of physical force as to the arbiter of nations, and under such an arbitrament women must always go under ... The sanction of brute force by which a strong nation "hacks its way" through a weak one is precisely the same as that by which the stronger male dictates to the weaker female.'[93] Swanwick saw the struggle for a peaceful means of resolving conflict as part of the longer-term effort by the women's movement to get men to stop using physical force. The connections she made in a number of her publications between the oppression of women and a culture of militarism and violence probably informed Virginia Woolf's heretical *Three guineas*, an essay on how and why to prevent war, published on the eve of the next one, in 1938.[94]

As they had planned, the Women's International Committee for Permanent Peace did reconvene when the war was finally over. But its next meeting couldn't happen in the same city as the official peace conference – Paris – because women from Germany, Austria and Hungary weren't allowed to enter France. Instead the women met, 160 of them from 16 countries this time, in Zürich in 1919. Helena Swanwick, unable to get her visa, missed the beginning of the conference, but arrived just in time for 'the most moving scene of all'. Lida Heymann from Germany had been making one of her amazing peace speeches, then Jane Addams quietly announced that the French delegate,

Jeanne Mélin, from Caringnan in the Ardennes (one of the districts invaded and occupied by Germany), who had been prevented from coming, had managed, after all, to get through, and was here. 'Jeanne Mélin came to the front of the platform. Lida Heymann leapt to her feet, with outstretched hands, her gaunt figure tense, her eyes and face burning with passion. The two "enemies" clasped hands and vowed to work evermore for peace. It was a rare moment. The delegates rose to their feet as one woman, and Emily Balch, the American, raised her hand aloft and cried, "I dedicate my life to the cause of Peace." Up shot all our hands and a great cry went up in many languages, "We dedicate our lives to Peace!"'[95] Florence Kelley said of the Zürich Congress, 'It was unbelievably wonderful. There were twenty-five English women sitting with the Germans in front, and the Irish at one side, alike engrossed in the common effort … Never have I seen so generous a spirit in any group of human beings.'[96] The symbol of women from opposite sides of the war acting together became a WILPF tradition: at the 1926 Congress, Camille Drevet, who had lost her husband in the war, and Frida Perlen, whose son had died fighting on the other side, together planted trees in the devastated region of France.

Although they refrained from talking directly about it, the post-war blockade had affected many of the women who went to the Zürich Congress. Britain's 'hunger blockade' against Germany, designed to starve Germany of foodstuffs and raw materials, was violent in its consequences. The effects of starvation on some of the women at Zürich meant that they didn't dare indulge in the good food spread in front of them; starved for too long, their digestions were simply unable to cope. Jane Addams described how she felt when she met in Zürich the Austrian delegate Leopoldina Kulka, whom she remembered from The Hague meeting four years earlier as a beautiful and blooming woman. Kulka, shrunken and marked by hunger and privation, was now almost unrecognizable. She died a few months later.[97] During the Zürich meeting delegates went to meet a trainload of 800 starved children from Vienna, who were being brought to Switzerland for emergency care. This is probably the occasion on which Maude Royden found her adopted son Freddie, and decided to take him home with her. Dr Ethel Williams, one of the first women GPs in Britain and a member of the British WILPF, had been to Vienna the previous year and had personally witnessed the extreme effects of war on the children. Almost all the younger ones had rickets and many had tuberculosis; the children were white faced, anaemic, all skin and bone: 'I think the thing which struck me most of all,' said Williams, 'was the fact that one saw no children playing.'[98]

Some of the women at the Zürich Congress had been directly involved in attempts at relieving hunger and distress. Almost from the first day of the war, Kate Courtney worked for the relief of ordinary German civilians trapped in Britain as enemy aliens; at the end of the war she helped to found the Fight the Famine Committee. Early in the war, Mary Sheepshanks and Chrystal Macmillan had organized a heroic attempt to feed Belgian refugees in Holland, personally buying hundreds of loaves of bread and tins of condensed milk, and other tinned food and chocolate from Lyons Catering Company, getting all this loaded onto a ship, crossing a U-boat-patrolled North Sea with it and delivering it to Flushing in Holland to thousands of refugees who were sheltering from the bitter cold in railway sheds.[99] In November 1918, four days after the armistice, two cables arrived in the US from German women. One was addressed to Mrs Woodrow Wilson and signed by Alice Salomon and Gertrude Baer; the other, signed by Anita Augspurg, was directed to Jane Addams: both cables protested against the hunger blockade and the seizure of 3,000 'milch cows' in Germany. Two members of the International Committee of Women for Permanent Peace then performed the amazing feat of getting one million rubber nipples sent to German mothers who were too starved to feed their babies.[100] Many such efforts were made during the war by women who, conscious of Aletta Jacobs' warning about a focus on relief detracting from the real challenge of stopping war, did what was needed on a practical front at the same time as campaigning for peace. The historiography of the First World War has neglected both these deplorable consequences of war and women's efforts at relieving them, choosing instead to celebrate men's sacrificial heroism.[101]

The Zürich Congress passed a strong resolution on famine and the blockade, asking for it to be lifted, for inter-allied machinery to provide relief, and for food rationing if necessary. But the Congress's main goal was to influence the terms of the peace. Despite the women's explicit demand in 1915 to be included in the peace negotiations process, the terms of peace were now being agreed by the male victors only. Addams brought with her on the train from Paris copies of the treaty that the men had just agreed in Versailles. The women at Zürich were the first international body to discuss the Versailles Treaty, and quite possibly the only ones to read the enormous document from beginning to end. Its terms were worse than anything they had anticipated. They condemned many of these, with no dissenting vote, recording their opposition to the principle of secret treaties to the conquerors, the rights of victors to the spoils of war and the denial of self determination. A major concern was that the proposed League of Nations was not to include all nations that wished to join; it was to be 'a league of conquerors against the conquered [which] would not save the world from future wars'.[102] In a 'wish list' appended to their comments, the women at Zürich recorded the importance to future world peace of total disarmament; protection for the civil and political rights of minorities; the abolition of child labour; complete sex equality; and abolition of capitalists' ability to profit from investments in foreign countries. After the Congress, they telegraphed their resolutions to Paris: 'The terms of peace can only lead to future wars … By the financial and economic proposals a hundred million people of this generation in the heart of Europe are condemned to poverty, disease, and despair, which must result in the spread of hatred and anarchy within each nation.'[103]

Unfortunately, nobody listened very much (again). Wars, and the treaties which end them, are patriotic nationalist projects. The language of victorious and vanquished nation-states is unable to admit women peace makers with an alternative vision of transnationalism that counters the very idea of 'national interest'. It seems also that most of the men at Versailles interpreted the women's appeals as essentially self-interested, that is, as about the suffrage.[104] However, or probably therefore, there was a small victory in Article 7 of the Covenant of the League of Nations, which declared that all positions in the League should be open to women. Following the same method as in the post-Hague envoy mission, a delegation of four women – Charlotte Despard and Chrystal Macmillan from Britain, Clara Ragaz from Switzerland and Rosa Genoni from Italy – was elected to accompany Jane Addams to Paris and, together with Frenchwoman Gabrielle Duchêne, present the resolutions in person to the male treaty makers. Helena Swanwick was given the task of trying to see Lloyd George in Paris. He never responded to her requests for a meeting. These were, she said, two of the most wretched days she had ever spent; her only consolation was to remember Zürich: 'the heavenly flowering spring there with meadows full of apple blossom, the kindly hospitable people, the crowds of pinched and white-faced children trooping in to be fed by the Swiss, from the countries we were still starving, and our noble and tragic colleagues returning to their work of peace-making in the midst of revolutions and murders and hunger'.[105]

Renaming themselves the Women's International League for Peace and Freedom, the women at the Zürich Congress decided to base their future headquarters in whatever town was selected for the League of Nations. They used the word 'League' in their new name deliberately to claim equal status with it.[106] Jane Addams was elected as International President, Emily Balch as International Secretary-Treasurer, and Lida Heymann and Helena Swanwick as International Vice-Presidents. Early in 1920 a charming old house, overgrown with creepers and with a little garden filled with a dripping fountain and a linden tree, was rented in the Rue du Vieux Collège in Geneva, on the slope of the hill where the old cathedral stands. They called it 'Maison Internationale', and in the ensuing years it became a centre for international encounters, discreet policy discussions and strategy sessions. Diplomats came to the Maison Internationale to consult WILPF women, many leaving imbued with the women's ideas. Emily Balch lived and worked there, on and off, for 12 years. During the Zürich meeting, she'd received a cable terminating her 20-year-long academic job at Wellesley College, on the grounds that she had been employed 'to teach economics, not pacifism'.[107] Left with no means of support and no pension at the age of 52, Balch had celebrated her dismissal by smoking a cigarette with Emmeline Pethick-Lawrence and the American lawyer Madeleine Doty; along with its dislike of independent women, Wellesley had a strict taboo on smoking.

The extent of the hazard these women's peace making and social reform activities was seen to pose was quite astonishing. It is, of course, one measure of their revolutionary nature – not in the sense of some hyped-up stereotype of communism or international socialism, but in their identification of radically different ways of living, founded on non-violence and social justice, and a different orientation to politics. At the Zürich Congress, Emily Balch shared a wry joke with the German delegates about how the war had permanently undermined 'the claim of men to possess sole competence to manage public affairs'.[108] 'For myself,' she said, 'I am not in love with governments as such. The sovereign State as we know it is a curious historical growth influenced both by certain by no means infallible political philosophers like Montesquieu and Austin and others, and by accidental occurrences. It is a clumsy irregularly developed instrument for joint action excessively colored by considerations of power and prestige.'[109] Mary Sheepshanks, in the pages of *Jus Suffragii* at the end of the war, argued that women's very newness to politics was an advantage: 'We have escaped party intrigues ... and the awe for traditional conventions, which have tied men's hands and led them to accept meekly the dictates of concessionaires, diplomats and armament firms. We are free to approach all the mystery-making of autocrats ... in a spirit of bold inquiry ... we can insist on fair dealing between nation and nation ... We can oppose the greed that masquerades as patriotism, and put the happiness and welfare of the masses before territorial or financial ambitions.'[110] Speaking from Calvin's pulpit in the old cathedral of Geneva in 1920, overlooking the very site of the Maison Internationale, Maude Royden observed to her congregation that, even as they were all still reeling from the terrible destruction of the war, statesmen in every country were preparing to rebuild society 'on the same foundations, unconscious, apparently, of any error in their building, or hopeless of avoiding it in the future'.[111]

The term 'international' in the name of the WILPF signified more than diversity of national backgrounds among its members: it connoted the withering away of nationalism, of the prime place the idea of the nation has in people's individual identities and in 'inter'-national politics. 'Lovers of our lands,' said Emily Balch in 1922, 'we are citizens of the world, conscious partakers in the sacrament of all human life or more truly of all sentient life.'[112] Alice Salomon said, 'I wanted the whole world to be my country';[113] Madeleine Doty's image characterized nations as being like blocks of ice that would melt and mingle, given the right conditions, then turn into internationalist steam.[114] Jane Addams called patriotism a 'tribal emotion'. For her the task of a 'new internationalism' required national communities to help one another adjust to new modes of life in an increasingly industrialized world. Such a rise in cooperative life would bring about a decline in nationalistic sentiments and would foster what she termed 'cosmic patriotism' – a feeling of pride in belonging to the world community.[115] It was *because* peace required just and equal social conditions and human relations that it called for the emancipation of women from oppression and of all citizens from the politics of nationalism.

In January 1918 Maude Royden sat in the Queen's Hall in London alongside Millicent Fawcett – the two women temporarily forgetting their differences – to celebrate the granting of the vote to some British women. The 1918 Representation of the People Act abolished the property qualification for men, but introduced it for women, who also had to be 30 or older (men could vote at 21). This limited victory for the suffrage movement was widely seen as marking the beneficial effect of the war in turning women into citizens. 'Jerusalem', composed by Hubert Parry especially for the occasion and set to William Blake's words, was played for the first time, conducted by the composer. 'That was a good hymn,' Royden told Parry afterwards. 'That was a better speech,' Parry replied.[116] Royden's speech put the winning of the vote into context: it was only one battle in a great campaign against the world's suffering.

SEVEN

'Our cosmic patriotism': diversity and the dangers of nationalism

When the British economic historian and pacifist Eileen Power travelled through Burma, China and India for her research in 1920–21, she wrote about her ascent to the Khyber Pass, the strategically hazardous mountain route separating what is now Afghanistan from the Indian subcontinent. In Power's day, women were forbidden access to the Khyber Pass, so she donned a 'hermaphroditic habit' and pretended to be a man.[1] Looking down from its heights onto the wide valley below, Power saw a landscape many men had invaded and conquered. It was a sight that exemplified the continuity and also the dislocations of history: the tangled interactions of nationalism, imperialism and militarism. 'Otherness' is a complex theme here, partly because it's also a feeling. What Power felt when she returned from the Khyber Pass to a reprimand from British officials for her geographical and gender transgression, we do not know.[2]

The story in this chapter is one about women being reprimanded by male politicians and governments for their iconoclastic ideas about the damages of the nation-state. It's a story about the meanings of citizenship, not just in one place but in the world. Eileen Power is a woman at the tail end of our story chronologically, but she's connected to it through her services to women's history, to a new methodology of *social* history and to the story of the LSE, a key institution in the evolution of the British welfare state. In the first decades of the 20th century, the LSE housed a number of significant women reformers and intellectuals. Eileen Power went there in 1911 and, after an interlude in Cambridge, she died in post as a Professor of Economic History at the LSE in 1940. The 20th century's most influential sociological text on citizenship was produced by a professor of sociology at the LSE, T. H. Marshall, in 1949. Marshall's *Citizenship and social class* signally failed to take account of the perspective and interests of women, including those of his cousin Catherine Marshall and her colleagues, prime movers in the women's peace movement.[3] Citizenship, for most male thinkers, has always foregrounded men, pushing women to the side as adjuncts or disturbing deviants.

Themes about civic rights, entitlement, welfare and citizenship were embedded in much Settlement sociology and practice, and are obviously raised most urgently when it comes to questions of war and peace. What does it mean to be a citizen? How is the status of citizen related to nationality? Does nationality entail nationalism? Why do some people have to endure, or sometimes choose, lives as displaced persons, refugees, immigrants or 'resident aliens'?

The British pacifist Emily Hobhouse travelled through Belgium and Germany in the middle of the First World War on a personal mission to investigate conditions for people whose nationality had put them in the wrong place – refugees, interned civilians and prisoners of war. On the border between Switzerland and Germany one morning in the late spring of 1916, she experienced a moment of heightened feeling about the absurdity of national frontiers: 'The foolishness of it all was startling – Nature had made no barrier – the earth and stones and grass were the same – one step only made the difference between the country of a friend and of an enemy. No barrier but man or at least Governments had put up landmarks saying "here is all mine, there is all yours, our interests are different and each must look after his own."'[4] Hobhouse's reflections on the man-made barriers dividing nations, and on the consequences of militarized nationalism for citizens of many kinds, were the abiding theme of her life. To the British government her activities were a major irritant, so much so that it subjected her to police surveillance, accused her of treason, withdrew her passport and at one stage had her forcibly deported, which provoked her into suing the government for assault and false imprisonment. Hobhouse's record of achievement, like many created by outspoken women in the early part of the 20th century, is missing from most histories of imperialism, which recite the exploits of men and male-led governments and scrutinize in minute detail the causes and processes of war, leaving women and ordinary citizens to one side as passive witnesses and victims of the nationalist project.

She had an unpromising beginning as the fifth surviving child of an Anglican rector in the tiny village of St Ive in Cornwall. Her mother, the daughter of a local baronet, died when she was 20, and she spent the next 15 years doing parish work and looking after her father, as women did in those days. With an education provided by her mother and 'incompetent' governesses, and only one term at school, Emily Hobhouse was, in 1895 when her father died, a 34-year-old spinster with no particular training for anything.[5] A photograph of her at the time shows her as a winsome young woman with an open, serious face: her eyes seem to look into the distance, to a different future, perhaps. Within a fortnight of her father's death she was on a ship to the US, bound for the remote mining town of Virginia in Minnesota, where it had been arranged that she would do welfare work among the miners who had emigrated there from Cornwall. Since there turned out to be rather few Cornish miners in the town of Virginia, Hobhouse spent her time working with the Finns and other Scandinavians, preaching to them off a sleigh on a frozen lake, trekking with her maid, a young Cornish woman called Mary Scourey, through bogs and creeks, deep into forests with lumber camps, and trying to wean the men off alcohol, a big problem in that cheerless landscape. She set up a temperance union and started a library, ran the church choir and a Sunday school, tried to sort out the local hospital, took miners and sick women into her home – all probably thoroughly influenced by a visit she had made en route to Minnesota to Jane Addams' Hull-House in Chicago: 'they have every sort of thing going on down in the low part of the city', she

7.1: Emily Hobhouse as a young woman

wrote excitedly to her sister, including a crèche, 'with babies of all nations'.[6]

The other thing that Emily Hobhouse did in Virginia was to fall in love. He was a storekeeper called John Carr Jackson, a mysterious figure with ambitions to stand for Congress, somewhat thwarted (though he did succeed in becoming Mayor of Virginia) by his propensity to run up debts. Jackson had friends in Mexico, and Hobhouse agreed to relocate there. In the autumn of 1896 she went alone to Mexico City, where she signed papers for a ranch with coffee plantations, pineapples, bananas and vanilla, and bought a concession for Jackson to deliver all the fresh meat to the city. But Jackson, on the verge of bankruptcy, never arrived. Hobhouse returned to London, where she took lodgings near the British Museum and became one of those women whose rustling skirts disturbed the men in its Reading Room. Her subject was the effects of factory legislation on children. In the winter of 1898 she went back to Mexico, this time accompanied by her wedding dress. Whatever subsequently happened with John Carr Jackson, it was not a wedding. Her family, who had campaigned against the prospect, were relieved. After another interlude in London working for Octavia Hill and for the Women's Industrial Council – producing, among other reports, the one on 'Dust-women' which ends Chapter Four – Hobhouse discovered the horrors of the Anglo–Boer War, the first major military conflict of the 20th century.

We must leave the detailed causes and character of this war to the historians of imperialism, but a brief outline is as follows: the farmers ('Boers') descended from the Dutch, Huguenot and German settlers of the Cape area of South Africa had moved north to set up two independent republics of the Orange Free State and the Transvaal earlier in the 19th century in an effort to free themselves from the colonial rule of Britain, which controlled the Cape. The discovery of gold in the Transvaal in 1886 threatened Boer independence with what can only be described as a global conspiracy between colonial administrators, the mining corporations and international financiers to deprive the Boers of their territory and take it for the empire.[7] Joseph Chamberlain, the British Prime Minister, Sir Alfred Milner, the British High Commissioner in South Africa, and Lord Kitchener,

Commander-in-Chief of the British Army in South Africa (from 1900) were confident of winning quickly, but the Boers fought back and Kitchener ordered his troops to engage in a policy of farm-burning, destroying Boer homesteads, livestock and crops, looting freely from every house, shooting (rather than taking as prisoners of war) all Boer fighters and herding more than 100,000 women and children into concentration camps in an effort to pressure the Boers into submission. The British government called them 'refugee' camps, but they were actually the first modern concentration camps – people were taken and kept there by force, and had no say in their living conditions, which were terrible. Conditions were worst for the wives and children of men still fighting, who were kept on half the meagre rations allowed to others.[8] There were 109 South African camps in all, with Black Africans kept separate from the Boer internees.[9]

Reports of farm-burning appeared in the British press by May 1900. A friend of Emily Hobhouse's, Leonard Courtney (the husband of the peace campaigner Kate Courtney), set up an organization called the South African Conciliation Committee; Hobhouse organized a women's section, holding a meeting in the Queen's Hall in London in the summer of 1900 that was attended by several thousand women (men were not allowed in, except for Leonard Courtney, who was permitted to listen behind a curtain – an experience inflicted on many women entering higher education for the first time). One of the attendees was Harriot Stanton Blatch, the daughter of women's rights campaigner Elizabeth Cady Stanton (Harriot appeared in Chapter Two, at the 1896 International Socialist Workers and Trade Union Congress in London). The women's meeting passed resolutions unequivocally condemning the Anglo-Boer War 'as mainly due to the bad policy of the Government', protesting against 'attempts to silence, by disorder and violence' freedom of speech and any criticism of government policy; they also expressed sympathy with the women of the Transvaal and Orange Free State, inviting them 'to remember that thousands of English women are filled with profound sorrow at the thought of their sufferings, and with deep regret for the action of their own Government'.[10] The immediate consequences of the Queen's Hall meeting, for Hobhouse, were unpleasant slogans chalked on the pavement outside her flat and a letter from her landlord warning her she had infringed the terms of her lease by running a business from it. Many more accusations were to follow – of lying, deception, treason, and the old one of hysteria: Chamberlain called Hobhouse a 'hysterical spinster'; Kitchener, later and more accurately, referred to her as 'that bloody woman'.[11] It all got much worse when she went to South Africa to see for herself.

Hobhouse's ship anchored at Table Bay in Cape Town two days after Christmas in 1900. It was a glorious summer morning there, and she was charmed by the scene: the vivid seas, the towering rampart of Table Mountain, the pale houses with purple and red bougainvillea, avenues of eucalyptus and evergreen oak. Sir Alfred Milner invited her to lunch. He was well known to her family and couldn't afford to ignore such a well-connected person: two of Emily's cousins, Charles Hobhouse and Henry Hobhouse, were MPs: Charles did a spell as private secretary at the Colonial Office, and Henry was permanent under-secretary at the Home Office (and was married to Margaret, yet another of Beatrice Webb's sisters). Another cousin, the Reverend Walter Hobhouse, was editor of the *Manchester Guardian* from 1900 to 1905; one uncle, Lord Arthur Hobhouse, was a Privy Councillor and another, Edmund Hobhouse, was a bishop in colonial New Zealand. Emily's brother Leonard was a well-known philosopher and writer; in 1907 he joined the welfare state intellectuals at the LSE as Britain's first professor of sociology. Carrying all these credentials of kinship, Emily Hobhouse told Alfred Milner firmly that the government policy of farm-burning was mistaken, and it was wrong to turn women and children into martyrs by putting them into concentration camps. She warned him that public opinion in Britain was getting uneasy. She wanted to go to the camps to study conditions there. Milner appeared helpful, but Kitchener would give her permission to go only as far as Bloemfontein, and he stipulated that she must go on her own.

Thus, on a moonlit night in January, Emily Hobhouse set off with a 12-ton covered wagon full of groceries, bedding and clothing attached to a military train on a journey from Cape Town, north-east through the Karoo desert to Bloemfontein, a 1,000-kilometre trip on which she was sustained by food given her by friends, mainly bread and a large tin of apricot jam, with a kettle lamp for making tea and cocoa. 'The land seemed dead and silent, absolutely without life as far as eye could reach,' she wrote, 'only carcasses of horses, mules and cattle with a sort of acute anguish in their look – and bleached bones and refuse of many kinds.'[12] In the Bloemfontein camp she found the barest necessities wanting: not enough water, meat crawling with maggots, poor sanitation, very crowded conditions with 8–12 people in small leaky bell-tents, women and children sleeping on the bare ground. In one of them she used her parasol to wound a snake. Milner, who had given her to understand that he would do something about the camps, did nothing, so she decided she must go back to Britain and conduct a publicity campaign.

Emily Hobhouse's *Report to the Committee of the Distress Fund for South African Women and Children, of a visit to the camps of women and children in the Cape and Orange River colonies* was published in 1901. Its 39 pages form a remarkable document, which in other contexts would be hailed as a fine example of qualitative research. It begins with a first-person diary, Hobhouse's description of her visits to six concentration camps as they happened, followed by her recommendations about what needed to be done to improve the situation. The second, longer part consists of 'Personal records, Applications for release, and Narratives.' It describes the standardized questions she asked the women in the camps (with the answers written down) about their personal circumstances. There was, for example, Mrs Van den B, a widow, who lived with her children in Jacobsdaal. The British came on 25 October and shot at the house, stealing money. When they came back a second time, they locked her and 10 other families in the schoolhouse without food. This was followed by three weeks' imprisonment in her own house. She and her children were then taken to a camp. Her only relative fighting was a brother; the Lieutenant, a Colonial Volunteer, told her she must suffer because of him.

The four detailed narratives at the end of Hobhouse's report use the women's own voices to demonstrate what Hobhouse deemed 'the wholesale cruelty' of the camp system.[13] In a paper published in *The Contemporary Review* in 1901 her anger is transparent. Kitchener, she says, attributes the high death rates of children in the camps to an epidemic of measles, but 'Lord

Kitchener's experience has not been gained in the nursery'. Perhaps in future Sandhurst [a military training academy] might like to add a couple of years' district visiting to its curriculum? The camps, she contended, needed medical resources and nurses, and some means for boiling water, but her requests for all of these were impeded by 'hideous red tapeism'.[14] In 1902 Hobhouse published *The brunt of the war and where it fell*, providing yet more statistics and reprinting much of her depressing correspondence with politicians. Like her friends in the peace movement, her position was that 'None of us can claim to be wholly civilised till we have drawn the line above war itself and established universal arbitration in place of universal armaments.'[15] A third book on the Anglo–Boer conflict, published in 1924, *War without glamour, or Women's war experiences written by themselves*, observes that history is lacking such accounts written by women, which are essential in order for us to understand just how wounding war is for those who do not fight.[16] *War without glamour* contains some 30 written narratives, about half of them translated from Afrikaans by Hobhouse herself.

History proved Emily Hobhouse right about the holocaust of the South African concentration camps (and the historical record is apt to omit the fact that the first concentration camps were a British invention). Some 28,000 people died in them; more children died than men fighting on either side.[17] The government's response to Hobhouse's relentless criticism was to appoint a special 'Ladies' Committee' to go and investigate: Hobhouse herself was excluded because of the 'suspicion of partiality'.[18] The Committee was headed by the politically conservative Millicent Fawcett (who considered Hobhouse a traitor and refused to meet her to discuss the camps). The other members were South Africa's first woman doctor, Jane Waterston; a nurse; two 'society ladies'; and Lucy Deane Streatfeild, one of Britain's first woman factory inspectors. The Ladies' report gave Milner a pat on the back, although it was critical of conditions and of camp administration. Streatfeild, approaching the matter as she would a factory inspection, disagreed with much of the Fawcett report and considered writing a minority report of her own.[19] 'It has been awfully difficult working with these good women,' she wrote to her younger sister Hyacinthe (one of the first woman education inspectors) from Durban in December 1901; all the time she had been 'one against five', but had she not struggled to get at least some of her recommendations accepted, their report 'would be even more "white-washy"'. Her opinion about the camps was clear: 'It is a huge object-lesson to the world in what not to do,' she explained to her sister. 'We brought the women in to stop them helping their husbands in the War and by so doing we have undoubtedly killed them in thousands as much as if we had shot them on their own doorsteps, and anyone but a British General would have realised this long ago.'[20] The Dutch doctor Aletta Jacobs was another who shared Streatfeild and Hobhouse's condemnation of the British government's role. Jacobs tried to go to South Africa to provide (self-financed) medical aid in the internment camps, but she was refused entry to the country on the grounds of her anti-government pronouncements.[21]

After the debacle of the Ladies' Committee, Emily Hobhouse returned to South Africa, or tried to. The Military Commander of Cape Town had been instructed by the British government to prevent her landing and to deport her instantly back to England. She refused to leave the ship and protested somewhat disingenuously that her 'words and works have been purely and consistently philanthropic in character and I have left politics severely alone'.[22] Her captors were not persuaded. Eventually three men were deployed to remove her from the ship by force and transport her to another one straight back to England. On 25 November 1901 *The Daily News* (which had published some of Hobhouse's material on the camps) gave its readers the facts with the apt editorial comment: 'Never, surely, has a great Empire allowed the doings of a lady to get so completely on its nerves; never, perhaps, before in British history has the whole machinery of Empire been brought to bear against a single unprotected woman.'[23] Once Emily was back in England, her uncle Arthur Hobhouse hired an eminent law firm to put forward an action for assault and false imprisonment against Kitchener, Milner and the officers who had taken her by force. St John Brodrick, Secretary of State for War, was uncooperative, and the Hobhouses concluded that, even if their action looked like succeeding, the government would probably introduce a Bill to indemnify it from the consequences of their misdeeds.[24]

But Emily Hobhouse wasn't done with her project of upsetting politicians by dissecting the damages of patriotism. In the next war of her lifetime, the First World War, she set out to counter anti-German propaganda by personally investigating the conditions of internment and prisoner-of-war camps. Invited by Jane Addams to the women's peace congress at The Hague in 1915, she'd been unable, like many British women, to secure a permit to travel, but she did manage to get one to go to Amsterdam in July, where she staffed the office of the International Committee of Women for Permanent Peace while Rosika Schwimmer and Aletta Jacobs were away on their envoy peace missions. The British ambassador in Rome, Sir Rennell Rodd, spoke for many British politicians when he warned the Foreign Office in June 1915 that Miss Hobhouse of Boer War fame was being a great nuisance again: 'It would be much better for these people to stay at home.'[25]

In 'a kind of year-long cat-and-mouse game' of ineffective argument and misplaced communication between the Home Office and the Foreign Office, they did try to keep Miss Hobhouse at home, but she defeated them and got to Bern in Switzerland with her project of visiting Germany and Belgium to see conditions in the ravaged cities and in the internment camps.[26] The British ambassador in Bern was instructed to remove her passport in 1916, but he couldn't find her. By the time he did, she had already been into Germany. The House of Commons debates of the time make entrancing reading, with desperately confused politicians asking how on earth Miss Hobhouse had managed to get into 'enemy territory' and what exactly she had been doing there, and should she, perhaps, be prosecuted for treason, since she was clearly talking to German officials and civilians?[27] Hobhouse examined the extent of destruction claimed by the Allies (much less than was claimed), and the effect of food shortages (much worse than people in Britain believed). She talked to the German Foreign Minister in Berlin, von Jagow, and visited the Ruhleben prisoner-of-war camp, which housed many subsequently famous men, including Catherine Marshall's cousin, Tom, he who would later be renowned for his theories of (male) citizenship. It was strange, wrote Hobhouse, to be in a camp again, 'with all its sordidness and all its artificiality, its neatness and its squalor, its dun colour and monotony, its forlorn efforts to find amusement and occupation, its shabbiness and the worn strained faces of the inmates'. She told the men off for keeping their barracks in such a dirty state – their excuse, which she didn't really swallow, was they didn't have the time for housework.[28] Following the methodology she had employed earlier in South Africa, Hobhouse then returned to Britain to publicize her findings and to suggest a scheme for the exchange of prisoners of war and the closing of internment camps by relocating remaining prisoners in a neutral country. In France, on the way, and again at Tilbury docks, she and her maid were strip-searched, and when she tried to see the Foreign Secretary, Sir Edward Grey, he refused to talk to her. Instead she was questioned by Scotland Yard, who advised the Home Office to intern her. In the end it didn't, probably because it saw the difficulty of making a cause célèbre out of someone who protested purely humanitarian motives (and who had friends and family in high places).

Emily Hobhouse worked best on her own: her biographers describe a strong personality, the propensity to make quick judgements, a certain lack of humour and a caustic tongue. Her radicalism eventually outran the patience of the WILPF, and she resigned. Accustomed to making enemies in the cause of contesting patriotism, she also parted company with her brother L. T. Hobhouse over their contrasting attitudes to war. In this she was paralleled by her fellow pacifist Charlotte Despard, whose own brother Sir John French devoted his whole career to fighting on behalf of the British empire. Yet, although Hobhouse was good at making enemies, she also made many friends. There she was, for example, in Berlin in 1916, where she had never been, not speaking the language, in her own words, 'a formidable old maid in a grey bonnet and a golf cape',[29] accompanied by the escort the Germans had forced upon her, a nervous young man who was obviously puzzled about how to prevent Miss Hobhouse from doing what she wanted. She had in her bag one address, that of Elizabeth Rotten, who had been born in Berlin, had lectured on German literature in Cambridge, been to The

Hague, co-founded the German League for Human Rights, and was now back in Berlin helping foreigners in Germany. When Hobhouse tracked her down, 'We fell on each other's necks with joy'.[30] Rotten suggested getting in touch with Alice Salomon and going to see Salomon's Arbeiterinnenheim (Female Workers' Home, a sort of Settlement where women reformers and trainee social workers lived with single working women). Salomon, a feminist and internationalist, had founded social work as a profession in Germany; some called her 'the Jane Addams of Germany'.[31] She invited Hobhouse to a light supper in her apartment. 'It was interesting,' Hobhouse reported, 'this peek of a German "professional" woman's flat. She had one maid and supper was ordered ... it certainly was light. In a moment I realized how short food was in private houses, there was an omelet made of one egg for the two of us, there were three very small and very thinly cut slices of bread – there was a very small dish of stewed cherries. In addition there was a small block of butter 3oz the total supply per head for two weeks. I realized I must only make a feint of taking any and just scraped it with my knife. As to the omelet we took tiny mouthfuls and eked them out with much conversation.'[32]

7.2: Alice Salomon, 1904

Alice Salomon and Emily Hobhouse wouldn't have been short of topics to talk about. Salomon was 44 when they met, 12 years younger than Hobhouse. The photographs that survive show her developing a progressively haunted look over the years: in the lightest one, shown in Figure 7.2, taken in 1904, she appears in a pale lacey dress topped with a veritable landscape of a hat. (This photo is interesting because it came from a studio in Munich called Hof-Atelier Elvira which was co-founded by the German feminist lawyer Anita Augspurg. The studio was an all-female establishment, and the first German company to have been set up by women.) Salomon was the daughter of a middle-class Jewish family in Berlin and had been active in feminist reform groups in Germany since the early 1890s. Her eyes had been opened by her early welfare work, which exposed the special hardships of poor women and children. When a mother she knew was convicted of manslaughter because one of her children had fallen into a washtub and drowned while she was out working in order to feed the family, Salomon defended her, criticizing public welfare for not doing more to help working mothers.[33] In 1899 she set up the first professional social work training course, followed in 1908 by a School for Social Work which continues today under the name of the Alice-Salomon-Hochschule Berlin. Its original curriculum, which Salomon designed, followed the scientific principles of the women sanitary scientists described in Chapter Five, placing practical knowledge of social problems in the broad context of accurate information about hygiene, public health, economic theory and history, law and civics. In the 1920s Alice Salomon developed a framework for supporting voluntary social service agencies with public funds that foreshadowed the German model of the welfare state. She wrote many books and articles about social work, social theory, research, education and the position of women, which were notable for their strong international theme: most of these have never been translated from their original German.

Salomon was able to penetrate international audiences in person through her involvement with the ICW. At the ICW Congress in London in 1899 she had shared a platform with Beatrice Webb, where they had both talked about protective labour legislation for women. She was upset by Webb's coldness: 'detached, unemotional, typically a scholar … She thought in different categories and dimensions from feminists and social workers.'[34] For the ICW congress in Canada in 1909, Salomon crossed the Atlantic for the first time, taking the northern route towards Montreal and passing icebergs in June. The ICW elected her Honorary Corresponding Secretary, and on the way back she took a train across the US, stopping in Chicago for an official luncheon hosted by the mayor, who introduced her to Jane Addams. 'Hull House and the stockyards were said to compete as the greatest attraction for visitors in Chicago,' noted Salomon. 'I went to see Hull House that time and lived there repeatedly as a guest in later years. The stockyards I left for others.'[35] She wrote enthusiastically about Hull-House in *Leben und Wirken*, the journal of the Baltic women's movement, and helped to secure a German translation of Addam's *Twenty years at Hull-House*, writing a new German preface. Salomon's research on stressors in family life borrowed the methods used by Sophonisba Breckinridge and Edith Abbott, whom she'd met at Hull-House; in turn, Jane Addams went to see Salomon in Berlin, giving a public lecture at the East Side Settlement there.[36]

Salomon's work for the ICW, in the tense years leading up to the war, taught her to understand 'what supranational work actually implies'. She learnt that 'people have not only different languages but different ways of expressing their thoughts'.[37] What satisfied one nation, another regarded as inappropriate or offensive. She also became aware of how militaristic some of her German colleagues were. She was in Dublin with her friends (made through the ICW) Lord and Lady Aberdeen when the war broke out, and found herself forbidden to leave the country and ordered to register at a police station as an 'enemy alien'. Back in Germany, she was horrified by the reactionary situation that greeted her: 'It was exactly as though they were preparing for some joyful festival and carried victory in their hands.'[38] She asked herself whether her patriotism had been corrupted by her international contacts, because she still loved Germany but absolutely could not approve of the war. 'Above all,' she wrote, 'war fosters attitudes which are the source of social injustice and distress. It annihilates respect for property, it drills men to requisition, loot and steal. It instills hatred in the population. It paves the way for cruelty, for domination, for a belief in the superiority of one nation over another ... Patriotism is not enough ... for the welfare of mankind.'[39]

Before she met Emily Hobhouse, Alice Salomon had tried, with other like-minded German women, to get permission to visit civilian and military prisoners' camps to see what might be done, but all their requests had been refused by the military authorities. She had also wanted to go to The Hague Congress in the spring of 1915, but the president of the German National Council of Women, of which she was a leading member, instructed that any woman who did so would thereafter be excluded from the Council. Salomon obeyed, later regretting her decision.[40] As anti-Semitism mounted in Germany, she and her friends were forced to close down their organizations; in May 1937 she herself was ordered by the secret police to leave Germany or be taken to a concentration camp. The main crime of which she was accused was the extent of her international travel – such networking among women was eminently suspicious. In addition, Salomon represented everything the Nazis detested: she was Jewish, Protestant, progressive, female and pacifically minded. Relocating to the US for the rest of her life, she wrote, saddened, 'it has been said so often that I hesitate to repeat it, the refugee loses caste'.[41] The career of the Dutch pacifist Rosa Manus, who was similarly persecuted by the Nazis, didn't survive the concentration camp threat; Manus was sent to Ravensbrück in 1941, and gassed sometime in early 1942.[42]

Salomon's articles about Hull-House for her German audiences singled out particularly its work for and with immigrants as 'the most peculiar and remarkable sign of the American sense of citizenship'.[43] Lillian Wald's Henry Street Settlement in New York had a particular reputation for work on cultural diversity. The Henry Street Settlement supported an early community theatre, the Neighborhood Playhouse, where Angelina Grimké's anti-lynching play, *Rachel*, was put on in 1917 – the first time a theatre in the US had presented a play by a Black author with a Black cast in front of an integrated audience. When Wald helped to set up the National Association for the Advancement of Colored People (NAACP) in 1909, she offered the Settlement for its first gatherings, which was important because of the prohibition in New York at the time against all integrated public meetings.

Documenting the histories, cultures and living circumstances of immigrant communities was a main plank of American Settlement work. For example, Italians, Slovaks, Lithuanians, Greeks and also 'Negroes' were the focus of attention in five of the ten meticulous studies of housing conditions published by Hull-House researchers between 1910 and 1915. In one set of 16 blocks of Chicago housing, 80% of the Greeks and Italians who lived there inhabited poorly repaired buildings; many were also overcrowded, with whole families huddled in gloomy, windowless rooms.[44] The economist Alzada Comstock, reporting on seven blocks mostly inhabited by 'negroes', found a much higher proportion of dilapidated, insanitary, rented accommodation than in other areas of Chicago, with families charged double the rents of other immigrant groups. 'Broken-down doors, unsteady flooring ... doors hanging on single hinges or entirely fallen off, and roofs rotting and leaking. Colored tenants reported that they found it impossible to persuade their landlords either to make the necessary repairs or to release them from their contracts.'[45]

Hull-House's most notable specialist on ethnic diversity and its implications for American citizenship was Grace Abbott, the younger of the two energetic, public-minded sisters who spent a decade living and working at Hull-House (page 49). Grace Abbott was present on the occasion when Theodore Roosevelt, embarking on the presidential campaign which ushered in the Progressive Era in American politics, is said to have been persuaded by Jane Addams, who had just had him to dinner in Hull-House, to support female suffrage.[46] Brought up by an enlightened lawyer-banker father and a feminist, abolitionist, Quaker mother, the Abbott sisters had not, unlike many other women in this book, had to make the case for taking up public reform work. The interests of the Abbott sisters overlapped, but their personalities differed. Edith was the thin, intensely intellectual one, the true scholar; Grace, more relaxed and fun-loving, was the one who translated knowledge into action.[47]

In a series of regular contributions to the *Chicago Evening Post* in 1909–10, Grace Abbott wrote passionately about the problem of poverty among immigrants. Her research on this employed both community involvement and in-depth interviewing. The study she did of Bulgarians in Chicago was carried out after 600 of them had marched on City Hall in 1908 demanding work; to find out more about their circumstances Abbott enlisted the aid of a young Bulgarian, Ivan Doseff, who had acted as their organizer and leader. Abbott and Doseff asked 100 of the men who'd marched to City Hall why and how they'd come to the US and what had happened to them since. Most of them were young, had been farmers in their native country, had wives and children there and had come in search of work with the aim of sending money home. But the American dream hadn't materialized: a third either had found no work at all or had spent just a few days shovelling snow. Most alarming of all was the role of the steamship companies in creating immigrants by making false promises of the riches to be found in America and offering expensive loans at interest rates of 40–50% for the men's passages.[48] Abbott's report of this study ended by calling for some better way of enabling Bulgarian immigrants to become valuable citizens of America. This emphasis on what immigrants have to offer was repeated in the study of Chicago Greeks she published in the *American Journal of Sociology* the same year. For this she depended on the services of 'a Greek-speaking woman' who visited Greek families in the neighbourhood around Hull-House, an area that contained a Greek Orthodox church with a school, a Greek bank, steamship-ticket office, notary public, employment agency 'and the coffee-houses, where the men drink black Greek coffee, play cards, speculate on the outcome of the next Greek lottery, and in the evening sing to the accompaniment of the Greek bag-pipes or – evidence of their Americanization – listen to the phonograph'. Carefully unpicking the allegation that Greek immigrants contributed disproportionately to the crime rate, Abbott recommends them as 'bright, industrious, and capable' people whose capacity for good citizenship will not be helped 'by the general condemnation which is too often meted out to "the stranger within our gates"'.[49]

A central method of women reformers' social science was to study problems at their source. In the summer of 1911 Grace Abbott joined the ranks of brave women travellers who transgressed the gender norms of their time by journeying alone in unfamiliar places. She sailed to England with her sister, leaving Edith there to renew friendships and do research, and proceeded to Germany, where she interviewed labour exchange officials in Stuttgart, Cologne, Nuremburg and Frankfurt and observed government housing projects for working people. Her visit took in highlights of the old Austro-Hungarian empire (Vienna, Budapest, Fiume, Krakow, Lemberg, Prague), and also remote villages, where she investigated factories, schools, churches, hospitals, prisons, and reform schools and was invited into people's homes. When she came back, Grace Abbott went to Washington to testify before a House Committee on immigration and naturalization on a proposal to restrict immigration. The condition of a literacy test, enacted by Congress, was vetoed by President Taft because of the evidence she gave.[50] The next year she was hired by the State of Massachusetts to direct a study of immigration that resulted in a powerful report, *The problem of immigration in Massachusetts*.[51]

Grace Abbott's status as an immigration expert was enhanced by her leadership of an organization she helped to found in 1908, the Immigrants' Protective League (IPL). Its aim was to help immigrants avoid the exploitation of avaricious landlords, employment agencies, ticket brokers and so forth, to support their rights to citizenship and to convince the American public generally that the cultures of different ethnicities must be respected both in themselves and because they had a valuable contribution to make to community life. A special concern of the IPL and of Grace Abbott was what happened to young women and girls who often travelled to the US on their own and were vulnerable to abuse and trafficking.[52] Some 20% of the women and girls leaving Ellis Island for Chicago simply disappeared, most, probably, into houses of prostitution. Abbott called it 'a little study'[53] but it was a fairly massive one, and its methodology clearly followed the general protocol of Hull-House research: investigators visited 178 of the 289 employment agencies licensed in Chicago in June 1908, studying in detail 110 of these which specialized in placing 'foreigners'. Under Abbott's leadership the IPL set up a system of organizing volunteers and interpreters to meet new arrivals and help them find homes and jobs. They persuaded the railroad company in Chicago to provide a building across from the main station and to direct new immigrants there, where IPL volunteers, speaking all the various languages, met them, endeavoured to contact the relatives and friends who were expecting them and then tried to ensure that they reached their destinations. In the five years from 1910 to 1915 more than half a million girls and young women arrived in the US, most under 21, and the IPL helped some 27,000 who came alone.[54]

Abbott wrote about this work, and about her own views on citizenship and nationality, in a book, *The immigrant and the community*, published in 1917. She drew on her experiences during her 1911–12 Balkan journey to explain what her earlier study of the Bulgarian community in Chicago had shown, that most immigrants were now coming to America not principally from economic necessity, but because of the prosperity, freedom and respect for individual initiative that America had come to symbolize. Some of the newest immigrants seduced by this dream were so young 'that their only work at home had been to watch the sheep and the cattle in the fields'.[55] One of many telling stories was of a Polish girl, deemed healthy after being examined by doctors at Ellis Island, who developed tuberculosis after a few months' factory work in Chicago and was taken to the County Hospital. She realized that her dreams of a good life in the US, of marrying well and sending for her mother to join her, had come to nothing: she asked only to go back home and be with her mother. The IPL arranged for this but, tragically, the girl died at sea.[56]

Through the medium of such case studies, Abbott engages the reader's sympathy and understanding. After the First World War she was appointed to a League of Nations permanent advisory committee on the suppression of the traffic in women and children. Proposing a full scientific investigation of the facts, she secured Rockefeller Foundation funds and then worked on the survey and on a report that helped to secure more effective international agreements.[57] She didn't hesitate to point out that not only had America treated immigrants badly, it had failed to remember that it was itself a country of immigrants, fashioned from many cultures. Thus, rather than participating in the European demand for nationalism, the US had the opportunity to work towards a democracy founded on internationalism: 'if we can respect those differences that result from a different social and political environment and see the common interests that unite all people, we shall meet the American opportunity. If instead we blindly follow Europe and cultivate a national egotism, we shall need to develop a contempt for others and to foster those national hatreds and jealousies that are necessary for aggressive nationalism.'[58] The circle of reformers and social scientists in and around Hull-House and other Settlements did much to soften the edges of American nationalism with messages of beneficial cultural diversity and a hard-hitting resolve to combat exploitation. What began as a process informed by traditional notions of 'assimilation' or 'Americanization' became over time a much more interesting internationalist project resting on the principle that all cultures are created equal.[59]

Cultures may be regarded as equal, but human beings tend to be monolingual; an enormously important aid to women's networking was the facility many had to speak several languages and develop some understanding of different national cultures. Women's membership of international organizations encouraged linguistic diversity, and communicating in other languages was regarded as crucial by (and, of course, enormously helped by membership of) organizations such as the ICW and the WILPF. The ability to speak other languages could be essential in campaigning work: the British pacifist campaigner Mary Sheepshanks, for example, was able to deliver speeches in three languages on her European suffrage tours. Rosika Schwimmer, the fiery, argumentative Hungarian pacifist, managed French, German and English in addition to her native Hungarian, and she could also read Dutch, Italian, Norwegian and Swedish, which meant that her translating skills were extremely useful at international congresses. The Dutch doctor Aletta Jacobs, and the pacifist and co-organizer of The Hague Women's Peace Congress in 1915, Rosa Manus, both spoke English fluently, but German rather less well, yet they took pains to use their German when writing to German colleagues.[60] The Abbott sisters had learnt German as children at their mother's insistence because Grand Island, Nebraska, where they lived, was a site of German settlement. The habit for middle-class families in Britain and America to send their young people for a period to European schools was another aid to language learning. The British pacifist Helena Swanwick, whose parents were British and Danish, went to a French boarding school; the writer Cicely Hamilton was bilingual in German and English as a result of being sent for a while to a German school. Hamilton was one of a number of women who did translations and gave language lessons to support her political and other work. Because medical training was open to women earlier in continental Europe than in Britain, many women doctors picked up German or French along with their medical education. Another route was research. Economist Emily Balch, who began with a childhood grounding in Latin, Greek, French, German and Italian, added some Dutch, Russian, Polish, Czech and Croatian in the course of her studies of different ethnic groups. *Jus Suffragii*, the newsletter of the International Women's Suffrage Alliance, had a Latin name because Latin was regarded as an international language, but objections about elitism were reasonably voiced by American women.[61] From time to time Esperanto was suggested, but the idea never gained much ground.[62]

The term 'cosmic patriotism' at the head of this chapter comes from Addams' *Newer ideals of peace*, a complex and in some ways surprising book published in 1907. Despite its title, Addams' book is not about peace, war and international relations, but about the 'new internationalism' Addams felt was being created in cities like Chicago, a kind of cosmopolitan humanitarianism arising out of the social practices of diverse ethnicities who were living and working closely with one another. 'Because of their difference in all external matters,' she wrote, 'the people in a cosmopolitan city are forced to found their community of interests upon the basic and essential likenesses of their common human nature … They are developing the only sort of patriotism consistent with the intermingling of the nations … There arises the hope that when this new patriotism becomes large enough, it will overcome arbitrary boundaries and soak up the notion of nationalism.' Optimistically, she believed this might eventually lead to the 'substitution of nurture for warfare'. It should mean the end of war, because you could no more wage war on a nation on the other side of the globe than you could on your next-door neighbour. A sense of 'cosmic patriotism' would hopefully be strong enough to move people 'out of their narrow national considerations and cautions into new reaches of human effort and affection'; it would be revolutionary, active and practical, an altruistic readiness to sacrifice narrow personal interests.[63]

Addams, Abbott, Balch and others enunciated an analysis of ethnic diversity that was aimed at changing mainstream white American perceptions of 'the immigrant'. One of its key strategies was to reposition the immigrant in the American mind as the bearer of gifts – of wise, rich, colourful 'other' cultures, of occupational skills and, above all, experience in that altruistic 'kindly relationship' that welds communities together.[64] This was a pragmatic and persuasive philosophy, albeit sometimes couched in a language that wouldn't today be regarded as politically correct. The extra input of African-American women was needed to shine the spotlight on the most fundamental ethnic division at the heart of American nationalism: between the white majority and the one-tenth of the population who were African-American. Ida Bell Wells-Barnett (commonly known as Ida B. Wells) and Anna Julia Cooper were both born as slaves. Their birth dates – 1862 and 1858 – place them within the same few years as some of the women whose stories feature most prominently in this book: Florence Kelley, Alice Ravenhill and Carrie Chapman Catt (all 1859); Jane Addams, Emily Hobhouse and Charlotte Perkins Gilman (all 1860); Vida Scudder (1861). But the names of Black women reformers and social scientists are even more dimly remembered than the others, having become detached from both histories of racism and canonical

narratives of women's struggles for emancipation – a word that does make absolute sense here, since it comes from the Latin verb *emancipare* (*e*- [variant of *ex*-] 'out' + *mancipium*, 'slave').

Consider, for example, the journey taken by Ida Wells from an impoverished slave homestead in Mississippi to becoming one of the first Black women to run for a state legislature and founding a transnational campaign against racism that connected the transatlantic crusade against

7.3: Ida B. Wells, c. 1893

slavery with modern civil rights movements. Among Wells' achievements were to join Jane Addams in campaigning successfully against the establishment of segregated schools in Chicago; to organize numerous clubs for Black women, including the country's first Black women's suffrage organization; to start her own Settlement, the Negro Fellowship League; to work as a probation officer for the Chicago Municipal Court; and she claimed, as she put it, to have been 'the only woman in the United States who ever traveled throughout the country with a nursing baby to make political speeches'.[65]

The eldest of eight children, Ida Wells faced the first big challenge of her life when both her parents and one of her siblings died in a yellow fever epidemic in 1876. With extraordinary determination, the 14-year-old Ida refused to allow her five surviving siblings to go into foster care and said she would bring them up herself. Lying about her age, she took a job as a schoolteacher in one of the schools that were springing up in the South in the wake of the law abolishing slavery that was passed when she was an infant. A few years later she moved the family to Memphis, where they lived with an aunt. On 4 May 1884 she bought a ticket for her usual train journey from Memphis to her school. Wells wrote an account of what happened in an unfinished autobiography later edited by her daughter:

> I took a seat in the ladies' coach of the train as usual. When the train started and the conductor came along to collect tickets, he took my ticket, then handed it back to me and told me that he couldn't take my ticket there. I thought that if he didn't want the ticket I wouldn't bother about it so went on reading. In a little while when he finished taking tickets, he came back and told me I would have to go in the other car. I refused, saying that the forward car was a smoker, and as I was in the ladies' car I proposed to stay. He tried to drag me out of the seat, but the moment he caught hold of my arm I fastened my teeth in the back of his hand … I had braced my feet against the seat in front and was holding on the back, and as he had already been badly bitten he

didn't try it again by himself. He went forward and got the baggage-man and another man to help him, and of course they succeeded in dragging me out. They were encouraged to do this by the attitude of three white ladies and gentlemen in the car; some of them even stood on the seats so that they could get a good view and continued applauding the conductor for his brave stand.[66]

Wells got off the train, went back to Memphis and hired the only Black lawyer in town to sue the railroad. After months of delay, she discovered he had been bought off by the railroad company. She hired a new lawyer and won the case in the local circuit court, being awarded $500 in damages. The local paper broadcast the news with the headline 'DARKY DAMSEL GETS DAMAGES'.[67] The decision in her favour was later reversed by the Tennessee Supreme Court on the grounds that she had intended to cause difficulty for the rail company. This was, after all, 71 years before the much better-known case of Rosa Parks, who similarly refused a segregated relocation on public transport.

Wells began to write pieces about race and politics, and in 1887 she was elected to the board of the National Afro-American Press Convention. She bought a half share in a Black newspaper, *Free Speech*, and became its editor, while continuing to teach, in both positions openly condemning segregationist policies, especially for their effect on education. The next defining political challenge of her life came in 1892 when three of her friends were lynched.[68] Before it happened to her friends, Wells had believed that lynching was simply used to punish criminals. But she knew that her three friends had committed no crime except for running a small grocery store that had taken customers away from white businesses. A group of angry white men had decided to destroy the competition, but the Black owners fought back, shooting one of their attackers. Wells' friends were jailed; a lynch-mob broke into the jail, dragged them away from town and murdered all three, gouging out the eyes of the man who resisted most fiercely.[69]

These horrors propelled Wells to conduct her own investigation into the extent of lynchings in the southern US. Her two months of travelling and asking questions would have been an extremely risky enterprise for a Black woman travelling alone, studying a practice that was endemic in the white male populations of many small southern towns. When *Free Speech* printed her editorial revealing some of the disturbing facts she'd discovered, a mob of white men broke into the office building and set fire to it, then posted a gunman at the station to shoot Wells, who was on a visit to New York.[70] Wisely, she stayed in New York. After this, she took a job on a Black newspaper in Chicago, and then married its editor and gave birth to four children. In Chicago, she worked with others to produce an attack on the racism of the 1893 Columbian Exposition, celebrating 400 years since Columbus supposedly discovered America. Ten thousand copies were handed out to visitors of the pamphlet she helped to produce, with the introduction in three languages, *The reason why the colored American is not in the World Columbian Exposition.*[71]

Wells' best-known publication on the subject of lynching has a suitably sarcastic subtitle, *A red record: Tabulated statistics and alleged causes of lynchings in the United States, 1892–1893–1894, respectfully submitted for the nineteenth century civilization in 'the Land of the Free and the Home of the Brave'*. The book covers in detail and by name all the 534 cases in which Black people had been lynched over the three-year period. She took her data from the records published in the *Chicago Tribune* and other local newspapers – 'statistics as gathered and preserved by white men'[72] – so that no one could accuse her of making them up. The cases are recited under headings – 'Lynched as a scapegoat', 'Lynched because the jury acquitted him', and so forth, and then, 'lynched for anything or nothing', a category which encompasses such cases as, 'Hanged for stealing hogs'. Descriptions of these atrocities, taken from the newspapers reporting them, expose a mass fascination for lynching as a public spectacle – what Wells called the 'barbarity' of American civilization: 'it is the white man's civilization and the white man's government which are on trial'.[73] For example, the public lynching described in *A red record* of one Negro, Henry Smith, who was accused without trial of murdering a small child in Texas in 1893, attracted a crowd 10,000 strong. They put Henry Smith on a carnival float and processed it through the city 'so that all might see the most inhuman monster'. Then they placed him, bound, on a scaffold and tortured him for 50 minutes with red-hot iron brands, burning out his eyes and cheering at every groan and contortion of his body. Finally they poured kerosene over him and set him on fire.[74]

Wells performed a major political service in connecting old reform sentiments in Britain with the case for opposing violent racism in the New World, a service that has mostly passed unnoticed by historians. Her studies of lynching drew her into a broad transnational network working against slavery and all forms of racist nationalism, particularly a group of British Quakers led by a quiet Somerset woman, Catherine Impey, who produced Britain's first anti-racist newspaper, *Anti-Caste*, from her own home: its most controversial issue, in January 1893, was the one which had on its cover a photograph of a lynched African-American in Alabama.[75] Impey travelled to the US and sponsored Wells' own visits to Britain in 1893 and 1894. She was a neighbour and relative of the Clark family, prominent Quaker shoemakers and reformers who included the historian Alice Clark and Hilda Clark, one of the early woman doctors. This was a network formed around the politics of abolitionism, temperance and women's rights, onto which was easily grafted the wider transnational campaign against racism. For example, Alice Clark and her mother spent some time in the US in 1900 visiting African-American community leaders and seeing the practices of segregation at first hand.[76] The Clark and Impey families had given refuge to escaped slaves in their Somerset homes – they helped to buy the freedom of the well-known abolitionist orator Frederick Douglass, who in turn was responsible for introducing Wells to Impey.

Wells' mission on her travels to Britain was to tell the British public about the horrors of lynching and racism in the southern US. She started in the Music Hall in Aberdeen, repeating her stories in more than a dozen cities in Scotland and England. In London, Wells took her message to many clubs, churches, drawing-room gatherings and dinner parties, including a large breakfast reception in the Westminster Palace Hotel for MPs and their wives, from whom she extracted the promise that English public opinion would thereafter endorse the right to a fair trial for all southern Negroes accused of any crime. An Anti-lynching Committee was set up, with links to parliamentary and suffrage leaders. Wells spared her audiences nothing, and especially drew their attention to the truth behind the myth that most lynching was of Black men for raping white women: she taught them instead that the bodies of Black women were a primary site for white aggression.[77] Newspapers, predictably, commented on Wells' youth, beauty and skin colour: 'Miss Ida B. Wells is a negress, a young lady of little more than twenty years of age, a graceful, sweet-faced, intelligent, courageous girl.'[78] She was actually 32.

Concentration camps and lynching are both unimaginable in the kinds of principled egalitarian communities espoused by women who worked for social justice. Hobhouse and Wells' contemporary, Anna Julia Cooper, presents a different and uniquely impressive example of someone who, just as they did, defeated enormous obstacles in hostile circumstances to voice unpopular convictions; but Cooper, more than either Wells or Hobhouse, produced a body of scholarly and sociological writings which contain the germs of modern theories about race, gender and power.[79]

7.4: Anna Julia Cooper, 1892

'My mother was a slave and the finest woman I have ever known,' she wrote.[80] Her mother had given birth to two sons by her wealthy slave-owner before probably being 'lent' to his brother, a prominent white attorney in Raleigh, North Carolina, who was Anna Julia Cooper's putative father.[81] She went to school at ten, to one of the new schools for Black children in the South, and the school saved her. She read everything and she learnt advanced mathematics, Greek and Latin, and then she proceeded to Oberlin College, one of the first to admit Black students, where she trained as a teacher. At 18 she married a minister, George Cooper, who died two years later. She took a teaching post at a Black high school in Washington, DC, the M Street School, where she designed an innovative curriculum intended to prepare Black students for entry to the élite universities. However, her very success at this task brought her the censure of the school's board and of other Black educationalists, particularly Booker T. Washington, who thought a liberal arts education inappropriate for Black students.[82] In 1906 the school relieved her of her contract and she took a position at Lincoln Institute in Missouri as professor of foreign languages.

Anna Julia Cooper's best-known publication, *A voice from the South by a Black woman of the South*, appeared in 1892. A collection of essays on racism, sexism and education, it spells out the anomalous position of women in a social system arranged on the axes of race and class. 'Why should woman become plaintiff in a suit versus the Indian, or the Negro or any other race or class who have been crushed under the iron heel of Anglo-Saxon power and selfishness?'[83] she asks. If Blacks are men, and women are white, then with what voice may a Black woman speak? The theoretical difficulty is rendered concrete, for example when Cooper, travelling in the South (and experiencing the same kind of physical harassment as Ida Wells), encounters two public toilets from which she must choose, one labelled 'FOR LADIES' and the other 'FOR COLORED PEOPLE'.[84] Under which heading, she demands, does she come? 'Race, color, sex, condition', she stated plainly, are 'the accidents, not the substance of life'; 'The cause of freedom is not the cause of race or a sect, a party or a class, – it is the cause of humankind.'[85]

In her response to a 1930s survey on Negro college graduates, Cooper described her vocation as 'The education of neglected people'.[86] In pursuit of this aim, she took part in all the normal reformist activities – co-founding or working with Black women's clubs, associations and charity organizations; contributing to Settlement life (the Colored Social Settlement, founded in 1902); and much public speaking (at which she was apparently very proficient), including a rousing speech at the first Pan-African Conference in London in 1900. While all this was going on, she adopted seven children, all relatives whose own parents were unable to care for them, and raised them on a teacher's salary. The childcare delayed her most remarkable educational achievement, which was the gaining of a PhD in 1925, at the age of 66, from the University of Paris; its title was 'The attitude of France toward slavery during the French Revolution', and it was written in French, a language in which Cooper had already amply demonstrated her proficiency by translating the epic 12th-century poem *Le pèlerinage de Charlemagne* from old to modern French.[87] Cooper worked in education full-time until she was 82, and after that continued to write and to publish until her death at 105. In her later years she composed a play about Black history for university students, *From servitude to service: contributions from the Negro peoples in American history, a pageant in three episodes and fourteen scenes*.[88] In the usual slight meted out to unusual women, commentators have subsumed her record under that of the nearest man – in this case W. E. B. DuBois, whose own landmark study of *The Philadelphia Negro* was conducted only because a woman suggested and supported it (see Chapter Three). Cooper, thereby renamed 'a female DuBois',[89] was certainly quoted by him, but anonymously; her public call for educated and energetic Black women to teach the world 'to be pitiful, to love, mercy, to succor the weak and care for the lowly' predated his own.[90]

The white imperialist race-based thinking, which Anna Cooper, Ida Wells and many others in this period took as their project to dissect and dismantle, flourished in a peculiarly extreme form in Haiti, a country that appeared on the radar of feminist peace makers in the WILPF in the early 1920s. Haiti had been under US control since 1915, ostensibly in order to prevent the island becoming a German submarine base and to dampen the political instability that had arisen among its leaders.[91] Haitian women in the WILPF wanted an investigation of the consequences of the US control, which had come to cover virtually every area of the nation's life. Haiti's history was prodigiously multicultural: Europeanized after Columbus' arrival in 1492, ruled by Spain and then by France, and populated by slaves imported from Africa to work on the lucrative sugar-cane plantations. The Haitian Revolution of 1791–1804 produced the only independent nation in the world ruled by non-whites and former captives. All Haiti's early leaders were ex-slaves, and by the time the US (in the form of Theodore Roosevelt's aggressively interventionist foreign policy) rediscovered an interest in the country in 1915, Haiti was controlled by French-speaking Black élites, the likes of which were unknown in the US itself. These Haitians, disrupting all the racist rhetoric about the unfitness of the Negro to govern, gave their American invaders an excuse for an unpleasantly hardened racial politics.[92]

In 1926, economist and anti-nationalist Emily Balch, on behalf of the WILPF, headed a six-person team which went to Haiti and published an influential report, *Occupied Haiti*, which put the case for ending the American occupation and returning the country to self-government. 'The most disconcerting aspect of the whole affair,' said the Committee in its preface to the report, 'is that it is possible to do what has been done in Haiti, directly contrasting as it is to all our principles and professions, without any popular demand for such action, without its ever being proposed or debated beforehand, and with so little realization in the US that it has been done.'[93] The team consisted of five women and one man; among the women were two African-Americans, Charlotte Atwood, a teacher, and Addie Hunton, representing the International Council of Women of the Darker Races. They spent three weeks in Haiti, interviewing officials and lay people and examining agriculture, healthcare, finance, education, civil rights and US military practices. It was an exercise in ethnography, as well as a political study; Balch, writing a chapter on 'Land and living' in their report, described the Haitian women, who did most of the buying and selling, and who came to market on long processions 'on donkey back, or afoot with amazing burdens on their splendidly poised heads … All alike are graceful, free-moving, very much alive, and often, to the seeing eye, very beautiful. They sit in the town square, perhaps in thousands, with their small stock of wares spread out before them.'[94] Yet the conditions of their industry were under the complete control of the US government. *Occupied Haiti* documented illegal imprisonment, forced labour, indiscriminate killing and many instances of aggression, abuse and violence towards women. Balch, who wrote much of the report, argued that the 'traditional' attitudes of the white men stationed in Haiti exemplified an extreme version of racialized and sexualized superiority.[95] What was happening there thus brought together all the 'isms': nationalism, imperialism, racism, sexism. It was a complete denial of that other way of living, which the women reformers had learnt through their own settlement in 'foreign' communities and by means of the close networks of relationships they had built to cross oceans and nations.

'Cosmic patriotism' was a learnt and lived experience. These women acted it and were involved in it, as well as applying their minds to understanding it. The men's understanding was much more likely to take the form of theories about how people's identities attach to places in such a way that citizenship can mean citizenship only of a self-aggrandizing nation-state. Far removed from Emily Balch's disturbing incursions into Haitian politics, the remarkable protests of women such as Anna Julia Cooper and Ida Wells, the attentive local studies of the Settlement sociologists and Alice Salomon's troubles with anti-Semitism, were the male social theorists in London, at the LSE. T. H. Marshall, the cousin of one of Britain's leading pacifists and the author of a highly theoretical statement about citizenship, might well have discussed his ideas with L. T. Hobhouse, the brother of 'that bloody Miss Hobhouse', who himself was interested mainly in theories of knowledge and the history of morality. Their residences at the LSE overlapped by some years in the late 1920s. In fact, Marshall took over both Hobhouse's chair in sociology at the LSE and the severely gendered theory about citizenship that Hobhouse proposed at the peak of the suffragist agitation in 1911.[96] Might the two men have sat in the heavy leather armchairs of the senior common room at the LSE exchanging the currency of intellectual debate and idly mentioning, from time to time, the (only) slightly disconcerting figures of their female relations? And perhaps Eileen Power, who had pretended to be a man in order to climb the Khyber Pass, and who had lately been occupied with researching women in medieval nunneries and complaining to the LSE administration about the unjust salaries paid to women staff, might have spied the men debating there and passed on, back to the truly gripping stories which engaged her of what brave, pragmatic, determined and compassionate women had actually done.

EIGHT

Deeds, not words: women reformers and healthcare

When Emmeline Pankhurst chose the famous slogan of the British Women's Social and Political Union (WSPU) in 1903, 'Deeds, not words', she was expressing the frustration suffrage campaigners felt at the unproductive political conversations that had been had for many years about whether women are sufficiently human to participate fully in the affairs of the male-run public world. 'Deeds, not words' was also the motto inscribed on the proscenium arch of a unique women's military hospital which opened in London in the spring of 1915. Healthcare is the main subject of this chapter: how women healthcare workers and reformers acted to enlarge and humanize the provision of health services; their scientific endeavours to understand and care for both physical and mental diseases; and the role the body played in their own struggles for emancipation.

This phrase 'deeds, not words' was a lot more than a slogan: it built on a thorough critique of masculine society, a critique that argued for an elision between both words and action and theory and practice in the effort to restructure social institutions and ideologies. Yet, what lingers in our historical memory is rather different: a crude mélange of images of indignant Edwardian ladies in beribboned hats squabbling among themselves and hurling bricks mindlessly through windows; emaciated suffragettes emerging from prison; and the repetitive complaints of men in authority about the inherent unreasonableness of women. As Louisa Garrett Anderson, daughter of Britain's first woman doctor, explained to the readers of the *British Medical Journal* in 1912, the reason why some women suffrage protesters decided to refuse food when imprisoned was completely understandable. The reason was 'political, not pathological', and the appropriate treatment was therefore not forced feeding but the granting of political rights.[1] Women doctors and prison reformers had especially close ties to movements for peace and citizenship rights. The issues they confronted are all embedded in the practice of welfare, and they were a pivotal part of women's collective attempts to transform the public policy landscape.

8.1: Marion Wallace-Dunlop, 1901

Marion Wallace-Dunlop, a British art nouveau sculptor and illustrator, joined the WSPU in 1908. The following summer she stencilled on the wall of St Stephen's Hall in the Palace of Westminster an extract from the Bill of Rights about the illegality of prosecuting people for claiming the right possessed by all subjects to petition the King. Imprisoned for this act, she decided to refuse food. Her complaint was that she was being treated as an ordinary criminal rather than a political prisoner. This classification made a huge difference to prisoners' conditions, since only 'First Division' (political) prisoners were allowed access to books and newspapers, letters and visits from family and friends.[2] Wallace-Dunlop was released after 91 hours of fasting but the idea of the hunger strike, which she introduced, caught on, and a few weeks later another three women arrested for disrupting a public meeting also refused food in prison. This time forced feeding was used: one of the three, Charlotte Marsh, was sentenced to two months' hard labour and force-fed by tube 139 times.[3]

Mahatma Gandhi met Wallace-Dunlop shortly after her release from prison and he noted that there was a 'great deal to learn from these ladies and their movement'.[4] Indeed, the suffragettes' example established the modern tradition of the hunger strike as a form of non-violent resistance to political control.[5] The practice of fasting as a form of political resistance was taken up by nationalists in India and Ireland, and then around the world.

It spread to the US, especially through the women's rights activist Alice Paul, who spent a few years studying in England, where she met the Pankhursts, joined the WSPU, was arrested, jailed, went on hunger strike and was herself forcibly fed. Returning to the US and founding the National Women's Party, Paul introduced in 1917 a method of non-violent civil disobedience designed to embarrass President Woodrow Wilson and his government (who were already fairly embarrassed by American women reformers, as we saw in Chapter Six).[6]

Suffragette militancy politicized women's bodies in a new, public way. A book written by an aristocratic suffragette called Lady Constance Lytton gives us a remarkable account of this form of torture. *Prisons and prisoners: Some personal experiences* (1914) was written with Lytton's left hand after she was half-paralysed by a stroke following her own prison treatment. She was born into the British aristocracy; her father was a diplomat, for 11 years the Viceroy of India, her mother a lady-in-waiting to Queen Victoria. Lytton's brother, the Earl of Lytton, was a member of the House of Lords; one of her sisters married the brother of Prime Minister Arthur Balfour. For her first 36 years, Constance Lytton lived the conventional version of an aristocratic daughter's life, receiving a limited education by governesses at home, acting as her mother's companion once her father had died, arranging flowers, polishing brasses and playing with dogs, although there were some saving graces, such as meeting Olive Schreiner on a trip with her mother to South Africa in 1892. (Schreiner would later dedicate her book *Woman and labour* to Lytton.) This life of enforced idleness changed when Lytton was left some money by a great-aunt. She chose to donate her inheritance to the revival of Morris dancing, a charitable act that brought her into direct contact with the suffragette movement through the Espérance Girls' Club, which had been founded by Emmeline Pethick-Lawrence and Mary Neal as a kind of Settlement for young women working in the London dress trade. In 1908 Pethick-Lawrence invited Lytton to join them on the annual Espérance summer holiday. At the 'Green Lady Hostel' in Littlehampton, the Club's holiday home, Lytton met the suffragette Kenney sisters, Annie and Jessie Kenney, the latter recently released from Holloway prison. Lytton was horrified by Jessie's account of her prison experiences, but not quite convinced about the need for militant tactics to gain the vote. She and Annie Kenney walked around the garden under dripping trees (it was a wet summer) and Lytton told Kenney that she considered class issues more important than issues relating to sex, to which Kenney replied that as a working-class woman she knew that the reverse was true.[7]

Lytton joined the WSPU in 1909. She was arrested twice but treated leniently because, she suspected, of her social connections. Thus she resolved a test case, rejoining the WSPU as Jane Warton, a seamstress, removing the initials from her underwear, having her hair cut short and buying a disguise, working on the principle she had observed during her first prison stays that ugly clothes and an 'unprepossessing' appearance attracted the worst treatment.[8] Her book, *Prisons and prisoners*, actually has two authors, Constance Lytton and Jane Warton. One is an elegant, upper-class woman wearing jewels and sophisticatedly coiffed hair, the other a no-nonsense woman with short hair, a dark hat, dark clothes and spectacles. Warton is Lytton's alter ego, an imaginative invention, a research strategy, like the disguises used by the women researchers who appear in Chapter Three. Lytton created her to make a point about the prejudiced, class-based practices of the criminal justice system.

8.2: Constance Lytton, 1908 and Jane Warton, 1910

Lytton/Warton took the train to Liverpool, selected some stones from a friend's garden, attended and spoke at a meeting outside the prison demanding the release of hunger strikers and proceeded to drop the stones over a hedge into the prison governor's garden. Arrested with two others, she was sentenced to two weeks in prison. On the fourth day of her refusing food the prison doctor came about six o'clock in the evening with five wardresses and the feeding apparatus. 'He urged me to take food voluntarily. I told him that was absolutely out of the question, that when our legislators ceased to resist enfranchising women then I should cease to resist taking food in prison.' Two wardresses took hold of her arms, one her head and one her feet. One helped to pour the food. 'The doctor leant on my knees as he stooped over my chest to get at my mouth, I shut my mouth and clenched my teeth ... The sense of being overpowered by more force than I could possibly resist was complete, but I resisted nothing except with my mouth.' The doctor plied her jaws open with a steel gag, breaking several teeth. Then he put a wide tube down her throat, causing her to choke and regurgitate the food that was poured down. As he left, the doctor slapped her cheek, 'not violently, but as it were, to express his contemptuous disapproval'. 'Then suddenly,' Lytton continued, 'I saw Jane Warton lying before me, and it seemed as if I were outside of her. She was the most despised, ignorant and helpless prisoner that I had seen. When she had served her time and was out of the prison, no one would believe anything she said, and the doctor when he had fed her by force and tortured her body, struck her on the cheek to show how he despised her! That was Jane Warton, and I had come to help her.'[9]

During one of Lytton/Warton's prison stays a fellow prisoner, the Welsh pacifist and suffragist Edith Mansell Moullin, gave her to read 'a wonderful book that had just come out' – Charlotte Perkins Gilman's *The man-made world*. 'I read it that night and found it all that she had said – a most remarkable book.'[10] Lytton was especially struck by the chapter on crime and punishment, which argues that all 'treatment' of criminals is retaliation, a punishment not at all effective in decreasing crime and which loses sight of crime's true causes: 'Everyone is a baby first, and a baby is not a criminal, unless we make it so. It never would be – in right conditions.' Moreover, such a system 'falls helpless' before the most far-reaching crimes: 'What of the crimes of poisoning a community with bad food; of defiling the water; of blackening the air; of stealing whole forests? What of the crimes of working little children; of building and renting tenements that produce crime and physical disease as well?'[11]

Other women took up the causes of child labour, housing conditions and environmental damage; Gilman's allegations about the retaliatory nature of the prison system were the cause célèbre of Britain's first woman inspector of prisons, Dr Mary Louisa Gordon. Gordon's book *Penal discipline*, published in 1922, outspokenly called the prison system 'a gigantic irrelevance', utterly failing in its aim of deterrence: 'If the system had a good effect on any prisoner, I failed to mark it … It appears to me not to belong to this time or civilisation at all.'[12] The whole system was 'a very expensive absurdity' whose true cost had never been estimated: people, expensively detained in prison, frequently went the round of other institutions as well – poor-houses, hospitals and asylums. But, most seriously, prisons create a criminal class, acting as a 'cradle and training ground' for the young criminal, and fostering that very recidivism they were supposed to prevent.[13] For Gordon, prisons were self-serving systems and their cardinal principle and sin was discipline. She wrote about the characteristics of women in prison: poor health, poverty, low self-esteem, substance abuse, self-harm; and she argued for the treatment of offenders to be based on science and the whole person rather than prejudice. Her case was built on the outrageously simple idea, borrowed from the methodological toolkit of other women social investigators, of talking to prisoners and asking them what would help them stay out of prison. This sometimes got an unexpected answer, such as from one woman who said she wanted to be sent to sea and live as a man. She didn't go to sea, but Gordon bought her a set of men's clothes and a train ticket for South Wales, where she got a job hewing coal, which seems to have done the trick.[14]

Photographs of Mary Gordon have proved elusive. She also left little information about her personal life. She was the eldest in a large Lancashire family; her father was a hide-and-tallow broker and her mother brought up 12 children. Gordon's family was opposed to her interest in medicine but she overcame this to become student number 171 at the London School of Medicine for Women (LSMW), the first medical school to train women doctors, which opened in 1874. Gordon's appointment in 1908 as 'His Majesty's Inspector of Prisons and Assistant Inspector of State and Certified Inebriate Reformatories' was probably one official response to the embarrassment caused by the imprisoned suffragettes, and it was a considerable responsibility. She had to inspect up to four times a year 47 institutions containing (in her first year) 40,195 female prisoners, supervise the training of women prison officers and manage 500 staff. In line with the government's general treatment of its female employees, it paid Gordon rather little – her maximum salary was below the minimum for male inspectors – and it didn't even give her an office. It also offered no special training for the work, so Gordon attached herself to a London prison and also visited women's prisons in France, the Netherlands and Belgium in an effort to base her practice on the best international evidence. In her first round of inspections she asked more questions 'than had been asked in the memory of official man'.[15] She was in many ways already well qualified for the job, given her background as a medical doctor, an ardent suffragist and friend of such activists as Constance Lytton and the Pankhursts, although about her suffragist connections she had to remain obediently quiet in her new post: 'I need not tell you that I have my work cut out, being a known suffragette and also a civil servant with a closed mouth,' she wrote to Pethick-Lawrence. 'I am closely watched and have to do my duty with all the tact I can get together.'[16] The supply of tact nearly ran out when Scotland Yard's special branch raided the headquarters of the WSPU on 23 May 1914, uncovering a file of Gordon's correspondence that contained evidence of her moral and financial support for the WSPU. When the Home Office asked her to disassociate herself formally from the militants, she refused on the grounds that the WSPU was not an illegal organization. There were calls for her dismissal, but government attention was distracted by the beginning of the war. When Gordon applied in June 1916 for paid leave to go to Macedonia with the Scottish Women's Hospitals, the Home Office readily granted permission, noting unkindly, 'she will not be missed'.[17]

Mary Gordon did succeed in making some significant changes in prison conditions, for instance, improving the lighting and ventilation of cells, replacing opaque with clear glass in windows and introducing notebooks and occupational training. She regarded informing prisoners about their rights and ensuring that they had as many comforts as possible as a key part of her job. But the radical philosophy of her *Penal discipline* was much too far ahead of its time to catch on; even among criminologists today, with whom her approach must resonate, there is widespread ignorance of the work she did. Like many of the forgotten women in this book, she was multi-talented, with diverse interests and achievements. Her novel *A jury of the virtuous* was published under the pseudonym 'Patrick Hood' in 1907.[18] It features a young man committed to prison for forgery whose subsequent attempts at rehabilitation prove Gordon's criminological point, that prisons confirm rather than cure criminality. Virginia Woolf, who didn't like her much, called her 'The hermaphrodite' because of her somewhat masculine appearance.[19] Women were the focus of Gordon's personal as well as her professional life. She wrote a semi-documentary account, *Chase of the wild goose: The story of Lady Eleanor Butler and Miss Sarah Ponsonby, known as the Ladies of Llangollen*, about two young women who in the late 18th century ran away from their families and set up home together for 50 years in a Welsh valley. Parts of this book echo Virginia Woolf's own hermaphroditic novel, *Orlando*, and Gordon herself wrote an unpublished novel about Orlando's son. *Chase of the wild goose* was dedicated to Gordon's friend, the psychotherapist and writer Emma Jung, wife of Carl Jung. Gordon's panoptic life extended to a Jungian analysis in 1920, and she studied analytical psychology with the Jungs in Switzerland.[20]

Mary Gordon had a counterpart in the US, Katharine Bement Davis, a woman of almost exactly the same age and equally manifold interests, who made similarly startling pronouncements about the imprisonment of women. The two women knew each other; they shared the platform at a six-week conference convened in New York at the end of the First World War concerned with women's medical work and women's health. Katharine Bement Davis's qualification for being involved in the Conference of Women Physicians was her role as secretary of the Bureau of Social Hygiene, which was funded by the Rockefeller

Foundation and was where much of her work concerning questions of women's physical and mental health was done. She wasn't a doctor by training; she had learnt sanitary science from Ellen Swallow Richards

8.3: Katharine Bement Davis, 1915

at Wellesley College. At the World's Columbian Exposition in 1893 Davis had put Richards' principles of good sanitation to work in designing a 'workingman's model home', which demonstrated that a family of five could live on $500 a year. She went on to train as an economist and was the first woman to gain a PhD in economics (in 1900) from that hotbed of intellectual feminism: the University of Chicago. Her photograph shows a slightly rotund woman, with piercing eyes, in a comfortably middle-class floral setting. Davis had a keen statistical mind and was methodologically inventive: her PhD on the causes affecting standards of living and wages used statistics, data from account books and other public records, interviews and participant observation to study economic life in Bohemia and Austria and among Chicago immigrants. A decade later, when the sociologist W. I. Thomas deployed a similar approach in his landmark study of *The Polish peasant in Europe and America*, his methodology, not hers, was hailed as original.[21] Davis had headed the College Settlement house in Philadelphia, where she worked with the civil rights sociologist W. E. B. DuBois, and she taught at Hull-House, where there was much interest in prison reform, especially from Edith Abbott, Jane Addams, Sophonisba Breckinridge, Florence Kelley and Julia Lathrop, who all wrote about prisons, crime, justice and the legal system.[22]

When a new reformatory for women was set up in Bedford Hills, New York in 1901 and a sociologically minded woman was needed to run it, Davis was an obvious choice. She turned the New York State Reformatory for Women into 'the most scientific institution of its kind in the world'.[23] Her interest was, like Gordon's, in looking closely at the ways in which the criminal justice system treated women. What account did the system and its institutions take of the backgrounds and needs of the women? Did the system stop women offenders offending? What evidence was there regarding the relative contributions of the environment and heredity? How could prisons become more humane institutions? Bedford Hills was an institution for girls and women aged 16 to 30 who were serving short sentences for minor offences. They were dressed uncomfortably in heavy ticking and shoes with no right or left; Davis got rid of both these insults. She supervised the erection and landscaping of new prison buildings on the cottage system, with no more than 28 inmates each; the cottages had gardens and kitchens equipped with good linen and china, so the women could cook and eat together, and they helped with the construction of all this, led by Davis, who learnt how to mix concrete and make foundations, paths and roads. 'Journalists, judges, and other visitors often marveled at the sight of women grading an embankment or draining a swamp.'[24] There were academic classes in basic skills, geography, history and current events, and Davis taught the women singing. On the vocational front, she started classes in cooking, sewing, hat-making, chair-caning, book-binding, painting, carpentry, masonry, road-building, ice-harvesting and farming. There was a working farm where sausages were made from the pigs, and arithmetic was taught using data from prison expenditure and supply books; there were lectures on law and democracy.

Davis, like Gordon, applied her penal philosophy to all prisoners, irrespective of gender. But her innovative research was devoted mainly to women 'criminals', who had long been subject to a litany of unevidenced claims about 'feeblemindedness'. The Italian criminologist Cesare Lombroso's widely acclaimed and deeply misogynist theories that criminals could be recognized by physical aspects of their heads and bodies stood out as particularly in need of attention. Davis hired two psychologists to study women inmates at Bedford Hills. Their research showed that the environment, especially 'crowded and unsanitary conditions', lack of education, 'unjust economic conditions' and the low moral standard of city men helped to bring women into the criminal justice system. Furthermore, Davis's study of 590 women sent to Bedford Hills on prostitution charges demonstrated that 'punishment' hardly deterred, since three-fifths of the women had a previous offence. On the basis of this research and her experience running the Reformatory, Davis developed 'a plan of rational treatment for women offenders'. She published her plan in the *Journal of the American Institute of Criminal Law and Criminology* in 1913.[25] A central element in it was a special expert state commission that would decide, prior to sentencing, the care of each female 'delinquent'. Among the people who were impressed by Davis' rational plan was John D. Rockefeller, who bought 71 acres of land adjacent to the Reformatory and in 1911 set up on it a Bureau of Social Hygiene, persuading Davis to become its director. She left the Bureau in 1914 for a temporary spell as Commissioner of Corrections for New York City, the first woman to hold such a post. One of her initiatives there was to use the technique of covert research in deploying two staff members to infiltrate New York's infamous prison 'The Tombs' in order to document the extent of drug-dealing, alcohol-smuggling and corruption.[26] Davis returned to the Bureau of Social Hygiene in 1918 and it was here that she conducted her magnificently original and thoroughly forgotten study of women's sex lives (for which see Chapter Ten).

Suffragette militancy, and political reaction to it, focused the minds of those with a more general interest in the functioning (or malfunctioning) of the criminal justice system. Edith Mansell Moullin, who had given Constance Lytton *The man-made world* to read in prison, was married to Charles Mansell Moullin, a surgeon and supporter of women's suffrage – it was he who operated (unsuccessfully) on Emily Wilding Davison after she fell under the King's horse.[27] But most medical doctors opposed women's suffrage, and most did not speak out against the treatment of women prisoners.[28] The web of patriarchal control was tightly woven, with the Royal College of Physicians, the King, and the prime minister forming a closed alliance against the suffragettes and in favour of forced feeding. Three doctors, Charles Mansell Moullin among them, examined the evidence about the consequences of this 'treatment'. Their 'Preliminary report on the forcible feeding of suffrage prisoners', published in the *British Medical Journal* in August 1912, looked at the experiences of 102 suffragette prisoners, 90 of whom had been force-fed. Prisoners suffered bruising through being held down by force, flung on the floor and tied to chairs and iron bedsteads; injuries to the nose and throat were common; most vomited; all had stomach cramps; many developed anaemia; sometimes food entered the larynx, causing pneumonia; the effect on the nervous system was always severe. It was hard to believe, said the authors of the report, that *any* doctor could support 'this form of prison torture'.[29]

The first author of the *BMJ* report was a woman doctor called Agnes Savill. One of the early Scottish medical women graduates, Savill specialized in dermatology and a subject known at the time as 'electro-therapeutics'. She was the author of a renowned volume on the life of Alexander the Great, an expert on the relationship between music and health and a pioneer researcher in the field of gas gangrene, 'the most terrible of all the horrors connected

8.4: Agnes Savill, 1907

with war which come under the notice of the surgeon'.[30] Savill did her gas gangrene research at one of many hospitals set up and staffed by women in Europe and Russia during the First World War. Flora Murray and Louisa Garrett Anderson, a formidably competent couple, established the first of these in a Parisian hotel in September 1914. The photograph opposite shows them with some of their colleagues outside the hospital.

Flora Murray was born in Scotland and educated in London and Germany; she attended the LSMW in 1907, went on to work in a large Scottish asylum and London hospitals for women and children, joined the WSPU and helped to look after suffragettes after they had been force-fed in prison. It was she who in 1909 stood surety for the first hunger striker, Marion Wallace-Dunlop. Murray's partner, Louisa Garrett Anderson, was the daughter of Elizabeth Garrett Anderson, a woman whose story is central to the mid-Victorian women's movement and whose famously determined struggle to become a doctor placed her as the first

8.5: Flora Murray (front row, second on right) and Louisa Garrett Anderson (front row, first on right), with colleagues outside the Hôtel Claridge, 1914

woman on the Medical Register in 1865. Louisa, herself a militant suffragette, arrived at the LSMW in 1892. Murray and Anderson found each other through the suffrage campaign. Their intimate companionship, 'effectively a marriage' marked by identical diamond rings, lasted until Murray's death in 1923; the gravestone in the churchyard near where they lived in Buckinghamshire bears the epitaph 'We were gloriously happy'.[31]

Perhaps it is strange to remember glorious happiness as a feature of these war-torn times, but the collective energy with which women professionals responded to the suddenly enlarged opportunities presented by the war was truly invigorating. Eight days after Britain joined the war, Murray and Anderson called at the French embassy in London and laid before one of its secretaries in an airless room inhabited by stale cigar smoke their plan to raise and equip a surgical unit to treat wounded soldiers in France. The French, knowing they lacked sufficient doctors and surgeons, agreed, and a month later, having raised all the necessary money and equipment, Murray and Anderson left Victoria station for France amid much bustle and handshaking, all of which was quietly observed by Louisa's mother in her last public appearance: had she not been in her late 70s, admitted

Elizabeth Garrett Anderson, she would have been on that train, too.[32] Murray's book about their war experiences, *Women as army surgeons*, is dedicated to Louisa Garrett Anderson and illustrated with riveting images, for instance, one of two white-coated women 'Searching for protozoa in the laboratory', and another, 'The Doctor-in-Charge sees men in her office'. This depicts Murray in her severe army clothes, studiously looking down, pen in hand, on a desk full of papers while three men await her attention. The men's blank faces are painted white by the light filtering through the slats of a window-blind behind Murray. The image's conscious artistry – the woman busy and in control, the men passive and uncertain – captures the tenor of the experiences described in the book.[33]

The paint on the walls of the Hôtel Claridge near the Champs-Élysées was scarcely dry when the contingent of women doctors arrived to take over its mirrored and chandeliered spaces. The ground-floor saloons became wards, the ladies' cloakroom an operating theatre and the grill-room a mortuary. A few weeks later Murray and Anderson were asked by the French to expand into a second hospital in Wimereux, near Boulogne. The Château Mauricien, built by an Englishman, had an English cooking range, a leaking roof and an obsolete drainage system.

8.6: Flora Murray at her desk in the Endell Street Hospital, 1915

There was an iconic moment when Anderson recognized one of the Wimereux hospital patients, an ex-policeman who had once arrested her for suffragette activities in Whitehall; he said, 'I wouldn't have mentioned it, Miss … We'll let bygones be bygones.'[34] Among the hospital's many visitors were two more women doctors, Elsie Inglis and Frances Ivens, who were on their way to set up another hospital in Royaumont Abbey, a 13th-century Cistercian monastery on the edge of the forest of Chantilly some 25 miles north of Paris. This was where Agnes Savill worked on the problem of gas gangrene. It was the brainchild of Elsie Inglis, who had founded the Edinburgh Medical College for Women. Inglis, born at the foot of the Himalayas to an East India Company family, and inspired to take up medicine by Elizabeth Garrett Anderson, was 'small and ramrod straight … her wispy hair, the colour of an autumn leaf … her eyes … the blue grey of an autumn bonfire that seems to be dying yet may at any moment crackle into blazing, all-consuming life'.[35] The hair is neatly tucked in beneath the hat with the tartan ribbon that features in the most-used photograph of Inglis. Through her position as secretary to the Scottish Federation of Women Suffrage Societies, she set up an organization called the Scottish Women's Hospitals. Offered the services of Inglis and her women colleagues early in the war, the British War Office responded with the memorable rebuff, 'My good lady, go home and sit still'. This was why Murray and Anderson had gone straight to the French with their proposal.[36] Inglis, declining to sit still, led the fund-raising for the Scottish Women's Hospitals, which went on to establish 14 field hospitals in Belgium, Corsica, France, Malta, Russia, Salonika and Serbia, employing more than 1,000 women as doctors, nurses, ambulance drivers, cooks and orderlies.

The French Red Cross's offering in France, Royaumont Abbey, had beautiful cloisters,

8.7: Elsie Inglis, 1918

vaulted halls and mullioned rose-coloured windows which cast a marvellous jewelled light, but it had been uninhabited for a decade and was impractically large, dusty and damp. One is impressed by the amount of DIY and housework that these women surgeons had to do before they could provide any medical care. It wasn't a building that gave itself easily to hospital work, as is clear in the photograph of neatly uniformed women tending to men in a vast ecclesiastical space. The writer Cicely Hamilton, who volunteered as a clerk and worked at Royaumont for two and a half years, remembered sleeping in a monk's moist cell with bats flying about and nightingales singing outside.[37] They drank coffee and wine out of the same enamel mugs to save washing up, recalled Louisa Martindale, another volunteer doctor.[38] This was a tight network of women doctors who lived and worked closely together, many trained at the LSMW, and all forced to finish their medical education abroad because of the restricted opportunities for women medical students at home. The British network was interwoven with networks in the US, where women doctors set up the first hospitals for women and children in the late 1850s and early 1860s.

At Royaumont Abbey, Agnes Savill was in charge of the X-ray and electro-therapy departments. The X-ray room was a cupboard, and X-rays had to be developed with a fish-kettle filled with water and a tiny and intermittent electricity supply.[39] No lesser person than Marie Curie advised on the installation of the X-ray equipment at Royaumont, and it was famous for a fully equipped mobile X-ray car that had been specially manufactured by Austins. The hospital received the wounded from the Western Front, who arrived by train at a station 12km away and were transported by Royaumont 'chauffeuses'. In the five years between 1914 and 1919, the Médicin-Chef, Frances Ivens, Agnes Savill and their team treated nearly 11,000 patients. During the battle of the Somme, Royaumont's women surgeons and doctors worked for eight days with only 16 hours' sleep, operating when necessary by candlelight. What was particularly pioneering about the hospital's treatment of gas gangrene was the close cooperation between radiologists, bacteriologists and surgeons, and the high standards of hygiene that led to low rates of infection and amputation.[40] Royaumont had the

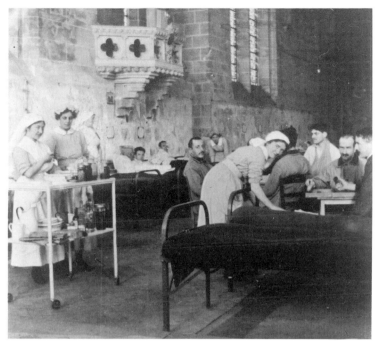

8.8: A ward in Royaumont Hospital, France, c. 1915

lowest amputation rate and the lowest mortality of all units on the Western Front. Wounded soldiers soon asked to be treated there, and military authorities sent it the most severe cases.[41] Once the staff had observed that patients accommodated in the open cloisters for want of space when the hospital was busy recovered more quickly, they also implemented a new, open-air wound treatment.[42]

Winston Churchill's admiration for this work generated one of his falsest prophecies, that Elsie Inglis and her staff would 'shine in history'.[43] On the contrary, their achievements have largely disappeared, and they don't feature at all in the official history of the war. Savill's reports, which she wrote with Frances Ivens, on the use of X-rays in gas gangrene were largely ignored by the medical establishment even at the time. The predominant characterization of these women medical pioneers was as patriotic, self-sacrificial figures – many reports even referred to them as nurses.[44]

One memorial to women doctors' war work was belatedly erected in 2008, in Endell Street, in the heart of London's Covent Garden. It marks the British War Office's final recognition that the women *were* doing something useful. Sir Alfred Keogh, director-general of the Army Medical Services, was eventually impressed by Murray and Anderson's successes in France and he gave them an old workhouse in St Giles, Bloomsbury, 'grey and sombre-looking', to run as a military hospital.[45] This was another building hardly fit for purpose, crammed with old furniture and apparatus for restraining the insane. The Endell Street Hospital opened in May 1915 with 17 wards containing 573 beds. Murray was the 'Doctor-in-Charge' and Anderson chief surgeon, although the War Office obstinately refused them any official rank (as it did for the staff of Royaumont). The Endell Street Hospital carried out 7,000 major operations and treated 26,000 patients, some suffering from illnesses that had nothing to do with the war (for instance, many victims of the 1918–19 influenza epidemic). It was particularly famous for the work of Mrs Banks, a forgotten medical artiste, who made magnificent splints, abdominal belts and other appliances out of papier mâché.[46] Here also Anderson studied and wrote up, together with pathologist Helen Chambers, a new method of treating septic wounds with bismuth-idoform-paraffin paste. Wounded men thus treated got better more quickly and none developed the terrifying gas gangrene or tetanus.[47] This attention to research and extending the evidence base of medicine in such trying circumstances was a feat to be marvelled at.

Endell Street and the two French hospitals that preceded it were run on rather different lines from other hospitals. In her autobiography the pacifist writer Evelyn Sharp, who visited Murray and Anderson's Wimereux venture, wrote penetratingly: 'something in the special understanding shown by the staff of the psychology of their patients seemed to accentuate the bitter irony of our civilization, which first compels men to tear one another to pieces like wild beasts for no personal reason, and then applies all its arts to patching them up in order to let them do it all over again … when the patching is done by women the ironic tragedy of the whole thing seems more evident'.[48] Murray explained that their patients were never operated on without being told exactly what was going to happen, and the surgeon always went to see them afterwards to discuss their surgery (both practices apparently being rare at the time). The hospital in Endell Street had flowers in the wards and the beds were covered with scarlet and blue blankets.

The style of medicine these women doctors practised was effective, scientific, caring and research-based. In that sense they established the basic architecture of welfare state health services. Dr Vera Scantlebury Brown, who worked at Endell Street, took the principles of this regime home with her to her native Australia, where she became the first woman to head a government department in the State of Victoria in 1926. Brown established there the universal structure of maternal and child health services which still exists today.[49] She was familiar with women's health work in another setting, New Zealand, whose Plunket Society, founded in 1907 originally as the Society for Promoting the Health of Women and Children, was run and staffed by women. Within a few years, its system of maternal and child health services had brought New Zealand's infant mortality rate down to half that prevailing in the UK or the US.[50] There were other scientific advances as a result of the women doctors' war work. For example, pathologist Helen Chambers pioneered radiotherapy treatment for cancer of the cervix, and Louisa Martindale worked on radium therapy for ovarian, uterine and breast cancer. Both Chambers and Martindale were prime movers in founding the Marie Curie Hospital in Hampstead, London (now the Marie Curie Hospice) in 1929, and they were unusual in conducting long-term follow-ups of their patients, eventually producing epidemiological data on 13,800 cases.[51]

Women doctors with a scientific eye as good as (or better than) any man's instigated practices that reduced mortality and improved health. The effects on women and families of incessant childbearing were obvious to anyone who had any contact with the poor: Settlement social science, feminist reformism and medical women's commitment to improving women's health coalesced to focus the spotlight on the great evil of maternal mortality. Deaths of women associated with pregnancy and childbirth were the exception to the great international decline in mortality that occurred between the end of the 19th century and the mid-1930s. General death rates, and the deaths of infants, all fell substantially, but maternal deaths scarcely shifted at all: in 1867, 1898 and 1934 alike, some four or five in every 1,000 childbearing women died of pregnancy or childbirth.[52] Sylvia Pankhurst, Emmeline Pankhurst's daughter, wrote a suitably polemical book called *Save the mothers* in 1930, in which she called the heavy loss of mothers in childbirth – some 39,000 women a year in England and Wales alone – 'as grievous an injury' to women as any other aspect of their political and social subjection, and one that should command 'the attention of the entire civilized world'.[53] The subject did command much attention from the first woman adviser at the Board of Education, Dr Janet Campbell, another graduate of the LSMW. Appointed in 1907, her report for the Carnegie UK trust in 1917 on the physical welfare of mothers and children, and her later reports on this and the protection of motherhood, provided facts and arguments that fuelled critical administrative reforms in the maternity services.[54]

Parenthood shouldn't be fatal in any welfare-oriented society, and most of all it should be a free choice. Aletta Jacobs, the first female Dutch physician, has flitted in and out of this book as a prominent peace campaigner, international conference attender and translator of key texts by Charlotte Perkins Gilman and Olive Schreiner. But in medical history her main claim to fame is that she started what was probably the first birth control clinic in the industrializing West, in the early 1880s, over 30 years before the much better-known Margaret Sanger and Marie Stopes got round to it. Jacobs' biography illustrates many of the key themes of this book: women's struggles to be accepted as citizens; the radicalizing nature of their contacts with the difficult lives of ordinary people; their enmeshment in international networks of like-minded crusading people; their understanding that *practices* of welfare mean more than *theories* about it.

She was one of 11 children, born to a Jewish family in a small Dutch village in 1854, and introduced to the medical life by her father, a country doctor.[55] Aletta and her sister Charlotte were the first female students at the University of Groningen in 1871, having got special permission from the Minister of Education to study there. Aletta got her medical degree in 1878, opening a small practice in central Amsterdam where she offered free care to poor women and children; if they were too sick to come to the clinic, she went to see them in their homes. Soon she found herself just as interested in her patients' lives as in their illnesses. She wrote a book for them in 1899 explaining their anatomy and reproductive system, an early version of many later feminist manuals.[56] There were many obstacles to be overcome in the early years

8.9: Aletta Jacobs, c. 1880

of her practice. One of them was that Kalverstraat, the main shopping street near her practice, was off-limits for women between noon and 4pm, because at these times men would enter and leave the Stock Exchange and any woman seen sauntering along the street was assumed to be a prostitute. Jacobs' habit of disregarding social norms embraced spreading the fashion for ice-skating among Amsterdam women (for whom it was considered improper), and bicycling stunts around Europe as a member of the International Cyclists' Association.

Hearing that women in Britain were struggling in their efforts to train as doctors, Jacobs went to see for herself in 1879. In London she was warmly greeted by her British counterpart, Elizabeth Garrett Anderson, and admired her new hospital in the Marylebone Road. During the four months of her stay, Jacobs attended Fabian Society meetings and many talks about the suffrage, which she found a great inspiration. She met many other reformers, such as Millicent Fawcett, and the birth control campaigners Annie Besant and Charles Bradlaugh. Many of Dr Jacobs' patients pleaded with her for some method of preventing unwanted pregnancy. She had no sensible solution to offer until she read an article in a medical journal in 1882 written by a

Dr Mensinga from Flensburg in Germany, who had developed, with the aid of a local instrument-maker, a rubber cap that fitted over the cervix. He had tried it in 12 women and it appeared to be effective. Jacobs immediately wrote to Mensinga and he sent her some specimens. She worked further on the design of these, perfecting what became known universally as 'the Dutch cap'. This she offered to some of the 'neediest' women in her practice, on condition that they let her monitor their health for some months to ensure that the devices did no harm. All seemed fine.

When Jacobs went public with the news that she could now offer safe, free contraception, and was effectively opening the world's first contraceptive clinic in 1882, she 'incurred the wrath of the entire medical establishment', which accused her of promoting abortion and adultery and of personally leading an immoral life.[57] Wandering around the beautiful green Vondelpark in Amsterdam, she wondered if she might truly be doing something dreadful; yet she knew how much hypocrisy surrounded her – how many men who spoke out against her publicly, privately sent their wives to secure her help. And some of the world *was* listening; for example, Margaret Sanger and Marie Stopes both travelled to the Netherlands to see her and examine the new invention. As to her personally immoral life, Jacobs had chastely married a radical MP, Carel Victor Gerritsen, in 1892. Their commitment to an equal relationship was probably cause for extra local scandal: Jacobs didn't change her name, and she and Gerritsen lived in two separate apartments in the same house (with a communal dining room and parlour). Most sadly for this woman who did so much for mothers, their only child died shortly after birth in 1893: 'But looking back, despite all the sorrow,' reminisced Jacobs, 'I still count myself lucky that I know how it feels to be a mother, that I have held my child in my arms, even though it was for but one day'.[58]

Jacobs knew more about the dangers of unchaste sexual liaisons than most of those who accused her of these. In her own clinic in Amsterdam, as the only woman doctor in the country, she was regularly consulted by prostitutes 'about diseases that I never even knew existed'. On her visit to London in 1880 the public health scientist and founder of the Malthusian League, Charles Drysdale, took her to one of the institutions where women suspected of prostitution were taken to be examined: 'I simply could not understand how a doctor could put himself in the position of judging whether these social outcasts should be allowed to continue their grim profession,' she reflected. When she spoke in 1909 at an international medical conference on prostitution, taking the line that it would be best prevented altogether, the audience dismissed her as just another hysterical woman.[59]

Aletta Jacobs' attendance at the ICW meeting in London in 1899 galvanized her into throwing herself into the suffrage struggle. She took on the presidency of the main Dutch suffrage organization and devoted more and more time to 'the cause'. In 1911–12 she went on a most extraordinary voyage throughout the Eastern hemisphere with the American suffragist and pacifist Carrie Chapman Catt: these two women, who had met at the IWSA Congress in Berlin in 1904, had both lost their husbands to illness in 1905. Together they circumnavigated the globe, visiting South Africa, the Middle East, the Philippines, Ceylon, the Dutch East Indies, Burma, China and Japan. Jacobs returned home via Russia and Catt went back to the US through Hawaii. The object of their journey was to find out about the position of women and spread the message of women's rights. In China, they were carried in sedan chairs to the only European hotel in Canton, and they held a suffrage meeting in the Palace Hotel in Shanghai. In South Africa, where they took a 1,700-mile journey into the interior, Jacobs went to see Olive Schreiner, while Catt took the suffrage meeting. Jacobs addressed women's meetings on prostitution in six South African cities. They took care to dress well, in their best velvet or satin dresses, even in the sweltering weather. In India they encountered Beatrice and Sidney Webb, and they argued with Beatrice about her signing of the anti-suffrage petition. At the end of it all, they totted it up: they had made suffrage speeches on four continents and on the ships of three oceans to audiences including 'Christian and Jew, Mohammedan, Hindu, Parsee, Buddhist, Confucian and Shinto'. 'I am tired,' commented Catt.[60] Jacobs' two-volume compendium of 700 travel letters about their experiences remains untranslated from its original Dutch and thus is a source very little used by scholars – and what a valuable source of information about all sorts of matters it must be.

Our next forgotten woman in the healthcare movement is a British woman, Annie McCall, the centre-piece of five children and the inventor of modern antenatal care. She was born in Manchester in 1859. Her father, an insurance agent, died of tuberculosis when Annie was four; her mother, a close friend of Elizabeth Garrett Anderson, took all the children to Germany to extend their education. McCall went to the LSMW in 1880, where she specialized in midwifery, completing her medical education in Bern and learning obstetrics in Vienna. Back in England, she worked first in South London, with a prison reformer called Susanna Meredith, who ran a rather industrial-scale enterprise for released women prisoners known as 'The Mission to Women' in the Wandsworth Road.[61] But McCall's real ambition was to care for childbearing women. In 1887 she initiated in her own home in Clapham what later became the Clapham Maternity Hospital. This was the third of 21 British hospitals opened and staffed by medical women between 1872 and 1929 and the first maternity hospital founded, staffed and funded entirely by women. Sixteen of these 21 hospitals, including McCall's, were still in existence at the start of the NHS in 1948 and thus became part of it.[62]

Surviving photographs of McCall depict a severe, dark-suited woman with a white shirt and tie, and grey hair pulled back from an unsmiling face: this was almost a studied version, a caricature, of a male doctor. Her rather autocratic personality was softened by the two women who supported her, Marion Ritchie, her cousin and a highly efficient hospital administrator, and Constance Watney, matron of the hospital for a time and McCall's 'close companion and business adviser'.[63] The hospital in Clapham was financed by private donations, the sale of headgear made by McCall's mother and McCall's own temperance lecture fees – she was a strong advocate of temperance, and neither alcohol nor smoking was allowed on hospital premises. Patients were charged five shillings, which went into a fund out of which an assistant was paid a guinea a week to help McCall teach midwifery pupils.

The hospital was open to all pregnant women, including the unmarried, breaking another convention of the time. Like other hospitals started by women, there was a dual motive:

to provide much-needed care and to enlarge opportunities for women medical students and doctors.

Annie McCall took both a holistic and a scientific view of maternity care. Her regime depended on regular antenatal supervision of women's health and health advice. She saw the main causes of maternal death as not enough trained maternity nurses; too

8.10: Annie McCall

much interference in labour (particularly too many internal examinations, increasing the risk of infection); and a lack of common-sense hygiene, feeding and exercise (she recommended a mostly vegan diet and three miles' walking daily). 'Everything must be done to allow the general function to proceed unimpeded,' she declared vigorously.[64] In her hospital there was scrupulous attention to hygiene: the labour room beds were fitted with removable wooden slats for easy cleaning, the hospital had its own laundry and each patient had her own numbered crockery and utensils to prevent cross-infection. Like the women doctors of Endell Street and the French military hospitals, McCall considered 'true friendliness' an essential element of effective care. When the hospital moved to a purpose-built site in 1915, the 12 wards had no more than four beds each, with colourful quilts and screens for privacy.

McCall and her colleagues took up another reforming cause which had much occupied Elizabeth Garrett Anderson, the low status of 'practical midwifery', which was not even regarded as worth including in medical education. McCall set up the first midwifery school run by women at a time when midwives were still unregistered and midwifery was unrecognized as a profession.

The Clapham School of Midwifery, which opened in 1887, trained midwives, monthly nurses and doctors in midwifery, and set its own examinations, which were marked by external women doctors. Many students came from Christian missions abroad: the first Nigerian arrived in 1912. 'It is character, not colour, that counts,' proclaimed McCall.[65] Students remembered her giving lectures in her garden in Clapham Road with its mulberry tree, the berries ripening and falling all around them – they were invited to gather these when the lecture was over. A list of Clapham Midwifery School students from 1874 to 1927 includes many prominent names in the women doctors' network of this period, and others from overlapping networks, for example, the painter, suffragist and pacifist, Mary Sargant Florence, who was a member of the committee for The Hague Congress in 1915 which produced the Women's International League for Peace and Freedom (WILPF).[66]

Annie McCall's achievements are completely absent from standard narratives of the origins of pregnancy care.[67] They were scientifically impressive. Clapham Maternity Hospital's overall maternal death rate was low in the 1890s at 1.65 per 1,000, less than half the national figure. In the first 1,205 cases, from October 1885 to October 1889, there were no maternal deaths, only four cases of septic infection (all the mothers recovered) and a forceps rate of 4%, a mere fraction of the 50–70% rate recorded in many deliveries managed by male doctors fond of the new fashion for using instruments.[68] Another measure of McCall's success was that when the Royal Colleges of Physicians and Surgeons finally decided that obstetrics and gynaecology were important and there ought to be a special diploma for qualified doctors, they wrote to her for advice.[69]

McCall sought out the best teachers in Europe and at home, and was especially fond of the work of Dr Alice Stockham, a Chicago obstetrician and gynaecologist, the fifth woman to qualify as a doctor in the US, a friend of Tolstoy and the British sex reformer Havelock Ellis, a promoter of dress reform, birth control, natural childbirth and some strange ideas about the importance of non-orgasmic sex. It was probably Stockham's *Tokology: A book for every woman*, published in 1886, and remarkable for its advocacy of practices taken up decades later by the feminist midwifery movement, that most interested Annie McCall.[70] She wrote her own advice manual for women, *What to do to have a healthy baby*, which was given to all the women who came to her hospital. Did McCall and Stockham actually meet? The trail runs cold, although Stockham, a much-travelled woman, does appear on passenger lists as visiting Britain in the 1890s.

Dr Alice Stockham would have been familiar with the work of the American women Settlement sociologists. Women reformers in continental Europe and across the Atlantic ocean had many of the same thoughts as their British colleagues about providing accessible and effective healthcare. In 1892 Lillian Wald, founder of the Henry Street Settlement in New York, was a young woman of 26 who wasn't sure what she wanted to do with her life. As a student at the Woman's Medical College in New York, and already a trained nurse, she underwent 'a baptism of fire' when teaching a weekly home nursing class to immigrant women on Manhattan's Lower East Side. A little girl led her from the school-room to a filthy rear tenement, housing a family of seven and several boarders in two rooms, where her sick mother lay on a 'wretched, unclean bed, soiled with a hemorrhage two days old'. After that encounter, Wald never returned to the Medical College. 'To my inexperience,' she wrote, 'it seemed certain that conditions such as these were allowed because people did not *know*, and for me there was a challenge to know and to tell.'[71]

8.11: Lillian Wald

Together with a fellow student, Mary Brewster, Lillian Wald set up a service of home-visiting nurses; this moved into a red-brick Georgian house in Henry Street in 1895, after which it was known as the Henry Street Settlement. 'We were to live in the neighborhood as nurses,' she said, 'identify ourselves with it socially, and, in brief, contribute to it our citizenship.'[72] The principles of their service were reciprocity – nurses and patients should know and respect one another; patients should be able to call on the nurses' help directly; the nurses should be independent of any other medical, religious or philanthropic institution; they should provide subsidized or free care. A flavour of their multifarious work is given in an account Wald wrote of a typical day's work for their wealthy sponsor, Jacob Schiff, in the summer of 1893:

> My first call was to the Goldberg baby whose pulse and improved condition had been maintained after our last night's care. After taking the temperature, washing and dressing the child, I called on the doctor who had been summoned before, told him of the family's tribulations and he offered not to charge them for the visit. Then I took Hattie Isaacs, the consumptive, a big bunch of flowers and while she slept I cleaned out the window of medicine bottles. Then I bathed her, and the poor girl had been so long without this attention that it took me nearly two hours to get her skin clean ... I made the bed, cooked a light breakfast of eggs and milk which I had brought with me ... Next, inspecting some houses on Hester Street, I found water closets which needed chloride of lime ... In one room, I found a child with running ears, which I syringed, showing the mother how to do it ... In another room there was a child with 'summer complaint' to whom I gave bismuth and tickets for a sea-side excursion. After luncheon I saw the O'Briens and took the little one, with whooping cough, to play in the back of our yard. On the next floor, the Costria baby had a sore mouth for which I gave the mother borax and honey and little cloths to keep it clean.[73]

This panoply of duties brings healthcare, welfare, education, nutrition, sanitation and simple human kindness together in a seamless web of service. Lillian Wald coined the term 'public health nurse' to stress the nurse's contribution to 'the civic culture' and to the broad struggle for effective and socially equitable health and welfare services. This was a 'new paradigm' for nursing, establishing it as political praxis.[74]

Like Annie McCall and others, Wald and Brewster monitored the outcome of their work carefully. In 1914, for example, the staff of Henry Street cared for 3,535 cases of pneumonia, achieving a mortality rate of 8.5%. This compared healthily with the record of four large New York hospitals, which reported 1,612 cases and a mortality rate of 31.2%.[75] After a while, they decided to focus on the problem of children excluded from school because of illness. So many children were being sent home that the Department of Education was accusing the Department of Health of emptying all the schoolrooms. Selecting four schools that had the greatest number of medical exclusions, Wald and her Henry Street colleagues arranged for one of their nurses, equipped only with 'the Settlement bag', to see all the children thought to need medical attention. Minor conditions were treated there and then, and in more serious cases the nurse visited the homes, taking children personally to the local dispensary for medicine if necessary. After one month's trial in 1902, they showed that it was possible 'to reverse the object of medical inspection from excluding the children from school to keeping the children in the classroom and under treatment'.[76]

Wald came from a Jewish family that had fled Central Europe in the late 1840s to escape anti-Semitism. She was open about her intimate relationships with women, which were many.[77] A special friend in the early years of Henry Street was Mabel Hyde Kittredge, a Park Avenue socialite and the most famous home economist of her day. Kittredge wrote books on household management with gripping titles such as *Housekeeping notes: How to furnish and keep house in a tenement flat* (1911), and was a crusader for school lunches, which fitted well with the public health side of Henry Street's work: a hot lunch programme was set up in New York City public schools in 1901, and was finally funded by the Board of Education in 1920. A feminist and pacifist, Kittredge represented the Henry Street Settlement at The Hague Congress in 1915, and she was a source of important financial support, living in the Settlement for some years in the early 1900s. She appears to have been somewhat needy in her relationship with Wald.[78] Her successor in Wald's affections, a lawyer called Helen Arthur, was also very generous, and a key support for another of Wald's ventures, The Neighborhood Playhouse, one of the first community theatres.[79]

Wald is remembered for founding public health nursing, but, like so many of the women in this book, she wasn't only a formidable influence on domestic public policy but also a major broker in the transatlantic exchange of ideas about health, education, welfare and politics. When she and Brewster moved into the building in Henry Street she arranged to have the magnificent mahogany doors in the entrance hall removed and turned into dining tables. Around these tables sat many of the international personalities that populate the history of the period. Vida Scudder, whom we met in Chapter Three, said that to turn the pages of Wald's guest book was 'to review international history'.[80] The British prime minister-to-be, Ramsay MacDonald, sat there with his wife, Margaret, on their honeymoon in 1897. Wald and MacDonald corresponded on a variety of public issues in the 1920s, and she was an important source of advice to him, especially when he became prime minister again in 1929. That year Wald and MacDonald's friendship achieved front-page status when *The New York Times* ran a story about MacDonald and his daughter Ishbel's visit to Wald's summer home in Westport, Connecticut. A canoe MacDonald had taken out onto Wald's lake became grounded and a detective walked in to free it without even taking his shoes off. To thank Wald for her hospitality, the MacDonalds gave her a dog, which she named Ramsay.[81]

Every day the residents of Henry Street met around those tables for breakfast at 7.30am. One morning in 1905, Florence Kelley, who had moved to Henry Street from Hull-House, read aloud a newspaper headline announcing that the Secretary of Agriculture was to investigate the protection of the cotton crop from the boll weevil. This was a small beetle that had been laying its eggs in the fruits of American cotton since it arrived from Mexico in the early 1890s. On hearing this story of the abuse of cotton by boll weevils, Wald decided it was time for the federal government to do something about the abuse of children by society: 'to take the child out of the realm of poetry and pure sentiment into the field of scientific, organized care and protection'.[82] The day that the Secretary of Agriculture went south in pursuit of the boll weevil, Kelley and Wald went to President Roosevelt to plead for a federal resource to protect the lives of children. This was the beginning of seven years' campaigning for what became the Children's Bureau, a key institution of the Progressive Era. As Wald put it in one of her political speeches, 'Ours is ... the only great nation which does not know how many children are born and how many die in each year within its borders; still less do we know how many die in infancy of preventable diseases ... There could be no greater aid to the reduction of infant mortality than full and current vital statistics of children, such as no one community can obtain for itself ... We can not say how many are in the jails or almshouses ... there is chaos in the treatment and punishment of difficult children ... Only the federal government can cover the whole field and tell us of the children with as much care as it tells of the trees or the fishes or the cotton crop!'[83]

Established in 1912, with a remit of investigating and reporting on all matters affecting children and child life, the Children's Bureau was the outcome of an alignment between Florence Kelley, Lillian Wald, Julia Lathrop and Grace Meigs, a doctor also associated with Hull-House who did a large and influential study of maternal mortality for the Bureau in 1917. With Lathrop its first director, the Children's Bureau was the first federal agency to be headed by a woman. Jane Addams wrote a mini-biography of Lathrop in order to publicize the achievements of a woman who seems to have caused almost no ripple of public attention either then or since (page 49).[84] When she took on the new Children's Bureau, Lathrop was a political unknown on Capitol Hill but, at the age of 54 and with nearly 25 years at Hull-House behind her, she had the advantage of an enormous network of professional and personal contacts.

Most notable in Lathrop's programme at the Children's Bureau were its field studies of infant mortality. In each of eight sites researchers collected all registered birth and infant-death certificates, adding in other sources such as local baby shows to find unregistered births. Home visits and interviews were carried out with every mother, and data were collected on the circumstances of the birth, infant feeding, socio-economic conditions and so forth. What emerged were correlations between infant deaths and low income, poor housing and inadequate sanitation. This was original social science research. Lathrop pioneered a strategy called 'the cohort approach', in which a whole birth cohort of babies was followed for a year, a practice subsequently followed in much epidemiological research.[85] Wald, Kelley, Lathrop and Meigs all played important roles in designing legislation for services to reduce infant and maternal mortality. The Maternity and Infancy Act (known as the Sheppard-Towner Act) of 1921, which proceeded directly from the Children's Bureau work, provided grants to states to develop health services for mothers and children.

By this time, leadership of the Children's Bureau had passed from Lathrop to Grace Abbott, sister of the economist Edith Abbott and another long-time resident of Hull-House, with her own inspiring history of citizenship activism and research. Grace Abbott brought to the Children's Bureau her particular background of work with the Immigrants' Protective League and researching child labour, but she had also undertaken one of the first empirical studies of midwifery practice in the US. Her midwife study sparkles with the methodological mix of systematic searching (for women practising as midwives), analysis of official records, interviews and questionnaires, and slightly invasive inspection of the midwives' bags. Twenty-one of these were found to be dirty, while a further 54 could be called only 'fairly clean'.[86] Many bags held instruments and/or pills both of which were against the Medical Practice Act.

Almost wherever we look in the history of these early cohorts of women healthcare workers, their paths lead us to services that met local need but that also later became part of state, federal or national health services. In Britain, Elizabeth Garrett Anderson had started St Mary's Dispensary for women and children in 1866, charging (for those who could pay) a penny per consultation: this became the New Hospital for Women and then the Elizabeth Garrett Anderson Hospital, which remains part of the NHS as a department of University College

Hospital in London today. Sophia Jex-Blake, the first woman doctor practising in Scotland and another leading campaigner for women's medical education, opened the Edinburgh Provident Dispensary for Women and Children in 1878, which migrated into the Bruntsfield Hospital, again a constituent of the NHS. Elsie Inglis started a small hospital for women and children in George Square, Edinburgh in 1894, which grew to provide maternity care and be one of the first hospitals to offer poor women anaesthetics for childbirth. Frances Ivens ran clinics in her home for the poor long before infant welfare clinics were set up. Before they embarked on their trail-blazing war service, Drs Murray and Anderson initiated the Women's Hospital for Children in the Harrow Road in London in 1912, which treated more than half a million children before it closed, due to lack of funds, in 1922. These are only a few of many examples.

It fell to another LSMW graduate, Helen Boyle, to specialize in the relationship between the body and the mind. Described as 'forbidding', but with a healthy sense of humour and dislike of medical paperwork, Boyle pursued a one-woman challenge to the existing legislation on insanity, which allowed no provision for the care of the mentally ill outside the asylum system.[87] She was a co-founder of the first dispensary offering free care to poor women and children in Lewes, Sussex, in 1899. In 1905 she attached to this a small hospital specifically for women 'suffering from any form of nervous breakdown'.[88]

8.12: Helen Boyle, 1939

Patients paid nothing, or what they could afford; nobody who could afford private treatment was admitted. This modest venture grew into the Lady Chichester Hospital for the Treatment of Early Mental Disorders, which survives today as a psychiatric day centre run by the local NHS Trust. Boyle worked there until 1948, when the NHS took over. Born in Dublin in 1869, she was hauled off by her mother for a linguistically useful education in Germany when her father went bankrupt. The same year that she got her MD in Brussels, 1884, she went to work at the Canning Town Mission, a Settlement in London's East End, where she became convinced that much mental ill-health was generated by the environment. She witnessed there, she said, 'mental patients being manufactured from the rough, as it were … I saw the impecunious and harassed mother of five (or ten as the case may be) with a nervous breakdown after influenza, or possibly child-birth, getting up too soon, with bad air, bad food, noise, and worry. I saw her apply for treatment, wait many weary hours, and get a bottle [of medicine] and the advice not to worry, and go home and rest. No hospital would take her because she had no organic disease; no asylum because she was not certified.'[89] Boyle read everything she could find about asylums and about the increase in nervous ailments but uncovered little recognition of the fact that 'insanity begins before a person is insane'; indeed, she was overwhelmed by the extent of 'chaos of opinion, thought, and practice' 'in this area, one of the outstanding increasingly important questions of public health'.[90] A key reason, she thought, was the totally unsupportable division between neurology and psychiatry, and the treatment of patients 'too much in bits', as collections of organs rather than as whole people.[91]

Boyle emphasized the treatment of women by women on the grounds that 'It is easier for a woman to understand a woman and the things that she does *not* say than it is for a man to do so',[92] but she did argue the need for an extension of the principles of her work to men (this happened in 1931). She dismissed the theories of the infamous Weir Mitchell, who had treated Charlotte Perkins Gilman and many clever and creative women by putting them to bed and forbidding all mental and physical exercise.[93] On the contrary, said Boyle, people with poor mental health need exercise, employment, occupation, distraction, amusement and open air. Her hospital had a small garden; patients went for walks on the Sussex Downs or by the sea, were offered bicycles and sea-bathing; they had a piano and music, sometimes a little dancing. When they could, they helped staff with the housework and care of the garden and with fund-raising. They were offered hydropathy, steam baths, electricity and massage. 'As far as I know,' wrote Boyle, 'this is a combination which is unique and unattainable elsewhere for poor people ... tied as they often are inexorably by their poverty to conditions which make recovery impossible.'[94] In its first four years, she and her staff treated women from varied social backgrounds: dressmakers, milliners, shop assistants, missionaries, nurses, box-makers, clergymen's wives, actresses, embroiderers, students. About half recovered; among those who didn't were 11 who were subsequently certified insane, two hypochondriacs, one who was 'phthisical [tubercular] and noisy' and a Russian who couldn't understand English and left after two days.[95] The hospital's *Annual Report for 1917* emphasized that it was still the only UK hospital to specialize in all forms of nervous breakdown among women and children, and that some 80% of those who ended up certified in lunatic asylums 'could have been saved such a fate and preserved as useful citizens and workers if they had been helped in time'.[96] Boyle was a founder of the National Council of Mental Hygiene, paying the first three years' office expenses herself: the Council eventually formed part of the organization known today as Mind. For the last 17 years of her life Boyle lived with her companion, Marguerite du Pre Gore Lindsay, in an isolated hilltop cottage outside Hove, defying further investigation of her private life (and frustrating all possible biographers) by issuing instructions that all her personal papers were to be burnt on her death.[97]

Boyle had run the first female GP practice in Hove, Sussex, with her friend Mabel Jones, who leads us to another in this cast of eccentrically colourful characters. Before Mabel Jones moved to Hove to work and live with Helen Boyle, she worked in Hull with Mary Murdoch, Hull's first woman doctor, an insightful, inspiring character who made no secret of her feminism, devotion to women or love of cars. Reputedly the first woman in Hull to own a car, she drove voters to the polls in the 1907 by-election in her open top car decorated with the colours of the suffrage movement. She was an awful driver. On one occasion when she was driving her then partner in practice (and lifelong close friend), Louisa Martindale, to Haworth, Murdoch got the gears confused and the car slid backwards and overturned, flinging them both out. It caught fire. Murdoch remarked casually to Martindale, 'Oh well, if you can't appreciate the scenery I shan't bring you out another time.'[98] Fortunately, when they went to study in Vienna they took their bicycles.

Cars feature prominently in the biography of Dr Ethel Williams, a pacifist and suffragist, Newcastle-upon-Tyne's first GP and first female car-owner, and co-founder of the Northern Women's Hospital in 1917: Dr Williams' car was of great use to the suffrage movement.[99] She was probably a better driver than Mary Murdoch. Murdoch's contribution to healthcare and public policy was broad: aside from her woman-centred practice, and research on pericarditis and vaccines, she helped to start the first crèche in Hull, founded the Hull women's suffrage society, a school for mothers and a lodging house for women, lectured on the suffrage, women's work and allied topics, and stood on an overturned box at the docks giving the male dock labourers the very modern advice that they ought to spend more time with their babies. She subscribed to the enlightened view that mothercraft is not instinctual, that women need antenatal care, good dentistry, pure milk, knowledge of food values, more female police, sanitary inspectors, health visitors, district and school nurses and should take every step to exterminate vermin and house flies, treating their dustbins regularly with borax.[100] When Murdoch spoke at a conference in Glasgow in 1909 on reforms needed in the health of nations, she talked about housing conditions in Hull as causes of local sickness: 'No through ventilation, no system of water drainage … the contents of the privies have to be carried through the living rooms.' Municipal housekeeping and sanitary science were essential elements in good healthcare. Unsurprisingly, Murdoch's approach earned her much abuse from Hull Corporation and local property-owners.[101] The women of Hull-House would have sympathized.

Characteristic of these communities of women doctors was the close link they made between research and practice, a hallmark, as we have seen, of the women's war-time medical service. Jane Walker, the Yorkshire daughter of a wool merchant, a student at the LSMW and the 45th woman on the General Medical Register, was responsible for importing from Germany a new open-air method for treating tuberculosis (TB). She opened a sanatorium in Suffolk in 1901 that, like Boyle's hospital in Sussex, was more of a community than a hospital. Patients were occupied with gardening, clerical work, baking, toy making and jewellery repair and manufacture; many ex-patients worked as members of staff.[102] Walker's East Anglian Sanatorium continued to treat TB until the 1950s. Dr Annie McCall started a TB dispensary where she administered, and became very enthusiastic about, the new treatment of tuberculin injections. So did Dr Hilda Clark, a member of the famous Quaker shoe-making Clark family, whose sanatorium in Street, Somerset also offered the tuberculin treatment. Most of the patients treated were working for the Clark boot-making business and had probably contracted bovine tuberculosis through working with leather.[103] The Clark sanatorium had some notable successes, among whom was Hilda Clark's own sister, Alice, whose classic of women's history, *The working life of women in the seventeenth century*, was mentioned in Chapter One.[104] Hilda Clark was an acknowledged authority on the treatment of TB, writing a textbook and medical articles on it, and being appointed TB officer by the public health authorities in Portsmouth. *Her* lifelong companion was a midwife, Edith Pye, trained at McCall's Clapham School of Midwifery. Pye's name appears on the list of women running war hospitals; at hers, in Châlons-sur-Marne in an old insane asylum 15 miles behind the fighting line, another water- and electricity-less establishment requiring yet more female DIY, Pye delivered 1,000 babies between 1914 and 1919. Mothers and midwives owe Pye a particular debt, since in the early 1930s she promoted a method of pain relief in the form of a chloroform tablet that could safely be given by midwives to women having babies at home.[105]

All these Ediths and Alices and Hildas and Marys and Louisas and Janes: the treasure trove of names and deeds and words overflows. This is a whole encyclopaedia of reform; not just an exercise in women proving their worth in male institutions, but a penetrating analysis of those accepted ideologies and practices that get in the way of a healthy life for all citizens. Health was seen as moulded by the environment, and its effective preservation as dependent on *both* a sound scientific base and democratic relationships between carers and the recipients of care.[106] In articulating this vision, women doctors relied on an energetic network of international friendships and connections that took in other women reformers in schools, prisons, science, journalism and literature.[107]

There was no room in any of this for violence of any kind. The last offering to be squeezed into this chapter concerns a highly newsworthy attack on the male system of medical education which was launched by two young Swedish women students at the LSMW in the early 1900s. 'Lizzy' (Emilie Augusta Louise) Lind-af-Hageby and Leisa Schartau had met at a lecture in Stockholm, and they formed a lifelong partnership devoted to opposing aggression against women, nations and animals. Lizzy is in the centre of the photograph, which was taken at the International Vivisection Congress of 1913. At the Pasteur Institute in Paris, a famous centre for medical research, in 1900, the two women saw vast rooms filled with cages containing suffering and dying animals. 'Now and then the young and amiable man who conducted us through the Institute opened the door of a cage, took out the dead body of a rabbit or guinea-pig, and threw it into a pail under the table.'[108] Two years later they enrolled as students at the LSMW with the intention of learning all they could about physiology in order to be better equipped for a campaigning life. Vivisection wasn't allowed at the LSMW, but it was rife everywhere else: indeed, live animals continue to be used in higher education today, and they feature also as tools in military combat training, with live pigs and goats being stabbed, shot, burned, fractured and amputated in order for soldiers to learn about trauma.[109]

Lind-af-Hageby and Schartau attended, with their notebooks, some 100 physiology lectures and 50 demonstrations on live animals in London. Their book, originally called *Eye-witnesses*, and then *The shambles of science: Extracts from the diary of two students of physiology*, caused a storm with its dramatic descriptions of the 'theatre' of the medical experimenter's art – no science, they said, but a display of butchery put on for entertainment that must not fail to brutalize the students exposed to it: 'The physiological theatre offers plays that are as exciting, thrilling, and entertaining as any others; there is quite enough of murderous attempts and of struggle for life, and the manager is anxious to bring the best performers on the stage.'[110] The best/worst play they laid before their readers was the case of the brown dog, an operation performed on a live, unanaesthetized terrier by two eminent medical men and compulsive experimenters, Ernest Starling and his brother-in-law, William Bayliss. In the original edition of *The shambles of science*, the case of the brown dog appeared in a chapter called 'Fun': 'A large dog, stretched on its back on an operation board, is carried into the lecture-room by the demonstrator … The animal exhibits all the signs of intense suffering; in his struggles, he again and again lifts his body from the board and makes powerful attempts to get free. The lecturer, attired in the blood-stained surplice of the priest

8.13: Lizzy Lind-af-Hageby (centre) at the International Anti-Vivisection Congress, 1913

of vivisection … is now comfortably smoking a pipe, whilst with hands coloured crimson he arranges the electrical circuit for the stimulation that will follow. Now and then, he makes a funny remark, which is appreciated by those around him.'[111] These discomforting revelations led to a much-publicized libel trial which the medical men won, the judge in the trial deeming *The shambles of science*, in a well-worn epithet, 'hysterical'.[112] According to a *Daily Mail* reporter who expected something different, Lizzy Lind-af-Hageby was 'a pretty, little, plump woman, with kind brown eyes, eyes that twinkle', and she wore a pretty blue dress.[113]

In feminist organizations of the period, Lind-af-Hageby and Schartau's vivisected dog on the operating board blurred into images of suffragettes forcibly fed, women forcibly deprived of their ovaries and uteruses as a cure for hysteria, or forcibly immobilized for childbirth and the unhygienic interventions of medical men.[114] The bizarre repercussions of the brown dog episode dragged on for years: a statue commemorating the unfortunate terrier, erected in Battersea, became the focus for brown dog riots orchestrated by crowds of male medical students in 1907, and had to be removed. A replacement now lingers in Battersea Park's Woodland Walk, where its location near the Old English Garden consigns it to a dead, rather than living, controversy. Yet more media attention was attracted to the anti-vivisection cause when, in 1913, Lind-af-Hageby sued the *Pall Mall Gazette* for libel because it had printed an unpleasant anti-anti-vivisection piece by the eugenicist physician Caleb Saleeby. Lind-af-Hageby argued her own case in court for three weeks (at a time when women weren't allowed to be lawyers), with an opening statement that lasted nine-and-a-half hours; she spoke, in total, *The New York Times* estimated, 210,000 words (more than the length of this book). The case was lost on the grounds that the Saleeby article wasn't nearly so unpleasant as Lind-af-Hageby considered it (George Bernard Shaw, himself a committed anti-vivisectionist and vegetarian, thought this misunderstanding occurred because Lind-af-Hageby, though by then a naturalized British citizen, was still linguistically a foreigner).[115]

Lind-af-Hageby and Schartau's disclosures about animal abuse in medical education did much to spread the message of animal rights. Lind-af-Hageby founded the Animal Defence and Anti-Vivisection Society in 1906, now the Animal Defence Trust, and ran it for 60 years. In the inter-war years she added the reform of slaughter-houses to her list of causes, visiting many abroad, especially in Chicago, the home of the inhumane slaughtering trade. She sported a few other eccentric interests, for instance, in premature burial, about which she lectured widely in England, Sweden and the US, informing her audiences that thousands of people were buried alive every year and that this tragedy could easily be prevented by affixing a device to coffin lids which would detect any sign of life and deliver air to the coffin, raising a flag above ground and thus alerting the need for rescue.[116] She was among the attendees at The Hague Congress in 1915, as determined a feminist and pacifist as she was an anti-vivisectionist, for these 'isms' were quite indissolubly linked in her world-view.

Annie McCall, asked to write her MD thesis on vivisection, objected that she couldn't possibly support something so cruel. It was a false principle in the building up of a true method of preventing ills of the body. In her *Prison and prisoners*, Constance Lytton had recited an experience of her own which drove home in a very vivid way this connection between the rights of animals and of women. One day in Littlehampton, Lytton had seen a sheep on its way to be slaughtered. It had escaped and was being mistreated by its two 'gaolers'. The sheep looked old and misshapen, but Lytton had a vision of what it should have been on its native mountain side with 'all its forces rightly developed, vigorous and independent'. A laughing crowd was watching while the sheep was caught and cuffed in the face. She had, she said, always burnt with indignation at unkindness to animals,

> But on seeing this sheep it seemed to reveal to me for the first time the position of women throughout the world. I realized how often women are held in contempt as beings outside the pale of human dignity, excluded or confined, laughed at and insulted because of conditions in themselves for which they

are not responsible, but which are due to fundamental injustices with regard to them, and to the mistakes of a civilisation in the shaping of which they have had no free share. I was ashamed to remember that although my sympathy had been spontaneous with regard to the wrongs of animals, of children, of men and women who belonged to down-trodden races or classes of society, yet that hitherto I had been blind to the sufferings peculiar to women as such, which are endured by women of every class, every race, every nationality.[117]

NINE

Dangerous trades: reforming industrial labour

Four interlinked problems beset late 19th-century industrial labour: employers worked their employees as hard and as cheaply as they could; this exploitation was at its most extreme in the 'sweated' trades, which were marked by long hours, poor wages and appalling conditions; sweating overlapped with home-work, where the production of goods and services for a pittance mingled uncomfortably with family life; and many of the manufacturing processes and constituents used in domestic and non-domestic workplaces actually poisoned or otherwise damaged workers' bodies. This was mainly a class-based, not a gender-based, exploitation. But women and children were especially vulnerable. Women made up the bulk of workers in the sweated trades; they had fewer rights, in fact almost no rights at all, at a time when workers in general were only in the process of discovering the power that might be exercised through the trade union movement. This chapter ventures into the attempts women reformers made to relieve the dreadful conditions of industrial labour. Although some paid special attention to the work of women and children, much of their effort was directed towards improving the world of wage labour in general. In the process, some women reformers also inaugurated campaigns which we think of as entirely modern – for example, the idea of boycotting goods produced by exploited workers.

The work of the main women who feature in this chapter – Britain's Clementina Black, Clara Collet, Margaret Bondfield and the early women factory inspectors, Sweden's Kerstin Hesselgren, and Crystal Eastman and Alice Hamilton in the US –

spans all the critical issues relating to the conditions of industrial labour in the late 19th and early 20th centuries. The trajectories of these women reiterate the theme of methodological inventiveness discussed in Chapter Three. In order to find out just how exploitative working conditions damaged workers, women researchers had to develop new tools of study and analysis. These were subsequently incorporated into economics, epidemiology and sociology as standard research techniques.

Thomas Oliver, a physician with a background in occupational diseases, edited a book called *Dangerous trades: The historical, social and legal aspects of industrial occupations as affecting health, by a number of experts* in 1902. Nine of its 60 chapters were written by women, eight of these by the first British women to be appointed as factory inspectors. The women wrote about the history of dangerous trade regulation and its variation across Europe; about infant mortality and factory labour; about laundry work, fish-curing and fruit-preserving and the dangers of rabbit down; and about the hazards facing workers in tinplate and aerated-water works. The latter industry was the only one officially scheduled as dangerous to life and limb at the time. Glass bottles, filled under pressure, tended to burst, sending fragments of glass at the workers and causing many to lose their eyes. In her chapter on rabbit down for Oliver's book, Rose Squire wrote that 'No description can convey any adequate impression of a fur-pulling room ... the universal grey, the haze of floating hair, the sickly disgusting odour of uncleaned skins – it must be seen, felt, and smelt, to be understood.' 'Sometimes the washing is done in a basement room, to light or ventilate which is practically impossible,' wrote Lucy Deane in her chapter on laundry workers, 'and one has only to stand in such a place, where ... proper drainage of the sloppy floor is impossible, where the heat in summer and the damp in winter are alike excessive, to realise vividly that of all industries laundry work is perhaps the least suitable to the home.'[1] The concept of a 'dangerous trade' was by then a technical term. In Britain it referred to a provision laid out in Schedule 8 of the 1891 Factory Act whereby 'any machinery or process' certified by the Secretary of State as dangerous or injurious to health required 'special rules' or measures to be introduced for the protection of workers. The evolution of interest in the dangers of dangerous trades in this period marked a significant moment in the progress of state intervention for public welfare.[2]

There was synergy, but also difference, in the interest women reformers took in industrial labour on either side of the Atlantic. For the British input, we will start with

9.1: Clementina Black

Clementina Black, born in Brighton in 1853, the eldest girl of eight children. Clementina was named after her paternal grandmother, whose husband had been naval architect to Tsar Nicholas I. Her mother's death when Clementina was 22, combined with her father's illness, gave her the responsibility of caring for her younger siblings. To this was later added her niece, the daughter of her brother Arthur, as a result of a mysterious tragedy in which Arthur killed his wife, his son and himself.[3] Clementina Black managed all this childcare at the same time as making history by writing more than 50 publications in which she investigated and analysed the conditions of women's work in the home and out of it, helping to found the women's trade union movement and proposing, as early as 1896, the radical idea of a legal minimum wage. She funded these activities and gained a living for herself and her family by writing seven novels, four biographies and many plays, short stories and poems, as well as translating books about art and politics from French and German. In her day, Black was well known, giving speeches and workshops across the country, travelling to congresses, lobbying in Parliament and producing the raw material of welfare legislation. All this was achieved with little formal education; she was proud of saying she had never passed a single examination.[4] She was also proud of remembering, as she neared the close of her life, once being kissed by Karl Marx at the end of a girls' evening with her friend Eleanor Marx; Marx himself, being engaged 'in high converse with a contemporary', and unaware of the girlish chatter going on in another part of the room, looked at Black vaguely when she got up to go, and 'some such as [sic] idea as "girl, niece" passed into his mind, and he dropped his avuncular kiss'.[5]

Clementina Black's first short story, 'The troubles of an automaton', published in 1876, was about a chess-playing machine which housed a man who was rendered exhausted by his labours, thereby demonstrating the evils of a systematized, mechanized society.[6] This was a theme which would occupy much of her non-fictional work. In London, Black and some of her sisters lived in a Bloomsbury apartment furnished and decorated 'after their own ideas'; Grace Black, an art student, did the decoration. As their friend, the poet Amy Levy, reported in a letter to another friend, 'Miss Black and her sister(s) are living on the top floor of a house in Fitzroy Street; they do their own housework & are quite & completely domestic, unless when they are attending Socialist or Anarchist meetings.'[7] Both Clementina and her sister Constance were members of the Fabian Society, and Clementina was heavily involved in the suffrage campaign; in 1906 she was responsible for organizing a Women's Suffrage Petition signed by 257,000 women. While Clementina did translations from German and French (as well as writing fiction) to earn money, Constance learnt Russian, and her translations of Tolstoy, Turgenev, Dostoyevsky and Chekhov would later introduce Russian literature to English-speaking readers across the world. A spatial centre for the multi-talented Black sisters' network was the Reading Room of the British Museum; Clementina got her reader's ticket in 1877, the same year as Eleanor Marx (see Chapter Three). The Keeper of Printed Books at the British Museum, Richard Garnett, provided useful connections for the sisters' translation work, and also a husband, Edward, for Constance. Constance and her 'Tolstoyan politics' were pivotal for the famous Bloomsbury group of writers, intellectuals and artists; Constance Garnett's son, David, who later married Virginia Woolf's niece, argued at a tribunal in 1916 that he should be let off conscription because he had been raised a pacifist and a socialist as a result of his mother's acquaintance with Tolstoy.[8]

The trade union movement was Clementina Black's route into the world of poverty research and industrial reform. She joined the Women's Trade Union Association in 1886 through her friend Eleanor Marx. As a member of the Investigation Committee of the Women's Industrial Council (WIC) (the body which took over the Women's Trade Union Association), and later its president and editor of its journal, the *Women's Industrial News*, Black spearheaded many detailed and revelatory inquiries into the conditions of women's work that in turn fed directly into policy and legislative change. This was effectively the model of Settlement sociology in the US as practised by reformers such as Jane Addams, Florence Kelley, Julia Lathrop, the Abbott sisters and many others.

According to the 1901 Census, some 13 million women and girls aged over ten years (a third of the female population) were employed in Britain, with the three biggest occupations being domestic service (41%), dressmaking (17%) and textile manufacture (16%).[9] Scores of books and articles and pamphlets were being written about women's work, some more evidence based than others. We remember the most famous ones – in Britain, Maud Pember Reeves' *Round about a pound a week* (1913), a moving scientific study of women's work in 42 poor South London households conducted with Dr Ethel Bentham and the Fabian Women's Group; and the equally persuasive *Maternity: Letters from working-women* (1915) compiled by Margaret Llewellyn Davies of the Women's Co-operative Guild.[10] But these were only the tip of the giant iceberg of investigations designed to bring the problems of labour in industrial society to public and policy attention.

By 1903 the WIC's own investigation committee had published studies of 25 trades in which women worked, ranging from cigar-making, hat-lining, box-making and artificial flower-making to laundry work, dressmaking, machining and typing. Typically, these reports included detailed descriptions of the work, statistics (for example, of wages) and recommendations for legislative and policy change. Emily Hobhouse's study of women workers in dust-yards, mentioned at the end of Chapter Four, was one of these reports. Another was meticulous research into artificial flower-making by Grace Oakeshott, who visited more than 20 flower-making workshops and factories to collect her data.[11] One of the WIC's most able and respected investigators, Oakeshott literally disappeared from its history when she staged her own death on the Brittany coast in 1907 to escape an unsatisfactory marriage.[12] Clementina Black's own *Sweated industry and the minimum wage*, published just as Grace Oakeshott wrote herself out of history in 1907, argued that the basic cause of workers being employed in dreadful conditions was the under-payment of both women and men.[13] The remedy was therefore payment of a minimum wage that would allow them to live decently. Following the example of a philanthropic society in Berlin, *The Daily News* sponsored a Sweating Exhibition in London in 1906. It attracted 30,000 people, commanding the attention 'of all serious students of our social system'.[14] Workers were shown actually making match-boxes and blouses, and carding hooks and eyes, with detailed information displayed about rates of pay, costs of materials and working hours. The exhibition led to the formation of the Anti-sweating League, with Black on its executive committee, and its aim of establishing a legal minimum wage and the creation of Trade Boards to set minimum wages for different industries.

Clementina Black's *Married women's work* was published in 1915, at a time when the employment of women as cheaper substitutes for men was rising. Her book, 'a temperate and graphic account of the lives of working women', according to the *British Medical Journal*,[15] is the WIC report for which she is best known. The problem was not that married women worked, but that the work they did was both scandalously ill-paid and often damaging to health, and it was added to the already heavy burden of unpaid domestic work: 'Few operations performed by women in factories are for instance so exhausting as the doing of the family wash with the appliances to be found in the ordinary poor home.'[16] In relation to the great historical theme of whether mothers working is bad for children, Black, with her keen eye for science, pointed out that the only general conclusion to be drawn from the available evidence was that poverty and population density are unfavourable to the health and survival of young children.

She was a social scientist, but also an imaginative writer of fiction, and her reports on women's work deploy these creative skills. In an article on 'Match-box making at home', published in *The English Illustrated Magazine* in 1892, and delightfully illustrated by the artist William Hatherell, Black describes a little patch of slums close to Shoreditch church in East London, an area once inhabited by French silk-weavers:

> In these streets live numbers of home workers, all in the deepest poverty ... Thousands of match-boxes pass in, unmade, every week ... and pass out again, completed. The women fetch out from the factory, or the middle-woman's, strips of notched wood, packets of coloured paper and sand paper, and printed wrappers; they carry back large, but light bundles of boxes, tied up in packets of two dozen. Inside their rooms the boxes, made and unmade, and half made, cover the floor, and fill up the lack of furniture. I have seen a room containing only an old bedstead in the very last stage of dirt and dilapidation, a table, and two deal boxes for seats. The floor and the window-sill were rosy with magenta match-boxes, while everything else, including the boards of the floor, the woodwork of the room and the coverings of the bed, was of the dark grey of ingrained dust and dirt. But the woman who lived here was quite cheerful; it was a sunny day, and her boxes could be dried without need of a fire. She worked while she talked, as such women always do.[17]

Match-box making was probably, said Black, the poorest industry of them all. A speech on match-girls' working conditions that she made to the Fabian Society in 1888 caught the attention of the socialist reformer Annie Besant, who was in the audience.[18] Besant's article on 'White slavery in London', about the big match-manufacturing company Bryant and May's treatment of its female workers, called for a boycott of its product, and so angered the firm that its actions provoked the famous match-girls' strike in 1888.[19] The unfair dismissal of an employee in the summer of 1888 brought the whole factory in Bow, East London, to a standstill, and the women were able to negotiate important changes to their conditions, including the abolition of fines and deductions, and a separate room for meals so that their food would no longer be contaminated by phosphorus. A Matchmakers' Union was formed, which was advised on all procedural matters by, of course, Clementina Black.

Like many social researchers of the period, Black was a methodological innovator. She gave details of how her inquiries were actually *done*. Here's an extract from her account of 'one hot day' in the life of a social investigator. It comes from *Makers of our clothes*, a report Black published with Adele Meyer, a social reformer married to a wealthy banker, who provided the funds for the study: 'We alighted from a municipal tram in a busy but not wide thoroughfare, hot and full of mingled odours from the fruit, meat, fish, cheese, onions and other comestibles displayed freely in open shop windows. Sweet shops glowed with wares of vivid and alarming hues; vendors shouted; trams went grinding by, and busy pedestrians hustled each other on the narrow pavements. We divided into two parties, one pair going to one church, the second to another.' They were in search of names and addresses of employers and workers to interview, having decided that the best way to select a sample was from people such as church and Settlement workers in the community, 'experience teaching very clearly how comparatively feeble is the appeal of pen and ink'.[20] After much chasing around they made a few useful contacts. They always explained to the workers the purpose of the inquiry and assured them that no names would be made public. It was necessary to let them tell their story in their own way. 'One has to hear far more than merely the industrial facts that one sets out to learn. The additional information is often very interesting – as a glimpse into any human life can hardly fail to be – but listening to it is apt to take a long time.'[21] All these comments will resonate with social researchers today. So also will Black's observations on the willingness of people to be investigated: 'The people upon whom we intrude are so busy, and they are – almost always – so kind. Our visits to them bear a painful resemblance to those of the enterprising agent who desires to sell a new variety of furniture polish. For our own purposes we enter their houses, demand their attention and take up their time. They, on their part, are not merely patient, they are often eagerly interested; sometimes they ... welcome us as friends. Some of them ... give us tea; and how thankfully we receive that refreshment few people can guess, unless they have made similar peregrinations.'[22]

This was another of Black's ideas: that 'consumers' should refuse to buy goods and services that were not ethically produced. It was an idea that radically challenged the conventional economic framework within which consumption is assumed to be a private act by self-interested individuals, whereas production is a site of public collective action.[23] As Black put it in her report on *Home industries of women in London*, which described the lives of 44 underpaid working-class women, we can hardly, 'comfort ourselves with a belief that the products thus wrung out of suffering are not in our own houses. To whom are not shoes sent home in boxes? Who does not buy matches, or tin tacks, or tooth brushes? Whose coals and potatoes are not put into sacks, or whose retail purchases not into paper bags? There is no person in this kingdom – or in any of the states that are called civilised – who does not partake in the proceeds of underpaid labour.'[24] The British Consumers' League was set up by Black in 1887, the first such organization anywhere, and the model for many later ones in the US, Belgium, France, Germany, Italy, Spain and Switzerland. This early consumer movement richly illustrated the transatlantic transfer of political ideas, which flowed from England to the US to France and other European countries and was facilitated by the frequent travels of early reformers such as Maud Nathan and Florence Kelley.[25] The principle was that consumers should be persuaded to boycott sellers of goods that had been produced by exploited labour, or were sold in exploitative ways (cheap overtime, child labour, Sunday trading and so on). For this purpose lists were circulated, either of sellers who performed well or of those who did badly, although the preference was for 'white lists' of sellers who behaved ethically. The original such list (of good sellers) in Britain was published in *Longman's Magazine* in August 1887.

First to copy Black's idea were a group of women in the Women's Trade Union League in the US, who adopted the same name, the National Consumers' League (NCL), despite its evident ambiguity – some people thought the main object of a consumers' league must be to get discounted goods, while others assumed it had something to do with tuberculosis.[26] In 1891 Maud Nathan and Josephine Shaw Lowell, two busy social reformers, sent out 1,400 letters to all retail, dry goods and fancy goods shopkeepers in New York City with copies of a statement about what 'a fair house' should do: give equal pay for work of equal value irrespective of sex; prohibit child labour; limit working hours; allow paid time for lunch and holidays; provide decent lunch and retiring rooms and sanitary facilities; supply seats for saleswomen. Employers were not interested. Only 30 forms were returned and, after inspection, only four of these employers conformed to the 'fair house' specification. There were some notable local victories, however. The wife of one of New York State's ex-governors, passing the counter of a 'high-class' department store one day, witnessed the fainting of a saleswoman. She followed her to the store's retiring room in the basement, where the afflicted saleswoman was laid on a bare concrete floor; she took the woman home and learnt that she had been nursing a sick mother, was severely sleep-deprived and unable to sit down at work as there were no seats, and it was against the store's policy to allow their saleswomen to sit at all. The next day this well-connected lady went to see the head of the firm and told him she would withdraw her account unless seats were provided. A consignment of three-legged stools promptly arrived and were distributed behind the counters, whereupon 'legend relates that when the girls saw the stools they ALL fainted'.[27]

The NCL in the US, which survives today, was a conspicuous success. Under the skilled leadership of labour reformer Florence Kelley, it quickly became a leading exponent of protective labour laws for women and children and the single most important political force behind the passage and enforcement of such legislation at both state and federal levels. Kelley's statement of the 'aims and principles of the Consumers' League', published in the *American Journal of Sociology* in 1899, repeated Black's case for the exercise of consumer power: 'The first principle of the league is universality. It recognizes the fact that in a civilized community every person is a consumer. From the cradle (which may be of wood or metal, with rockers or without them) to the grave (to which an urn may be preferred), throughout our lives we are choosing, or choice is made for us, as to the disposal of money … all of us, all the time, are deciding by our expenditures what industries shall survive at all, and under what conditions.'[28] The NCL aimed to moralize these purchasing decisions, and in so doing it provided a claim to a form of citizenship for women: 'consumer citizenship'.[29] Consumers have rights, and these include the right to intervene in capitalism. Kelley, Black and others who took up this cause repeated the mantra of the sanitary scientists, that individual purchasers can never be properly equipped to judge articles on their merits: 'What housewife can detect, alone and unaided, the injurious chemicals in her supplies of milk, bread, meat, home remedies? What young girl, selecting silk for her adornment knows that oil-boiled taffeta is more durable than common silk at twice its price; or why it is so?'[30] The New York Consumers' League's inquiries into working conditions were presented in a series of 'Behind the scenes' reports, using the covert investigation techniques favoured by many reform-minded researchers. Its 1921 study of hotel workers, for example, depended on League investigators taking jobs and actually living as staff in ten New York State hotels.[31] A study of women laundry workers required the researcher to take jobs in nearly every branch of the laundry industry in Manhattan.[32] The first woman to get a master's degree in sociology in the US, in 1897, Annie MacLean, worked for the NCL using this methodology to investigate two Chicago department stores. In two weeks of employment she notched up 175 hours for around 6 cents an hour, earning a surplus of 1 dollar 4 cents after her bills were paid: 'At that rate it would take a long time to earn enough to buy a pair of boots.'[33]

The success of Clementina Black's model in the US wasn't matched in her own country, where the Consumers' League lasted only a few years, for reasons that aren't clear (although one of them was Black's decision to concentrate on lobbying for the minimum wage).[34] Maud Nathan, talking about the League's work at the ICW in London in 1899, blamed 'tradition and conservatism' for hampering the growth of the seed that had flowered so well in the US.[35] Encouragingly, a French writer, suitably called Madame Blanc, who was in the audience, took the idea back home, where La Ligue Sociale d'Acheteurs was set up in Paris; its 'listes blanches' were also distributed on transatlantic liners and in the US so that visiting shoppers would know where to go. Madame Blanc, otherwise known as Thérèse Bentzon, was a friend of the British writer and pacifist Vernon Lee (Violet Paget, see Chapter Six). Bentzon made her living from journalism and fiction, and when she visited the US in 1893 to report on the condition of women there she met, as everyone did, Jane Addams.[36] One of the French Ligue workers, Henriette Brunhes, who lived part of the year in Switzerland, started a League there, which appropriately began its work by looking at conditions in chocolate factories. This led to disquieting revelations about slave labour in West Africa. Nathan's address in German at the 1904 ICW Congress in Berlin produced Der Liga von Konsumenten, its name changed later to Der Kaüferbund (Buyers' Federation), thus removing the association with consumption as a disease. Although the Consumers' League languished in Britain, an important example of the transatlantic exchange of ideas is mentioned by Nathan in her history of the movement. Clementina Black, disheartened by the failure of a Bill improving the conditions of shop assistants' work, heard that such a law had successfully entered the statute book in New York State; she told the chairman of the House of Lords Committee, the Marquis of Salisbury, about this, and the Marquis requested a copy from the US ambassador in London, who couldn't find it, so Nathan, who was in London, supplied it, and was then asked to give evidence before the House of Lords Committee. The Seats for Shop Assistants' Act was passed in the summer of 1899 (although whether it resulted in the delivery of milking-stools is not known).[37]

Clementina Black, giggling away with Eleanor Marx in the augustly distracted company of Karl, started out as a serious, young bespectacled women, handsome but unsmiling in her photographs, and by the time her book *A new way of housekeeping* was published in 1918, she had become what her biographer described as a 'little bent bespectacled old lady'.[38] This, Black's final book, returned to the subject of housework, central to any discussion of industrial labour. As an occupation in which two-thirds of British women were engaged, it was, she asserted, an enormously wasteful and inefficient one. One problem was the design of houses, which were riddled with what Black called 'domestic idiocies'. These included stone steps requiring daily cleaning; brass fittings on front doors; grooved and moulded doors and window frames; insanitary floor coverings 'congenial to insects and mice'; wainscoting; fancy staircase balusters; grooved earthenware sinks; lavatories with inflow holes 'covered by some projecting ornament such as a simulated cockle-shell' and the whole business of locating a lavatory in a bathroom, which ought to be prohibited by the sanitary authorities.[39] She must have driven house-sellers and agents mad, since she herself inspected nearly 200 dwellings before finding one with sufficiently few of these idiocies to live in herself. Black's comments on the inefficiency of housework remind us of Charlotte Perkins Gilman, whose many fictional and non-fictional tracts against housework were widely read at the time. Black and Gilman met during Gilman's visit to Britain in 1896, and again at the 1899 ICW Congress in London, where Black talked about domestic service. Her solution to the problem of wasteful housekeeping wasn't the same as Gilman's, however: it was to establish loose federations of around 50 households, which would collectively operate domestic centres fitted with storerooms, kitchens, dining rooms and offices run by scientifically trained manageresses. Meals would be conveyed to the federated houses in 'some sort of heat-retaining box, probably on little wheeled trucks',[40] a plan that does sound suspiciously like Gilman's; indeed, Black notes that such a suggestion appears in Gilman's novel *What Diantha did*, which is about an enterprising young woman who profits personally from a socialized housekeeping enterprise.[41] These women constantly wrote novels about their non-fictional ideas, and about each other. Black's own 'social realism' novel, much admired by Eleanor Marx, was *The agitator*, about the vicissitudes of a strike leader.[42] Their friend Amy Levy's novel *The romance of a shop*, which portrayed four sisters who set up a photography business together, was said to be in part based on the experiences of the Black sisters as New Women in rapidly changing times.[43]

9.2: Clara Collet

A near contemporary of Clementina Black was Clara Collet, one of the first female civil servants, a distinguished economist and specialist on all matters relating to women's employment. They were born eight years apart, Black in 1852 and Collet in 1860, with their mutual friend Eleanor Marx in the middle, in 1855. Both Black and Collet visited the Marxes in their crowded, argumentative household in North London, and both were actors in the 'Dogberry Club', a group of family and friends founded by Clara Collet and Eleanor Marx in 1877 to read Shakespeare plays. Named after Mr Dogberry, the self-important constable in *Much ado about nothing*, the Club's performances were, like much of what went on in the Marx household, subject to the nice irony of surveillance by Scotland Yard.[44]

Clara Collet was a serious economist and statistician, trained at University College in the accepted neo-classical economics of the time. Her obituary in the *Journal of the Royal Statistical Society* describes her as 'an ardent social investigator in the cause of women's welfare'. It noted her 'vigour, alertness of mind and body, sincerity and directness, practical commonsense, independence of judgement', and her refusal to be fettered by convention, as illustrated by her arrival, in a hearse, at the Ministry of Labour during the General Strike; this was simply the most efficient way of getting there.[45] She founded the Economic Club at University College in 1890, which later included the young William Beveridge, whose ideas about the welfare state were probably greatly fertilized by the discussions Collet organized and to which she contributed. He may not, however, have sympathized with her negative views about the aspirations of the 'grandiose' new LSE, to which he took the Club in 1920 when she handed it over to him.[46] Collet was a founder member of both the Royal Statistical Society and the Royal Economic Society, a governor of Bedford College and the first woman to be made a fellow of University College, in 1896. Many of her contributions to debates about women's employment were made in the form of statistical analyses and reports during the 27 years (1893–1920) she spent as a civil servant in the Board of Trade and the Ministry of Labour. Typical of her rigorous approach was an investigation she carried out in 1899 into how much 'indoor' domestic servants were paid. She managed to get information from 2,067 households employing 5,453 women and 326 men, and then compiled wage statistics according to age, type of household and work.[47] This was the first time any such data had been collected. When scholars today set the scene for discussions of British women's lives in the period from the 1880s through the early decades of the 20th century, it is Clara Collet's statistics that they use.

Collet came from a long radical family. Her father, Collet Dobson Collet, was a newspaper editor, a campaigner for a free press and director of music at the South Place Ethical Society, a centre for radical thinkers. He edited a paper called *The Free Press: A Diplomatic Review*, to which Karl Marx contributed. Clara Collet's mother, Jane, ran a laundry in the family home, which lay in the fields between Archway and Hornsey Rise in North London. Clara was the second daughter and fourth child, and she went to North London Collegiate School, where she was taught statistics by Edward Aveling, who would later form a tense relationship with her friend Eleanor Marx. All the Collet children were sent to France for a year to learn French. After her school years the formidable head of North London Collegiate School, Frances Mary Buss, dispatched Clara Collet, fortified by nothing more than 'a petrified bun from Kentish Town Station', to teach at a new girls' school in Leicester.[48] During her sojourn there she heard the young Arnold Toynbee talk in March 1882 on the subject of 'Are socialists radicals?' and this inspired her to enter the world of radical social research. While teaching, she took her first degree, and then in 1887 an MA in moral and political philosophy (which, given the quaint disciplinary divisions of the period, included economics and psychology).

Her grand-niece, Jane Miller, remembers Clara Collet as 'small, neat and formidable, with an impressive double chin and chilly ways'.[49] In her 'retirement', Collet contributed a chapter on 'Domestic service' to a *New survey of London life and labour*, following up Charles Booth's original inquiry, moved herself and her siblings to a bungalow on a hill in Sidmouth, Devon, learnt Hindustani, had breast cancer surgery by Maynard Keynes' brother Geoffrey (she survived for 12 years, which was exceptional at the time) and began a study of pre-Victorian novels. Despite all her achievements, this 'neglected daughter of Adam Smith'[50] is most often remembered for her 11-year relationship with the novelist George Gissing, whom she met in 1892, when she was 33 and Gissing 36. She sent him her articles for comment, and they went boating on the river from Richmond to Kingston, but Gissing was married to his second wife. Within months Collet had become embroiled in a three-way relationship with the couple not unlike that which Maude Royden enjoyed with her vicar and his wife (see Chapter Six). These are engaging stories about how single women of the time negotiated the blurry boundaries of private and public lives and – in Clara Collet's case – the pull of fiction and non-fiction.[51] Collet was attracted by Gissing's social realism fiction, recognizing in its characters many of those individuals whom she had met in her East End work (and Gissing went to the British Museum Reading Room to read Charles Booth's volumes on London poverty). Gissing's habit of forming liaisons with working-class women who didn't understand him (nor he they), and of needing the solace of unattainable middle-class women to confide in, led him to engage in many alliances during the time Collet knew him, including with yet another of Beatrice Webb's sisters, Rosalind (Rosie) Williams. In terms of the narrative of this book, it's a nice touch that Gissing's last visit to England, in 1901 (he had relocated to France with his third partner, who was French), was to recuperate in the East Anglian sanatorium that had just been opened by one of the early women doctors, Dr Jane Walker.

At a time when economics was becoming increasingly statistical and technical, Clara Collet promoted a more straightforward 'useful knowledge' approach which had much in common with the perspectives of the economists who worked in Settlement sociology networks in the US. Collet corresponded regularly with Edith Abbott of Hull-House, who published around this time various studies of women workers in industries such as cigar-making and the manufacture of boots and shoes.[52] Abbott visited Collet in England in 1907 and they, too, boated together on the river in Richmond.[53] Collet also knew well Julia Lathrop and Sophonisba Breckinridge. They all shared news about the evidence they put forward to policy makers, reviewed each other's books, exchanged books and papers and met one another's families. In 1908, Sophonisba Breckinridge was in England and took back to Abbott 'nice news' of Collet. Abbott had just been reading Collet's piece in the *Statistical Journal* about 'Women occupiers'. 'I should think the Lancashire and Cheshire Committee would reprint that as a very influential tract,' observed Abbott. 'It does seem to me that our census ought to get the statistics that yours does with regard to numbers of families keeping servants. Perhaps I could get Miss Breckinridge to put it up to the authorities.'[54]

The most famous finding of Charles Booth's mammoth investigation of urban poverty was that around a third of Londoners were living in some degree of poverty, caused mainly by structural factors such as industrial depression, disorganized labour markets and low wages.[55] In her 70-page chapter on 'Women's work' in one of the survey's 17 volumes, Collet takes a strictly analytic view of working conditions and wants to understand the economic and social factors determining these: the nature of the trade; the effect of competition among employers; the skill required; the home-worker's private circumstances.[56] The same analytical mind is at work in her attempt to document the whole problem of access to accurate data about women's work, a necessary prerequisite for all reforming efforts. In a key paper read before an august audience at the Royal Statistical Society in 1898, she looked at the generic problem of collecting and using statistics about women's work. Census data, for example, may mislead as to women's ages, occupations and employment status, since only a small proportion of women actually fill in their own Census returns; most are completed by their fathers, husbands or employers, who don't necessarily tell (or know) the truth. The greatest problem with Census data is the absence of information about the occupations of married women, who are returned merely as 'wives'. More than a third of Collet's text is taken up with the issue of maternal employment and infant mortality, a constant preoccupation of Royal Statistical Society discussions. Taking an unusual angle, she shows that a circumstance more closely connected with infant mortality than women's industrial employment is the proportion of indoor domestic servants kept – 'the lower the percentage of domestic servants, the higher the rate of infant mortality'. Servant-keeping, in other words, is a proxy measure of social class.[57] Collet's argument that blaming mothers masked the real reasons for high infant mortality inaugurated a shift in policy makers' approach from descriptive to explanatory social and economic statistics.

The clarity Collet brought to these much-debated social questions made her a widely recognized expert on the position of women. She pioneered the rooting of arguments about women's employment in both accurate statistical evidence and systematic interviewing, and in a catholic use of sources, including Census and factory inspectors' returns. As Mary Paley Marshall, wife of the Cambridge economist Alfred Marshall, put it in her review of one of Collet's books, 'She is not holding a brief for women, but evidently wants to get at the truth, whether it tells for or against them.'[58] Some of this truth involved the evidence of history. Census data contradicted popular assumptions in showing that women's employment was actually declining, not increasing.[59] Moreover, the notion that women ought to idle their time away at home was entirely new. For this argument Collet commanded the support of some of the forgotten texts mentioned in Chapter One of this book. Historian Annie Abram's *Social England in the fifteenth century* demonstrated that no trade in the later medieval period had been closed to women, who had worked in all sorts of occupations as drapers, grocers, merchants, embroiderers, tailors, midwives, barber-surgeons, apothecaries, shipwrights and so forth. Lina Eckenstein wrote about the independence and educational contribution of women living in religious settlements in Anglo-Saxon times.[60] American sceptics of the value of academia, such as Jane Addams, would have enjoyed Eckenstein's conclusion that the main factor ending women's equal participation in the intellectual life of the times was the rise of the secular university. It was Collet's approval of robust historical evidence that underlaid her own cutting remarks about Charlotte Perkins Gilman's *Women and economics* – full of 'stirring appeals' and 'high-minded delusions' with little respect for logic or social and statistical reality.[61]

In 1891 Clara Collet was one of four women asked by a Royal Commission on Labour (RCL) to compile evidence on the employment of women. This was the first British commission to look at women's employment as a separate category. It began as an all-male commission and the inclusion of women and their work came about only as a political afterthought, a response to pressure from the women's trade union movement. The RCL was set up in the aftermath of the London dock strike of 1889, and the aim of the women's commission was to document the differences in men's and women's wages and to examine women's 'grievances' and the effects of their industrial employment on their health and morality and the home. The most senior of the four women invited to consider women's employment was a radical lawyer, Eliza Orme, the first British woman to earn a law degree. Prevented as a woman from practising as a lawyer, Orme ran a flourishing legal conveyancing and patent business with another legal graduate, Mary Richardson. These two women were also the first women to be directors of a building society.[62] As an outspoken agent of change, Orme was the model for the cigar-smoking actuary daughter Vivie Warren in George Bernard Shaw's *Mrs Warren's profession*. Orme's opinions on the subject of 'strong-minded women' remain apt today: 'Society has adopted the word ["strong-minded"] to describe the abnormal result of its own over-restrictions. How, then, can we speak of women who can take a journey by railway without an escort, who can stand by a friend through a surgical operation, and who yet wear ordinary bonnets and carry medium-sized umbrellas?' The correct term, she decided, should be 'sound-minded'.[63]

Orme's role on the RCL was to supervise and read her women colleagues' work, as well as conducting investigations herself into the work of barmaids, waitresses and bookkeepers in hotels and restaurants, and women's work in Wales and the Black Country. At some point in her career as a social investigator, Orme asked her friend Alice Ravenhill, the sanitary reformer, to find out about women in the fish-curing industry. Ravenhill had never done a survey before, but she thought it would be useful experience, so she went to Grimsby, where she sought the help of the local rector to locate the sheds where the fish-curing women worked. He 'professed ignorance of a class of women he described as the lowest, and of the conditions of their work, which he considered as both degrading and unpleasant'.[64] Ravenhill went to a bookshop and got the address of a nonconformist minister, who took her to the sheds and introduced her. She found women in roughly built, ill-lit and freezing buildings standing for hours in salty and filthy water, their hands and shins covered in exposure sores.

The RCL reports on *The employment of women* were published in 1893, and enthusiastically greeted in the pages of *The Economic Journal* as 'a treasure-house of well-authenticated facts' illuminating all sorts of economic questions.[65] Clara Collet's own work on the RCL led directly to her entry into the civil service as an expert on women's work. In 1893 she was appointed a labour correspondent to the Board of Trade, becoming a senior investigator for women's industries there a decade later. In this post she was responsible for many inquiries, investigations and collations of policy evidence on earnings and hours, fair wages, sweated industry and trade boards. The RCL's report also provoked a hugely important development in the situation of women workers and the legislation and policies which led to the welfare state: the appointment in 1893 of the first women factory inspectors.

The idea that women should join the British civil service as inspectors for women's trades wasn't new – it had long been advocated by the Women's Trade Union League – but it had been misogynistically opposed by male civil servants and politicians on the grounds that such duties would be incompatible 'with the gentle and home-loving character of a woman': indeed, their petticoats might even get caught in the machines.[66] This latter fate actually befell, not infrequently, the limbs of children and adults exposed to the awful conditions that the women inspectors found once they had embarked on their pioneering work. May Abraham, the first woman inspector to be appointed, had been a colleague of Collet's on the RCL, where her input had included investigating 170 textile mills in Lancashire and

Cheshire, many textile and clothing trades in Manchester and Yorkshire, and silk mills in Macclesfield – all industries rife with poor sanitary facilities, inadequate ventilation and a system, beloved by employers, of deducting from paltry wages fines for being late and for such minor sins as talking and laughing at work.

By 1896 there were five women inspectors, a close-knit, adventurous, hard-working, imaginative group: May Abraham, Adelaide Anderson, Lucy Deane (later Streatfeild), Mary Paterson and Rose Squire, all born in the 1860s, all from solidly middle- or upper-middle-class families, all single women who needed to earn their own living. They met in each other's homes, or in that of Elizabeth Garrett Anderson, who was Adelaide Anderson's aunt, and they learnt to cycle together, setting out on bicycles or trains or 'Irish jaunting cars' (light two-wheeled carriages drawn by a single horse) or on foot to do battle against multiple, unacknowledged health hazards and industrial dangers.[67] Mary Paterson worked in the early years of the job in her home country, Scotland, and later became one of the first national health insurance commissioners for Scotland. Deane and Squire had an earlier existence as the first women sanitary inspectors in Kensington, where they had chafed at the restrictions of the sanitary role; factory inspection was much closer to the heart of the policy-making process. They had both been students with Alice Ravenhill, taking the diploma of the National Health Society. Adelaide Anderson, the only one of the five with a university education, headed the group as Principal Lady Inspector from 1897. The Committee on Dangerous Trades, set up in 1895, recognized Anderson's expertise and appointed her a member; its chairman, Jack Tennant, later

9.3: Three of the first women factory inspectors in Britain: May Abraham, Lucy Deane Streatfeild, Mary Muirhead Paterson

married her, thus causing her resignation from the inspectorate: the iniquitous 'marriage bar', requiring women to give up work on marriage, wasn't abolished in the Home Civil Service until 1946 (1973 in the Foreign Service).

Another notable addition to the first cohort of women in the factory inspectorate was Hilda Martindale, sister of Louisa, whom we met in Chapter Eight. Their mother, also called Louisa, was a reformer, a women's rights activist and a most determined mother. In 1900 she had taken her daughters on a year's world tour, the high point of which was their visit to Chicago, where they met Jane Addams and were introduced to the buzzing reform factory of Hull-House.[68] Once back in Britain, Henrietta Barnett asked Hilda to talk at a public gathering about work for children in the countries they had visited, and Adelaide Anderson, who was in the audience, offered Hilda a post as factory inspector. Hilda Martindale was initially stationed in the Potteries, and then she joined Deane and Squire in Ireland, becoming Resident Lady Inspector for Ireland in 1904.

Unlike the men inspectors, whose assignments were geographical, the women had the whole field of women's trades across England, Wales, Scotland and Ireland to inspect. Their mission was to identify violations of Factory Acts, prosecute offending employers, report on industrial hazards and make recommendations for improvement. Lucy Deane, appointed in November 1894, was another reformer with a sister in a cognate occupation; Hyacinthe Deane worked as an inspector of domestic science and was one of the first women inspectors in the Department of Education. Lucy Deane recorded in her diary the support network that helped her own baptism into the new role. For example, a few days before she started the new job she 'went, by apt, to see Miss Orme at Bedford Park. So *thankful* I went. She is quite charming & has helped me more than any one. We had a long conversation & she gave me advice, invaluable of course, of which the upshot was – "keep clear of public speaking or sympathy with anything political or Trades Unions etc ... Keep tabulated reports (showed me some of hers & Miss Collet's and Miss Abraham's) ... Don't believe without evidence, without personal thorough investigation".' A few days later, 'Went to tea with Miss Abraham. She is very bright and sensible looking & handsome, dark with fire, fond of riding, said we could work a great deal in each other's hands ... Went to see Mrs. Bondfield.'[69] Lucy never really heeded Eliza Orme's advice to stay out of politics (nor, indeed, did Orme herself).

The women inspectors carried an enormous workload. In 1894, for example, Deane and Squire visited 2,358 factories, 4,590 workshops and 4,500 laundries.[70] They and their colleagues interpreted their brief very widely to cover actively informing workers about their rights, encouraging them to come forward with complaints, and exposing the many subterfuges that employers resorted to in their efforts to avoid the law. It was not uncommon for workers to lose their jobs and be blacklisted because they had been seen talking to the women inspectors. This resulted in the women inventing a few subterfuges of their own. For example, in 1897 Lucy Deane was dispatched to Ireland, where it had been reported that women handkerchief embroiderers were being paid not in money but in goods or credit at the local shop, which constituted an offence under the Truck Acts. Deane shipped her bicycle ahead of her – in 1896 the Home Office had cautiously sanctioned factory inspectors' use of bicycles at the reimbursement rate of a penny a mile – and travelled to Ardara, a small, isolated town in Donegal, where she obtained some inside information from a local embroiderer. She then took her colleague Mary Paterson, dressed as a country girl, to mingle with the women as they brought their embroidery into the local agent's shop. Paterson was thus able to witness them being 'paid' with packets of poor tea or eggs or credit notes.[71] There's a fine line between these manoeuvres and the covert investigations of women journalists and social scientists explored in Chapter Three.

Rose Squire told an engrossing tale in her autobiography of the lengths to which she went in the endeavour to find employers who were operating illegally: 'On one occasion, after an absence of some weeks from a small town in the Midlands where I knew the railway station was watched (to catch the government lady), I arrived after dark by a road from a distance, hurried into an hotel and engaged a room from whence I had a view of the factory windows. Watch was kept on the lighted windows until after ten o'clock, when I crossed the street and entered an unguarded door as someone came out. I was found half an hour later by the astonished employer (who had been hastily fetched from his house) among the workgirls, taking their names and addresses in preparation for the inevitable prosecution.'[72] At Dungloe, a coastal village, Squire stayed in a hotel full of English trout fishermen, going out daily on her bicycle equipped with camera, sketch book and sandwiches to talk to country women in their cottages, and allaying suspicion by letting the other hotel guests believe she was an 'authoress'.[73] Prosecuting offenders was one of the women inspectors' duties, and it was one at which they excelled, despite having no legal training: in 1898, for instance, the 'lady inspectors' launched 128 prosecutions against negligent employers and got 125 convictions. Squire was particularly impressive in court. In a case involving exploitative working hours in a smart Regent Street shop, she raided the shop after midnight and presented an elaborately wrapped box of chocolates as evidence in the prosecution of the employer who required women, after a full day's work selling chocolates, to stay on packing chocolates in ornate, beribboned boxes and hampers. She won the case, sharing the box of chocolates with her colleagues.[74]

The women weren't hired for their excellence as amateur lawyers, but they were hired partly because it was thought they would be better than men at getting access to the facts about women's work. This proved particularly true with respect to the dangers to workers' health of the match-making industry. Three times as many women as men, many of them under 18, were involved in making and packing matches.[75] The plight of the Bryant and May match-girls to which Clementina Black had drawn attention in 1888 was a matter of occupational disease as well as low pay and savage working conditions. The phosphorus used to make matches caused a form of bone cancer known as 'phossy jaw' in which the side of the face turned green and black, discharging foul-smelling pus and leading eventually to death. On the grounds that banning phosphorus would impede free trade, the British government had refused to follow the example set by other countries.[76] Investigating this industry in 1898, Rose Squire watched workers trying to cram as many matches as speedily as possible into boxes which, when overfilled, ignited and were dropped on the floor, giving off deadly fumes. The process of match-dipping, which involved phosphorus spread on a plate, also meant poisonous fumes. As Squire remembered, 'In a certain town, by following up hints thrown out by frightened girls, I dug out cases of men and women hidden away in the slums ... Some of the sufferers had toothless gums. One woman had completely lost the lower jaw, a young girl in an earlier stage of the disease was constantly in great pain while the suppurating jaw bone was gradually decaying.'[77] Some victims were given hush money by employers. As a result of Squire's investigation, medical experts in the Home Office carried out an exhaustive study of phosphorus poisoning that led to structural changes in factories to remove fumes, other changes such as medical examinations and dental care, and eventually the substitution of safer alternatives for the deadly phosphorus.

Machine safety was another unladylike concern. 'It is evident that ... the tact and sympathy of lady inspectors is invaluable,' noted Bessie Hutchins and Amy Harrison in their *A history of factory legislation*, 'and they do not disdain to spend time and thought over such matters as adapting of a "face guard" or a respirator.'[78] Rose Squire remembered a young girl of 15 whose hair got caught in a shaft driving a factory sewing machine, and who lost her scalp and most of the skin on her face, lay in the London Hospital for three months and then died.[79] In 1899, Lucy Deane began systematically to collect and analyse accidents in laundries in West London, using accident reports and her own observations. Most laundries were small businesses located in the basements or on the ground floors of multi-occupancy houses, with not more than a dozen workers, although many were crammed into back kitchens, with machines connected to a little gas engine tightly wedged in a dark broom cupboard under the stairs. Houses quivered and shook, and the laundries were damp and steamy affairs, with windows sealed to stop smuts descending on clean linen. Workers put in more than 60 hours in a six-day week, with few breaks allowed and often much night work. It was arduous and hazardous work, with the risk of scalds from hot water and steam, and burns from irons. The air, laden with particles of soda and ammonia, was very thirst-inducing, and 'beermen' brought cans of beer from the local public house twice a day, a habit seemingly not found in any other trade.[80] Hazards multiplied with the introduction of new, steam-powered equipment that included hydro-extractors, mangling and starching machines, shirt-bosom polishers, blouse-ironers, gophering (ironing) machines and drying closets, driven by systems of belts and pulleys and powered by small steam engines. In 1896, when the first accident figures were collected, 81 out of 84 reported laundry accidents were caused by machinery.[81] Lucy Deane went to the site of all the 37 laundry accidents reported in West London in 1900–01, and she worked with laundry managers and engineers to develop, test and monitor different types of machinery guards. Through a series of successful prosecutions, management was made to take responsibility for compensating workers who had been injured by machines lacking adequate guards. A reduction in laundry accidents followed.[82]

Lead was a major industrial poison: white lead works were known as 'white cemeteries'.[83] Lead gained the attention of the women inspectors mainly through its use in the pottery industry, where it was a constituent of enamels and glazes. It got into workers' bodies through the pores of the skin and through the inhalation and swallowing of lead dust. Poisoning could be either chronic (colic, paralysis, cramps, cirrhosis, degeneration of the brain, blindness) or acute (severe colic, constipation/diarrhoea, anaemia and delirium). The *British Medical Journal* was not alone in suggesting that girls and women with these symptoms were simply being hysterical.[84] A similar unpreparedness to take women seriously was behind the dismissal of women silk-workers' claims that they were coughing up not just silk dust but actual silkworms.[85] Suggestions for lead control, such as requiring that women change their boots before going home, made little sense, as Mary Paterson observed, since very few of the women employed in white lead industries possessed more than one pair of boots.[86] She and Lucy Deane looked at the reproductive histories of 77 married women in the pottery industries in 1896–97 who had been identified as suffering from lead poisoning. Of these 77 women, 35 shared 90 miscarriages, 8 reported stillbirths, and 15 had no living children. Of the 36 women who had given birth to 101 living children, only 61 of their children were still alive.[87] Deane and Paterson's report, which recommended the development of leadless glazes, was highly influential in the campaign to reduce the use of lead in the pottery industry.[88]

The hazards of industrial labour were an international problem. Adelaide Anderson made a particular study of factory regulations in Germany and Austria; she translated Germany's special rules for the bichromate industry and for letterpress printing works, and her study of practice in France contributed to the inclusion of all laundries in the British Factory and Workshop Act of 1907.[89] Another of Anderson's achievements was to highlight the industrial hazard of label-licking, which she observed in a country thread mill during her first year as a factory inspector. In one large Lancashire thread mill, the tickets for bobbins were almost entirely moistened by 12 young, full-time workers licking up to 50 gross of labels a day, and 35 half-timers licking up to 25 gross a day. Many workers had swollen neck glands and other symptoms, a syndrome known colloquially as 'stamp lickers' tongue'. Anderson reported this to the Dangerous Trades Committee, which identified the same practice in the silk and aerated-water industries. Sweet-packing, siphon-labelling, tin-labelling and cigar-banding all entailed vast quantities of licking. 'In 1903,' wrote Anderson victoriously in her autobiography, 'I was able to give an account of a good power-driven machine for punching labels and pasting them onto thred-spools which I had seen that year at work in silk mills in the Grand Duchy of Baden, a health and time-saving machine doing the work very efficiently.'[90] Anderson and Deane spent their leave in 1897 attending the first meeting of the Congrès International de Législation du Travail in Brussels. (One is tempted to comment that with all this unpaid overtime the Home Office must itself have been breaching some Act or other.)

What all this added up to was a substantial decline in the dangerousness of the dangerous trades to women, children and men as a direct result of the women factory inspectors' work. The scrupulous evidence they amassed, the reforms they advocated, and their awareness of developments in continental Europe, were fundamental to debates and developments in late 19th- and early 20th-century social reform, and they led to greater state regulation of industry. 'Facts accurately observed and recorded are the stuff out of which effective laws are framed,' as Squire remarked.[91] The women inspectors were pioneering a methodology at the forefront of developments in occupational health at the time: systematic recording of statistics; careful observation; tracking the relationships between structural factors and workers' health. Their habit of making home visits to ascertain hidden sufferers and the causes of accidents and illness was not replicated in the male inspectors' reports.[92]

This was a critical moment at the end of the great modern transition between the old miasmatic theory of disease and the new understanding that many diseases could be attributed to specific germs or particular environmental factors. It was also the beginning of the time when more precise scientific tests were becoming available. The women inspectors worked with scientists to establish precise criteria for air quality and good ventilation, and they collected air samples and sent them off for analysis. This work intensified with the arrival in 1905 of the first scientifically qualified woman factory inspector, Mildred Power, a graduate of the Royal Commission on Sewage Disposal (on which she served as an assistant bacteriologist). Interestingly, and sadly, the laboriously gained insights and wisdom of the women inspectors have been condemned to a different interpretation in much feminist historiography – that here was a group of moralizing, middle-class women who were acting as agents of the state in demanding cleanliness and the 'protection' of vulnerable women workers as solutions to the damages of industrial labour.[93] The debate about whether women should be a protected class of workers, and potentially endure a curtailment of their rights as a result, was one that certainly occupied much reforming time and attention, and it divided those who were otherwise agreed that much needed to be done. It did not, however, detract from the women reformers' role as scientists (of both the natural and social sort) who had a real impact on industrial conditions and on policy and legislation.

Links between social reform, the social and medical investigation of industrial work, the trade union movement and the networks of women connected to the suffrage and peace movements were common. Kerstin Hesselgren was the first woman factory inspector to be appointed in Sweden, in 1912. She was known as 'Kerstin the First' because of the number of firsts for women she achieved: aside from the factory inspectorate, she was Sweden's first female parliamentarian and the first Swedish woman delegate to the International Labour Organization and the League of Nations.[94] Our knowledge of her life,

9.4: Kerstin Hesselgren, c. 1900

particularly for English speakers, is restricted by the absence of a biography and by a focus on her political career rather than her extensive social reform, research and policy work, which seems to have followed a very similar pattern to that of women reformers in Britain and the US.[95] Hesselgren was the daughter of a rural doctor, and she trained in nursing, hygiene and household economy at the Karolinska Institute in Stockholm and in Germany, acquiring, it is said, a certificate as a barber-surgeon. While head of the School of Domestic Science in Stockholm, she took a year's absence in 1904 to attend Bedford College in London, where she gained a sanitary inspector's diploma. Hesselgren did her factory inspector's job for 22 years and was a strong supporter of the trade union movement, setting up a number of unions herself. She was a passionate pacifist and supporter of the women's peace meeting in The Hague, arguing that 'humanity has to destroy war before war destroys humanity'.[96] In the early 1920s her stringent criticism of defence spending in the Swedish Parliament successfully moved money out of the military budget and into paying for radical social reforms.[97]

The American lawyer Crystal Eastman had a distinguished legal career, as well as being an outspoken pacifist, socialist and feminist – although histories of the period often mention her merely as an adjunct of her much more famous brother, the writer and political activist Max Eastman. Crystal Eastman's study of work accidents is a classic of epidemiology that paved the way for the first Workmen's Compensation Law in the US. Her *Work accidents and the law* (1910) was written as part of a mammoth survey of urban conditions in Pittsburgh. Eastman had studied sociology at Columbia University and then law, and had worked in the Settlement movement. For her input to the survey she took one year's data on industrial fatalities and three months' on industrial accidents occurring in Allegheny County, Pennsylvania, in 1906–07. She studied the total of 1,035 cases in detail, using coroners' and hospital records, and family, neighbourhood and workplace interviews, deploying Italian and Slavic investigators as necessary. 'Poor people do most of the hazardous work in the world,' observes Eastman, factually.[98] Her report is illustrated with

9.5: Crystal Eastman, c. 1915

many tables, graphs and blurry black-and-white photographs of machinery and people ('the problem of a railroad widow', 'One arm and four children'), and it carries a compelling appendix by Eastman recording her personal experiences of visiting afflicted families. This approach of meshing observations and statistics runs throughout the six volumes of the Pittsburgh Survey. It's especially marked in 'One of the most vivid and heart wrenching pieces of reform scholarship of the early 20th century', an account by another investigator, Margaret Byington, of steel workers' living conditions.[99]

The investigative work of the Hull-House women, especially Florence Kelley, also had an enormous influence on the enactment of state labour laws curtailing unhealthy and dangerous working conditions, and considerable impact on the political agenda of the Progressive Party and the New Deal in the US.[100] But the main campaigner against dangerous trades in the Hull-House community was Dr Alice Hamilton. Her reading of Thomas Oliver's *Dangerous trades* in 1907 dispatched her immediately to the library to find out all she could about the hazards faced by industrial workers. What she found there shocked her deeply: in the early 1900s industrial medicine simply did not exist in the US. There was no need for the subject, she was told, because workers were treated well here. But Hamilton, living where she did, in Hull-House, 'could not fail to hear tales of the dangers that workingmen faced, of cases of carbon-monoxide gassing in the great steel mills, of painters disabled by lead palsy, of pneumonia and rheumatism among the men in the stockyards'.[101] She had read a study of phossy jaw among match workers – and Jane Addams had seen some cases in London in the 1880s and had told her how awful the deformities were. From this beginning, Dr Alice Hamilton became a leading national and international expert on industrial toxicology, the founder of the field in its modern form.

In a photo taken in her late 80s, Hamilton is well dressed, seated at a tidy desk with an inkwell and papers, against a background of bookshelves, and despite her advanced years she looks clear-sightedly and wisely at you as though she knows exactly who you are and what you're up to. One of five children brought up in Indiana by liberal parents who didn't believe in formal education, Hamilton was taught a little mathematics by a governess, but otherwise learnt languages and the habit of poring over books from her parents. Her paternal grandmother was passionate about the temperance movement and about women's suffrage and she counted Susan B. Anthony among her friends. Hamilton and her three sisters all had to earn their own living because of diminishing family finances. She chose medicine,

9.6: Alice Hamilton, 1957

not because she loved – or knew anything about – science, but because she believed that as a doctor she would be able to go anywhere she pleased and be useful at the same time. She went to do medicine at the University of Michigan, and then to Germany with her sister Edith Hamilton in 1895 to study bacteriology and pathology. The professor in Munich conceded that she might attend his lectures, provided that she arrived before the other students and sat in a separate chair in the corner. Returning home to the US, she got a job teaching in the women's medical school at Northwestern University in Chicago, which allowed her to fulfil her dream of living at Hull-House. Hamilton had met Jane Addams when Addams came to speak in Hamilton's home town of Fort Wayne, and it was after hearing Addams speak that Hamilton and her sister decided to take up Settlement life. Alice Hamilton lived in Hull-House for 22 years, returning every year thereafter, and acting as Addams' personal doctor, until Addams died in 1935.[102]

Her early years at Hull-House were very busy: she opened a well-baby clinic, bathing the local babies in the basement of Hull-House (which was difficult as some of them came sewn into their clothes for the winter and had Italian mothers with an unwholesome fear of water). She taught classes in anatomy and physiology, and English to Russian and Greek immigrants, directed men's fencing and athletic clubs, visited sick children at home and helped with the duty of tending the door and showing visitors around. At Hull-House they consulted Dr Hamilton about everything medical and she became embroiled in a fight against local drug dealers who sold cocaine – 'happy dust' – to schoolchildren. Lawyers defending the dealers constantly argued that the substance wasn't cocaine, and the only way to prove them wrong was to test it – at first on rabbits, but then, when she was accused of cruelty to animals, Hamilton took the powders herself, the proof being disconcerting dilatation of the pupils of her eyes.[103]

In the autumn of 1902 Chicago experienced a typhoid epidemic, and Hull-House appeared to be the epicentre. Jane Addams asked Hamilton to find out why so many people in the neighbourhood were dying of typhoid. Hamilton prowled about the streets and ramshackle wooden tenement houses, observing the outdoor privies, forbidden by law, sometimes set below the level of the street, and overflowing in heavy rains; she saw the wretched indoor water closets, perhaps one for four to five families, filthy and with broken plumbing, and swarms of flies everywhere. Her hypothesis was that flies were the problem. They were feeding on typhoid-infected excreta and then alighting on food and milk. Two Hull-House residents, Maud Gernon and Gertrude Howe, helped Hamilton to test her theory. The three women embarked on the engaging task of scooping up flies from filthy privies and water closets and kitchens. They dropped the flies into broth, and Hamilton took them to the laboratory to incubate them and plate them out. Triumphantly, she found the typhoid bacillus, and proceeded to write up the discovery for presentation to the Chicago Medical Society. A subsequent public inquiry led to the complete reorganization of the Health Department under a chief loaned by the Public Health Service. Hamilton said that she gained more kudos for her typhoid discovery than for anything else accomplished in a long and distinguished medical life. This is ironic, given the sting in the tail of the story. Flies had little or nothing to do with it. The cause was simpler, but also so much more discreditable that the Health Department didn't dare reveal it. A local pumping station had developed a break that resulted in the escape, over three days, of raw sewage into the water pipes.[104]

In Hamilton's view, industrial poisoning was, next to tuberculosis, the great destroyer of the working class, and it was as endemic in poor industrial areas as malaria was in swamps.[105] As was the case with many women reformers, her work exposed her to adventures considerably at odds with prevalent definitions of womanhood. She bought beers for workers in order to interview them in saloons where women were not expected to go; she climbed dangerous catwalks, wore workers' overalls to descend deep into mine shafts and spent nights in workers' shacks, being mistaken for a prostitute.[106] Her studies of lead and mercury poisoning had immense impact in terms of reforming public policy and industrial toxicology. She showed decisively that the US had higher morbidity and mortality rates from industrial poisons than did its European counterparts, attributing this to less effective factory inspection-systems. Charles Henderson, a Chicago sociologist, had been studying sickness compensation in Germany, and he persuaded the state government of Illinois to set up an Occupational Disease Commission in 1908, with Dr Alice Hamilton its token woman member. In her role on the Commission, Hamilton directed a team of 23 assistants inquiring into the dangers of lead, arsenic, brass, carbon monoxide, turpentine and the cyanides. Hamilton and her assistants visited 304 establishments and found more than 70 industrial processes that exposed workers to lead poisoning. In one factory that they studied, 41% of the workers were poisoned.[107] They visited plants, read hospital records, interviewed labour leaders and doctors and apothecaries, and discovered all sorts of unrecognized lead trades such as making freight-car seals, coffin trims, and polishing cut glass. Hamilton had to report back in such a way that no factory referred to could be identified, but she never felt that this was the end of her responsibility. 'I was the only one who had seen the men ... sandpapering the lead-painted ceilings of Pullman cars, shoveling the white lead from the drying pans. How could I hope that a cold, printed report which would satisfy the Commission would serve to do away with these pressing dangers? So, from the first, I made it a rule to try to bring before the responsible man at the top the dangers I had discovered in his plant and to persuade him to take the simple steps which even I, with no engineering knowledge, could see were needed.'[108]

Alice Hamilton knew that you often had to see the workers in their own homes in order to get the facts: 'Life at Hull-House had accustomed me to going straight to the homes of people about whom I wished to learn something and talking to them in their own surroundings, where they have courage to speak out what is in their minds.'[109] Through this work, Hamilton developed her characteristic technique of 'shoe-leather epidemiology', which combined thorough investigation of workplaces, the correlation of symptoms with specific industrial processes and the compilation and verification of diagnosed poisoning cases.[110] The lead survey resulted in the documentation of 578 cases of poisoning and a report that provoked an occupational disease law requiring safety measures in workplaces, regular medical examinations and reporting of illness to the factory inspectorate.[111]

The First World War brought Hamilton an active involvement in the peace movement. Like the British women factory inspectors, her pacifism directed her professional attention to hazards in munitions factories; she identified thousands of workers poisoned by nitrous fumes and trinitrotoluene (TNT, an explosive chemical). It was grotesque, declared Hamilton, that men died producing goods designed to kill others, and that people made a profit out of this. Pacifism always helped her to find her real place and leave muddled thinking behind.[112] In 1918 Alice Hamilton's work was recognized in her appointment as the first woman professor at Harvard University, a stronghold of masculinity (female medical students were not admitted until 1945). The Harvard School of Medicine wanted to expand its public health work and Hamilton was the only suitable candidate. She agreed to forgo perks such as access to the Harvard Club and football tickets in order to relieve the men's anxiety about the admission of a woman. Instead of football, she embarked on a new investigation of mercury-producing and mercury-using industries. In one hat-making town in Connecticut, 43% of workers examined had the tremors, twitching, delirium and confusion known as 'hatter's shakes' and commemorated in the phrase 'mad as a hatter'.[113] In the 1920s she turned her attention to environmental conditions in General Electric Company works, was invited to Soviet Russia to advise about public health, publicized the early cases and dangers of radium poisoning and joined, as its only woman member, the Occupational Health Committee of the League of Nations, whose nationalism she was never able to get used to. Despite all this, Harvard University never promoted her, and she remained an assistant professor until she retired at 65.

The protection of workers was an international issue. The strength of women reformers' networks shows itself powerfully here, connecting fact–gathering research on working conditions with political interest groups and campaigns. The first two women in the Western world to be appointed as members of government cabinets both had a background in industrial reform and the consumer movement: Frances Perkins in Washington in 1933, and Margaret Bondfield in London in 1929. Perkins, Secretary of Labor from 1933 to 1945 and the 'Mother of social security' in the US, offers a prime case study in the interwoven threads of research, reform and policy making stitched together by the strong fabric of the women's network. Her story is told later, in Chapter Eleven. This chapter ends with Margaret Bondfield, the British trade unionist, the first woman minister (in the 1924 Labour Government) and the first female Minister of Labour and cabinet member (after the 1929 election). In the photograph, she's campaigning from the back of a car in 1918 with the compelling confidence that was one of her trademarks.

Bondfield was the tenth child of a Somerset laceworker and she entered the world of work at the age of 14 with a job as a shop assistant in Brighton. There Hilda Martindale's mother, Louisa, had already decided that shop assistants were an oppressed group, and she invited some of them to her house. Among these was Bondfield, 'an eager, attractive, and vividly alive girl of

sixteen', as Hilda Martindale recalled. Bondfield told the Martindales all about the evils of the living–in system, whereby many shop owners provided accommodation, often substandard, for their shop workers. It meant 'sleeping in bare, dingy, stuffy dormitories, intolerably hot in summer, miserably cold in winter; never being alone ... no place to keep one's things ... fines for entering the dormitory during the day-

9.7: Margaret Bondfield, c. 1930

time; nights spent with a poor consumptive girl, who coughed and coughed, and with a middle-aged woman, who led a bad life and liked talking about it'.[114] Bondfield wrote about her experiences surreptitiously at night by the light of a candle concealed from her room-mates by a towel, publishing articles and stories under the pseudonym 'Grace Dare' in the magazine *The Shop Assistant* and in the *Daily Chronicle*. Louisa Martindale lent Margaret Bondfield books on social issues, and, when she had saved enough money to go to London, Bondfield joined the Ideal Club in Tottenham Court Road, where many such issues were debated by the likes of Beatrice and Sidney Webb and George Bernard Shaw. One day she bought fish and chips in Fitzroy Street, and the newspaper they were wrapped in contained a letter from the secretary of the National Union of Shop Assistants, Warehousemen and Clerks, urging shop assistants to join the Union. Bondfield, who was then working a 65-hour week for scarcely enough money to afford fish and chips, promptly did so. The WIC, hearing through the Ideal Club of this 'exceptionally level-headed' young shop assistant, took her on for two years to carry out an investigation of shop assistants' work.

Bondfield's mission was to use the undercover method of social research to obtain engagements in various shops, staying long enough to judge working conditions. Her reports formed the basis of articles written by the journalist and economist Vaughan Nash in the *Daily Chronicle*, which were used by the Liberal politician Sir John Lubbock as material for legislation to improve shop assistants' working conditions.[115] Bondfield also published descriptions of shop work (under her own name) in places such as *The Economic Journal* (1899) and the *Journal of the Royal Sanitary Institute* (1904): 'I think it is not sufficiently understood that the nature of the work in connection with serving customers is irritating and fatiguing to the last degree,' she remarked politely in one of these. Analysing the 1,280 medical certificates received by the central office of the Shop Assistants' Union in 1903, she showed that one in five shop workers who had registered as sick suffered from 'anaemia and debility' and 'digestive diseases', and more than twice as many reported respiratory illness.[116] When the feminist writer Cicely

Hamilton produced her play about the shop worker's burden, *Diana of Dobson's* in 1908, Bondfield was consulted about its 'living-in' setting. The Diana of the title is a young woman, Diana Massingherd, who conceives a 'fierce resentment against the system that aimed at transforming living flesh and blood into the mechanism of a profit-mongering drapery machine', and whose inheritance of some money leads her to discover how the other half lives.[117] It was written as a farce, but the prominence of the campaign to improve the shop workers' lot turned it into a widely acclaimed political documentary.

Margaret Bondfield went to the US for the first time in 1910 to talk about the trade union movement. She had already met Edith Abbott in Oxford through Clara Collet, so it was entirely logical that in the US she should go directly to Hull-House. On arriving there, 'We were invited to proceed immediately to a Suffrage meeting, but we decided to go to bed at once. We were very tired.'[118] Bondfield and her friend, the suffragist Maud Ward, were caught up in the maelstrom of activities that usually greeted visitors to Hull-House: they were taken to the Hull-House theatre and the Labour Museum; they fitted in a visit to Chicago's fruit market, where they witnessed bananas ripening in 'electric-lighted caves'; they met Carrie Chapman Catt and Rose Schneiderman at the Women's Trade Union League offices, the progressive politician Robert La Follette and his daughter Fola, the labour activist sisters Margaret Robins and Mary Dreier, and Professor DuBois, author of the study of *The Philadelphia Negro*, at 'Miss Ovington's'.[119] Bondfield lectured to Sophonisba Breckinridge's class at Chicago University on her investigation into married women's employment, and, despite her disinclination that first evening, she did speak at several Hull-House suffrage meetings. Jane Addams invited Bondfield and Ward to her room for intimate conversations, telling them some of the things she'd been up to with the assistance of Julia Lathrop and Florence Kelley.

This was a woman who 'just lived for the trade union movement'.[120] She became assistant secretary of her union in 1898, learning to smoke 'in self-defence as the men's pipes were awful' during the long drawn-out union executive meetings.[121] She was an executive member of the Women's Trade Union

League and, with her friend Mary Macarthur, she established the first women's general union, the National Federation of Women Workers. She was the first woman elected to the Trade Union Council Executive and its first female Chairman. In 1912 she and Macarthur were members of the Advisory Committee on the Health Insurance Bill and were able to secure the inclusion of maternity benefit in the 1911 National Insurance Act. She never lost her class allegiance. During her first European trip in 1904, when she attended the ICW Congress in Berlin to talk about factory and workshop conditions, she felt distinctly out of place at the grand dinner presided over by Lady Aberdeen at a table laden with orchids and six glasses each for wine. A photograph of the occasion testifies to its grandiosity and to the now forgotten habit of hat-wearing while dining. However, Bondfield did appreciate the opportunity to meet Charlotte Perkins Gilman, Rosika Schwimmer and Alice Salomon.[122] In 1915 she was one of the 100 British women who signed an 'open letter' to women in Germany and Austria appealing for their support in calling an end to the war. Bondfield and Lucy Deane could both claim the distinction of being on the list of those refused passports to attend the 1915 women's peace congress in The Hague.

9.8: International Council of Women Congress dinner, Berlin, 1904

Margaret Bondfield's friend Molly Hamilton wrote a biography of her in 1924. Its opening chapter recalled the start of the 1918 Labour Party campaign at the general election when, at a meeting in the Albert Hall marked by great chaos, clamour and dissension, 'a tiny woman' came forward, 'hands thrust deep in the pockets of a rose-red jersey coat, no manuscript, no notes even', instantly bringing the meeting to order with her clear and compelling voice and asking it to consider what had happened to the great labour movement and its capacity for a new kind of government.[123]

Clara Collet's advice to Margaret Bondfield was, 'Concentrate on anything you like, but shut out everything else; concentrate on the subject chosen and stick to it.'[124] All the women who contributed to the reduction of dangerous trades, both those named in this chapter and many others, were skilled in the art of persistently focused work. Together they authored a formidable account of the class and gender injustices perpetrated by a profit-driven economic system. 'As one gets older, the meaning of the story slowly reveals itself,' wrote Bondfield in her autobiography. 'We ourselves are not the authors of the drama – we are only the actors. We are liable to be as much astonished at it as anyone else. I foresaw nothing. Only towards the end did I begin to realize how intricate a construction my life had been – how carefully it had been fitted together, and made to yield certain results.'[125]

TEN

Domestic relations: female attachments, homes, and the trouble with marriage

Marriage, argued writer, actor and feminist Cicely Hamilton at the height of the suffrage campaign in 1909, is a leading cause of the economic and social disabilities suffered by women. 'It is ridiculous to suppose that nature, who never makes two blades of grass alike, desired to turn out indefinite millions of women all cut to the regulation pattern of wifehood.' Marriage, for women, is a compulsory trade, simply an exchange of persons for the means of subsistence, and thus akin to prostitution. Its reality as 'a sweated trade' and the status of women as 'class wives' is concealed and maintained by a variety of subterfuges on the part of men: the idea of women's natural domestic instinct, of a 'natural' division of labour, of women's deficient rationality, of women as nothing more than breeding machines and 'the necessary adjunct to a frying pan'.[1] Hamilton's case is argued with uncompromising logic and a healthy dash of humour, and it includes the point, crucial to the reformers of both sanitary science and municipal housekeeping, that a trade thus exercised is hardly likely to be an efficient one, since the care of homes and families requires education, expertise, science and respect for the individual human dignity of those whose work it is.

Cicely Hamilton's *Marriage as a trade* was a major document of Edwardian feminism. It provided an analysis of patriarchy without using the term, and it drew people's attention to the economic subjection of women in the home as considerably more important than the vote. It was one of many texts on this theme, and Hamilton was one of many women who cast a critical eye over the conventional division between public and private worlds. Just as the women considered how the conduct of public life often favours warfare over welfare, so they thought it essential to look at how the conditions of home life interfere with the promotion of welfare. There were three tasks: to analyse what marriage and conventional family life does to people; to interrogate the status of children and childhood; and to re-envision the material and administrative design of homes. This chapter takes a journey through all these topics. It aims to show how some women reformers' objections to militarism, aggression and power inequalities were reflected in their perspectives on personal life. Cicely Hamilton's story offers an entrée to an unfamiliar land of female attachments and cooperative coexistence that was in turn connected to ideas about a material restructuring of homes and domestic labour. All this was 'utopian' in the sense of the radically different world imagined by Charlotte Perkins Gilman, but some of it was real, and it did really happen.

Published in 1909, Hamilton's book followed one of Gilman's significant non-fiction texts, *Women and economics* (1898), and it preceded a third, Olive Schreiner's *Woman and labour* (1911). Gilman knew, and admired, Hamilton's *Marriage as a trade*, and she sent her a signed copy of her own book; Hamilton, in response, told Gilman, 'My own work owes so much to you that I am glad to know that you are not ashamed of your follower.'[2] *Women and economics* proposed that women's economic dependence on men had caused a morbid and 'excessive sex-distinction' in women and a 'pathological' form of motherhood which ill serves the interests of the child. On the other hand, 'A mother economically free, a world-servant instead of a house-servant; a mother knowing the world and living in it, – can be to her children far more than has ever been possible before.'[3] Schreiner's *Woman and labour* was dedicated to the British suffrage campaigner and writer of painful prison narratives, Constance Lytton (see Chapter Eight). Schreiner's book has a sad history: the main text of *Woman and labour* was complete by 1899, but it fell victim to the Boer War and was burnt when British troops looted Schreiner's house in Johannesburg.[4] In reconstructing her text, Schreiner places great emphasis on the notion of 'sex-parasitism' – the condition of women's dependence as wives and mothers on their 'sexual function alone'. Like Gilman, but unlike Hamilton, Schreiner idolizes, rather than dissects, the personal relationships of men and women.

Cicely Hamilton's own trade was practised mainly in the theatre as a playwright and an actor, and in fictional forms of writing. Her own experience of family life was disorganized, with a mother who disappeared, probably into a lunatic asylum, when Cicely was ten, and a father whose career in the army led him to consign his four children to the care of relatives. One of these paid for the teenage Cicely to go to school in Bad Homburg

10.1: Cicely Hamilton

in Germany for a year, which made her bilingual, a handy skill enabling her to earn a small living from teaching German and doing translations. She tried work on the stage, but was only moderately successful, deeming her face 'unfortunately … not of the type that induces theatrical managers to offer engagements on sight'; her autobiography, published in 1935, carries a photograph of a square-faced woman with blown hair and a sleepy cat. Hamilton discovered that female actors had to pay for their own clothes, which male actors didn't, and there was a pronounced shortage of good roles for women. She joined the suffrage movement 'not from any faith in the magic of the vote' but 'to write and speak against the secondary existence of women', and she started writing plays which featured real, interesting female characters.[5]

One of her creations was *A pageant of great women*.[6] This was mainstream suffrage drama, a huge spectacle performed originally in London and then all over Britain to raise funds for the Actresses' Franchise League. The play is about a central mission of this book: the attempt to restore to the historical record important and world-changing but forgotten lives. *A pageant of great women* enlists a cast of between 50 and 90 historical characters from women's history (the number of parts depended on the performance) who all add their voices to modern women's cause. Its effect, in bringing together women from different countries, times and places, is to present a commanding visual statement about female solidarity. Hamilton resisted the call by American suffragists to extend the list to take in American women's history, so the Americans put on their own version.[7] Negotiations between Hamilton, the Hungarian pacifist Rosika Schwimmer and Countess Iska Teleki, a leading light in the Hungarian suffrage movement, for a Hungarian version to be performed at the IWSA congress in Budapest in 1913, fell foul of copyright problems, although Schwimmer did do the translation.[8]

In her radical text on marriage, Hamilton pointed out one of its inequities, which was a cause célèbre of the women's movement: married women's loss of their own nationality. The 1870 Naturalisation Act imposed on British women the obligation to take on the nationality of their husbands, whether they wanted to or not. Women who lost British citizenship on marriage to 'foreign-born' men had no automatic right to get it back, even if they divorced. 'Foreign-born' men and unmarried women could apply for British nationality, but married women were classed with 'lunatics and children' as 'under a disability', and therefore ineligible. Hence the American feminist Harriot Stanton, daughter of the famous Elizabeth Cady Stanton, who met a 'tall, dark, Englishman' on her way back to the US from her travels in Europe in 1882 and married him, found that, as Harriot Stanton Blatch, she was no longer an American, but an Englishwoman: her nationality had been stolen from her, and there was nothing she could do about it.[9] This remained the situation until 1948, despite the heroic efforts of many, led in Britain by the Scottish barrister Chrystal Macmillan, to do something about it. 'The right to nationality in one's own person is the most fundamental political right,' declared

Macmillan.[10] She headed the Nationality of Married Women Committee of the IWSA and was tirelessly involved in drafting bills, writing pamphlets and articles, lecturing at women's meetings and heading deputations to the Home Office. The absurdity of the situation was highlighted in 1914 when British women, deprived of their nationality on marriage, were classed as 'aliens', had to register with the police and were unable to get passports. Macmillan cited the real-life cases: 'Mrs. E., before the War married a man who had been in England since he was two months old but was born in Germany. She had no idea he was not British, and the question never arose until the war broke out, when he was interned and his business ruined. The wife was compelled to endure all the hardship inflicted on Germans at that time, although she had never been out of the country … Mrs. F., an English woman of considerable wealth, married a German after the Armistice, and so lost her British nationality. Under certain of the provisions of the Treaty of Versailles, which authorised the confiscation of private property, the British Government deprived her of her possessions on the ground that she was an enemy alien.'[11] American women's organizations were similarly involved in efforts to get the law on gender and nationality cleaned up in their own country, a campaign in which lawyer Sophonisba Breckinridge of Hull-House was a leading light.[12]

In Hamilton's *Pageant of great women* the role of St Hilda, the 7th-century abbess and royal advisor, was originally played by Charlotte Despard, the wonderfully contradictory president of the Women's Freedom League (WFL). In her lifetime Despard espoused suffragism, pacifism, socialism, communism, Catholicism, vegetarianism, theosophy, anti-colonialism and Home Rule for Ireland and India, and some rather trickier ideas such as the transmigration of souls, a belief that enabled her to seek the political advice of the dead Italian politician and proponent of equal rights for women, Giuseppe Mazzini. Despard and Hamilton both also enter the historical record through their membership of the Tax Resistance League (TRL), a direct action group founded in Dr Louisa Garrett Anderson's drawing room in 1909 and affiliated to the WFL. With its slogan 'No vote no tax', the TRL pledged its members to refuse payment of all taxes on the grounds that the government had refused women citizenship. The tax resisted was mainly tax on the income of middle-class women, but other taxes were also declined: Emma Sproson, for example, later the first woman councillor for Wolverhampton, twice refused to pay her dog licence, was imprisoned and went on hunger strike (her dog was shot).[13] Cicely Hamilton wrote about the problems her own membership of the TRL caused her in her autobiography. She had informed her local collector of income tax that as a suffragist she was withholding tax as a protest. After some weeks of letters, he turned up on her doorstep, saying he thought he would like to talk things over with her, as she wrote such very nice letters. Eventually she received a communication to the effect that her goods and chattels would all be sold. Since she was self-supporting and had never earned very much, she owned only some books, a strip of elderly carpet and a kettle, which she told the tax office she would get ready for auction.[14] Hamilton's friend, the writer Evelyn Sharp, was less fortunate, having a bailiff installed in her flat for six weeks (she converted him to women's suffrage), her mail intercepted and all her possessions, save for her clothes and her bed, removed and sold.[15]

These were acts of violence against women on the part of the masculine state. They demonstrated how ideologies about women's roles in the home and family were inseparable from their second-class citizenship. In her *Marriage as a trade* Hamilton didn't confront the problem of personal male violence, but another member of the TRL, another Settlement researcher, Anna Martin, did do so in her *The mother and social reform*, published a few years after Hamilton's tract on marriage. Like Hamilton, Martin takes the line that married women are in 'the disadvantageous position of being tied to only one possible employer' and thus they suffer from two fundamental disabilities: 'firstly, the law does not enforce contract for her as against her employer-husband; secondly, it does not, save in the feeblest and most inefficient way, protect her from his personal violence'. It's not easy, says Martin, after years of living in the Bermondsey Settlement in South London, to discover the full amount of marital cruelty to which English wives are subjected. Generally, the higher the social standing of the family, the less willing is the woman to say her husband mistreats her. "'My husband hit me on the side of my head two years ago,' said Mrs. S., a most respectable woman who has managed to rear a strikingly fine set of girls amidst indescribably squalid surroundings, "and I've never been out of pain since, but he would never forgive me if he knew I had told you".[16]

Anna Martin and Cicely Hamilton both lived with women. They are the first two examples of an extensive roll-call of female-partnered names that laces its way through this chapter. Anna Martin's lifelong partner was Laura Robinson, a fellow worker in the Bermondsey Settlement.[17] Cicely Hamilton herself lived entirely in a world of relationships with women, although discerning her closest intimacies is hard because, like other public women of the time, she left, probably deliberately, few traces of evidence – an uninformative autobiography, but no private papers or diaries and few letters. Her most intimate friend was probably Elizabeth Abbott, a married Scottish suffragist and a leading figure in a number of suffrage organizations.[18] Many women involved in social reform, research, feminism and pacifism in the 19th and early decades of the 20th century did share their lives with other women.[19] It is impossible to understand these linked stories of the suffrage campaign, the effort to create world peace, respect the rights of children, take humane health-care to those who need it, reform labour conditions, housekeep the cities, introduce science into the home, and secure living wages and support for motherhood, without taking into account the ways in which women were able to cooperate and collaborate and love one another. The personal aspect of their lives was not something divorced from their work and world-views, but was deeply and thematically connected. Personal relationships between women marked their solidarity as a class – Hamilton talked about 'class consciousness' and 'trade unionism' among women as particular threats to the masculine state.[20] There were ructions and ruptures, of course, and disagreements and disaffections, but the power of sisterhood, so celebrated in feminism's second-wave, was realized in a much stronger and more practical shape during its first wave.

There are many reasons for rejecting marriage, and most of them are illustrated in the biographies of the women who feature in this book. Yet, of all these reasons, the *choice* to relate primarily to another woman, or women, carries a note of special offensiveness in any male-oriented culture. Hence the genesis of the term 'Boston marriage', introduced in the US in the 19th century, which effectively imposes a heterosexist lexicon on what is clearly not a heterosexual experience. The term 'Boston marriage' is usually associated with Henry James' novel *The Bostonians* (1886), which features a close relationship between two women (based on James' sister Alice and her female companion, Katherine Loring); yet, intimate long-term partnerships between women have a very much longer history.[21] In the period covered by this book, women's enmeshment in various national and international webs of connection (suffrage, peace, temperance, abolitionism, trade unionism and so forth) gave them multiple opportunities for forming close bonds with other women. Vida Scudder, English literature expert and founder of the first Settlement in the US, Rivington Street in New York, discussed women's friendships in her autobiography *On journey*: 'The devoted loyalty they engender, their persistence from youth to age, through evil and good report, are moving to watch. Endless in variety, they wait their chronicler.'[22]

10.2: Jane Addams (left) and Mary Rozet Smith (right), 1923

Institutions and organizations such as Settlements and clubs, universities and professional or campaigning associations, all gave women membership of communities that bridged the public world of work and politics and the private one of colleagues, friends and intimate companions.[23] The clearest examples of this are the female communities of the Settlement houses. Hull-House in Chicago had at its centre Jane Addams, its co-founder, with her childhood friend Ellen Starr, and then her lover Mary

Rozet Smith, 'the great woman behind a great woman'.[24] These two stand prosaically and comfortably together wearing matching raincoats in their photograph. The Rozet-Smith–Addams legend is well-known: Mary Rozet Smith came from a wealthy Chicago family and helped to support both Jane Addams and Hull-House financially for 40 years. She and Addams shared their lives and work, and also a double bed, and were known in the women's international network and outside it as a couple.[25] The Dutch doctor Aletta Jacobs once engagingly remarked that she would have fallen in love with Rozet Smith, had she been a man.[26] Also in the Hull-House set, the fiery Florence Kelley had an intimate and 'profound' alliance with the reformer Julia Lathrop; and Sophonisba Breckinridge's closest friends were, first, the sanitary sociologist Marion Talbot and then the economist Edith Abbott.[27] Economist Emily Balch recorded her ambivalence about the attentions of *her* childhood friend Helen Cheever, who wanted to live with her permanently, but the two were nonetheless recognized as intimates.[28] The physician Cornelia de Bey, who worked with Jane Addams, also worked with her partner Kate Starr Kellogg to reform the Chicago educational system,[29] and the sociologists Virginia Robinson and Jessie Taft (Taft had worked at Hull-House), were hired by the prison

10.3: Jessie Taft (left) and Virginia Robinson with their adopted children, 1923

reformer Katharine Bement Davis to undertake research on female criminals: their partnership lasted more than 50 years and included two adopted children.[30] Adopting children was a surprisingly common feature of these relationships; the renowned social researcher, biographer, suffragist and pacifist, Katharine Anthony, adopted five children with her lover, Elisabeth Irwin, a radical New York schoolteacher.[31] Anthony's feminist biographies of women such as Queen Elizabeth I, Catherine the Great and Marie Antoinette scandalized many with their outspoken attention to details of private lives. She and Irwin shared a home in California and dubbed themselves 'The gay ladies of Gaylordsville' in a deliberately modern use of the term 'gay' – in fact it has been suggested that they were responsible for the first adoption of this term among American radicals.[32]

Vida Scudder lived for 35 years with the writer Florence Converse, her 'comrade and companion'.[33] They taught and did Settlement work together, and wrote fiction drawing on their relationship. Their friends Katharine Coman and Katharine Lee Bates, professors of economics and sociology, and English, respectively, co-founders of the Rivington Street Settlement, and partners for a quarter of a century, left Bates' celebrated and loving poetic memoriam of Coman's illness and death from breast cancer, the earliest such record in American literature.[34] Many women, including Jane Addams, wrote to Bates to thank her for having written so movingly about 'a woman's love for a woman'.[35] The labour reformer Anna Rochester, a 'special agent' for the New Jersey Consumers' League and the researcher for an influential report on poverty and infant mortality, met her partner, Grace Hutchins, through Scudder and the Denison House Settlement in Boston. Rochester and Hutchins' shared 45 years embraced most conceivable revolutionary enterprises, including a women's commune, 'the Community House' shaped around an ethic of shared housekeeping, and otherwise dubbed 'the unsettlement house.'[36] In the Henry Street Settlement in New York, Lillian Wald had 'intimate, physical relationships' with women. Her friends included the domestic science expert Mabel Kittredge, a generous donor to Henry Street, and Helen Arthur, an equally generous lawyer, who became business manager of the Neighborhood Playhouse and often cross-dressed in high collars and ties to please her lover.[37]

Many British women's partnerships were quieter and less exotic affairs, but their prevalence is still remarkable. In one of the early women's Settlements in Liverpool, the British family allowances campaigner Eleanor Rathbone met her partner, Elizabeth Macadam, and the two worked for the next 17 years to put the Settlement on a sound footing and transfer its training of women social workers to the University of Liverpool. The photograph shows the two women sitting companionably in the garden of the cottage where Rathbone wrote her anti-government book about foreign policy in the 1930s.[38] In 1919 Rathbone and Macadam moved to London, where they lived together for the rest of Rathbone's life, Macadam, it is said, increasingly adopting the role of 'political wife' (a role that may have led to a certain downplaying in the historical record of Macadam's own worthy achievements as a social reformer).[39] The labour politician and trade union activist Margaret Bondfield met Maud Ward at Oxshott in Surrey at Whitsuntide in 1906: Ward was a socialist and a suffragist, an expert on health insurance and successor to factory inspector Lucy Deane Streatfeild: she

10.4: Eleanor Rathbone (left) and Elizabeth Macadam, 1937

dug out facts from blue books (official government reports) for Bondfield, housekept for the two of them, and was Bondfield's travelling companion.[40] Lizzy Lind-af-Hageby and Leisa Schartau's lifelong liaison, most of it lived in Britain, was built around the anti-vivisection, animal rights and environmental rights movements, to which they saw the issue of women's rights as intimately linked.[41] The suffragist and poet Eva Gore-Booth met her partner, Esther Roper, in Italy in 1896 when they were both in their late 20s, and they formed a permanent union around a joint commitment to working women's rights.[42] Like Cicely Hamilton, the pacifist Mary Sheepshanks spent all her life enmeshed in a web of relationships with like-minded women; she met Margaret Bryant, who worked for the Royal Institute of International Affairs, during the First World War, and Margaret became 'my greatest friend'. As Sheepshanks' biographer, Sybil Oldfield, remarks, 'We must believe Mary's declaration ... we know nothing more.'[43] Eglantyne Jebb, founder of Save the Children, declared herself unable to live without Margaret Keynes, the 'strikingly beautiful' sister of the famous economist John Maynard Keynes: 'Whatever happens, I am yours,' inscribed Jebb: '[Y]our face is the most beautiful one in the world and the nicest to kiss and kiss'. The two women left a voluminous, 20-year correspondence: 'My sweetheart, I have had no letter from you today,' Margaret complained at Christmas 1910, perhaps the suffragettes had been at the postbox? They arranged to share a bed whenever possible, and Margaret, with two bisexual brothers, would have been no stranger to such shared-sex intimacies, which in her and Eglantyne's case covered the discussion of a joint house and a 'marriage'.[44] Eventually, however, Margaret was persuaded to marry a man, and she went on to have four children, to whom Eglantyne, no personal lover of children, despite her diligent international work for them, declared she didn't wish to be an 'auntie'.

When Cicely Hamilton took herself off to scrub the floors of Royaumont Abbey for the Scottish Women's Hospitals during the First World War, she found herself in the midst of yet another network of formidably women-connected women. Flora Murray, physician to the suffragettes, lived with Dr Louisa Garrett Anderson (page 211). Before that, Murray lived closely with Dr Elsie Inglis, founder of the Scottish Women's Hospitals, in Edinburgh.[45] Surgeon Louisa Aldrich-Blake, nicknamed 'Madame la Générale' during the time she spent at Royaumont, lived with her friend Rosamond Wigram.[46] Dr Helen Boyle, the founder of mental healthcare in Sussex, had a series of relationships with women, including Drs Mabel Jones and Mary Murdoch.[47] Dr Ethel Williams' lifelong companion, with whom she lived in Northumberland, was the mathematician Frances Hardcastle.[48] Dr Louisa Martindale enjoyed a lifelong relationship with the Hon. Ismay FitzGerald, whom she met in 1910. The two women found each other on the doorstep of a dinner party with a barrister friend of Millicent Fawcett's, 'and we laughed', recalled Martindale, 'because we were both attired in cream lace dresses'. When FitzGerald's mother died, Martindale invited FitzGerald to visit for a fortnight and she stayed for 35 years.[49] Dr Hilda Clark met the midwife and international relief organizer Edith Pye in 1907 when Clark started work for her medical degree: 'To this day,' wrote Pye, 50 years later in another love-at-first-sight memory, 'I can see her as she came down the attic stair in the old house in Westminster, the gold glint in her brown hair and eyes lightened up by the flame of the candle she carried.'[50] The relationship was sustained through many separations, as both Clark and Pye engaged in war-relief work in Europe. They wrote to each other in the delightful 'plain language' of the Quakers: hence Clark to Pye in Geneva from London: 'While I miss thee dreadfully here I know it is worse being away and alone ... I am glad thou has good friends there ...'[51]

Dr Ethel Bentham, who started the first child welfare clinic in London to offer both advice and treatment, shared her house and life with the Labour Party activist Marion Phillips: Bentham and Phillips were prominent in local politics and among the first generation of women MPs.[52] Dr Christine Murrell, about whom Christopher St John wrote a biography, joined forces with her 'beloved friend and colleague' Dr Honor Bone early in her professional life and lived with her for over 30 years, the last of these spent in a ménage à trois with Marie Lawson, a printer, editor and tax resister.[53] Murrell and Bone worked in general practice together in West London; Murrell, who also used the forename 'Christopher', ran one of the first infant welfare clinics, helped with the aftercare of imprisoned suffragettes and became the first woman elected to the Council of the British Medical Association in 1924 and to the General Medical Council in 1933.[54] And back in the very first generation of women doctors, Sophia Jex-Blake, the first woman doctor in Scotland, fell in love with the housing reformer Octavia Hill in 1860. Hill wasn't quite the staid, conservative matron she is often made out to be (see Chapter Three). She taught Jex-Blake bookkeeping, and Jex-Blake reciprocated with tutoring in mathematics. From this unpromising beginning developed what can only be described as a passionate love affair, whose outlines we can (again) only surmise, due to the wholesale suppression of evidence by Hill and her family.[55] 'I believe I love women too much ever to love a man,' reflected Jex-Blake.[56] It seems that their connection was disrupted by parental intervention: Hill's mother didn't like Jex-Blake, and so instructed Octavia to end the relationship.

Evelina Haverfield wasn't a doctor, but the founder of the Women's Emergency Corps and the Women's Volunteer Reserves and a colleague of Elsie Inglis's in Serbia and Russia. Despite being married twice, she was the lover of the exotically colourful character Vera 'Jack' Holme, who, aside from being an actor, performed a key role as the WSPU chauffeur from 1909. Holme holds the qualification of being recognized in the industry magazine *The Chauffeur* as the very first female chauffeur in Britain.[57] A wealthy supporter of the WSPU had donated money to buy Emmeline Pankhurst a motor car. The qualifications of chauffeurs like Holme at the time were limited to coping with the frequent mechanical breakdowns that occurred and the confusions caused by horse traffic: compulsory driving tests weren't introduced until 1935. Holme and Haverfield lived together from 1911 until Haverfield's death in 1920. After that, when Holme was working in Serbia in the 1920s as an ambulance and relief lorry driver for the Scottish Women's Hospitals, she met two women, Margaret Greenlees and Margaret Ker, with whom she later formed a ménage à trois in Scotland. They were known as the 'Ladies of Lochearnhead'.[58] And it was, of course, Dr Mary Gordon, the British prison reformer, herself partnered by a woman, who publicized the story of the 'Ladies of Llangollen', the two young women who ran away together in 1778 and set up home for half a century in a Welsh valley. The twosome was actually a threesome: the ladies are buried together in the graveyard of St Collen's Church in Llangollen together with their servant, Mary Carryl. The sculpted marble relief of the two ladies that sits there is reputedly modelled on Gordon herself and the sculptor, Violet Labouchere, who was probably Gordon's own lover.[59]

Homes are traditionally places of inequality in more ways than one. How did the women reformers in this book manage their magnificently adventurous and influential lives? Domestic servants are shadowy figures in the background, and they tend to be mentioned in passing, if at all. Unusually, Cicely Hamilton included in her autobiography a photograph of *her* housekeeper, 'Mrs Hainsby' together with Hamilton's cat. Emily Hobhouse's domestic accomplice on her first expedition to Minnesota was Mary Scourey, a young Cornish woman, whom she dragged across unwelcoming landscapes in search of men to reform (see Chapter Seven). Later, in Europe during the First World War, Hobhouse complained a lot about a maid called Phoebe, 'A truly impossible girl'. Phoebe had much packing and transporting and conveying of letters to diplomats to do, which gives some idea of how necessary such aides must have been in supporting the women's activities, particularly on the lengthy journeys many made.[60]

10.5: The Ladies of Llangollen, sculpted marble relief in St Collen's Church, Llangollen

There is no great evidence that women in the network pondered much on the ethics of servant-keeping. Charlotte Perkins Gilman's friend Helen

10.6: Cicely Hamilton's housekeeper, 'Mrs Hainsby'

Stuart Campbell warned housewives about the dark secrets of some American domestics – prostitution, venereal disease and so forth – although she was also probably the first progressive reformer to address the unpleasant question of sexual relationships between male employers and domestics in the bourgeois home. Gilman herself considered domestic helpers ignorant, gossipy and unnecessary, especially in her radically redesigned homes which would require little housework, yet she was plainly capable of a more democratic attitude: in her short story 'Turned', the mistress of a house finds a servant pregnant with her husband's child, and the two women leave the household and raise the child together.[61]

Large swathes of this world featuring female attachments defy easy classification. Many overtly defied or queried conventional cultures of gender. This was a task central to women's general goal of reform; fiction, fantasy and facts about gender were all bundled together in a play of alliances that met both personal and political needs. One of the most surprising examples was the relationship between the American actor and writer Elizabeth Robins, and a member of the British landed classes, the author and social investigator, Lady Florence Bell. Robins is best known for introducing Ibsen's *Hedda Gabler* and *The master builder* to Britain (she learnt Norwegian in order to do this), and as the author of many 'suffrage' novels. Florence Bell's name crops up most often as the author of a 30-year-long social investigation called *At the works*, about the lives and work of more than 1,000 families in Middlesbrough, the site of her husband's ironworking factory. *At the works* was dedicated to Charles Booth, but it rejected an approach dominated by statistics, relying chiefly on the observations of 'female visitors', including Bell herself, who engaged the families in 'friendly and continuous intercourse'.[62] Bell was a prolific writer of drama, fiction and biography and she was also an accomplished multilingual translator. She and Robins were poles apart in age, wealth, social standing, life-style and political attitudes, but they loved each other, confided in each other and worked intensively together, producing plays and translations that helped to secure Robins' reputation as an actor; introduce Ibsen's drama to British audiences; make up for the deficit of good female parts; and place on the stage some of the big social issues of the day.

Their first joint enterprise, performed in 1893, was a play called *Alan's wife*, a short tragedy in three scenes about a woman whose husband dies and who gives birth to and then smothers a handicapped child.[63] It was a play about the dangers of industrial work (the husband is mangled by a factory machine) and the collision between idealized family life and the harsh economic and social conditions other reformers made the subject of their research. It was a play about motherhood, about female sexuality, about the New Woman and about female independence, and it puzzled and disturbed its audiences.[64] *Alan's wife* was based on a Swedish short story, but Bell and Robins relocated it to the north of England, where Lady Bell lived in a rambling arts and crafts house near the sea in the Yorkshire resort of Redcar with her husband and children; she had her family, and

Robins a long-standing liaison with Dr Octavia Wilberforce, whom Robins helped to put through medical school when Wilberforce's father disinherited her (the convolutions of these relationships are impressive).[65] Bell and Robins published *Alan's wife* anonymously, Robins not wanting to confuse her acting and writing reputations, and Bell mindful that her husband would rather she didn't engage in such exploits. It took them 30 years to acknowledge their authorship.[66] They revelled in the intimacy of their long professional and personal association, much of which was kept from the public eye: 'I love you all the hours of the day' confessed Robins to Bell, who admitted to 'a wild longing' for Robins. They wrote letters to each other several times a week for the best part of 40 years.[67]

'Romantic friendships' and intimate long-term relationships between women reformers were transnational markers of their labours. In continental Europe, the German Federation of Women's Associations (Bund Deustcher Frauenvereine), the organization which forbad Alice Salomon's attendance at the 1915 women's peace congress at The Hague (see Chapter Seven), featured yet another devoted couple, the feminist pedagogue Helene Lange, and the writer and politician Gertrud Bäumer: Lange and Bäumer lived together for more than 30 years and they share a 'Grave of honour' in a Berlin cemetery.[68] A particularly evocative photograph, taken at the Zürich WILPF Congress in 1919, gives us Charlotte Despard, always eccentrically dressed in a black lace mantilla, standing between the German feminist Lida Heymann, who wears a masculine hat, and *her* lover, the radical lawyer and Germany's first woman judge, Anita Augspurg, whose attire is even more manly. Heymann always recalled her first sight of the woman who would become her lover for 40 years, a figure in brown velvet with a powerful voice and sparkling, clear-sighted eyes standing at a lectern.[69] Augspurg and Heymann are another couple who have been tracked down by assiduous biographers to the habit of staying in double rooms. They went everywhere together, including to visit Addams and Rozet Smith at Hull-House.[70] The British Mary Sheepshanks considered the German couple 'extreme' women, but keener and abler than many others, besides which, 'German men are exasperating and would infuriate one'.[71] Heymann and Augspurg's memoirs

10.7: Anita Augspurg (left), Charlotte Despard (centre) and Lida Heymann (right) at the WILPF Congress in Zürich, 1919

give a powerful picture of how these two determined women lived and worked and pursued a radical social vision together, travelling extensively throughout Europe and North Africa, and arguing that the central mistake of much feminism is to ape the social lives of men.[72]

Augspurg and Heymann's ideas and writings directly opposed conventional ideas about heterosexual private life, and would undoubtedly have given German men a heavy dose of infuriation. Along with the German radical thinker Helene Stöcker, they were significant figures in the early 20th-century feminist movement in Germany, which brought together theoretical and practical understandings of domestic relationships more clearly, perhaps, than movements in other countries.[73] Helene Stöcker, the daughter of a pious Calvinist household – she said that the Song of Solomon was her introduction to sex – had studied the history of literature, philosophy and national economy at the University of Berlin, and followed to Glasgow Alexander Tille, a professor of German who had been in Berlin researching the legend of Faust and who suggested, when his wife died, that Stöcker might like to marry him and mother his children for him. Attempting to do this opened Stöcker's eyes to Tille's chauvinism and to the immense difficulty of combining motherhood with public work; it galvanized her into considering what might be done to enable mothers to lead more satisfactory lives.[74] She combined an unrelenting opposition to war and violence with campaigns on behalf of single mothers and their children, birth control, sex education and the decriminalization of abortion and of homosexuality, all of which contrasts with her decidedly matronly appearance – curled hair, a full, round face, a little overweight behind her furs and jewels. In her determinedly argued views, Stöcker recognized her debt to Charlotte Perkins Gilman. She herself rejected affiliation with any political party, operating as a member of left-wing intellectual networks and belonging to many peace organizations, including the WILPF (she was at The Hague Congress in 1915).

Stöcker is recognized today as a major influence on the Federal Republic of Germany's welfare legislation, although much of her reputation is confined to, and trivialized as, a defence of 'free love'.[75] This is a common strategy for downgrading women's achievements: personalizing and domesticating them. Following Stöcker's escape from the exhausting experience of mothering Tille's children, she returned to Germany and offended public opinion by living with, but not marrying, a lawyer, Bruno Springer: for many years the couple inhabited two apartments on the same floor.[76] Springer helped Stöcker with the legal side of the organization she co-founded in 1905, the Bund für Mutterschutz und Sexualreform (BfM), whose name is usually translated as 'the Society for the Protection of Motherhood', which misleads us as to its nature and purpose: the wholesale reform of sexual ethics on both a theoretical and practical level. The American feminist and writer Katharine Anthony, who produced a book introducing German and Scandinavian feminism

10.8: Helene Stöcker, c. 1900

to English-speaking audiences in 1915, called the founding of
the BfM 'the most important historical event in the history of
the woman movement since the American Woman's Rights
convention at Seneca Falls in 1848'.[77] BfM stood for both the
right to motherhood and the right to reject it, and was especially
concerned with the situation of single mothers, proposing birth
clinics and shelters, a scheme of maternity insurance, the legal
equality of legitimate and illegitimate children, equal status for
both parents, the legal recognition of 'free' relationships and
the greater responsibility of fathers: altogether the creation of a
concept of motherhood appropriate to the changing patterns of
the era which had been named by the Swedish reformer Ellen
Key 'the century of the child'.[78] Key's ideas about the reform
of marriage and family life were very influential in Germany:
she spoke at the founding of the BfM in Berlin in 1905. Her
argument was that motherhood is so important that it needs
to be supported by the state, rather than by individual men;
and it should be enjoyed by unmarried women who live with
female friends, just as much as by those in heterosexual marital
unions. The promotion of welfare legislation by the BfM and
by Stöcker, as its intellectual leader, was accompanied by a
denunciation of a patriarchal social order in which marriage
and prostitution operate as complementary institutions. German
feminism of this period embodied a particularly radical attack
on the whole notion of the family as a private realm separate
from civil society, insisting that the idea of citizenship rights must
be applied to the home. The German Civil Code was notably
uncivil on this issue; as the sociologist Marianne Weber, the
intellectually powerful wife of the famous sociological theorist
Max Weber, explained, the Code dictated that: 'The will of the
mother must always yield to that of the father. He can, if he
wishes, decide entirely independently how children are to be
cared for, supervised and fed, which school they should attend,
which profession they should adopt, indeed he can even take
them away from the mother against her will and entrust them
to the care of a third party.'[79]

Perhaps nothing illustrates quite so well the patriarchal
politics of marriage about which Cicely Hamilton in England
complained than what history has done with Marianne Weber's

legacy. Her writings and public persona made her by far the better-known half of the Weberian couple in the early 1900s. She was a highly regarded public figure who was actively involved in German feminist politics. In 1904, when the Webers visited America, it was Marianne who was more eagerly welcomed by the women Settlement sociologists and reformers. Soon after arriving in New York, the Webers were dining at Hull-House with that 'quite extraordinary and engaging' woman, Jane Addams; Marianne, feeling much at home there, returned to Hull-House for a meeting of the Women's Trade Union League, while Max, enticed by Baedeker's listing of the stockyards as a tourist spectacle, went to watch the mechanization of industry in 'an ocean of blood'.[80] Back in Germany, it was Marianne Weber's lecture on 'What America offers to women' rather than Max Weber's perorations on American political life that drew the bigger audiences. Her landmark book, *Ehefrau und Mutter in der Rechtsentwicklung* (*Marriage, motherhood, and the law*), on the historical development of women's legal rights, took women's experiences as the starting point for analysing social systems. Max wrote about *The Protestant ethic and the spirit of capitalism*, while Marianne observed that his analysis of these institutions left women and human relations unexplored.[81] In a later reverse historical narrative, and despite their unconsummated and childless marriage, Marianne becomes the helpmeet wife, steering Max through his recurrent mental crises and forgiving his extra-marital 'enchantments', especially with Else Jaffé, his first female student (and Germany's first female factory inspector), with whom Marianne, in another three-way relationship, also became intimate. That Marianne herself was complicit in this reframing of their roles, acting as the guardian of her husband's sociological reputation, the editor of 10 volumes of his work and the author of a selective monumental biography of him (giving 'birth to him out of my own powers' is how she put it[82]), would probably not have surprised the English author of *Marriage as a trade*. Cicely Hamilton might simply have observed that this is what marriage does to women.

Charlotte Despard had a totally different response from Marianne Weber's to widowhood. Despard was known for her unflagging energy for welfare initiatives, a tenacious opposition to all aggressive behaviours and a tremendous capacity to capture the attention of audiences wherever she spoke. Charlotte French, as she was born, was one of six daughters in a wealthy naval family that prized its only son much more, and consequently left the girls to enjoy an unruly childhood. Charlotte married a successful but unhealthy and impotent Anglo-Irish businessman, Maximilian Despard, and for 20 years she behaved like a good, upper-middle-class woman, writing, at his suggestion, highly romantic novels replete with racist stereotypes and complex plots, cardboard characters and improbable happy endings: her one social realism novel, *A voice from the dim millions*, remained unpublished. After Max died, Charlotte abandoned his principles and their wealthy home and adopted a life of poverty and devotion to her enormous range of radical causes, at first in the Nine Elms area of Battersea, a desperately poor place enclosed by railway lines and overlooked by the gasometers of the London Gas Light Company, and later in Belfast at the foot of Stormont Castle and in Dublin, where she moved at the age of nearly 80 to live with the luminously beautiful Irish revolutionary Maud Gonne. Remembered mainly as the poet Yeats' muse, Gonne was herself a startingly radical woman who founded a new nationalist organization called Inghinidhe na hÉireann ('Daughters of Ireland') that campaigned for welfare services. Despard and Gonne's house in Ireland acted as a refuge for a floating population of homeless prisoners, Irish Republic Army gunmen and assorted refugees, and so was frequently the target of police raids. In Nine Elms, Despard's main concern had been the children, on whose behalf she created a mini-welfare state, hiring a nurse to treat sick children, most of whom were sick because of malnutrition, providing gyms, play equipment and country holidays, and setting up school clinics and feeding programmes. The nurse, Rosalie Mansell, who worked with her for years, was also left in charge of Despard's adopted daughter Vere, but Mansell turned out to be addicted to laudanum and so Vere suffered. Despard's remarkable life is marked by this tendency of hers not to get everything right.[83]

Direct action was the Despard method. When the Boer War began, she took the boys of Nine Elms to hear her speak at an anti-war meeting in Battersea Town Hall. When, as a Poor

Law Guardian for Vauxhall, she discovered that orphaned boys were being sent to Canada for agricultural training under the auspices of Dr Barnado's, she set off (in 1902) to and through Canada by train, stage-coach and horse-buggy to check out what had happened to them, and was deeply disturbed, but possibly not entirely surprised, to find they were just being treated as cheap labour. When (in 1899) she got herself elected as a manager of the two elementary schools in Nine Elms, she put forward her theory that ill-fed children would never learn properly, and suggested that three unused rooms in one of the schools should be used to cook and serve food. The School Board protested that money could not legally be spent on such a venture, but Despard wasn't giving up. She provided a stove, saucepans, tables and benches, and enough volunteers to set up a school meals service, after which the School Board accepted responsibility.[84] Despard's reaction to what she and others saw as the autocratic behaviour of the Pankhursts was to lead the move to create a new organization, the Women's Freedom League, in 1907, with a much broader programme of reform than the WSPU's. Its attempts to respond to public opinion included a series of postcards aimed at countering the suspicion that activist women ignored their homes. In Figure 10.9 an aproned woman activist makes pastry, leaving her plenty of time for other pursuits. The WFL was dedicated to non-violence and to pacifism, and based on the premise that claiming the vote implied far too narrow a vision of necessary social change: it soon had twice as many members as the WSPU. At the 1918 general election, Despard and two other members of the WFL stood (unsuccessfully) as independent women's rights anti-war candidates with a commitment to gender equality. The WFL survived until 1961 and remains a strangely neglected strand in women's reform history.

Despard's story is interesting from another point of view. Her welfare initiatives were accompanied by an uncomfortably personal collision with the war-making masculine state: her brother was Sir John French, a high-ranking member of Britain's Committee of Imperial Defence. French, 'a short man with the bow-legged swagger of a cavalry officer',[85] made his reputation as a fighting army general in the Boer War, leading the troops that

SUFFRAGETTES AT HOME.—(I.) Mrs. Snow Makes Pastry.

10.9: Women's Freedom League postcard, 'Mrs Snow makes pastry'

burnt farms and homes and mistreated women and children in ways that gave Despard's fellow pacifist Emily Hobhouse much cause for discomfort. Of his sister's alliances, French said, 'we have tried all we could to keep her from mixing up with these foolish women'.[86] While French defended the state's right to impose its authority undemocratically, Despard resisted it. She refused to accept that the state had rights when it didn't grant these in return. When the Decennial Census was due in 1911, she proposed that women should be uncompliant, providing no information as to their marital status, children or people in the household. 'There are times and seasons in human history,' she pronounced, 'when civil disobedience is the highest duty we can offer to our generation.'[87] Some 15,000–20,000 women followed her injunction. Since they had to be absent from their homes when the Census was delivered, theatres and halls were booked for all-night entertainments: in Lancashire, groups of Census-resisters cycled through the night, and in London the Aldwych ice-skating rink was on night duty.[88] The Census protest was a logical extension of tax resistance, another movement Despard helped to found. The tax resister who got the most publicity – more than either Cicely Hamilton or Evelyn Sharp – was another of Despard's lovers, a deaf physiotherapist and mother of three, Kate Harvey, who refused to buy a National Insurance stamp for her servant, who memorably carried the same name – Asquith – as the prime minister. When Harvey was sent to prison, Despard wrote, 'The miss of my darling always greater ... I think of her first at noon and latest at night ... sad and first thoughts always of her, my darling.'[89] They shared many interests, and their lives and work, closely for nine years. Together they went to the IWSA Congress in Budapest in 1913, a crucial gathering for the affirmation of war-time transnational women's networks. Then Despard went to Ireland to take up the cause of Irish independence, and a relationship with Maud Gonne. When Gonne was imprisoned and on hunger strike, Despard, 'as old as the hills and twice as wrinkled',[90] kept another prison vigil outside Kilmainham jail. Her brother was by now Lord-Lieutenant of Ireland, having been dispatched by Lloyd George to impose Home Rule on Ulster by force. While French was recruiting the notorious Black and Tan troops to quell civil unrest, Despard was doing all she could to encourage it. Her brother never forgave her and refused to see her, even on his death bed.

Charlotte Despard's idiosyncratic dress signalled the intersection of two social movements which together ate at the conventions of gendered family life: feminism and dress reform. In Germany, the Deutscher Verband für Neue Frauenkleidung und FrauenKultur (German Union for New Clothing for Women and Women's Culture) had branches in 26 cities by 1915, a biennial congress and its own specialist journal. The information the Union handed out about the dangers of conventional dress incurred the wrath of local corset-makers who knew their livelihood was threatened.[91] The precepts of the dress reform movement make many appearances in Charlotte Perkins Gilman's utopian trilogy, especially when Ellador from the women's world of Herland visits the real world of Ourland and, shocked by its clothing habits, asks the male sociologist to imagine what it would be like as a man to dress like a woman, 'wearing open-work lace underclothing, with little ribbons all strung through it; wearing dresses never twice alike and almost always foolish; wearing hats'.[92] 'The Hat' has a chapter all to itself in Gilman's *The dress of women*, published in 1915. The argument is that women's conventional dress impedes the social development of the wearer: 'This is its heaviest injury, even beyond the ill effects to health, the interference with comfort and freedom, the continual insistence on sex-distinction.'[93] Women's demand for the ballot would, maintains Gilman, never be taken seriously by men who saw before them such silly feminine creatures.

Along with dress reform and same-sex unions went cross-dressing as both personal statement and political protest. The German women and their female friends had short haircuts, wore bloomers, drove cars, rode bicycles and sat astride horses rather than side saddle. Frances Kellor, an investigator at Hull-House and at the Rivington Street Settlement in New York, and a shaper of much Progressive Era welfare legislation, met Mary Dreier, a prominent labour reformer and trade unionist, in 1904 and set up house with her for the 47 remaining years of her life; a photograph of Kellor and Dreier in a high-seated open motor car presents almost a caricature of the heterosexual couple: Kellor, in a man's cap, shirt and tie, is the man behind the wheel, Dreier is the long-skirted decorous feminine person seated beside. In Britain, Dr Octavia Wilberforce described Dr Louisa Aldrich-Blake as 'a tall, massive individual who wore a stiff collar and a tie like a man's'. Aldrich-Blake enjoyed boxing and cricket, and was a skilled mechanic[94] – the fondness and fearlessness of women in relation to cars is a pronounced

10.10: Frances Kellor and Mary Dreier

sub-theme here (see Chapter Eight for Dr Mary Murdoch's adventures with her car). Dr Annie McCall, who pioneered antenatal care and who lived with her companion and business adviser, Constance Watney, dressed in a dark suit, shirt and tie, with short, combed-back hair.

Cicely Hamilton's own closest friends in the suffrage network were Edy (Edith) Craig and Christopher St John (Christabel Marshall), who lived together, and then later in another 30-year-long ménage à trois with 'Tony' (Clare) Atwood, a painter of some distinction, a trio known to their friends as 'Edy and the boys'.[95] The adopted male names were accompanied by masculine dress: 'Miss Craig,' wrote Virginia Woolf in her diary, 'is a rosy, ruddy "personage" in white waistcoat, with black bow tie & gold chain loosely knotted.'[96] Virginia Woolf's own lover, Vita Sackville-West, with whom St John was besotted, described Edy Craig as 'the most tearing old lesbian'.[97] She compared her to Radclyffe Hall, one half of the most celebrated public lesbian couple of the 20th century, and a famous masculine dresser. Radclyffe Hall and her lover, Una Troubridge, were close friends of Edy and the boys, and of Cicely Hamilton. Troubridge, recalling her meeting with 'John', as Radclyffe Hall had been named by her first (female) lover, remembered the 'rough country clothes; heavy short-skirted tweeds unusual in those days, collars and ties and … a queer little green Heath hat'.[98] Troubridge herself was monocled and shingled and wore trousers. There is something very moving about the photograph opposite in Hamilton's autobiography of her and Christopher St John dressed as George Eliot and George Sand, respectively, for a fancy-dress ball in 1911. The past, when recovered, is replete with demonstrations that claiming citizenship is so much easier if you pretend to be a man. Ethel Smyth, the feminist composer with whom Cicely Hamilton worked (she put words to Smyth's suffragist melody *March of the women*, which Smyth is renowned for conducting with a toothbrush in Holloway prison), often wore men's clothes and had multiple passionate attachments to women, including Emmeline Pankhurst and Virginia Woolf. Woolf, who was flattered by Smyth's attention, called her a 'valiant truculent old mosstrooper of a woman'; watching Smyth conduct her music with a pencil, with a drip at the end of her nose and knocking her hat from side to side, Woolf wondered if Smyth might actually be a great composer.[99]

The history of women's relationships with women shows that marriage and intimate female friendships were by no means incompatible. Carrie Chapman Catt, co-founder in 1902 of the IWSA, had two husbands who predeceased her, but at her request she was buried next to her friend Mary Garrett Hay. Their grave in

10.11: Cicely Hamilton and Christopher St John as George Eliot and George Sand, c. 1911

the Bronx, New York, bears the inscription, 'Here lie two, united in friendship for 38 years through constant service to a great cause'.[100] The great woman preacher and pacifist, Maude Royden, who adored her Rutland vicar for decades before managing an extremely brief marriage to him (see Chapter Six), loved not only him but his wife, and a woman she met when a student at Oxford in the 1890s, Kathleen Courtney, herself a great peace campaigner and suffragist. Of Effie, the vicar's wife, Royden wrote, 'I fell in love with her, too, at first sight'.[101] Royden's letters to Courtney from the vicarage in South Luffenham were sprinkled with passionate endearments: 'Dear little Kathleen I do so awfully want to see you. Consider yourself kissed!'; 'Oh beloved, rejoice with me! I am so fearfully happy here, but I want you dear, so badly, & don't *ever* seem to have had as much as I am hungry for'; 'There is a kiss in the envelope. Did you find it?' she asked from a hotel in Bellagio on an Italian holiday.[102]

Protestations of love and intimacy hold a key place in women's correspondence, both nationally and internationally. 'My dear, precious friend', 'much love, dearest heart', wrote Carrie Chapman Catt to Aletta Jacobs.[103] 'I love you and I have admired you from the first day I have met you ... With many kisses,' wrote Jacobs to Catt.[104] 'You can never know,' wrote Mary Rozet Smith to Jane Addams, 'what it is to me to have had you and to have you now.' 'I miss you dreadfully, and am yours 'til death,' said Addams.[105] Lillian Wald's correspondence with Mabel Kittredge is 'replete with passages of ardor and longing'.[106] In an attempt to preserve their privacy, Octavia Wilberforce and Elizabeth Robins excised the endearment-intense beginnings and ends of the letters they left behind.[107] Charlotte Perkins Gilman fantasized about the newspaper headlines that might result from the discovery of *her* love letters to the journalist and reformer Adeline Knapp: 'Mrs. Stetson's Love Affair with a Woman'.[108]

The endearments of women have puzzled historians. Should we call these lesbian relationships? Does it matter? Historians haven't been good at attending to the ways in which women themselves described their intimate relationships.[109] Here is Kathleen Courtney, reflecting on her intense relationship with Maude Royden, formed in their university days: 'We made great and lasting friendships but they were not lesbian (of course we did not know that word in those days). Our friendships were founded on some sort of affinity, a community of mind.'[110] Interrogated in her 90s about the nature of the relationships enjoyed by women at Hull-House, Alice Hamilton said there was no open lesbian activity, but she went on to point out that the very question presupposes a preoccupation with sex that would have struck the women of Hull-House as strange.[111]

There were, however, some women who were interested, scientifically, in sex. A quarter of a century before Alfred Kinsey got round to it, the American economist and prison reformer Katharine Bement Davis effectively brought the science of sex into the public domain for the first time when she published in 1929 a study about the sex lives of American women. *Factors in the sex life of twenty-two hundred women* took Bement Davis almost 10 years to research and write; the result was a 450-page book that was both commended for its scientific approach and condemned for its shocking revelations of private experiences, and probably also implicitly for its undermining of ideas about the exclusive heterosexual nature of marriage.[112] There were two samples: 1,000 married and 1,200 unmarried women. Most were college educated, and they provided information via an eight-page questionnaire that included such questions as 'Have you at any time experienced intense emotional relations with other women?' to which 50% of the unmarried and 31% of the married answered yes. Fifty-two per cent of the unmarried women and 51% of the married ticked the boxes indicating that the relationships had been accompanied by sexual contact beyond 'hugging and kissing'. Nearly half of Davis' text was taken up with the topics of homosexuality and masturbation (61% of the unmarried and 38% of the married admitted to masturbating), which helped to create a picture of 'normal' female sexuality considerably at odds with the prevailing stereotype. Some of the detail might have been received as uncomfortably graphic for the time, as in the account of one young married woman who had been deploying water from the bath tub hose to masturbate since the age of 10, and who continued this practice when marital intercourse was unsatisfactory or her husband was away in France. Davis' study was methodologically ground-breaking in its use of questionnaires for probing sensitive topics and in combining what are now called 'qualitative' with 'quantitative' methods. An appendix on the work of a psychiatrist, Elizabeth McCall, who helped Davis with the project, compared the data yielded by questionnaires with those obtained from face-to-face interviews, finding much higher rates of masturbation, premarital sex and physical relationships with other women declared using the anonymous and impersonal questionnaire strategy, an important methodological conclusion forgotten by most modern methodologists.[113]

From sex to children: the importance of *choice* about whether to have children or not put birth control and sex education at the heart of many women reformers' initiatives. We often don't know why, but even among heterosexually married reformers there was a striking absence of children; perhaps the work they did was possible only because they were free from the encumbrances that came with motherhood. For some, such as

Aletta Jacobs and Ada Salter, non-motherhood was not a choice: their only children died; others, for example Henrietta Barnett, Charlotte Despard and Marianne Weber, were involuntarily childless (although all went on to adopt, Weber taking on her sister-in-law's four children after the latter's death). The First World War yielded a rash of adoptions among women reformers: there was Maude Royden's Freddie (see Chapter Six), and the Pankhursts' ambitious adoption enterprise: a home for female orphans in London's Campden Hill, furnished luxuriously with chaises longues and elaborate armchairs. The home was run by Annie and Jessie Kenney, who were instructed by Emmeline Pankhurst to deploy scientific feeding and the Montessori method. She herself adopted three girl babies, naming one of them after the doctor and prison reformer Mary Gordon, and Christabel adopted one.[114]

Concern for the social and economic position of children, especially children in the working-class world of sweated, casual and underpaid labour, was always a prominent feature in women reformers' programmes. Much Settlement work in many countries was given to supplying children with better food, clothes, education, homes and healthcare. Women reformers identified the absurdity of dividing the nurture, education and healthcare of children as separate domains of policy: a conference on 'The needs of little children' held in London in 1912 by the Women's Labour League, for example, had on its agenda speeches by Margaret McMillan urging 'the grave necessity for continuous supervision of the childhood of the nation by some one authority', by Dr Ethel Bentham on the 'neutralisation' of education by the poor housing in which many children were forced to live, and by Ada Salter, the socialist and 'municipal beautifier' (see Chapter Four), who quoted the results of a Glasgow study showing that boys living in two-roomed homes were 8.2 pounds lighter and 3.2 inches shorter than those from four-roomed homes (the figures for girls, 10.7 pounds and 3.8 inches, were even more shocking).[115]

Children and their welfare were recognized as an important research topic. The British household science educator Alice Ravenhill (see Chapter Five) carried out what was probably the first scientific study of children's sleep. She presented the results at the First International Congress on School Hygiene in London in 1907: this was a three-year investigation, including 3,500 boys and 2,680 girls, from which data Ravenhill reached the entirely modern conclusion that the conditions of family and school life were depriving children of between 2.75 and 3.25 hours of much-needed sleep every day.[116] In the US, the plight of children was at the root of some of the most ambitious of the women's welfare initiatives, especially the Children's Bureau, which emerged from the industry of the Hull-House group in the US in 1912 under the able leadership of Julia Lathrop.

The *condition* of children called for a welfare state, but underlying this the condition of *childhood* demanded a new conceptual vision. 'We should bear in mind in studying children that we have before us a permanent class, larger than the adult population,' wrote Charlotte Perkins Gilman in her *Concerning children*, published in 1900. Yet, 'As members of society, we find that they have received almost no attention.' Consequently, says Gilman, anticipating her utopian trilogy, 'A visitor from another planet, examining our houses, streets, furniture, and machinery, would not gather much evidence of childhood as a large or an important factor in human life.'[117] Houses are not designed for children, or, rather, they are designed to be full of *dangers* for children – stairs to fall down, windows to fall out of, doors to jam little fingers in, furniture to bump into. Adults are ignorant of the need to treat children as people with human rights, including the right not to be physically chastised. In an almost elegiac passage in her later book, *The home: Its work and influence*, Gilman takes up her favourite theme, the incompatibility of housework and childcare: 'What is the real condition of the home as regards children – its primal reason for being? How does the present home meet their needs? How does the homebound woman fill the claims of motherhood? As a matter of fact, *are* our children happy and prosperous, healthy and good, at home? ... The mother loves the child, always and always; she does what she can, what she knows how; but the principal work of her day is the care of the house, not of the child.'[118] So, says Gilman, if the ordinary conditions of household life are unsuitable for children, 'it is for us to so arrange those conditions as to make them suitable'.[119] With this framing of the problem, Gilman is anticipating what would later become the sociology of childhood.

Childhood as a status that comes with its own citizenship rights arrived on the British scene of welfare undertakings in the early 20th century mainly through the efforts of Eglantyne Jebb, lover of Margaret Keynes and co-founder with her sister Dorothy Buxton of the Save the Children Fund. Jebb was the fourth child of an élite landowning family in Shropshire, the prettiest of the daughters, with periwinkle eyes and red–gold hair. She managed an Oxford education, a term behind Maude Royden and Kathleen Courtney at Lady Margaret Hall; then she tried out, as they did, Settlement life in working-class London. The latter did not suit her: 'I do not like the poor,' she concluded.[120] Jebb's 1,098 page 'slum novel' featuring a relationship between two young women, a social worker and a leisured daughter at home, remained unpublished because the publisher said it was too long, and Jebb, an unrelentingly stubborn woman, refused to cut it. After Oxford, she tried teaching, and working for the Charity Organization Society (which is how she met Margaret Keynes), but nothing seemed to satisfy her until she became involved through her brother-in-law, Charles Roden Buxton, a liberal MP, in relief work in Macedonia. This bred in her a burning antipathy to all war. During the First World War, Jebb helped her sister with the 'hugely daring pacifist venture' of translating and publishing German and other foreign anti-war material in the form of a weekly leaflet called *Notes from the foreign press*.[121] This was a domestic industry, overseen by Buxton from the attic of her home in Golders Green, North London, and involving a team of expert linguists and typists translating from

10.12: Eglantyne Jebb, c. 1925, and the poster she handed out in 1919

over 100 Finnish, French, German, Hungarian, Italian, Romanian, and Russian newspapers. The focus was on the impact of the war on social and economic conditions. No one reading the *Notes* could avoid appreciating that what the war and the economic blockade had produced was a giant, Europe-wide humanitarian crisis encompassing many millions of starving, sick and dead children. Margaret Keynes' brother Maynard resigned from the Versailles Peace Conference when his proposals for lifting the blockade, raising a loan to feed starving Europe and instituting an ambitious regeneration programme to kick-start the devastated continental economies were rejected. Retreating to Virginia Woolf's sister's home in Kent, he reached a large international audience with his book *The economic consequences of the peace* (1919), a copy of which Margaret Keynes inscribed to Eglantyne Jebb.[122] The same year that Keynes' book was published, Jebb and Buxton joined forces with others to found the Fight the Famine Council, a single-issue pressure group aimed at persuading the British government to end the blockade.

The Save the Children Fund, the centre and driving ambition of Eglantyne Jebb's life, was originally set up under the aegis of the Fight the Famine Council to raise money for the feeding of German and Austrian children. Its first publicity stunt, planned with the help of the WILPF, saw Jebb handing out leaflets in Trafalgar Square bearing pictures of starving Austrian children (page 314). This act led to her being fined for 'unpatriotic behaviour' – there was widespread opposition in Britain then to the feeding of starving children who belonged to former 'enemy' nations.[123] These initiatives to save the children of Europe involved many women reformers, among them Emily Balch, Hilda and Alice Clark, Kate Courtney, Kathleen Courtney, Margaret Llewelyn Davies, Gabrielle Duchêne, Mary MacArthur, Catherine Marshall, Jeanne Mélin, Maude Royden, Olive Schreiner, Mary Sheepshanks and Helena Swanwick. The Save the Children Fund is another legacy that survives today, working in over 120 countries around the globe.

But it was Eglantyne Jebb alone who formulated the text of the 'Children's Charter' adopted by the League of Nations in 1924. According to the legend, on a cloudless summer's day in 1922 she climbed to the summit of Mont Salève, on the edge of Geneva, where she had located her Save the Children organization, close to the central office of the WILPF in the Rue du Vieux Collège, and, looking across the lake to the League of Nations building on the opposite shore, she took out pencil and paper and drafted a succinct document laying out the key objectives of a charter for the world's children. Her list decreed that they should be fed, sheltered and succoured; provided with healthcare; 'reclaimed' if delinquent; prioritized in times of distress; enabled to earn a livelihood; protected from all forms of exploitation; and reared to abide by the principle of service to others.[124] Her original objectives were expanded by the United Nations (UN) and adopted as a Declaration on the Rights of the Child in 1959; this, in turn, was one of the main inspirations behind the 1989 UN Convention on the Rights of the Child, 'the most universally accepted human rights instrument in history'.[125] It does seem unlikely that a woman who was not especially keen on the language of human rights, nor on children, should occupy such a position in history. The answer is that Jebb understood that advancing the welfare and rights of children was a way to create better citizens. Constructive child welfare could promote reconciliation between nations and encourage the moral ethos of 'supranationalism'.[126] Her emphasis on the duties as well as the rights of citizenship – duties that carry the obligation of altruism and a sense of community – was in this respect akin to the radical social philosophy worked out by Jane Addams.

If children are to become altruistic, peace-loving citizens, both the education system and the domestic system of teaching gender roles, with their emphasis on militaristic masculinity, need to change. Lizzy Lind-af-Hageby, campaigner against animal experimentation, wrote in her passionate *Be peacemakers: An appeal to women of the 20th century to remove the causes of war* (1924), that 'It is folly to expect peace whilst every child is subjected to suggestions and associations of war. Tin soldiers and toy guns prepare the way for a teaching of history in which conquests and losses in battle play the most prominent part … There is ceaseless recruiting of the minds of the young; boys in grammar schools are dressed in khaki and drilled with rifles and bayonets. Cadet corps are formed and trained in special military practices.' She invited all women to pledge that they would do everything in their power 'to teach children that war is incompatible with civilization', which meant discouraging the use of military toys and games, and military precepts and training in schools and colleges.[127]

Peace education appeared on the agendas of many women's organizations of the time. In 1914 the Peace and Arbitration Committee of the ICW urged mothers (fathers weren't mentioned in this context) to banish from nurseries 'toys that teach children the mimicry of warfare', and urged them and teachers to ban the use of stories extolling military and naval heroes, focusing children's attention instead on 'the heroic services of men and women in the Ordinary Peaceful occupations of life'.[128] One of the WILPF's resolutions at the Hague in 1915 was 'the necessity of so directing the education of children that their thoughts and desires may be directed towards the ideal of constructive peace'.[129] The WILPF set up an International Council for Education at its Zürich Congress in 1919. This drafted proposals for consideration by the national sections recommending the exclusion from school books of 'anything which tends to hinder international understanding ... or to arouse hate and scorn for foreign peoples'.[130] Outlining the requirements for a new peace organization in 1922, the WILPF went further, suggesting that any book inciting to hate should be subject to the same legal penalties as apply to impure foods. Just as polluted food can damage the body, so polluted ideas about citizenship can injure the mind, with ravaging consequences for the prospect of international harmony.[131]

Two American protagonists of children's peace education, Fannie Fern Andrews and Lucia Ames Mead, were prominent members of the WILPF. Andrews had a PhD in diplomacy and international law and wrote a well-regarded two-volume study of the mandate system in Palestine. Her work as a teacher in Boston public schools convinced her that children of different ethnic cultures had to be helped to understand one another, and that this recasting of citizenship would lay the foundations for avoiding war in the future. She founded the American School Peace League in 1908, using her home as a base of operations, although she also travelled a great deal across the US and in Europe to promote the idea of international peace education. After her visit to London a British School Peace League was set up; French school-teachers also adopted the idea.[132] In Sweden, Selma Lagerlöf and Matilda Widegren, two other WILPF enthusiasts, both took up the cause of peace education.

Lagerlöf's writings, for which she won the Nobel Prize for Literature in 1909, are shot through with the themes of peace and altruism, a feat she achieved partly through her union with the writer and translator Sophie Elkan – she and Elkan engaged in relentless criticisms of each other's works.[133] Matilda Widegren co-founded the Swedish Schools Peace Association in 1916, with the result that a new national curriculum for schools was issued by the government in 1919, specifying that history instruction in schools had to be carried out in such a way 'that its leading thread is peaceful cultural and societal development': any heroes celebrated had to be heroes of peace.[134]

Fannie Fern Andrews in the US worked with four colleagues to develop a comprehensive 400-page curriculum guide for teachers. *A course in citizenship* contained month-by-month lesson outlines designed to shape children into companionate citizens of an interconnected world community. Grade 1 children, for example, would be taught in September, 'Kindness to playmates', followed by 'Kindness to animals' in October, 'Responsibility for cleanliness and care' in November and 'Making others happy' in December. Children were urged to respect the natural resources of the earth as a component of peace culture. The guide suggested as 'peace heroes', figures in science, medicine, education and social reform whose work was about nurturing and preserving life instead of taking it.[135] Lucia Ames Mead's *How the war system affects women* observed that patriotism has 'no more to do with a gun than it has to do with a broom': thus, 'A five-year-old who learns not to throw his banana skin on the sidewalk and not to mark his neighbor's fence with chalk is learning the first lesson in that service which is the corner-stone of patriotism.'[136] Mead, 'a tiny, red-haired disciple of peace',[137] was a splendid publicist for the peace education cause, speaking at many gatherings, producing much written propaganda, and inventively using any opportunity she could; thus, in the early 1900s she paid for advertisements in Boston street cars warning the public that some 70% of government revenues was devoted to past or future wars.

A new world of domestic units containing equal and equally peace-loving men, women and children called for new ways of designing homes. Some of these have appeared in earlier chapters of this book: Charlotte Perkins Gilman's kitchenless homes; Clementina Black's federated houses, with their wheeled food containers and underground service tunnels; the strategies for scientific efficiency promoted by women sanitary scientists, with their interest in how domestic relations are constantly spoilt by germs, bad air and dirt. Ideas about reformulating the traditional family so as to liberate women, diffuse the power of heterosexuality and alter the rules of gender, came from many different directions and took different shapes. But at the root of most was a *theoretical* analysis of The Family's responsibility for tying together women's servitude in the home with their secondary social position, and the effect of this in obstructing the citizenship that women needed in order to turn the cast of the social order fully towards welfare. 'Utopian' housing schemes were both pragmatic answers to pressing questions of personal and public health and far-sighted plans for accommodating new kinds of 'family' relationships. Two British women, Jane Hume Clapperton and Henrietta Barnett, born in 1832 and 1851 respectively, approached the idea of new housing design from contrasting viewpoints. Clapperton's goal was the eradication of 'servant-wives', and Barnett's the dissolution of class barriers, but both women understood that *where* people live is a powerful determinant of *how* they are able to live.

Jane Hume Clapperton was in her 70s when Hamilton's *Marriage as a trade* and other key texts of the women's movement were published, yet she anticipated most of their ideas in an astonishing book, *Scientific meliorism and the pursuit of happiness*, which was published in 1885.[138] In Clapperton's book we have: the need for factual evidence to support social reform; the damages inflicted on the social fabric through the predatory pursuit of wealth; reform of the economic system to decrease social gaps in earnings and life-chances; a critique of forms of masculinity emphasizing competition and aggression; the goal of remedying an over-vindictive criminal justice system; dissolving the inequities of marriage and traditional divisions of gender; respecting motherhood as a public service that should be publicly endowed; developing less punitive and more pacifist methods of child-rearing; and a new public spirit to mend the fractured attempts of philanthropists and the state to provide welfare. We know rather little about Clapperton's personal life (and she left no accessible portraits): her father was a merchant and local liberal politician, she was the tenth of 12 children, and was sent to a boarding school when she was 12. She did philanthropic work, was a committed suffragist and had a close friendship with the artist and social reformer George Gaskell.[139] She never married, considering marriage a claustrophobic institution that turned women into a 'parasitic' class. At the heart of Clapperton's melioristic plan are what she calls 'unitary homes'. She spoke about these at the International Socialist Workers and Trade Union Congress in London in 1896, where she met Charlotte Perkins Gilman. Clapperton's unitary homes were establishments made up of some 40 families who live communally, sharing refectories, nurseries and facilities (music, art, dancing, chess, whist, reading, mechanics and smoking rooms), while retaining some private space, use of which is governed by strict rules: 'For instance, that no one shall enter the private room of another, except by special request; that no one shall smoke where it interferes with the comfort of others; that no one shall talk in a reading-room; that dirty boots in carpeted rooms are not permissible; that punctuality at the dinner hour and other set times is essential.' Housework is shared between the sexes and generations. A unitary home, in short, is 'a social organism superior to the family in its power of promoting human happiness'.[140]

Clapperton turned the script of her unitary home into a novel, *Margaret Dunmore; Or, a socialist home*, published in 1888 and set just two years into the future.[141] No straightforward utopian text, this chronicles the personal and social obstacles that have to be dissolved before cooperative living is possible. In a house called 'La Maison' – because the English word 'home' has so many outdated associations – Margaret Dunmore and her friends pledge to promote the happiness of humanity, living without wealth, luxury or idleness, and adopting a system of childrearing in which every tendency to domination, anger, revenge, hatred or greed is nipped in the bud. La Maison is a three-storey building, with the first floor used for education, culture, amusement and public service, the second for domestic affairs and the third for cooking and dining. A committee of two men and two women elected every six months run the place, assigning members of the household their individual tasks and ignoring all conventional gender divisions. Nonetheless, as the story unfolds, we see that some of the men do find it difficult to relinquish their old ideas about women and housework. Clapperton's characters struggle (realistically), with their author's uncompromising conviction that reforming the conditions of domestic life will change both individual character and the wider social ethos.

In the same year that Jane Hume Clapperton talked about unitary homes in London, Henrietta Barnett, who is remembered mainly for her role in setting up the first British social Settlement, Toynbee Hall, went to Russia with Canon Barnett, and on the ship she met a man who told her of plans to extend the London tube network. This would bring trains closer to the refuge from their East End work that she and her husband had bought, overlooking Hampstead Heath. Henrietta's horrified reaction was to decide that many additional acres of open space must be secured for the Heath so that its harebell-strewn meadows, verdant hedgerows, grazing lambs and woodland birdsong would be inviting and accessible to all. She also decided to erect a garden suburb of her own design. Barnett's 'beautiful green-golden scheme' for social integration, Hampstead Garden Suburb, was 'one of the most imaginative and innovative housing developments ever created'.[142] Once off the ship and back in London, she and her faithful companion, Marion Paterson, set up a committee, wrote 13,000 letters and organized dozens of deputations to local authorities and city companies, in a five-year-long campaign. Much land was owned by Eton College, so Barnett approached Mr Sanday of the Eton College trustees: 'Mr Sanday was a tall, grave man, and after I had told him all my hopes, and we had studied maps and discussed prices, he looked down on me and said, "Well, Mrs Barnett, I know you, and I believe in you, but you *are only a woman*, and I doubt if the Eton College trustees would grant the option of so large and valuable an estate to a woman! Now, if you would get *a few men* behind you, it would be *all* right".' So she did, and it was.[143]

Barnett called it 'a national duty' to demand the best for poor people: 'Do not let us put up with repaired slums, unsuitable huts, huge block buildings, or cheap substitutes. Demand the best. Cottages surrounded with gardens; fruit trees; open spaces; rest-arbours for the old, and playing-fields for the young; flowering hedges, tree-lined roads. Demand the best. Homes, not habitations.'[144] These were years of increasing interest among planners in garden cities. In Britain, there was already, in 1903, Letchworth Garden City, where the animal rights campaigner Lizzy Lind-af-Hageby was delighted to establish a model abattoir employing a humane method of mechanically stunning animals.[145] For her own utopian development in Hampstead, which began to be built in 1907 on the newly acquired Heath extension, Henrietta Barnett hired the Arts and Crafts architect Raymond Unwin, who had worked on the Letchworth plan. She asked him to combine her vision of a community that would mix the social classes with an emphasis on nature not found in conventional urban developments. Her idea was that the way homes were designed would encourage residents to live together 'in helpful neighbourliness'.[146] Barnett wanted schools and cottage homes for orphans, communal homes for the disabled and cooperative housing for single and retired people. Five acres were set aside for a church, chapel, library and social centre. Inspired by American housing design on her 1891 visit to that country, Barnett specified that there should be no borders between the gardens, but this was too much for some of the trustees, so they compromised on hedges of sweet briar, holly, yew and wild rose.

Barnett's utopia exists as a strongly middle-class enclave today, thus rather signalling the failure of her vision. She was too much of a believer in environmental determinism, and also quite unrealistic about what the working classes wanted. They wanted rents that were lower than her utopia could offer, and they wanted houses that were easier to clean and care for than many of hers were, and they didn't want the ban on alcohol that she imposed (as a keen supporter of the temperance movement, she gave them a tea house instead), nor did they particularly warm to the lectures and classes in bookkeeping, dressmaking, rambling and so forth put on at the social centre. Much more practical were the housing ideas of Labour Party activist Marion Phillips, who began at the other end of the problem with the views and experiences of house-dwellers themselves. Appealing to women's new sense of citizenship, Phillips, together with a colleague, Averil Sanderson Furniss, produced in 1917 some 50,000 copies of a four-page leaflet that asked women what was wrong with their housing and what they would like for the future. Detailed questions probed issues of plumbing and sanitation, heating, lighting and cleaning, and most importantly house design and layout. The book the two women wrote, *The working woman's house*, had a section called 'Cooperative house management' that proposed municipally owned and run restaurants, kitchens and laundries, in order to yield economies of scale and increase efficiency.[147] Some 100 National Kitchens had been established by the Ministry of Food and local authorities during the war, and these, said Phillips and Sanderson Furniss, should be extended and replicated in every district; at the one in New Bridge Street, in the very centre of London, for example (pictured in their book as a sparklingly clean but rather spartan establishment), customers purchased tickets at the door, then served themselves from a sensibly cheap bill of fare – boiled tongue and parsley sauce for 6d, fruit salad and custard for 4d. 'The ideal arrangement is a double one,' pronounced the authors, tactfully: food and laundry facilities should be provided communally for those who wanted it, while these functions would also be retained in the home.[148] Marion Phillips was a member of a body called the Women's Housing Sub-Committee, an all-female body appointed by the Ministry of Reconstruction in 1918 to comment on plans for post-war working-class housing. Its work had a big impact on post-war housing policy in Britain.[149]

There was an obvious logic in home reform being the responsibility of women. The first American woman to graduate as a civil engineer, and later to set up her own practice as an architect, was Nora Stanton Blatch, a woman with such tremendous trail-blazing credentials that she has to provide a suitable end to this chapter. Blatch was the grand-daughter of Elizabeth Cady Stanton, who helped to organize the declaration of women's rights at Seneca Falls in 1848, and she was the daughter of Harriot Stanton Blatch, whose efforts on behalf of equality and pacifism have made several appearances in this book. Nora was named after Nora in Ibsen's *A doll's house*, which a friend of her grandmother's had translated into English and which reformers such as Clementina Black and Eleanor Marx eagerly went to see when it was performed in London. Blatch was born in Basingstoke, England, 'a very benighted conservative town', according to her grandmother,[150] to parents whose transatlantic marriage meshed two cultures of welfare activism. As a child, Blatch played with both Emmeline Pankhurst's daughter, Sylvia, and with Charlotte Perkins Gilman's daughter, Katherine Stetson. Of the former, Blatch wrote, 'We climbed trees together while our mothers conferred.' Lots of well-known people ventured out to Basingstoke, including Beatrice and Sidney Webb, and a 'young man in rather baggy tweed clothes and a beard' – George Bernard Shaw.[151] In her adult life, Nora Stanton Blatch didn't publish much, being presumably over-occupied with architecture and also with bringing up three children. Yet the titles of two of her pamphlets say it all: *World peace through a people's parliament* (1944) and *Women as human beings* (1946).[152] The latter is a plea for equal opportunity in which Blatch returns us to the unfulfilled precepts of her grandmother's time at Seneca Falls. In a short marriage to radio and TV inventor Lee de Forest, Nora Stanton Blatch found herself with a husband who railed unpleasantly against his wife's working and campaigning on the equality front. She left him. When the American Society of Civil Engineers refused her full membership, she sued it and lost. But 99 years later, in 2015, the Society changed its mind and admitted her posthumously as a Fellow.[153] Posthumous recognition may not be much of a prize, but women who played so creatively with society's most sacrosanct social arrangements could hardly expect to be properly appreciated in their lifetimes.

ELEVEN

New deals: women reformers in the 1920s and 1930s

It was February, 1933. Franklin Roosevelt had recently been elected President of the United States. A woman with whom he had worked, and whom he had known for over 20 years, was coming to see him at his home in Hyde Park, New York, a lavish Italianate mansion which he had remodelled in colonial revival style. Roosevelt drove Frances Perkins around the Hyde Park estate in his hand-operated automobile – necessary because of the damage polio had inflicted on him. He pointed out the new trees and other improvements, of which he was very proud, and they discussed the grave industrial and social problems of the US and what might be done to solve them. She knew that he wanted her to be his new Secretary of Labor, the first female member of a presidential cabinet, but he didn't know just what she intended to accomplish in such an important political position. She told him. The package included unemployment insurance, old age insurance and health insurance. 'I remember he looked so startled, and he said, "Well, do you think it can be done?"' She told him she didn't know, but she wanted to try. She wanted his authorization. He gave it. She could try. And that was how it all began.[1]

In so far as the US has ever had a welfare state, most of the credit for its federal legislative origins should go to Frances Perkins. She served as Secretary of Labor from 1933 to 1945, during all four of Franklin Roosevelt's administrations, and was directly behind most of the social legislation associated with what is known as 'the New Deal' era in the US. Behind her were the achievements of many of the women reformers who appear in this book. Through her, the sociology of Settlement women that emphasized the need for evidence-based federal government action to promote social justice came to inform government values and policies. But, while we remember Franklin Roosevelt, most of us have never heard of Frances Perkins: her role as the principal architect of the New Deal is missing from most histories of that time. Because we don't know who she was or what she did, we are also excluded from knowing about the history that connects her to the transnational networks of women reformers who developed the tools of social science and a shared commitment to a just public policy. In being forgotten, Frances Perkins joins a large contingent of other women reformers. Her accomplishments, like theirs, once excavated, provide some kind of answer to the question: what difference did the women make? This chapter looks at how the work of women reformers bore fruit and continued into the 1920s and 1930s and beyond. Their labours and their ideas formed a living tradition, and can't simply be treated as a short-lived moment in social history.

Frances Perkins was a distant relative of the visionary Charlotte Perkins Gilman, and she was connected in other ways to the women reformers' networks. She was born to a middle-class family in Boston in 1880 and educated at a women's college. An early inspiration was the labour reformer Florence Kelley, who, as president of the National Consumers' League (NCL), braved the rigours of winter travel in New England in 1902 to visit Mount Holyoke College, where Perkins was a student, and address 'a little handful of girls studying economics or sociology', telling them about her programme for industrial and human social justice.[2] Perkins and Kelley met again later, at Hull-House, and Kelley recruited her as the executive secretary of the New York Consumers' League in 1910. Here Perkins learnt the well worked-out strategies for influencing the relationship between research, activism and policy that had been developed by this and other large-scale women's reform organizations. An event on Saturday, 25 March 1911 changed her life. Perkins was at a small tea party at an address in New York's Washington Square when the guests were distracted by the sound of fire engines and people screaming. The eighth floor of a nearby factory building, a sweatshop where women's tailored blouses were made, had caught fire. As the tea party guests rushed down the steps and towards the fire, the trapped workers started to jump. The overloaded fire escape had given way, only one of the elevators was working and the stairway was locked because the management was trying to stop trade union organizers getting in. Most of the 146 workers who died that day were young immigrant women. Later Perkins would say that the Triangle Shirtwaist Factory fire was the day the New Deal in American politics was born.[3]

Franklin Roosevelt took office in the midst of the Great Depression, and the New Deal promised a resolution of the structural problems that had produced a 25% unemployment rate and the collapse of much industry. It offered relief of hardship through social programmes that would also address the social and economic inequities of capitalism so intensively studied by reformers. Perkins thought that Franklin Roosevelt's compassion, a quality without which he probably would not have given such wholehearted support to her New Deal, derived from his experience with polio. His wife, Eleanor, had a different explanation: her husband became a more caring human being after she took him on a visit to the Settlement where she was working in New York; there, Roosevelt had carried a sick child up several flights of stairs in a terrible tenement building and had been profoundly shocked by the circumstances in which ordinary people had to live.[4] Possibly both women were right.

Perkins' four goals as 'Madam Secretary of Labor' were reviving the economy, preventing further depressions, improving the public welfare and stabilizing social order. She believed that 'government in a democracy is a service agency for these essential activities of human cooperation'.[5] To this end, she upgraded and professionalized the Bureau of Labor Statistics, enabling the US government for the first time to collect high-quality workforce data. Her creation of the Division (later Bureau) of Labor Standards – an initiative naturally involving the expertise of the industrial toxicologist Dr Alice Hamilton – was the first attempt to focus properly on workplace safety. With the Social Security Act of 1935, Perkins established unemployment benefits, old age pensions and welfare benefits for the poor. With the Fair

Labor Standards Act of 1938, she introduced the first federal minimum wage and overtime legislation, and the standard 40-hour working week. She worked to reform the laws governing child labour and provided a strategy for the government to cooperate with the trade unions instead of fighting them. So it was, really 'Perkins' New Deal' not Roosevelt's.[6] This was a 'cradle to grave' plan for the American people – a phrase that Britain's William Beveridge may just possibly have appropriated after his visit to the White House in 1934.[7]

The photograph below shows Frances Perkins standing behind Roosevelt in a group of men as he signs her Social Security Act into law. The public representation is symbolic: the men dominating the picture. Perkins is wearing her trademark tricorn hat, with its deliberate symbolic associations to the dress of the revolutionary colonists, and the plain black clothes she said she favoured on the grounds that men respond best to powerful women if women dress like men's mothers. But in the photo here she looks distracted, rather than pleased at her achievement. The explanation is that her husband, who was in a sanatorium with what would now be called bipolar disorder, had just escaped, and immediately after the signing she had to go to New York to find him. Perkins had married Paul Wilson, an economist in New York City politics, in 1913; Florence Kelley offered them her

11.1: Frances Perkins and the signing of the Social Security Act in the US, 1935

sea-view cottage in Maine surrounded by blueberry bushes for a honeymoon. Perkins defied convention by not changing her surname on marriage, and for most of it she provided financial and emotional support for Paul, and then for their daughter, who was also diagnosed with bipolar disorder. She kept these frailties of her private life as private as she could, but of course the media were obsessively interested in all the details (did she use perfume? What did she eat for breakfast? Could she cook?).[8]

Frances Perkins, together with Eleanor Roosevelt and another indomitable political activist, Molly (Mary) Dewson, were the triumvirate at the centre of the influential New Deal political sisterhood. Eleanor Roosevelt's spell as America's First Lady, 1933–45, was the same as Perkins' reign as America's Secretary of Labor, and both women profited from Molly Dewson's dedicated and strategic sponsoring of network women for key public posts. Dewson's background was in household management, criminal justice, the minimum wage movement and the NCL. She headed the Women's Division of the Democratic Party, and she made it her job to find government posts for female party workers so that they could see the goals for which they had long worked, in organizations such as the NCL and the Women's Trade Union League, realized in public policy. It was Dewson who orchestrated a major campaign to persuade President Roosevelt that Perkins was the only possible candidate for the job of Secretary of Labor, deploying what she later admitted was the somewhat 'deceptive' tactic of getting their friends in the network to write him fervently supportive letters.[9] 'About the most important letter I ever wrote you,' scribbled Dewson in the margin of one she addressed to Eleanor Roosevelt in April 1933 that contained the names of 23 women who simply had to be given government jobs.[10] By April 1935 there were more than 50 women in such positions. Dewson's plan worked, just as did most of the plan Frances Perkins laid before Franklin Roosevelt that day at Hyde Park.

Eleanor Roosevelt, welfare worker, diplomat, politician, pacifist, as well as an advocate of rights for women, African-Americans and refugees, would eventually become the first chair of the United Nations Commission on Human Rights and the main drafter of the Universal Declaration of Human Rights.

Her introduction to the women's welfare reform project came in an unlikely place, at a boarding school in England called Allenswood, where she was sent in 1899. The school was run by a friend of Beatrice Webb's, Marie Souvestre, a woman whose intellectual method stressed independent thinking, humanism and commitment to justice, and who made no secret of her intimate relationships with other women.[11] Eleanor Roosevelt herself lived out her commitment to marriage with her cousin Franklin, but with difficulty, owing to his recurrent marital infidelities. Her discovery in 1918 of his relationship with her secretary provoked Eleanor into a role as a public person and an independent woman (not forgetting, of course, her five children and all the housekeeping responsibilities of the White House and Hyde Park).[12] Eleanor Roosevelt wasn't intimate with Frances Perkins or with Molly Dewson (whose lifetime partner, the 'stunningly beautiful' Polly Porter,[13] supported her emotionally and financially), but she did have a close and politically important relationship with a journalist called Lorena Hickok.

Hickok, known as 'Hick', was the nation's best-known, hard-drinking, cigar-smoking, ribald-talking female reporter, and she had been assigned to follow Eleanor Roosevelt's side of the presidential campaign in 1932. Eleanor helped her to be appointed as Chief Investigator for the newly constituted Federal Emergency Relief Administration. By 1933 the two women met almost daily and dined together most evenings; when not away from Washington, Hickok slept on a daybed in a room adjacent to Eleanor's. Eleanor's first biographers were totally unable to deal with this relationship, but the publication in 1998 of some of the 3,500 extant letters between the two women makes the nature of their relationship and the importance of the political work they plotted together abundantly clear.[14] It was Hickok, with her inside knowledge of how the media shaped public opinion, who suggested to Eleanor the weekly press conferences and regular newspaper columns by means of which the First Lady told all the ladies of America what she thought they ought to think. It was at these conferences – the first held two days after her husband became president, and the last a few hours before he died – that Eleanor announced the appointments of network women and outlined the contents of their programmes. At Hickok's suggestion, Eleanor excluded male reporters from her press conferences, thereby forcing newspapers to keep female reporters on staff.[15] Hickok encouraged all Eleanor's efforts to reach as wide an audience as possible. The First Lady's 1933 book, *It's up to the women*, is a mongrel compendium of household advice (try to get one maid if you can, greet your husband with a smile in the evening, consult the local home economics college for cheap, nourishing menus, and take your holidays on bicycles as they do in England) and serious appeals to women to join the movement for social justice, become unionized, set up consumer groups and enter politics. It laid out the First Lady's priorities, which were those of most of the Settlement sociologists, peace makers and welfare workers who have appeared in this book: peace, the abolition of poverty, a concern for youth, women's rights and the rights of minorities generally.[16] The New Deal sisterhood were clever strategists, playing to, rather than confronting, prevailing gender conventions. When any of the network women wanted something done they told Eleanor, and she told Franklin. 'I never tried to exert any political influence on my husband or on anyone else in the government,' she remarked once, disingenuously.[17]

So this is one answer to the question: what was it all for? What did the manifold, intrepid and trail-blazing efforts of the women reformers in this book add up to in the end? The New Deal was a particular expression in the US of many of the women reformers' hopes, visions and labours. It wouldn't have been possible without the affiliations they had built with one another. To understand a little more about how Perkins' New Deal happened, it's useful to go back to another hopeful era, another Frances and another Roosevelt. As Governor of New York in 1898 Theodore Roosevelt (a cousin of Franklin's and uncle of Eleanor, this was a tight-knit family) had formed many links with women reformers. He was sympathetic to some of their causes – for instance, helping to get through Congress funding for a comprehensive inquiry promoted by Mary McDowell, Edith Abbott and Sophonisba Breckinridge into the working conditions of women and children (Roosevelt complained that this turned the Department of Labor into 'practically a Department of Sociology').[18] The other Frances, Frances Kellor, who has put in fleeting appearances earlier in

this book, would have very much approved of this result. Kellor
was a lawyer, a sociologist of crime, a pioneer of work on the
status and social conditions of immigrants, and a script-writer
for Progressive Era legislation. (See page 307 for a photograph
of her as a chauffeur with her long-term partner, Mary Dreier.)
Kellor combined a legal training – hard won, since she came
from a poor, single-mother family – with the study of sociology
at the University of Chicago, funded by a scholarship awarded
by the Chicago Women's Club. She knew about Settlement
work, living at Hull-House intermittently for a number of years.
Her work on unemployment, crime and race relations yielded
a powerful environmental analysis of social problems at a time
when biological theories were an obstacle to the extension of
state welfare. Her research methods are a familiar story: the
use of disguise and covert ethnography alongside large-survey
data-gathering to expose the unsavoury underside of urban life.
Kellor helped to draft successful legislation for New York State to
correct the maltreatment of immigrants and African-American
women who travelled north to find work, and she set up and/
or headed various civil rights organizations in the early 1900s.
Democratic inclusion, a new international version of citizenship:
these were the guiding principles of her work.[19]

She first met Theodore Roosevelt through the arch-networker
Lillian Wald of the Henry Street Settlement in New York and
Maud Nathan of the NCL. When Roosevelt decided to form
a new party, the Progressive Party, during the 1912 election
campaign, Frances Kellor, Jane Addams, Florence Kelley and
Margaret Dreier Robins wrote the social justice proposals for his
presidential platform. Kellor and Addams both became members
of the party's National Committee and, along with Kelley, made
up his 'Female Brain Trust'. The 1912 election was a moment
seized by leading women reformers, who recognized that non-
alliance with any political party was increasingly limiting the
scope and reach of their reform goals. Jane Addams put it like
this: 'a worthy code of social legislation can only be secured
through the co-operation of the nation and state, held to a
common purpose through party unity'.[20] She also thought that
supporting the progressives would be a much-needed way of
educating the public about social reform. The suffrage became a

huge campaign issue, dividing the Republican Party and testing Theodore Roosevelt's own lukewarm approval of it, but it was clear that the support of the women reformers could be crucial to the men's political success. There is a sense in which the clash of the genders, with all that women had learnt about the humanitarian need for social justice, and all that the men held onto about narrow notions of the state and political practice, was what actually gave birth to modern welfare states.[21]

It's scarcely a coincidence, as noted in Chapter One, that large-scale state welfare programmes and women's social action movements both began to happen around the same time in countries such as the US, France, Germany and Britain.[22] Social policy is often the result of the transnational circulation of ideas, 'travelling knowledge',[23] and an adequate history requires abandoning narrow concepts of the nation-state. Many theorists have, however, followed the German sociologist Max Weber's extraordinarily restrictive but historically accurate definition of the state as 'a relation of men dominating men, a relation supported by means of legitimate (that is, considered to be legitimate) violence'[24] – a definition that surely his sociologically competent feminist wife Marianne would have complained about. How, then, can the state be redefined so as to be about the non-hierarchical relationships of peaceful equals? This was the essence of the women reformers' project. In pursuing this, they had to confront the deep-rooted injuries of patriarchy, with its masculine definitions of states, subjects and citizens, hardened during the First World War into the idea that soldiering and working (not mothering and housekeeping) can be the only proper entitlement to citizenship rights.[25] Hull-House's Sophonisba Breckinridge pointed out in the 1920s that tests for naturalization were male-biased because they didn't ask about 'the principles of community association' and care that women know about through their everyday experiences. If a mother is fit to care for her children, if she knows how to be a good neighbour, then she should be regarded as fit to be a citizen: these qualifications are more relevant than being able to recite the US constitution or the names of men holding public office.[26] Britain's L. T. Hobhouse, the liberal philosopher and brother of Emily Hobhouse, the woman who gave the British government so much trouble in and after the Boer War, spoke for many when he said that the duty of the modern state is to provide the conditions that enable a man to keep himself and his family.[27] The women reformers' counterpoint about enlarging citizenship, dissolving the boundaries between private activities and public roles and questioning the whole absurd notion of bearing arms as a qualification for political rights was bound to cause a certain uneasiness, if not an actual humungous clash of perspectives.

One of Frances Kellor's almost totally under-referenced achievements was to be in the vanguard of what, in the 1990s in Europe and the US, became the evidence-based policy movement.[28] Kellor articulated the historically neglected principle at the heart of many women reformers' work: that policy should be founded only on facts systematically gathered in well-conducted research. She was scandalized by the existing situation – 'little more than a mass of disorganized, numberless, separate investigations, which have little correlation with lawmaking bodies or the needs of the public'. In 1914 she asked, 'Why should the party, the administrator, and the State depend so largely upon the initiative and recommendations of the voluntary efforts of social welfare organizations? ... Why should they not have their own laboratories for ascertaining facts?' Her vision of a laboratory 'manned by experts', undertaking social research and acting as a 'general clearing-house for information, as well as a power for the most intelligent and courageous governmental action', took the women reformers' experiences and turned them into a very modern plan of governmental action. Her model for the social sciences was the natural sciences. An effective political laboratory, she insisted, 'must be as scientific, as thorough, as dispassionate in its personnel, methods, and findings as are the laboratories of other sciences'.[29] Her view of public policy was that politicians had no business inflicting on the public programmes that had not been shown to achieve the ends they were supposed to.

These ideas were realized in an organization Kellor set up and headed in 1912, called the National Progressive Service (NPS), an ambitious and complex outfit with four departments, 16 expert committees, two permanent bureaux dealing with education and legislation and many local agencies at state level. The NPS conducted research, consulted with experts, prepared legislation, ran conferences, produced publications and did vast amounts of dissemination to 'the people', including supplying to 'motion picture companies' scenarios of plays written by well-known authors dealing with problems and social conditions 'as they actually exist in prisons, mines, sweat-shops, and factories where child labor is employed'.[30] Women such as Jane Addams, Edith Abbott, Grace Abbott, Emily Balch and Mary McDowell all had formal posts in the NPS, which was based in the Progressive Party headquarters in New York and was noted for its incredible pace of activity – work ceased only at midnight, when the elevators stopped running. The NPS seems to have had a successful couple of years and then it ran into trouble, with complaints about too much bureaucracy and the inconvenient time lag between getting research done and needing it to inform policy – an issue familiar to many researchers in the evidence-based policy field today. It's said that Kellor was bossy, and that people didn't like working for a woman: she was known for her men's clothes and for her skills in sport, as a basketball coach and the author of a book on athletics for women.[31]

Post-hoc excuses cover up whatever might be the true story of this early attempt to lock policy and evidence firmly together, but it does seem that the alliance of many women in the NPS with the peace movement ultimately drove the nail in the coffin of their relationship with Theodore Roosevelt, for whom the women's pacifism was simply 'silly and base'.[32] *This* Roosevelt's problem was that he wanted to champion both virility and reform, but virility had the upper hand. Roosevelt's *Hunting trips of a ranchman* (1885) carried a symbolic photograph of the author as a manly Western ranchman, complete with large gun and bullet belt, a pose he also adopted in his foreign policy.[33] Kellor herself emerged from the experiment of the NPS to make another critical contribution to pacifism (these women were nothing if not persistent). In 1926, she founded the American Arbitration Association, an organization specializing in alternative dispute resolution that continues to flourish today. Since belligerent nations in the First World War had failed to sit round the negotiating table, as the WILPF said they should, a scientific organization was called for which would cultivate a spirit of arbitration, teaching people and nations about it and thereby, hopefully, helping to reduce conflict, litigation and violence.[34]

Despite the view, repeated in many historical accounts, that women's collective activism ceased once the vote was gained, their cross-border social and political activism increased in the 1920s and 1930s.[35] The debilitating terms of the Versailles Treaty (and other treaties dealing with the 'losers' of the First World War) caused starvation and shortages throughout Europe well beyond the war's official end, and many women reformers went to help. They could see with their own eyes that this was a fragile peace, and they issued multiple warnings that, since the 'organized war system' hadn't been dismantled, it would all happen again. Talking at the WILPF Congress in Vienna in 1921, Aletta Jacobs noted sombrely: 'Let us not forget that we are still living in the midst of war in all parts of the world and that the present terms of peace will soon be producing a new war, more immense and more inhuman than the last one … we are sitting on the edge of a volcano.'[36] The German feminist-pacifists Anita Augspurg and Lida Heymann told the Bavarian Minister of Domestic Affairs in 1923 that Hitler (who was Austrian) ought to be deported from Germany; they warned the minister that he would live to regret it if he ignored their advice.[37] Rosika Schwimmer wrote to her friend Lola Maverick Lloyd in October 1930: 'It is the old thing. The militarists act and prepare for war by their actions, and the pacifists sit at pink teas, and study books and plans. That is why we are going to have another world war and a worse one.'[38] Three years later she wrote to President Roosevelt about the dangers of 'Fascism of the Hitler variety' conquering one country after another. She issued similar warnings about Mussolini after Italy invaded Ethiopia in 1935, organizing an international campaign that involved sending hundreds of letters and copies of a flyer at the end of which she proposed the establishment of 'the United States of the World, the only means to save mankind from self-destruction'.[39]

The work of the WILPF continued. Major campaigns were waged against the opium trade, and for the internationalization of waterways; sharing the world's natural resources; the protection of minorities; the control of chemical weapons; and universal disarmament. It was one of the first organizations to urge the peaceful utilization of Antarctica under international control. Fact-finding missions in which WILPF members went to Ireland (1920), Haiti (1926), Indo–China and China (1927), the Ukraine (1930) and Palestine (1930) yielded a constant stream of reports identifying the errors of male-dominated imperialist politics.[40] Theologian Maude Royden's last campaign, in the early 1950s when she was approaching 80, was on behalf of the Arabs in Palestine. She wrote to the Duke of Edinburgh and to Mrs Pandit in India to tell them both that the Balfour Declaration was wrong and that the British should never have given away what wasn't theirs to give in the first place.[41] (There's no record of a reply.) Other women reformers persisted, like Royden, with their pacifist message well into old age: Dr Alice Hamilton was 94 when she signed an open letter in 1963 calling for an end to American involvement in the Vietnam War.[42]

Age was no barrier to the pursuit of long-held goals or to the realization of new ones. As examples of territorial expansion, consider the final careers as advocates of minority rights of two British reformers whose work appears in this volume: sanitary educator Alice Ravenhill and the radical economist Mabel Atkinson. After Ravenhill's career in the science of household reform and the revolutionary enterprise of the KCHSS (see Chapter Five), she emigrated with her family to Canada, where she continued lecturing in household science. Then, after 'retirement', she took on a new career as an authority on aboriginal culture and defender of native rights in British Columbia. As befits a household science specialist, she began with needlework, reproducing indigenous Indian designs on rugs, bags, cushions and so on. In her late 70s she started giving talks about indigenous arts and crafts in schools. This resulted in a course on 'British Columbian Indians' being added to the grade school curriculum. Ravenhill published two books on the topic, the second at the age of 85 after three years' intensive research.[43] Her stress on the importance of appreciating pre-industrial artistic skills was part of her more fundamental social critique of contemporary society, which took issue with the prevailing treatment of Indian children – corralling them in special schools and forcing on them an alien education disrespectful of their own cultural traditions.[44]

The economist Mabel Atkinson, who changed her name to

11.2: Mabel Palmer (formerly Atkinson)

Palmer after a short marriage to an Australian journalist, lectured in economics for the Workers' Educational Association and also at the KCHSS, where she would have met Alice Ravenhill. Like Ravenhill, she emigrated, first to Australia and then, after abandoning her marriage, to South Africa, where she embarked on career number two as a race relations activist and the founder of university education for Non-Whites in Natal. She began by holding classes, unpaid, in her sitting room. Supported by her British friends, Beatrice and Sidney Webb, Palmer proposed that Durban should host a global Institute of Inter-racial Economics. At meetings of the University of Senate of South Africa she was a legendary figure, given to knitting when bored, wearing thick glasses and a green eye-shade and exposing everyone to her formidable, single-minded intellect.[45] Mabel Palmer published her last book, *The history of the Indians in Natal*, when she was 81.[46] Many women reformers would have applauded endeavours such as these of Ravenhill and Palmer to promote minority rights and the value of ethnic and cultural diversity.

Fertilized by the strength of alliances already formed, new groupings also emerged and new organizations were set up. The Medical Women's International Association (MWIA) arrived at a conference of women physicians that was convened in New York for six weeks in 1919. The aim of the conference was to draw on women health-care workers' war-time experiences of solidarity and underscore the role of science as a vehicle for international cooperation.[47] Thirty-eight women doctors from 16 countries talked about women and children's health; about sexuality and contraception; about workplace safety; and about accident and maternity insurance and other legislative reforms. They discussed sex and dietary education, the importance of regular medical examinations and healthy dress (without corsets and with sensible shoes), and spent a certain amount of time debating whether or not female homosexuality was due to a 'psychic arrest of the libido', as the new Freudian psychology was claiming.[48] Jane Addams was there, and Charlotte Perkins Gilman; the only non-doctor on the programme committee was the prison reformer and scientific student of sex, Katharine Bement Davis. Her transatlantic colleague from England, Dr Mary Gordon, talked about international friendship. The conference published its proceedings in six volumes[49] and resulted in the formation of two organizations, one of which, the Medical Women's International Association, is still alive today. In the photograph the women are meeting in Geneva at their first international conference in 1922; hats are much in evidence, as always, the shoes look sensible – and about the corsets we can only guess.

In the same year as the MWIA got off the ground, another transnational initiative bound together academic women in an organization called the International Federation of University Women (IFUW). Like the MWIA, its motive was the promotion of international collaboration and understanding. Seven women from Britain made the ocean voyage to New York in the autumn of 1918 to visit 46 universities and colleges over six weeks and produce proposals for productive British–US exchanges. Unfortunately, two of them, Caroline

11.3: First meeting of the Medical Women's International Association, Geneva, Switzerland, 1922

Spurgeon, the first female university professor in Britain at Bedford College in London, and Rose Sidgwick, an English lecturer at Birmingham University, caught flu (this was during the 1918–19 flu epidemic) on board ship. Sidgwick died, but Spurgeon survived, convalescing in the home of New York college dean Virginia Gildersleeve, with whom she formed an intimate personal and professional attachment for the rest of her life. The IFUW was the brainchild of these three women, aided by other members of existing networks, including Alice Masaryk from Czechoslovakia.[50] Its first convention was held in the summer of 1920 at Bedford College in London, with representatives from 15 countries. Spurgeon's address framed its mission as the development of sympathetic and mutually helpful links between nations and 'the organized training of women to be citizens of the world'.[51] Their method expanded the existing women's network logic of shared interests and sociability. There were to be cultural exchanges of women students, teachers and researchers; fellowship programmes; and a network of international clubhouses and individual international hospitality. In the 1930s, IFUW members made phenomenal efforts to rescue academic women from Germany and German-occupied Europe. Renamed Graduate Women International in 2015, this organization has also survived, pressing today for equality, empowerment and equal access to education and training. In 1945 Gildersleeve was appointed by Franklin Roosevelt to the US delegation that was writing the United Nations Charter. She managed to insert into the Charter, 'universal respect for human rights and fundamental freedoms for all without distinction as to race, sex, language, or religion', and she also insisted that a Commission on Human Rights be set up, which it was, to be directed by Eleanor Roosevelt, who wrote the Universal Declaration of Human Rights three years later, in 1948.[52] In the photograph opposite Gildersleeve watches, smiling, again the lone woman in masculine company, as the United Nations Charter is signed in 1945.

Wheels turn full circle; network structures connect stories, biographical journeys and public achievements. The International Industrial Relations Institute (commonly shortened to IRI, rather than IIRI), 'A remarkable but scarcely known organization',[53]

11.4: Virginia Gildersleeve and the signing of the United Nations Charter, 1945

came a little later than the IFUW and the MWIA, in 1922. Like them, it was propelled into existence by women reformers' disappointment in the ability of national governments to act in the interests of welfare and international peace. 'We are tired of seeing economic power used by a few instead of for the benefit of many,' declared Mary van Kleeck, an industrial sociologist and the radical director of the IRI. The war and the peace alike, she said, demonstrated the failure of government to act in the public interest.[54] Van Kleeck was a friend of 'Madam Secretary of Labor' Frances Perkins and was inspired, like her, by Hull-House's Florence Kelley. She shared Frances Kellor's view of scientific social research as a vehicle for social transformation, although she took it further. Van Kleeck was critical of the New Deal, arguing that it didn't go far enough and, indeed, couldn't, because government, in the existing political and economic system, would never be able to secure real equality and democratically distributed welfare.

In 1934 Van Kleeck delivered a good dose of both heat and light to a conference of social workers, in an address entitled 'Our illusions regarding government'. There are two theories of government, she told the social workers: in the first – an

11.5: Mary van Kleeck

approach favoured by Beatrice and Sidney Webb in Britain – governments can pass and administer laws that will equalize the distribution of wealth and guarantee fair standards of living for workers. In the second – which accords with American experience – 'government essentially is dominated by the strongest economic power and becomes the instrument to serve the purposes of the groups possessing that power ... government tends to protect property rights rather than human rights'.[55] She personally drafted a proposal called the Frazier-Lundeen Bill in 1934–5 which outlined a much more comprehensive insurance plan than Franklin Roosevelt's/Frances Perkins': a federal system for unemployment insurance and aid to dependent children; guaranteed wages until a new job was found; 16 weeks of paid maternity leave for women; and national criteria for unemployment and welfare, all to be funded by an inheritance tax on wealthy individuals and corporations. Van Kleeck formed the Inter-professional Association for Social Insurance to promote the Bill and its underlying philosophy, which had widespread left-wing support and came close, but not close enough, to being passed.[56]

The IRI was 'a two-woman transoceanic operation' run by van Kleeck and Mary Fleddérus, a Dutch activist and personnel manager of a glass factory in the Netherlands.[57] The two women shared their lives as well as their work, directing the IRI from offices in The Hague and New York. The organization was a conglomeration of disparate interest groups committed to international economic planning: personnel managers, factory inspectors and welfare workers; forward-thinking employers; modernist architects, engineers and doctors; trade union leaders and 'Taylorites'.[58] Kerstin Hesselgren, Sweden's Chief Factory Inspector, was one of those involved, and so was Adelaide Anderson, Principal Lady Inspector of Factories in Britain. The IRI sponsored ideas, plans, meetings, conferences and publications, acting as a networking platform for key figures in industrial welfare internationally.

The origins of the IRI lay in Van Kleeck's work in the Rivington Street Settlement, where Eleanor Roosevelt had shown her husband how the other half lives, and as director of industrial studies for the Russell Sage Foundation. Van Kleeck became convinced that a more rational system was needed to replace the haphazard and paternalistic way industry was run, which affected women workers disproportionately. Arbitrary power was the problem, and science should replace the authority of power with the authority of knowledge. In this Van Kleeck followed the teaching of Frederick Taylor, pioneer of scientific management, but she adapted his ideas to incorporate the women reformers' values of care, welfare and dialogue, insisting that workers' well-being and the health of industry could not be divorced from one another. Van Kleeck's radicalism wasn't shared by all around her, but it did prompt a new movement in social work critical of the interests of government.[59] The IRI's last international conference was held in 1947; the organization was effectively killed off when the Germans occupied Holland in 1940 and ordered its headquarters to be destroyed and replaced by defence works.[60]

In 1957, aged 73, Mary van Kleeck sat in the US Passport Office, being interrogated. She was trying to regain her passport, which had been withdrawn because she was suspected of communist sympathies. Van Kleeck told her interrogators that they had no idea about the important work of her generation in international affairs, or about the depth of its concern for social justice.[61] This confrontation points us to one well-worn mechanism for closing the door of memory on the contributions of women reformers: labelling them as dangerous. Fredrika Bremer of Sweden, calling for a world peace alliance of women in 1854, was deemed dangerous; so was Emily Hobhouse, exposing the violence of the British government in the Boer War of the early 1900s; so were most of the women who went, or tried to go, to The Hague Peace Congress in 1915. The passionate protector of minority rights and director of the Children's Bureau, Grace Abbott, was pilloried for her association with the pacifist and suffrage movements, and was alleged to be involved in a sinister alliance with the Russian communist revolutionary Alexandra Kollontai, People's Commissar for Social Welfare in the new Soviet republic in 1917.[62] The Military Intelligence Division of the US War Department deployed undercover agents among women peace workers throughout the First World War – Jane Addams and Alice Hamilton were two of the many who knew they were the objects of official surveillance.

In 1923 a US War Department librarian, Lucia Ramsey Maxwell, developed a 'spider web chart' based on War Department files that linked 17 women's organizations and 20 individual women in a supposed international socialist–pacifist–feminist conspiracy designed to bring Bolshevism to the US. Top of the list was the WILPF. Jane Addams was now 'the most dangerous woman in America'.[63] She did have excessive trouble with the ultra-right-wing Daughters of the American Revolution (DAR), who used the spider-web chart to point the finger at Hull-House and at the WILPF as organizations operating in a world revolutionary movement aiming to destroy with 'the poison of liberalism' the government of the US.[64] It's no coincidence that among the 87 'doubtful speaker' names on the DAR list are many of the women who appear in this book: as well as Jane Addams there were Grace Abbott, Gertrude Baer, Emily Balch, Harriot Stanton Blatch, Sophonisba Breckinridge, Carrie Chapman Catt, Madeleine Doty, Alice Hamilton, Julia Lathrop, Lola Maverick Lloyd, Maude Royden, Rosika Schwimmer, Vida Scudder, Mary Simkhovitch and Lillian Wald.[65]

The suppression of radical women's voices in the McCarthy era in the US exceeded anything experienced by their British sisters, but pacifism in women has always tended to be an upsetting matter, since it queries the nationalism of the masculine state. Indeed, the reason why women peace makers had been excluded from the 1919 peace negotiations was precisely because it was feared they would support peace rather than the best interests of their own nations.[66] This was a contest over citizenship and nationalism as key frameworks for welfare states, as much as it was over the antagonistic claims of war and peace. No story demonstrates this better than Rosika Schwimmer's. As a Jewish radical feminist and pacifist, Schwimmer was thoroughly entangled in the spider web; she was labelled a Bolshevik agent or a German spy or a seditious communist or a swindler of Henry Ford, duping him into the peace-ship ruse (see Chapter Six) and stealing his money.[67] Once Britain had ejected Schwimmer as an enemy alien in 1914, she went to the US, where her mail was secretly opened by the State Department and a 13-page US intelligence report on her activities was compiled and distributed widely to women's and peace groups in an effort to stop them working with her. Schwimmer probably *was* the most thoroughly radical woman in this book. She called herself 'a very very radical feminist', 'an uncompromising pacifist' and 'an absolute atheist' and rejected all allegiance to political parties, considering them too masculine and contaminated with concepts of authoritarian and violent leadership.[68] She was self-confident, stubborn, extremely quarrelsome and enormously persistent.

Schwimmer was also, in a spectacularly forgotten episode, the first woman ambassador in history. In 1918 she was appointed by Count Mihály Károlyi in Hungary to the National Council in what proved to be a short-lived pro-western liberal/pacifist government, and was then sent to Bern in Switzerland as Hungarian ambassador. In Bern her diplomatic mission was immediately blocked by the male diplomats, some of whom were explicitly instructed by their governments not to deal with a woman; the Swiss president acknowledged openly that 'he was very reluctant to break with the tradition under which diplomatists are of the male sex'.[69] Schwimmer resigned, the Karolyi government fell to Béla Kun's communist regime and she was smuggled to the US by English and American Quakers. She applied for US citizenship in 1924, declaring that, although a world government was preferable, the US was the best democracy she knew. This battle lasted five years and was ultimately unsuccessful. The Supreme Court barred Schwimmer from citizenship, ostensibly because she refused to answer affirmatively question 22 of the oath of allegiance, 'If necessary are you willing to take up arms in defense of this country?' She said no. 'If ... the United States can compel its women citizens to take up arms in the defense of the country – something that no other civilized government has ever attempted – I would not be able to comply with this requirement of American citizenship ... I have no sense of nationalism, only a cosmic consciousness of belonging to the human family.'[70] The Supreme Court decision was not unanimous, Justices Brandeis, Holmes and Sanford dissenting, and considering Schwimmer 'a woman of superior character and intelligence, obviously more than ordinarily desirable as a citizen of the United States'.[71]

Rosika Schwimmer remained single-mindedly committed to peace, to the transcendence of nationalism and to the idea of world government. Having officially become 'a woman without a country', she continued with her transnational work. Her efforts to launch a World Center for Women's Archives featured in Chapter One. During the 1930s also, Schwimmer began, with her friend Lola Maverick Lloyd, a campaign for world government and world citizenship.[72] In 1937, Schwimmer's friends, led by Lloyd, presented her with an unofficial World Peace Prize, to substitute for the Nobel Peace Prize that she was never offered.[73]

TWELVE

Ways of forgetting: women reformers as missing persons

The Australian feminist Dale Spender complained in her invigorating (but sadly not well remembered) *Women of ideas, and what men have done to them* (1982), that there was no way in which the research for her book could be regarded as comprehensive: 'Had I decided to wait until I had pursued every clue … I would never have come to write the book, for every fragment uncovered points to many more.'[1] The account offered in *Women, peace and welfare* is only one among many that might have been constructed. The contents of this book have been made out of what it has proved possible to find in a limited amount of time and with limited resources. Stitching the stories of different women in different places together in the shape of a single project runs the risk of over-emphasizing sameness at the expense of difference; yet what is most remarkable is how women of different political persuasions in different places did share similar ideas. They rejected violence towards people and nations as a form of human interaction, and they wanted communities and populations, not just their own social groups, to prosper and claim civil rights. In doing this they found alliances with other women a major source of solidarity and friendship. They thought deeply about what it means to be a citizen in relation to cultures, genders, geographies, nation-states and our habitation of planet earth. In their thinking they sometimes reproduced uncomfortable ideas about eugenics, evolution, class, colonialism and the 'essentialism' of women's maternalist ethics – in that sense they were, as we would expect them to be, creatures of their time. They may not have achieved what they hoped for – a blueprint for a new, good society – but they did offer a powerfully argued alternative approach to social problems. This is at least as relevant today as it was in their lifetimes, as we confront a global politics of terrorism, international conflict, environmental destruction and violence, and the apparent inability of even the most 'advanced' welfare states to abolish gross inequalities of income, justice and citizenship. The resonance of the women reformers' ideas extends to the way some of these have actually seeped into transnational thinking about welfare and peace. For example, United Nations peace-making policy today contains most of the conclusions women reformers arrived at over a century ago, when they met against a background of ferns at the International Women's Congress in The Hague zoo. Their resolutions anticipated modern principles of human security and positive peace and a discourse of social justice and human rights flowing across and beyond national borders.[2]

Ways of forgetting are as thoroughly entangled with cultural values as are ways of knowing. But perhaps we know more about knowing than we do about forgetting. I began my quest to find out more about the lives and work of women reformers wondering why my lengthy liberal education as a white, middle-class British woman had taught me so little about them. I end my journey through the stories contained in this book simply amazed by the extent of this act of cultural forgetting. This final chapter discusses some of the strategies which have been used to relegate these ground-breaking women to the 'missing persons' list. It introduces one more name – that of an American philosopher – and one more organization – the Women's Organisation for World Order – which in their different ways took the radical frameworks of the women reformers even further in outlining novel understandings of the social system that has managed so comprehensively to forget them.

Five main strategies have combined to create a general amnesia about the lives and labours of women reformers. The first has been just to ignore what they did: we don't remember it because it didn't happen. This strategy applies particularly to those of the women reformers' activities that were unconnected with the suffrage or with traditional philanthropy; it also marks the period after women got the vote, which is said (incorrectly, see Chapter

Eleven) to have ushered in a period of quiescence in female activism. Denying women's activism is connected to a second manoeuvre for forgetting, which is squashing their achievements into a small box labelled 'feminism'. The more one pokes around in the dark undergrowth of standard historical accounts, the more obvious it is that the overwhelming preoccupation with what feminism is and what women qua women have done has created a concealing shrubbery of colossal proportions. The fallacious logic here is that whatever is feminist can't possibly be of mainstream importance. If the exploits of the women reformers in this book (and many others besides) are classed as feminist, then by implication they are only of interest to historians of feminism. The women weren't taken in by this subterfuge, understanding that their work was of enormous importance to the public health; neither, then, should we be.

The third device for reducing women to an obliterated history, another strategy for sticking them in the shrubbery, is to call them 'social workers'. Most (if not all) of the women whose stories feature in this book are called 'social workers' by many of the historians and commentators who have inscribed their lives. Social work is a deserving profession, but this appellation is almost a term of abuse when considered in the light of the women reformers' intellectual appetites for major social change.[3] The term 'social worker' implies small-scale, local, practical action; it certainly doesn't denote the culturally valued work of thinking, analysing and theorizing. But this is what they did. They analysed the nature of democracy and the meanings of citizenship (Jane Addams, Sophonisba Breckinridge, Crystal Eastman, Helena Swanwick, Mary van Kleeck), particularly in relation to ethnic and cultural diversity (Jane Addams, Grace Abbott, Mabel Atkinson, Emily Balch, Alice Ravenhill), the development of social welfare (Florence Kelley, Alice Masaryk, Alice Salomon); and theories and methods of knowledge (Jane Addams, Frances Kellor). They took careful and systematic looks at the institutions of marriage and the family (Anita Augspurg, Jane Hume Clapperton, Charlotte Perkins Gilman, Cicely Hamilton, Lida Heymann, Helene Stöcker, Marianne Weber); economic models and theories in relation to production and reproduction (Mabel Atkinson, Clementina Black, Clara

Collet, Charlotte Perkins Gilman, Florence Kelley); theology and gender (Maude Royden); sociological concepts/theories and gender (Marion Talbot, Marianne Weber); the criminal justice system (Edith Abbott, Jane Addams, Katharine Bement Davis, Sophonisba Breckinridge, Mary Gordon, Florence Kelley, Julia Lathrop). Their work may justly be called 'visionary', but they were not dreamers;[4] they were powerful intellectuals with an incisive curiosity about social systems, and especially about how these operate in an exclusionary manner to omit women, children, Black and ethnic minority people, the poor and disadvantaged, and manual and domestic labourers from the rights and privileges assigned to advantaged white men. The principle was not just 'add women and stir'. It was a radical approach to social knowledge, a revisionist and transformative project that has been removed from that disciplinary terrain devoted to theories of knowledge, in part, at least, because women's theorizing always tends to be seen as of less value than men's.[5]

This, then, has been a fourth device for making women reformers' contributions disappear from the landscape: they did good works, but they weren't intellectuals. Yet, on the contrary, theories about the nature of democracy and the good society, and about the existence and effects of class, race and gender divisions, arose out of, and were applied to, women reformers' activism and research. Original theories erupted in unexpected places. The writer Vernon Lee, whose wildly pacifist *Ballet of the nations* appears in Chapter Six, published articles on economics, politics and international affairs in widely respected British and American periodicals, as well as writing plays, novels, ghost stories, poetry and philosophy: she was known in her time as 'the cleverest woman in Europe'. Lee's work disputed two conventional separations that have helped to push the contributions of women reformers into the shadows: the division between fiction and non-fiction; and between art and politics. One of Lee's most startling and forgotten achievements was to introduce the word 'empathy' into the English language in 1912.[6] She lived most of the time in Italy, where she was much given to visiting churches, museums and galleries; doing this in the 1890s with her lover, the painter Clementina Anstruther-Thomson, she decided to undertake a study of what happens to the human body when the mind is occupied with the vista of an aesthetic object: a building, a decorative jar, a painting. Anstruther-Thomson kept a diary in which she recorded her reactions, how looking at art made her *feel*. She noted her respiration and heart rate, balance, muscular tension, the manner and speed with which her right and left lungs filled with air. For example, looking at the Gothic-Renaissance façade of Santa Maria Novella in Florence one day, she observed that her balance changed and her breathing deepened.[7] The composer Ethel Smyth, who had also had a relationship with Lee, made snide comments about what Lee and Anstruther-Thompson were doing, 'experimenting' in art galleries.[8] What they were doing was developing a theory of aesthetic empathy as a kind of knowledge that dissolves the boundaries between individuals, and between individuals and their environment. The states we perceive as qualities of another thing or person are our own states. This feat of bringing a new concept into the English language may seem an odd one for an 'irascible, outspoken, brilliantly critical',[9] lesbian nonconformist to have accomplished. Yet understanding the physiological and psychological processes underlying our connections to things and people outside ourselves fills a gap in theories that women such as Jane Addams were developing about how cooperation and participatory democracy are possible.

Another forgotten theorist, the American philosopher and sociologist Mary Parker Follett, extended the insights of Settlement sociology by studying social connectedness. Follett's book *The new state: Group organization, the solution of popular government*, was written during the First World War and it provided plenty of evidence for her main thesis that human

12.1: Mary Parker Follett

beings hadn't yet learnt to live effectively together.[10] Follett argued that people needed to give up their addiction to individualism and develop a truly collective life. Her theories reflected her experience. Like many other American women of her class and generation, she put her liberal education at élite universities in the US, England and France to work in Settlements in poor urban areas, worrying away at what could be done to improve social and economic conditions. She established a mini-Settlement in Boston, and she founded what became known as the schools centres movement, persuading local authorities to agree that school buildings could be used after hours as community centres.[11] This straightforward political activism gave rise to a somewhat complex and elegant theory of group dynamics. At its core was an argument about the differences between 'power with' and 'power over', and about neighbourhood relations as the building blocks of a just and conflict-free democracy. A new 'principle of association' was needed, said Follett: we must study and learn how people can be helped to understand one another, work politically together and deal with conflict, which is really only difference, and we must help people to negotiate solutions which aren't mere compromises. The result will be a 'deepening' of citizenship. Follett's *A new state* suggests that a greater sense of democratic unity could replace the lure of war for men, who fight neither out of hatred nor out of love for fighting, but just because war provides an opportunity to join with other men in a common cause.[12] Putting forward the notion of 'a world-ideal, a whole-civilization' that nations need to work towards, Follett adds, 'I am told that this is mysticism. It is the most practical idea I have found in the world.'[13]

Mary Parker Follett applied her ideas to the field of industrial relations, and this is where they have most flourished, especially in Japan, where management theorists in the 21st century find an affinity between her philosophy and the set of Japanese culture.[14] She travelled a good deal, disseminating her ideas; her transatlantic journeys were furthered by the relationship she developed in the 1920s with a British woman, Katherine Furse, a leader of the Girl Guide movement, with whom she shared a house in Chelsea for a time.[15] Follett was the first woman to lecture at the LSE, in the newly formed Department of Business Administration.[16] Did William Beveridge, then the director of the LSE, come to hear her? What about historian and internationalist Eileen Power, or sociologist Tom Marshall, whose theories of (male) citizenship would probably not have much impressed her? Follett's legacy has been repeatedly forgotten and rediscovered; she was, above all, a philosopher and sociologist of *networks*, a woman who gave full credence to the idea that much of human welfare derives not from our lives as atomized individuals, but through our social connections with others. It could be said that Follett provided the theory behind the women reformers' all-important praxis of network building and network-nurturing.[17]

Describing what women reformers did in one or two keywords was difficult then and it remains difficult now. A central problem is the issue of science versus care. Conventionally, men do science, and women do the caring. Because it's much easier to dismiss as of marginal importance anything that reeks of 'women's work', we stumble here on a fifth strategy for evicting women from centre stage: they were unscientific. Edith Abbott, who became dean of the Chicago School of Service Administration in 1924, complained that 'some of our social science friends are afraid we can't be scientific because we really care about what we're doing'.[18] Can one both care and be scientific? It's obvious from the case studies in this book that the answer is yes. It's important not to be misled here by the strategy that reformers themselves sometimes resorted to of claiming that they were doing and saying only what good women ought to: the municipal housekeeping movement, for example (Chapter Four), clearly appealed to a separate-spheres ideology in which women's interest in public matters was justified as an extension of their caring role in the home, yet it was also, equally clearly, tremendously important public health work, and the women themselves were under no illusions about this. Women reformers weren't much interested in labels: science, social work, welfare theory, economics, policy research – it was for them a single enterprise. 'Please don't think of me as a sociologist,' pleaded Sophonisba Breckinridge, memorably.[19] Yes, she had worked in sociology, economics, the law and government, but she didn't want to be seen as a sociologist. This may have had something to do with the hostility of male academic sociologists in Chicago at the time. Robert Park, one of their leaders, and still revered today as a founder of Chicago sociology, said, equally memorably, that the greatest damage done to the city of Chicago wasn't by criminals or corrupt politicians but by women reformers. Park intensely disliked both women and 'do-gooders', regarding them as 'lower than dirt'.[20] His quarrels with Edith Abbott and Sophonisba Breckinridge retain such power that when the sociologist Mary Jo Deegan started asking questions about them more than half a century later, in the 1980s, she was told that she would lose her future in sociology if she persisted.[21] Park's view of society inflated its bias against women, peace and welfare into a sociological model of competition, conflict and dominance; in such a model, war becomes a socially important form of relaxation: 'what man wants is not peace but battle'.[22] The disregard for women reformers' work led *Hull-House maps and papers*, a pivotal founding moment of sociology, to be dismissed as 'unscientific', on the grounds that it was concerned only with the feelings of slum-dwellers.[23]

The local result in Chicago of this gender stereotyping was an institutional divorce between male and female sociologists that put the men in the prestigious academic positions and the women in a School of Social Service Administration.[24] The situation elsewhere in the US and in Britain and other European countries reflected different local contexts, but the effect was very similar: a sustained gender gap that prioritized mainstream theoretical work over more mundane empirical research ('mundane', meaning 'of the world', ought surely to be a term of praise here). One effect of this gendering process was an 'origin myth' that leans heavily on men as the central actors and revered ancestors of modern social science.[25] This continues to be repeated in textbooks today; it surfaces in bland assertions that calling women reformers such as Jane Addams 'early sociologists' must surely constitute an 'unplausible hypothesis'.[26] Much of women reformers' theoretical and empirical work was interdisciplinary, and conducted outside academic institutions. This gave them freedom from the institutional constraints of academia, but it also cut them loose from a mooring in institutional memory – how disciplines keep alive (at least a version of) their own origins.

Consigning the labours of women reformers to cobwebbed corners of historical basements labelled 'feminism' or 'social work' and disparagingly describing them as atheoretical and unscientific makes the act of retrieval notoriously difficult. That's why it must mean going back, as far as possible, to the original accounts, to the records inscribed at the time. Our inability to trust the standard historical interpretations applies equally to histories of social policy and welfare states, to those charting the development of social science and to narratives about people's efforts to purge social relations of militarism and aggression. In seeking to understand how women's contributions have been allowed (encouraged?) to fade from historical vision, there are probably other, more covert and therefore fugitive, reasons, such as the women's self-sufficiency in communities bound together by close female partnerships. This strike for independence of thought and action was mostly not intended as defiant, but it could easily have been read as such by many men, both then and now. The disconcerting spectre of an independent woman might also be a strand in that equally perplexing story about why, among the many women who are forgotten, there are some who are remembered: Florence Nightingale, for example, although for her feminine nursing care rather than for her innovatory statistical expertise; Beatrice Webb for her partnership with Sidney, rather than for her career as a founding social science methodologist.

This book began with the *Herland* trilogy of utopian fiction by Charlotte Perkins Gilman, a set of novels which acted as a vehicle for transmitting ideas about the kind of equal and peaceful welfare society towards which Gilman and her contemporaries worked. After the efforts described in this book, women fiction writers were more likely to take dystopias as their theme. Cicely Hamilton, playwright, pacifist, tax resister and author of the hyper-critical *Marriage as a trade*, wrote one in 1922. *Theodore Savage* is named after its main character, and it was republished a few years later under the more sinister title *Lest ye die: A story from the past or of the future.*[27] Hamilton's novel is a fable about civilization and patriarchy; it reflects the real distress that many reformers of her generation felt at the failure of the political world to heed what they had to say, particularly after the exclusionary episode of the Versailles Treaty. This was a moment of nation-making for a new world order which repeated and multiplied the mistakes of the old one. Not only did the Treaty further the chances of more warfare, it pushed women's voices further back in time, re-domesticating them instead of taking them seriously as the public intellectuals and policy strategists they had shown themselves to be (15 European countries actually introduced *new* laws depriving women of their nationality on marriage to men from other nations).[28]

One might, at first reading, believe that the Women's Organisation for World Order (WOWO) also belongs in the tradition of utopian fiction. It could do; but it doesn't; instead its social origins redirect us to that fire of optimism that runs through so many of the stories in this book. WOWO was founded in a hotel room in Geneva in 1935, lasted four years and has left virtually no mark in any history or archives. Its instigator was the Swedish environmental reformer Elin Wägner – at least, she is known as an environmentalist, but she was much more than that. She was a novelist and a playwright, a political writer and public intellectual, a pacifist (she went to The Hague Women's Peace Congress in 1915) and a suffragist.[29]

The object of WOWO was to establish an intellectual forum for drafting a new world order. The 23 women at the founding meeting came from Austria, Czechoslovakia, Denmark, England, Hungary and Sweden, and many of them had been involved in organizations which fed into early welfare states: 'We women refuse to follow statesmen who are not capable of shaping an economic and social order that excludes war and injustice,' they said.[30] WOWO demanded that money devoted to weapons of destruction should go to construction projects, and that everyone should be guaranteed a sufficient level of subsistence for the duration of their lives. Housework should be salaried; abortion, birth control and divorce should be easily available; and civil rights and all occupational positions should be equally distributed between men and women. The people of earth should elect a world parliament for legislative purposes and a world government to prevent the production of munitions and run the economy; the aims of production should be human need, not profit, and the value of human life would be paramount. Anyone who wanted to farm the land should be given some, but it must be worked organically; and a land tax should be paid and used to fund benefits for mothers until children reached working age. WOWO undertook a survey of women's attitudes and experiences that was printed in several languages, but distribution was a problem, since censorship of mail and publications had already begun in

Germany. The survey asked leading political questions: 'Do you think there always has to be war?' 'Why is women's experience of managing the household, which is thousands of years old, not used when it comes to managing the world?'[31] Some discussion of the survey results was published, but no evidence lingers of a systematic analysis.

Another WOWO aim was an international encyclopaedia of women's achievements: the manuscript of this disappeared when one of its writers, Anna Askanasy, was persecuted by the Nazis and fled to Canada. Askanasy, also known as Helena Mahler (she was the niece of the composer Gustav Mahler), had been active in the peace movement of the First World War, operating in the same networks as women such as Rosika Schwimmer, Mary Sheepshanks and Mary Beard. She tried to keep WOWO going in Canada and wrote a lengthy, unfinished text, *The catastrophe of patriarchy*. This is a curious mixture of over-simplistic evolutionary anthropology and modern wisdom about the connections between environmental destruction, masculine aggression and the gender system. The manuscript combines some oddly named sections – for example, 'Nausea' (which is about the suppression of natural body odours) – with more obvious references to patriarchal customs ('The wedding night in literature and fact') and acute observations such as a remark about the clear historical alliance between movements for hygiene and sanitation, on the one hand, and the intellectual awakening and emancipation of women, on the other.[32]

Askanasy is in no doubt that a patriarchal social system is to blame for most distortions of right-minded living. WOWO's abandoned agenda reconnects the core ideals of democratic welfare, justice, equality and peace that brought together many women during the period covered in this book. They shared an incisive analysis of political and social systems; a belief in a better future that human beings can bring about through their own efforts; a consistent devotion to the documentation of experiences, obstacles and goals; and an ethos and practice of human friendship. All of this leaves us a hugely inspirational legacy today.

The capacity of these women reformers to join hands and find common grounds for thought and action is poignantly

12.2: Henrietta Barnett and Jane Addams in Hampstead Garden Suburb, 1900

and symbolically displayed in the last photograph in this book, a little-known one of Henrietta Barnett and Jane Addams holding hands in Barnett's own utopia, Hampstead Garden Suburb. They had met originally through the Settlement movement, with Addams propelled into founding Hull-House in Chicago by seeing Henrietta and Samuel Barnett's Toynbee Hall in London, and the Barnetts visiting Hull-House on their own world tour in 1890. When Henrietta went back to the US on her own in 1920, she found Addams' habit of constantly entertaining any visitors who chose to flow through the house most unsettling. 'They stroll in and out with a freedom that I should have found trying at Toynbee Hall, sit down, and seem unable to go away,' she remarked.[33] Jane Addams might have said that was exactly the point: Hull-House was open to everyone. The two women had different views about how Settlements ought to be run, and Barnett didn't share Addams' radical views about war and peace. In the photograph, she clutches Addams' hand firmly and she seems to be pointing at something which might be only a rose bush, or perhaps it's something less prosaic. She's smiling, but Addams always did look uncomfortable in front of the camera.

Difference doesn't have to mean division. It's the struggle that counts. On the night of the Decennial Census in Britain in 1911, enumerators were sent out to collect details of every household in the country; the suffragettes mounted their refusal to participate – 'If women don't count, neither shall they be counted'. On that night, the composer Ethel Smyth stood with her friend Emmeline Pankhurst at the window to watch the dawn. In their dressing gowns, they saw the sun rise beyond the river and fight its way through the mist. 'She was on the eve of some terrible venture that would end in rough usage and prolonged imprisonment,' recalled Smyth of her friend. It was a collective struggle, a memorable and meaningful one.

Their foreheads pressed against the window, they realized that Pankhurst's championing of downtrodden women, her hope of better things to come, Smyth's music and their friendship, were all 'part of the mystery that was holding our eyes. And suddenly it came to us that all was well; for a second we were standing on the spot in a madly spinning world where nothing stirs ... Neither of us ever forgot that dawn.'[34]

Appendix: list of women reformers

Note: The women listed below are those who feature in this book, including the names of their partners and associates, where these are also mentioned and information is known. For other names, see the general index. The names listed are those by which the women were generally known; titles are omitted. In a few cases, dates of birth and/or death are not known. Page numbers in bold indicate a photograph.

Abbott, Edith (1876–1957) US **page 49**

Abbott, Elizabeth (1884–1957) UK

Abbott, Grace (1878–1939) US **page 49**

Aberdeen, Lady, see Hamilton-Gordon, Ishbel **page 35**

Abraham, May (1869–1946) UK **page 261**

Abram, Annie (1869–1930) UK

Addams, Jane (1860–1935) US **page 46**, **80, 149, 288**

Aldrich-Blake, Louisa (1865–1925) UK

Alice, Princess, of Hesse-Darmstadt (1843–78) UK and Germany

Anderson, Adelaide (1863–1936) UK

Anderson, Elizabeth Garrett (1836–1917) UK

Anderson, Louisa Garrett (1873–1943) UK **page 211**

Andrews, Fannie Fern (1867–1950) US

Anstruther-Thomson, Clementina (1857–1921) UK

Anthony, Katharine (1877–1965) US

Anthony, Susan B. (1820–1906) US

Arthur, Helen (1879–1939) US

Askanasy, Anna (also known as Helena or Helen Mahler) (birth and death dates not known, active 1930–70) Austria and Canada

Atkinson, Mabel (married name Palmer) (1876–1958) UK **page 338**

Atwood, Charlotte (birth and death dates not known) US

Atwood, Tony (Clare) (1866–1962) UK

Augspurg, Anita (1857–1943) Germany **page 299**

Baer, Gertrude (1890–1981) Germany

Balch, Emily Greene (1867–1961) US **page 38, 157**

Banks, Elizabeth (1872–1938) US

Barnett, Henrietta (1851–1936) UK **page 62**

Barrett, Janie Porter (1865–1948) US **page 61**

Bates, Katharine Lee (1859–1929) US

Bäumer, Gertrud (1873–1954) Germany

Beard, Mary Ritter (1876–1958) US **page 11**

Beecher, Catherine (1800–78) US

Bell, Florence (1851–1930) UK

Bentham, Ethel (1861–1931) UK

Besant, Annie (1847–1933) UK

Bey, Cornelia de(1865–1948) US

Black, Clementina (1853–1922) UK **page 243**

Black, Constance (married name Garnett) (1861–1946) UK

Blanc-Bentzon, Thérèse (also known as Madame Blanc, and as Th. Bentzon) (1840–1907) France

Blatch, Harriot Stanton (1856–1940) US

Blatch, Nora Stanton (married name Barney) (1883–1971) US

Bly, Nellie (Elizabeth Cochrane Seaman) (1864–1922) US **page 67**

Bodichon, Barbara (1827–91) UK

Bondfield, Margaret (1873–1953) UK **page 276**

Bone, Honor (1874–1950) UK

Booth, Mary (1847–1939) UK

Bosanquet, Helen (1860–1926) UK

Boyle, Helen (1869–1957) UK **page 231**

Boys-Smith, Winifred (1865–1939) UK and New Zealand

Breckinridge, Sophonisba (1866–1948) US **page 49**

Bremer, Fredrika (1801–65) Sweden **page 128**

Brewster, Mary (1864–1901) US

Brown, Vera Scantlebury (1889–1946) Australia

Brunhes, Henrietta (1872–1914) France

Bryant, Margaret (1871–1942) UK

Buss, Frances Mary (1827–94) UK

Butler, Josephine (1828–1906) UK

Buxton, Dorothy (1881–1963) UK

Byington, Margaret (1877–1952) US

Campbell, Helen Stuart (1839–1918) US **page 124**

Campbell, Janet (1877–1954) UK

Catt, Carrie Chapman (1859–1947) US

Chambers, Helen (1879–1935) UK

Clapperton, Jane Hume (1832–1914) UK

Clark, Alice (1874–1934) UK

Clark, Hilda (1881–1955) UK

Collet, Clara (1860–1948) UK **page 254**

Coman, Katharine (1857–1915) US

Comstock, Alzada (1888–1960) US

Converse, Florence (1871–1967) US

Cooper, Anna Julia (1858–1964) US **page 193**

Courtney, Kate (Catherine) (formerly Potter) (1847–1929) UK

Courtney, Kathleen (1878–1974) UK

Craig, Edy (1869–1947) UK

Crane, Caroline Bartlett (1858–1935) US **page 89**

Creighton, Louise (1850–1936) UK

Curie, Marie (1867–1934) Poland and France

Davies, Margaret Llewelyn (1861–1944) UK

Davis, Katharine Bement (1860–1935) US **page 207**

Davison, Emily (1872–1913) UK

Deane, Hyacinthe (1867–1903) UK

Deane, Lucy, see Streatfeild, Lucy Deane

Despard, Charlotte (1844–1939) UK **page 299**

Dewey, Annie Godfrey (1850–1922) US **page 107**

Dewson, Molly (1874–1962) US

Doty, Madeleine (1875–1963) US

Dreier, Mary (1875–1963) US **page 307**

Drevet, Camille (1860–1969) France

Duchêne, Gabrielle (1870–1954) France

Dummer, Ethel Sturges (1866–1954) US

Eastman, Crystal (1881–1928) US **page 270**

Eaton, Isabel (?–1938) US

Eckenstein, Lina (1857–1931) UK

Eckhard, Edith (1885–1952) UK

Elkan, Sophie (1853–1921) Sweden

Elliott, Sophronia Maria (1854–1942) US

Faithfull, Lilian (1865–1952) UK

Fawcett, Millicent (1847–1929) UK

Federn, Else (1874–1946) Austria

Fitzgerald, Ismay (1870–1946) UK

Fleddérus, Mary (1886–1977) Netherlands

Florence, Mary Sargant (1857–1954) UK

Follett, Mary Parker (1868–1933) US **page 351**

Forbes-Mosse, Irena (1864–1946) Germany

Frederick, Christine (1883–1970) US

Fry, Margery (1874–1958) UK

Furniss, Averil Sanderson (1873–1962) UK

Furse, Katherine (1875–1952) UK

Genoni, Rosa (1867–1954) Italy

Gernon, Maud (married name Yeomans) (1865–1920) US

Gildersleeve, Virginia (1877–1965) US **page 341**

Gillmore, Inez Haynes (formerly Irwin) (1873–1970) US

Gilman, Charlotte Perkins (formerly Stetson) (1860–1935) US **page 22**

Glücklich, Vilma (1872–1927) Hungary

Goldmark, Pauline (1874–1962) US

Gonne, Maud (1866–1953) UK

Gordon, Mary Louisa (1861–1941) UK

Gore-Booth, Eva (1870–1926) UK

Grant, Clara Ellen (1867–1949) UK **page 60**

Greenlees, Margaret (1880–1952) UK

Griffith, Mary (1772–1846) US

Grimké, Angelina (1805–79) US

Hall, Radclyffe (1880–1943) UK

Hamilton, Alice (1869–1970) US **page 272**

Hamilton, Cicely (1872–1952) UK **page 283, 309**

Hamilton, Edith (1867–1963) US

Hamilton, Molly (1884–1966) UK

Hamilton-Gordon, Ishbel (1857–1939) UK **page 35**

Hardcastle, Frances (1866–1941) UK

Harkness, Margaret (1854–1923) UK

Harrison, Amy (married name Spencer) (circa 1874–1970) UK

Harvey, Kate (1870–1946) UK

Haverfield, Evelina (1867–1920) UK

Hay, Mary Garrett (1857–1928) US

Hesselgren, Kerstin (1872–1962) Sweden **page 269**

Heymann, Lida (1868–1943) Germany **page 299**

Hickok, Lorena (1893–1968) US

Higgs, Mary (1854–1937) UK **page 67**

Hill, Octavia (1838–1912) UK **page 64**

Hobhouse, Emily (1860–1926) UK **page 169**

Holme, Jack (Vera) (1881–1969) UK

Hoodless, Adelaide (1857–1910) Canada

Howe, Gertrude (1847–1928) US

Hunton, Addie (1866–1943) US

Hutchins, Bessie (E. L. Hutchins) (1858–1935) UK

Hutchins, Grace (1885–1969) US

Impey, Catherine (1847–1923) US

Inglis, Elsie (1864–1917) UK **page 213**

Irwin, Elisabeth (1880–1942) US

Ivens, Frances (1870–1944) UK

Jacobs, Aletta (1854–1929) Netherlands **page 219**

Jaffé, Else (formerly Else von Richthofen) (1874–1973) Germany

Jebb, Eglantyne (1876–1928) UK **page 314**

Jex-Blake, Sophia (1840–1912) UK

Jones, Mabel (1870–1923) UK

Kelley, Florence (1859–1932) US **page 49**

Kellogg, Kate Starr (1854–1925) US

Kellor, Frances (1873–1952) US **page 307**

Kenney, Annie (1879–1953) UK

Kenney, Jessie (1887–1985) UK

Ker(r), Margaret (1879–1957) UK

Key, Ellen (1849–1926) Sweden

Keynes, Margaret (1890–1974) UK

Kittredge, Mabel Hyde (1867–1955) US

Knapp, Adeline (1860–1909) US

Kollontai, Alexandra (1872–1952) Russia

Kulka, Leopoldina (1872–1920) Austria

La Follette, Belle Case (1859–1931) US

La Follette, Fola (1882–1970) US

Lagerlöf, Selma (1858–1940) Sweden

Lang, Marie (1858–1934) Austria

Lange, Helene (1848–1930) Germany

Lathrop, Julia (1858–1932) US **page 49**

Lawrence, Maude (1864–1933) UK

Lawson, Marie (1881–1975) UK

Lee, Vernon (Violet Paget) (1856–1935) UK **page 146**

Levy, Amy (1861–89) UK

Lind-af-Hageby, Lizzy (1878–1963) Sweden and UK **page 237**

Lindsay, Marguerite du Pre Gore (1890–1977) UK

Lloyd, Lola Maverick (1875–1944) US

Lowell, Josephine Shaw (1843–1905) US

Luxemburg, Rosa (1871–1919) Poland and Germany

Lytton, Constance (1869–1923) UK **page 202**

Macadam, Elizabeth (1871–1948) UK **page 291**

Macarthur, Mary (1880–1921) UK

McCall, Annie (1859–1949) UK **page 223**

MacDonald, Ishbel (1903–82) UK

McDowell, Mary (1854–1936) US **page 80**

MacLean, Annie (1869–1934) US

Macmillan, Chrystal (1872–1937) UK **page 157**

McMillan, Margaret (1860–1931) UK

Malvery, Olive (1877–1914) UK **page 67**

Mansell Moullin, Edith (1859–1941) UK

Manus, Rosa (1881–1942) Netherlands

Marsh, Charlotte (1887–1961) UK **page 9**

Marshall, Catherine (1880–1961) UK

Marshall, Mary Paley (1850–1944) UK

Martin, Anna (1858–1937) UK

Martindale, Hilda (1875–1952) UK

Martindale, Louisa [mother] (1839–1914) UK

Martindale, Louisa [daughter] (1872–1966) UK

Martineau, Harriet (1802–76) UK

Marx, Eleanor (1855–98) UK

Masaryk, Alice (1879–1966) Czechoslovakia **page 96**

Masaryk, Charlotte Garrigue (1850–1923) Czechoslovakia

Mayor, Flora (1872–1932) UK

Mead, Lucia Ames (1856–1936) US

Meigs, Grace (married name Crowder) (1881–1925) US

Mélin, Jeanne (1877–1964) France

Meredith, Susanna (1823–1901) UK

Meyer, Adele (1855–1930) UK

Mitchell, Maria (1818–89) US

Morgenstern, Lina (1830–1909) Germany

Mott, Lucretia (1793–1880) US

Mumford, Mary (1842–1935) US

Murdoch, Mary (1864–1916) UK

Murray, Flora (1869–1923) UK **page 211**

Murrell, Christine (1874–1933) UK

Nathan, Maud (1862–1946) US

Neal, Mary (1860–1944) UK

Nightingale, Florence (1820–1910) UK

Oakeley, Hilda (1867–1950) UK **page 117**

Oakeshott, Grace (1872–1929) UK

Orme, Eliza (1848–1937) UK

Ovington, Mary White (1865–1951) US

Palmstierna, Ellen (1869–1941) Sweden

Palthe, Mien (1875–1960) Netherlands

Pankhurst, Christabel (1880–1958) UK

Pankhurst, Emmeline (1858–1928) UK

Pankhurst, Sylvia (1882–1960) UK

Parsons, Elsie Clews (1875–1941) US

Paterson, Mary Muirhead (1864–1941) UK **page 261**

Paul, Alice (1885–1977) US

Payne-Townshend, Charlotte (1857–1943) UK

Perkins, Frances (1880–1965) US **page 328**

Perlen, Frida (1870–1933) Germany

Pethick-Lawrence, Emmeline (1867–1954) UK **page 142**

Phillips, Marion (1881–1932) UK

Pillow, Margaret (1859–1929) UK

Pinchbeck, Ivy (1898–1982) UK

Playne, Mary (formerly Potter) (1849–1923) UK

Plunkett, Harriette (1826–94) US

Porter, Polly (1884–1972) US

Power, Eileen (1889–1940) UK

Power, Mildred (married name Gordon) (1878–1953) UK

Pugh, Sarah (1800–84) US

Pye, Edith (1876–1965) UK

Ragaz, Clara (1874–1957) Switzerland

Ramondt-Hirschmann, Cor (1871–1957) Netherlands **page 157**

Rathbone, Eleanor (1872–1946) UK **page 291**

Ravenhill, Alice (1859–1954) UK **page 104**

Rawson, Helen (1886–1964) UK and New Zealand

Reeves, Maud Pember (1865–1953) UK

Rice, Harriet (1866–1958) US

Richards, Ellen Swallow (1842–1911) US **page 107, 111**

Robins, Elizabeth (1862–1952) US and UK

Robins, Margaret Dreier (1868–1945) US

Robinson, Laura (1861–1906) UK

Robinson, Virginia (1883–1977) US **page 289**

Rochester, Anna (1880–1966) US

Roosevelt, Eleanor (1884–1962) UK

Roper, Esther (1868–1938) UK

Rotten, Elizabeth (1882–1964) Germany

Royden, Maude (1876–1956) UK **page 131**

Rucker, Thereza (1863–1941) UK

Sackville-West, Vita (1892–1962) UK

St John, Christopher (Christabel Marshall) (1871–1960) UK **page 309**

Salomon, Alice (1872–1948) Germany **page 178**

Salter, Ada (formerly Brown) (1866–1942) UK **page 93**

Sanger, Margaret (1879–1966) US

Savill, Agnes (1875–1964) UK **page 210**

Schartau, Leisa (1876–1962) Sweden and UK

Schneiderman, Rose (1882–1972) US

Schreiner, Olive (1855–1920) South Africa

Schwimmer, Rosika (1877–1948) Hungary **page 138, 157**

Scudder, Vida Dutton (1861–1954) US **page 43**

Seaman, Elizabeth, see Bly, Nellie **page 67**

Sharp, Evelyn (1869–1955) UK

Sheepshanks, Mary (1872–1960) UK

Sidgwick, Rose (1877–1918) UK

Simkhovitch, Mary Kingsbury (1867–1951) US

Smith, Mary Rozet (1868–1934) US **page 288**

Smyth, Ethel (1858–1944) UK

Solomon, Hannah (1858–1942) US

Souvestre, Marie (1830–1905) France and UK

Sproson, Emma (1867–1936) UK

Spurgeon, Caroline (1869–1942) UK

Squire, Rose (1861–1938) UK

Stanton, Elizabeth Cady (1815–1902) US

Starr, Ellen Gates (1859–1940) US

Stephens, Alzina (1849–1900) US

Stöcker, Helene (1869–1943) Germany **page 300**

Stockham, Alice (1833–1912) US

Stopes, Marie (1880–1958) UK

Stowe, Harriet Beecher (1811–96) US

Streatfeild, Lucy Deane (1865–1950) UK **page 261**

Strong, Ann Munroe Gilchrist (1875–1957) New Zealand

Swanwick, Helena (1864–1939) UK **page 160**

Sweet, Ada Celeste (1853–1928) US

Taft, Jessie (1882–1960) US **page 289**

Talbot, Marion (1858–1948) US **page 122**

Teleki, Iska (1864–1937) Hungary

Notes

Chapter One

[1] See Bartley, P. (2002) *Emmeline Pankhurst*, London: Routledge, p 5; Holton, S. S. (1992) 'The suffragist and the "average woman"', *Women's History Review*, 1 (1): 9–24.

[2] See Bock, G. and Thane, P. (1991) 'Introduction', in Bock, G. and Thane, P. (eds) *Maternity and gender policies: Women and the rise of the European welfare states, 1850s–1950s*, London and New York: Routledge, pp 1–20; McDonald, L. (1994) *The women founders of the social sciences*, Ottawa, Canada: Carleton University Press.

[3] See Lewis, J. (1994) 'Gender, the family and women's agency in the building of "welfare states": the British case', *Social History*, 19 (1): 37–55.

[4] Koven, S. and Michel, S. (1990) 'Womanly duties: maternalist politics and the origin of welfare states in France, Germany, Great Britain, and the United States, 1880–1920', *The American Historical Review*, 95 (4): 1076–108, p 1076.

[5] Skocpol, T. and Ritter, G. (1991) 'Gender and the origins of modern social policies in Britain and the United States', *Studies in American Political Development*, 5: 36–93.

[6] Deegan, M. J. (2011) 'Archival methods and the veil of sociology', in Stanfield, J. H. (ed) *Rethinking race and ethnicity in research methods*, Walnut Creek, CA: Left Coast Press, pp 123–40.

[7] Martin, J. (2005) 'Gender, the city and the politics of schooling: towards a collective biography of women "doing good" as public moralists in Victorian London', *Gender and Education*, 17 (2): 143–63; Martin, J. (2014) 'Intellectual portraits: politics, professions and identity in twentieth-century England', *History of Education*, 43 (6): 740–67.

[8] Parker, J. (1988) *Women and welfare: Ten Victorian women in public social service*, Basingstoke: Macmillan; Lewis, J. (1991) *Women and social action in Victorian and Edwardian England*, Aldershot: Edward Elgar Publishing Limited.

[9] Gordon, L. (1992) 'Social insurance and public assistance: the influence of gender in welfare thought in the United States, 1890–1935', *The American Historical Review*, 97 (1): 19–54; Gordon, L. (ed) (1990) *Women, the state and welfare*, Madison, WI: University of Wisconsin Press.

[10] Lengermann, P. M. and Niebrugge, G. (1998) *The women founders: Sociology and social theory, 1830–1930: A text/reader*, Long Grove, IL: Waveland Press,

Inc; Deegan, M. J. (1991) *Women in sociology: A bio-biographical sourcebook*, Westport, CT: Greenwood Press.

[11] See, for example, Rappaport, R. I I. (2001) *Encyclopedia of women social reformers*, Santa Barbara, CA: ABC-CLIO, Inc; Law, C. (2000) *Women: A modern political dictionary*, London and New York: I. B. Tauris & Co, Ltd; Crawford, E. (2001) *The women's suffrage movement*, London: Routledge; Dimand, R. W., Dimand, M. A. and Forget, E. L. (eds) (2000) *A biographical dictionary of women economists*, Cheltenham: Edward Elgar; Ouditt, S. (2000) *Women writers of the First World War*, Abingdon, Oxfordshire: Routledge; Oldfield, S. (2001) *Women humanitarians: A biographical dictionary of British women active between 1900 and 1950*, London: Continuum; Harvey, J. and Ogilvie, M. (2000) *The biographical dictionary of women in science*, London: Taylor & Frances.

[12] Oldfield, S. (2010) 'Sybil Oldfield at seventy-two: humanistic feminism – or thinking back through our grandmothers', *Women's History Review*, 19 (5): 741–58, p 750.

[13] Oldfield, S. (1984) *Spinsters of this parish: The life and times of F. M. Mayor and Mary Sheepshanks*, London: Virago.

[14] Oldfield, S. (1986) 'German women in the resistance to Hitler', in Reynolds, S. (ed) *Women, state and revolution: Essays on power and gender in Europe since 1789*, Brighton: Harvester Wheatsheaf, pp 81–101.

[15] Beard, M. R. (1931) *On understanding women*, London, New York, Toronto: Longmans, Green and Co., p 483.

[16] Oldfield, 'Sybil Oldfield at seventy-two', p 755.

[17] Martin, J. (2008) 'Engendering city politics and educational thought: elite women and the London Labour Party, 1914–1965', *Paedagogica Historica*, 44 (4): 397–413, p 398.

[18] Oldfield, 'Sybil Oldfield at seventy-two', p 755.

[19] See, for example, Oakley, A. (2002) *Gender on planet earth*, Cambridge: Polity Press; Oakley, A. (2000) *Experiments in knowing: Gender and method in the social sciences*, Cambridge: Polity Press.

[20] Oakley, A. (2014) *Father and daughter: Patriarchy, gender and social science*, Bristol: Policy Press.

[21] Beauman, K. B. (1996) *Women and the settlement movement*, London: Radcliffe Press, p 205.

[22] http://www.naswfoundation.org/pioneers/t/towle.htm.

[23] Gordon, L. 'Fitting Charlotte Towle into the history of welfare thought in the U.S.', The social welfare history project, http://socialwelfare.library.vcu.edu/issues/towle-charlotte-fitting-her-into-the-history-of-welfare-thought-in-the-u-s/.

[24] Hegar, R. L. (2008) 'Transatlantic transfers in social work: contributions of three pioneers', *British Journal of Social Work*, 38: 716–33.

[25] Kendall, K. A. (1989) 'Women at the helm: three extraordinary leaders', *Affilia*, 4 (1): 23–32.

[26] Committee on Un-American Activities, U.S. House of Representatives (1949) *Review of The Scientific and Cultural Conference for World Peace arranged*

by the National Council of the Arts, Sciences and Professions and held in New York City on March 25, 26 and 27, 1949, Washington, DC: United States Government Printing Office.

[27] Towle, C. (1952, first published 1945) *Common human needs,* New York: American Association of Social Workers; see also Posner, W. B. (1995) 'Common human needs: a story from the prehistory of government by special interest', *Social Service Review,* 69 (2): 188–225.

[28] Charlotte Towle Papers, Special Collections Research Center, University of Chicago Library, diary entry for 27 January 1955, Box 20. On Barbara Wootton, see Oakley, A. (2011) *A critical woman: Barbara Wootton, social science and public policy in the twentieth century,* London: Bloomsbury Academic.

[29] Rathbone, E. F. (1940) *The case for family allowances,* Harmondsworth: Penguin.

[30] Rathbone, E. F. (1924) *The disinherited family: A plea for the endowment of the family,* London: E. Arnold & Co; Pedersen, S. (2004) 'Rathbone, Eleanor Florence (1872–1946)', *Oxford Dictionary of National Biography,* Oxford: Oxford University Press.

[31] Stewart, J. (2006) 'Psychiatric social work in inter-war Britain: child guidance, American ideas, American philanthropy', *Michael Quarterly,* 3: 78–91.

[32] Myall, M. (2004) 'Marsh, Charlotte Augusta Leopoldine (1887–1961)', *Oxford Dictionary of National Biography,* Oxford: Oxford University Press.

[33] Stanley, L. (1992) 'Romantic friendship? Some issues in researching lesbian history and biography', *Women's History Review,* 1 (2): 193–216, pp 198–9.

[34] Crocco, M. S. (1997) 'Forceful yet forgotten: Mary Ritter Beard and the writing of history', *The History Teacher,* 31 (1): 9 31. Crocco observes that the books Mary Ritter Beard wrote jointly with her husband were often attributed to him alone.

[35] Beard, *On understanding women,* p v.

[36] Beard, *On understanding women,* p 32.

[37] See, for example, Mayreder, R. (1913) *A survey of the woman problem,* London: William Heinemann; Zimmern, A. (1909) *Women's suffrage in many lands,* London: Woman Citizen Publishing Society.

[38] Lane, A. J. (1977) 'Part one: Mary Ritter Beard: an appraisal of her life and work', in Lane, A. J. (ed) *Mary Ritter Beard: A sourcebook,* New York: Schocken Books, pp 1–72, pp 45–8.

[39] Lane, 'Mary Ritter Beard', p 49.

[40] Eckenstein, L. (1896) *Women under monasticism: Chapters on saint-lore and convent life between A.D. 500 and A.D. 1500,* Cambridge: Cambridge University Press; Abram, A. (1909) *Social England in the fifteenth century,* London: G. Routledge & Sons; Clark, A. (1919) *Working life of women in the seventeenth century,* London: George Routledge and Sons, Ltd; Pinchbeck, I. (1930) *Women workers and the Industrial Revolution,* London: Routledge.

[41] Cited in Oldfield, S. (2004) 'Eckenstein, Lina Dorina Johanna (1857–1931)', *Oxford Dictionary of National Biography,* Oxford: Oxford University Press.

42 See especially Addams, J. (1907) *Newer ideals of peace: The moral substitutes for war*, New York: Macmillan.

43 Woolf, V. (1938) *Three guineas*, London: Hogarth Press.

44 Berg, M. (1992) 'The first women economic historians', *Economic History Review*, XLV (2): 308–29, p 308.

45 Goldberg, J. (2013) 'Some reflections on women, work, and the family in the later medieval English towns', in Telechea, J., Bolumburu, B. and Andrade, A. (eds) *Ser Mujer en la Ciudad Medieval Europea*, Logrono: Instituto de Estudios Riojanos, pp 191–214.

46 See Berg, M. (1996) *A woman in history: Eileen Power, 1889–1940*, Cambridge: Cambridge University Press.

47 Perry, E. I. (2002) 'Men are from the Gilded Age, women are from the Progressive Era', *The Journal of the Gilded Age and Progressive Era*, 1 (1): 25–48, p 27.

48 See Berg, 'The first women economic historians'.

49 Woolf, *Three guineas*, p 197.

50 Sandell, M. (2015) *The rise of women's transnational activism*, London: I. B. Tauris & Co Ltd.

51 Anthony, K. (1916) *Feminism in Germany and Scandinavia*, London: Constable & Company Ltd, p 3.

52 Letter dated 17 September 1935, cited in Relph, A. K. (1979) 'The world center for women's archives, 1935–1940', *SIGNS*, 4 (3): 597–603.

53 Lane, 'Mary Ritter Beard', p 35; see Wernitznig, D. (2017) 'Memory is power: Rosa Manus, Rosika Schwimmer and the struggle about establishing an international women's archive', in Everard, M. and de Haan, F. (eds) *Rosa Manus (1881–1942)*, Leiden and Boston: Brill, pp 207–39.

54 Downey, K. (2009) *The woman behind the New Deal*, New York: Doubleday, pp ix–x.

55 Malvery, O. C. (1906) *The soul market*, London: Hutchinson & Co., p 8.

56 See Bosch, M. (ed) (1990) *Politics and friendship: Letters from the International Women's Suffrage Alliance, 1902–1943*, Columbus, OH: Ohio State University Press; D'Itri, P. W. (1999) *Cross currents in the international women's movement, 1848–1948*, Bowling Green, OH: Bowling Green State University Popular Press; Jonsson, P., Neunsinger, S. and Sangster, J. (eds) (2007) *Crossing boundaries: Women's organizing in Europe and the Americas, 1880s-1940s*, Uppsala, Sweden: Acta Universitatis Upsaliensis, Uppsala Studies in Economic History, volume 80; Rupp, L. J. (1997) *Worlds of women: The making of an international women's movement*, Princeton, NJ: Princeton University Press.

57 Addams, J., *Newer ideals of peace*, p 15.

Chapter Two

1 Edwards, C. (1896) 'International Socialist Congress', *The Economic Journal*, 6 (23): 460–5; *Full report of the proceedings of the International Workers' Congress, London, July and August 1896*, London: The Labour Leader.

2   Gilman, C. P. (1991, first published 1935) *The living of Charlotte Perkins Gilman: An autobiography*, Madison, WI: University of Wisconsin Press, p 203.

3   Gilman, C. P. (2002, first published 1915, Hill, M. R. and Deegan, M. J. (eds)) *The dress of women: A critical introduction to the symbolism and sociology of women's clothing*, Westport, CT: Greenwood Press.

4   Magarey, S. (2003) '"The colour of your moustache" or have feminists always been humourless?' *Journal of the Association for the Study of Australian Literature*, 2: 141–56, p 144.

5   Hill, M. A. (1980) *Charlotte Perkins Gilman: The making of a radical feminist, 1860–1896*, Philadelphia, PA: Temple University Press, p 277; Jacobs, A. (1996, first published in Dutch 1924) *Memories: My life as an international leader in health, suffrage and peace*, New York: The Feminist Press, p 125.

6   Foster, M. S. (1896) 'Women at the International Congress', in *Full report of the proceedings of the International Workers' Congress London, July and August, 1896*, London: The Labour Leader, pp 82–4, p 84.

7   Gilman, *The living of Charlotte Perkins Gilman*, p 229.

8   Gilman, *The living of Charlotte Perkins Gilman*, p 71.

9   Ward, L. (1991, first published 1935) 'Foreword', in *The living of Charlotte Perkins Gilman*, p xliii.

10 Hayden, D. (1982) *The grand domestic revolution*, Cambridge, MA: The MIT Press, p 183.

11 Sinclair, A. (1965) *The emancipation of the American woman*, New York: Harper and Row, p 272.

12 Gilman, C. P. (1981, 'The yellow wallpaper' first published 1892) *The Charlotte Perkins Gilman reader: The yellow wallpaper and other fiction*, London: The Women's Press.

13 Hill, M. A. (1980) *Charlotte Perkins Gilman: The making of a radical feminist, 1860–1896*, Philadelphia, PA: Temple University Press, pp 122–3.

14 Wood, A. D. (1973) '"The fashionable diseases": women's complaints and their treatment in nineteenth century America', *The Journal of Interdisciplinary History*, 4 (1): 25–52.

15 Gilman, *The living of Charlotte Perkins Gilman*, p 95.

16 Sharpe, M. and Wessely, S. (1998) 'Putting the rest cure to rest – again', *British Medical Journal*, 316: 796.

17 Poirier, S. (1983) 'The physician and authority: portraits by four physician-writers', *Literature and Medicine*, 2: 21–40; Bassuk, E. I. (1985) 'The rest cure: repetition or resolution of Victorian women's conflict?' *Poetics Today*, 5 (1/2): 245–57.

18 http://www.branchcollective.org/?ps_articles=anne-stiles-the-rest-cure-1873–1925.

19 Sicherman, B. (1984) *Alice Hamilton: A life in letters*, Cambridge, MA: Harvard University Press, p 127.

20 Lane, A. J. (1979) 'Introduction', in Gilman, C. P. (first published 1915) *Herland*, New York: Pantheon Books, pp v–xxiv, p vi.

[21] Gilman, C. P. (1903) *The home: Its work and influence*, New York: McClure, Phillips & Co., pp 52–3.

[22] Degler, C. N. (1956) 'Charlotte Perkins Gilman on the theory and practice of feminism', *American Quarterly*, 8 (1): 21–39, p 36.

[23] Gilman, C. P. (2011 edition) *The Herland trilogy: Moving the mountain, Herland, With her in Ourland*, Blacksburg, VA: Wilder Publications; *Moving the mountain*, pp 1–116, p 5.

[24] Gilman, *Moving the mountain*, p 11.

[25] Gilman, *Moving the mountain*, p 105.

[26] Lengermann, P. M. and Niebrugge, G. (1998) *The women founders: Sociology and social theory 1830–1930*, Long Grove, IL: Waveland Press, Inc., p 3.

[27] Hayden, D. (1978) 'Two utopian feminists and their campaigns for kitchenless houses', *SIGNS*, 4 (2): 274–90.

[28] Beard, C. A. and Beard, M. R. (1927) *The rise of American civilization*, London: Jonathan Cape.

[29] Gilman, *Herland*, pp 117–234 in *The Herland trilogy*, p 166.

[30] Gilman, *Herland*, p 194.

[31] Gilman, *With her in Ourland*, pp 235–350 in *The Herland trilogy*, p 298.

[32] Utopian writing by women was relatively uncommon in the late nineteenth century; less than 10% of the 150 utopian novels published between 1888 and 1900 were by women. See Roemer, K. M. (1972) 'Sex roles, utopia and change: the family in late nineteenth-century utopian literature', *American Studies*, 13 (2): 33–47.

[33] Gillmore, I. H. (1914) *Angel island*, London: G. Bell & Sons.

[34] See Schwarz, J. (1986) *Radical feminists of Heterodoxy*, Norwich, VT: New Victoria Publishers.

[35] Griffith. M. (1836) *Three hundred years hence*, Boston; Bellamy, E. (1890) *Looking backward, 2000–1887*, London: Routledge & Sons.

[36] Stowe, H. B. (1852) *Uncle Tom's cabin*, Cleveland, OH: John P. Jewett & Company

[37] Allen, J. A. (2009) *The feminism of Charlotte Perkins Gilman: Sexualities, histories, progressivm*, Chicago, IL: University of Chicago Press.

[38] Ward, L. (1970, first published 1903) *Pure sociology: A treatise on the origins and spontaneous development of society*, New York: Augustus M. Kelley, p 275.

[39] Allen, J. A. (2004) '"The overthrow" of gynaecocentric culture: Charlotte Perkins Gilman and Lester Frank Ward', in David, C. J. and Knight, D. D. (eds) *Charlotte Perkins Gilman and her contemporaries*, Tuscaloosa, AL: University of Alabama Press, pp 59–86, p 8.

[40] Gilman, C. P. (1911) *The man-made world; Or, our androcentric culture*, New York: Charlton Company, pp 213, 216, 221.

[41] Gilman, C. P. (1904) *Human work*, New York: McClure, Phillips & Co., p 16.

[42] Gilman, *The living of Charlotte Perkins Gilman*, p 285.

[43] Ward, 'Foreword', p xliv.

[44] Allen, P. W. (1988) *Building domestic liberty: Charlotte Perkins Gilman's architectural feminism*, Amherst, MA: University of Massachusetts Press, p 17.

[45] Webb, Mrs S. (1913) 'Introduction', in 'The awakening of women', *The New Statesman* (special supplement), 1 November, pp iii–iv, p 193.

[46] Butlin, F. M. (1899) 'International Congress of Women', *The Economic Journal*, 9 (35): 450–5.

[47] Clapperton, J. H. (1885) *Scientific meliorism and the evolution of happiness*, London: Kegan Paul, Trench & Co., p 153.

[48] Jacobs, *Memories*, p 125.

[49] Rupp, L. J. (1997) *Worlds of women: The making of an international women's movement*, Princeton, NJ: Princeton University Press, p 189.

[50] D'Itri, P. W. (1999) *Cross currents in the international women's movement, 1848–1948*, Bowling Green, OH: Bowling Green State University Popular Press, p 126.

[51] https://www.nobelprize.org/nobel_prizes/peace/laureates/1905/suttner-facts.html.

[52] Butlin, 'International Congress of women', pp 454–5.

[53] http://thenewinquiry.com/blogs/the-austerity-kitchen/the-peoples-kitchen/.

[54] Campbell, H. (1970, first published 1887) *Prisoners of poverty: Women wage-workers, their trades, and their lives*, New York: Garrett Press.

[55] Campbell, H. (1889) *Prisoners of poverty abroad*, Boston, MA: Roberts Bros., pp 140–1.

[56] Campbell, *Prisoners of poverty abroad*, p 246.

[57] Randall, M. M. (1964) *Improper Bostonian: Emily Greene Balch*, New York: Twayne Publishers Inc, p 88, p 90.

[58] Randall, *Improper Bostonian*, pp 20–1.

[59] Randall, *Improper Bostonian*, p 346.

Chapter Three

[1] Lengermann, P. M. and Niebrugge-Brantley, J. (2002) 'Back to the future: Settlement sociology 1885–1930', *The American Sociologist*, Fall: 5–20.

[2] See Collette, C. (1998) *The international faith: Labour's attitude to European socialism, 1918–39*, Aldershot: Ashgate Publishing Limited.

[3] Woolf, V. (1929) *A room of one's own*, New York: Harcourt, Brace & World, p 26.

[4] Hoberman, R. (2002) 'Women in the British Museum reading room during the late-nineteenth and early-twentieth centuries: from quasi- to counterpublic', *Feminist Studies*, 28 (3): 489–512.

[5] Flanagan, M. A. (2006/2007) 'The workshop or the home? Gender visions in the history of urban built environments: Canada and the United States', *London Journal of Canadian Studies*, 22: 59–83.

[6] Marx Aveling, E. and Zangwill, I. (1891) 'A doll's house repaired', *Time*, March: 239–53; Bernstein, S. D. (2007) 'Radical readers at the British Museum: Eleanor Marx, Clementina Black, Amy Levy', *Nineteenth-Century Gender Studies*, 3 (2) http://www.ncgsjournal.com/issue32/bernstein.htm.

[7] Frederick, P. J. (1970) 'Vida Dutton Scudder: the professor as social activist', *The New England Quarterly*, 43 (3): 407–33.

8   Spain, D. (2006) 'Octavia Hill's philosophy of housing reform: from British roots to American soil', *Journal of Planning History*, 5 (2): 106–25.

9   Picht, W. (1914) *Toynbee Hall and the English Settlement movement*, London: G. Bell and Sons Ltd, p 29.

10 Beauman, K. B. (1996) *Women and the Settlement movement*, London: Radcliffe Press.

11 Scudder, V. D. (1937) *On journey*, London: J. M. Dent and Sons, pp 109–10.

12 Scudder, *On journey*; Davis, A. F. (1967) *Spearheads for reform: The social settlements and the progressive movement, 1890–1914*, New York: Oxford University Press.

13 Barnett, H. (1919) *Canon Barnett: His life, work, and friends*, Volume 2, London: J. Murray, p 31.

14 Marks, N. (1890) 'Two women's work: the Misses Addams and Starr astonish the West Siders', *Chicago Tribune*, May 19: 1–2.

15 Addams, J. (1961, first published 1910) *Twenty years at Hull-House*, New York: Signet Classics, p 81.

16 The gravestone in Cedarville Cemetery, Illinois, reads 'Jane Addams of Hull-House and the Women's International League for Peace and Freedom'.

17 Thomas, H. P. (1910) Review of Addams, *The spirit of youth and the city streets*, *American Journal of Sociology*, 15 (4): 550–3, p 553. On Addams' shrewd business sense, see Davis, A. F. (1973) *American heroine: The life and legend of Jane Addams*, New York: Oxford University Press, p 106.

18 Bulmer, M., Bales, K. and Sklar, K. K. (1991) 'The social survey in historical perspective', in Bulmer, M., Bales, K. and Sklar, K. K. (eds) *The social survey in historical perspective, 1880–1940*, Cambridge: Cambridge University Press, pp 1–48, p 36.

19 Hill, M. A. (1980) *Charlotte Perkins Gilman: The making of a radical feminist 1860–1896*, Philadelphia, PA: Temple University Press, p 276.

20 Addams, J. (1899) 'A function of the social settlement', *The Annals of the American Academy of Political and Social Science*, 13: 33–55, p 38, p 54; Addams, J. (1910) 'Charity and social justice', *The North American Review*, 192 (656): 68–81.

21 Deegan, M. J. (2011) 'Jane Addams, the Hull-House School of Sociology, and social justice, 1892 to 1935', *Humanity & Society*, 37 (3): 248–58.

22 Lathrop, J. (1895) 'The Cook County Charities', in Residents of Hull-House (1895, new edition Schultz, R. L. (ed) (2007)) *Hull-House maps and papers*, Urbana and Chicago, IL: University of Illinois Press, pp 120–9.

23 Shannon, D. A. (ed) *Beatrice Webb's American diary, 1898*, Madison, WI: University of Wisconsin Press, pp 107–9.

24 Cited in Goldmark, J. (1953) *Impatient crusader*, Urbana, IL: University of Illinois Press, p v.

25 Sklar, K. K. (ed) (1986, first published 1927) *The autobiography of Florence Kelley: Notes of sixty years*, Chicago, IL: Charles H. Kerr Publishing Company, p 31.

26 Sklar, *The autobiography of Florence Kelley*, p 66.

27   Blumberg, D. R. (1966) *Florence Kelley: The making of a social pioneer,* New York: Augustus M. Kelley, p 89; Perkins, F. (1954) 'My recollections of Florence Kelley', *Social Service Review,* 28 (1): 12–19, p 18.

28   Florence Kelley says in her autobiography that she met Engels only once (p 69). Blumberg's (1966) biography records two meetings, in 1886 and 1888 (p 57, p 95).

29   http://florencekelley.northwestern.edu/documentbrowser/?nodeId=57703.

30   Sklar, *The autobiography of Florence Kelley,* p 77.

31   Kelley, N. (1954) 'Early days at Hull House', *Social Service Review,* 28 (4): 424–29, p 424.

32   Florence Kelley to Friedrich Engels, 7 April 1892, cited in Blumberg, *Florence Kelley,* p 127.

33   Blumberg, *Florence Kelley,* p 100.

34   Blumberg, *Florence Kelley,* p 128.

35   Sklar, K. K. (1991) 'Hull-House maps and papers: social science as women's work in the 1890s', in Bulmer, M. et al., *The social survey,* pp 111–47, p 111.

36   Bales, K. (1991) 'Charles Booth's survey of Life and Labour of the People in London 1889–1903', in Bulmer, M. et al., *The social survey,* pp 66–110.

37   Webb, B. (1979, first published 1926) *My apprenticeship,* Cambridge: Cambridge University Press, pp 246–7.

38   Webb, *My apprenticeship,* p 316.

39   Blumberg, *Florence Kelley,* p 149.

40   Kelley, F. (1887) 'The need of theoretical preparation for philanthropic work, Part I', *The Christian Union,* 35 (22), and 'The need of theoretical preparation for philanthropic work, Part II', *The Christian Union,* 35 (23), reprinted in Sklar, *The autobiography of Florence Kelley,* pp 91–104.

41   Kelley, F. (1887) 'A reply', *The Christian Union,* 35 (25): 27.

42   Balch, E. G. (1910) *Our Slavic fellow citizens,* New York: Charities Publication Committee.

43   Coman, K. (1904) 'The Negro as a peasant farmer', *Publications of the American Statistical Association,* 9 (66): 39–54; (1912) *Economic beginnings of the Far West: How we won the land beyond the Mississippi,* New York: Macmillan Co; (with E. Kendall) (1894) *The growth of the English nation,* New York: Flood and Vincent; (1891) 'The tailoring trade and the sweating system', *Publications of the American Economic Association,* 6 (1/2): 144–7; (1911) 'Government factories: an attempt to control competition in the fur trade', *American Economic Review,* 1 (2): 368–88; (1911) 'Some unsettled problems of irrigation', *American Economic Review,* 1 (1): 1–19; (1903) 'The history of contract labor in the Hawaiian Islands', *American Economic Association,* pp 485–545.

44   Abbott, G. (1909) 'A study of the Greeks in Chicago', *American Journal of Sociology,* 15: 373–93.

45   http://www.upenn.edu/spotlights/web-dubois-penn.

46   Deegan, M. J. (1988) 'W. E. B. DuBois and the women of Hull-House, 1895–1899', *The American Sociologist,* 19 (4): 301–11.

[47] Scotland, N. (2007) *Squires in the slums: Settlements and missions in late-Victorian London*, London: I. B. Tauris.

[48] Cited in Vicinus, M. (1985) *Independent women*, London: Virago, p 215.

[49] Woods, R. A. and Kennedy, A. J. (1911) *Handbook of Settlements*, New York: Russell Sage Foundation, p vi.

[50] Johnson, C. (1995) *Strength in community: An introduction to the history and impact of the international settlement movement*, International Federation of Settlements & Neighbourhood Centres; Roivainen, I. (2002) 'Settlement work – carrying out socially committed work', *Nordisk Sosialt Arbeid*, 4: 217–25; Imai, K. (2012) 'The women's movement and the settlement movement in early twentieth century Japan: the impact of Hull House and Jane Addams on Hiratsuka Raichō', *Kwansei Gakuin University Humanities Review* (Nishinomiya, Japan), 17: 85–109; James, C. (2001) 'Reforming reform: Toronto's settlement house movement, 1900–20', *The Canadian Historical Review*, 82 (1): 55–90; Soydan, H. (1993) *Det Sociala Arbetets Idéhistoria*, Lund: Studentlitteratur (Soydan points out that there has been little research on the Nordic settlements).

[51] Malleier, E. (2006) 'The Ottakring Settlement in Vienna', in Gilchrist, R., Jeffs, T. and Spence, J. (eds) *Drawing on the past: Studies in the history of community and youth work*, Leicester: The National Youth Agency, pp 123–31. Marie Lang brought the Settlement idea to Viennese women in 1898 after attending the abolitionist congress in London. In the summer of 1900 her friend Else Federn spent time at the Women's University Settlement in London.

[52] Koengeter, S. and Schroeer, W. (2013) 'Variations of social pedagogy – explorations of the transnational Settlement movement', *Education Policy Analysis Archives*, 21 (42), http://eric.ed.gov/?id=EJ1015369.

[53] Delap, L. and DiCenzo, M. (2008) 'Transatlantic print culture: the Anglo-American feminist press and emerging "modernities"', in Ardis, A. L. and Collier, P. (eds) *Transatlantic print culture, 1880–1940*, Houndmills, Basingstoke: Palgrave Macmillan, pp 48–65, p 56.

[54] Feustel, A. (2006) 'The significance of international relations and cooperation in the works of Alice Salomon', trans. Siepman, S. Original German version in *Ariadne: Forum für Frauen und Geschlechtergeschichte* (2006), 49: 24–9.

[55] Rathbone, E. (1909) *How the casual labourer lives. Report of the Liverpool Joint Research Committee on the domestic condition and expenditure of the families of certain Liverpool labourers*. Read before and published by the Liverpool Economic and Statistical Society, Liverpool: The Northern Publishing Co Ltd.

[56] Grant, C. E. (n.d.) *From 'me' to 'we' (forty years in Bow Common)*, London: Fern Street Settlement, p 10.

[57] Farthing bundles continued until the 1960s, and the Fern Street Settlement survives today as a community centre in Tower Hamlets.

[58] Grant, *From 'me' to 'we'*, p 68.

[59] Davis, V. (2005) *Inspiring African American women of Virginia*, New York: iUniverse Inc.

[60] Blair, T. D. (2015) *Building within our borders: Black women reformers in the South from 1890 to 1920*, The University of Southern Mississippi, Dissertations, Paper 188.

[61] Dinwiddie, E. W. (1903) *The tenants' manual: A handbook of information for dwellers in tenement and apartment houses and for settlement and other workers*, New York: 26 Jones Street (Greenwich House).

[62] Flanagan, 'The workshop or the home?' p 66.

[63] Yeo, E. J. (ed) (1998) *Radical femininity: Women's self-representation in the public sphere*, Manchester: Manchester University Press.

[64] Barnett, H. (1894, first published 1886) 'The poverty of the poor', in Barnett, S. and Barnett, H., *Practicable socialism: Essays on social reform*, 2nd edn, London: Longmans, Green, and Co, pp 12–19, 17–19.

[65] Creedon, A. (2006) *'Only a woman': Henrietta Barnett: Social reformer and founder of Hampstead Garden Suburb*, Chichester: Phillimore & Co Ltd, p 92.

[66] Cited in Lewis, J. (1991) *Women and social action in Victorian and Edwardian England*, Aldershot: Edward Elgar, p 220.

[67] Webb, *My apprenticeship*, p 278.

[68] Cited in Bell, E. M. (1942) *Octavia Hill: A biography*, London: Constable & Co., p 78.

[69] Hill, O. (1871) 'Blank Court; or, landlords and tenants', reprinted in O. Hill (1875) *Homes of the London poor*, New York: State Charities Aid Association, no. 8, p 36.

[70] Walker, S. P. (2006) 'Philanthropic women and accounting. Octavia Hill and the exercise of quiet power and sympathy', *Accounting, Business and Financial History*, 16 (2): 163–94.

[71] Wohl, A. S. (1971) 'Octavia Hill and *The Homes of the London poor*', *The Journal of British Studies*, 10 (2): 105–13.

[72] Freeman, M. (2001) '"Journeys into Poverty Kingdom": complete participation and the British vagrant, 1866–1914', *History Workshop Journal*, 52: 99–121.

[73] Webb, *My apprenticeship*, p 156.

[74] Webb, B. (1888) 'Pages from a work-girl's diary', reprinted in Ross, E. (2007) *Slum travelers: Ladies and London poverty, 1860–1920*, Berkeley, CA: University of California Press, pp 266–79, 268–9.

[75] Higgs, M. (1906) *Glimpses into the abyss*, London: P. S. King & Son, pp ix, 89.

[76] Higgs, M. (1904) *How to deal with the unemployed*, London: S. C. Brown, Langham & Company, Ltd, p ix.

[77] http://www.pixnet.co.uk/Oldham-hrg/members/carol-talbot/mary%20higgs/narrative.html.

[78] Higgs, M. and Hayward, E. E. (1910) *Where shall she live? The homelessness of the woman worker*, London: P. S. King & Son, p 186.

[79] Higgs, *Glimpses into the abyss*, p 255.

80 Beveridge, W. H. (1906) 'Review of Mary Higgs, *Glimpses into the abyss*', *The Economic Journal*, 16 (64): 581–3.

81 Pottle, M. (2004) 'Malvery, Olive Christian (1876/7–1914)', *Oxford Dictionary of National Biography*, Oxford: Oxford University Press.

82 Walkowitz, J. R. (1998–9) 'The Indian woman, the flower girl, and the Jew: photojournalism in Edwardian London', *Victorian Studies*, 42 (1): 3–46.

83 Koven, S. (2004) *Slumming: Sexual and social politics in Victorian London*, Princeton and Oxford, NJ: Princeton University Press, p 202.

84 Malvery, O. C. (1905) 'Gilding the gutter', reprinted in Ross, *Slum travelers*, pp 139–47, 143.

85 Malvery, O. C. (1906) *The soul market*, London: Hutchinson & Co, p 186.

86 Malvery, *The soul market*, p 108.

87 She was born Elizabeth Cochran, and later added the 'e' because she thought it was more sophisticated. See Peko, S. N. (2016) *Stunt girls: Elizabeth Bisland, Nell Nelson, and Ada Patterson as rivals to Nellie Bly*, MSc thesis, Ohio University: The Scripps College of Communication, p 1.

88 Bly, N. (1887) *Ten days in a mad house*, New York: Ian L. Munro Publisher.

89 Rosenhan, D. (1973) 'On being sane in insane places', *Science*, 179 (4070): 250–8.

90 Goodman, M. (2013) *Eighty days: Nellie Bly and Elizabeth Bisland's history-making race around the world*, New York: Ballantine Books.

91 http://aoghs.org/transportation/Nellie-bly-oil-drum/.

92 Kroeger, B. (1994) *Nellie Bly: Daredevil reporter, feminist*, New York: Times Books.

93 Peko, *Stunt girls*, p 5.

94 Banks, E. L. (1894) *Campaigns of curiosity: Journalistic adventures of an American girl in London*, London: Cassell & Co.

95 Margaret Harkness's best-known novels (published originally under the pseudonym John Law) are: (1887) *A city girl*, London: Vizetelly; (1888) *Out of work*, London: Swan Sonnenschein; (1889) *Captain Lobe: A study of the Salvation Army*, London: Hodder and Stoughton. See Diniejko, A. 'Margaret Harkness: a late Victorian new woman and social investigator', *The Victorian Web: Literature, history, and culture in the age of Victoria*, http://www.victorianweb.org/gender/harkness.html.

96 Engels to Harkness in London, Marx-Engels Correspondence 1888, early April, http://www.marxists.org/archive/marx/works/1888/letters/88_04_15.htm.

97 Scudder, V. D. (1903) *A listener in Babel: Being a series of imaginary conversations held at the close of the last century and reported*, Boston, MA: Houghton, Mifflin & Co.

98 Scudder, *On journey*, p 138.

99 Kellor, F. (1914) 'A new spirit in party organization', *The North American Review*, 199 (703): 879–92, p 883.

Chapter Four

[1] Wilson, H. E. (1928) *Mary McDowell: Neighbor*, Chicago, IL: University of Chicago Press, p 144.

[2] Flanagan, M. A. (1996) 'The city profitable, the city livable: environmental policy, gender, and power in Chicago in the 1910s', *Journal of Urban History*, 22 (2): 163–90.

[3] Mumford, M. E. (1894) 'The place of women in municipal reform', *The Outlook*, 31 March: 587–8, p 587.

[4] Wilson, *Mary McDowell*, p 23.

[5] Mitchell, R. C. (1980) *Alice Garrigue Masaryk 1879–1966: Her life as recorded in her own words and by her friends*, Pittsburgh, PA: University of Pittsburgh Center for International Studies, p 50.

[6] Hill, C. M. (ed) (1938, facsimile edition, India, 2015) *Mary McDowell and municipal housekeeping: A symposium*, 'Compiler's preface', p x.

[7] Hard, W. (1906) '"Five maiden aunts": women who "boss" Chicago said to do so to much advantage', *New York Tribune*, 17 September.

[8] Melosi, M. V. (1981) *Garbage in the cities: Refuse, reform and the environment, 1880–1980*, College Station, TX: A&M University Press, p 15.

[9] The figures are for Greater London, http://www.londononline.co.uk/factfile/historical/.

[10] Breckinridge, S. P. and Abbott, E. (1911) 'Housing conditions in Chicago, IL: Back of the yards', *American Journal of Sociology*, 16 (4): 433–68, p 435.

[11] http://www.socialwelfarehistory.com/people/mcdowell-mary/.

[12] See Phillips, H. E. (1938) 'Mary McDowell as we knew her in the yards, part II', in Hill, *Mary McDowell*, pp 120–32.

[13] Phillips, 'Mary McDowell as we knew her', p 120.

[14] Melosi, *Garbage in the cities*, p 45.

[15] Cited in Wade, L. C. (1967) 'The heritage from Chicago's early settlement houses', *Journal of the Illinois State Historical Society*, 60 (4): 411–41, p 415.

[16] McDowell, M. (1938) 'City waste', in Hill, *Mary McDowell*, pp 1–10, p 2.

[17] McDowell, 'City waste', p 3.

[18] Platt, J. (1992) '"Acting as a switchboard": Mrs. Ethel Sturges Dummer's role in sociology', *The American Sociologist*, 23 (3): 23–36.

[19] Thomas, W. I. (1923) *The unadjusted girl*, Montclair, NJ: Patterson Smith. Dummer commissioned and funded the work, also providing Thomas with case material and analytic ideas.

[20] McDowell, 'City waste', p 4.

[21] McDowell, 'City waste', p 4.

[22] Washington, S. E. (1999) 'Gender, technology and environmental policy', *Bulletin of Science, Technology & Society*, 19 (5): 365–71.

[23] McDowell, M. (1938) 'Our proxies in industry', in Hill, *Mary McDowell*, pp 39–61, p 58.

[24] 'Poverty delays garbage boards', *Chicago Daily Tribune*, 7 August 1913.

[25] Gregory, T. (2015) 'Plan to restore Bubbly Creek stalls amid contamination concerns', *Chicago Tribune*, 26 June.

[26] 'Tell of unclean alleys', *Chicago Daily Tribune*, 17 March 1896.

27 Breton, M. J. (2000) *Women pioneers for the environment*, Boston, MA: Northeastern University Press, p 65; 'Buttons for street work', *The Marin Journal* (San Rafael, CA), 15 April 1914.

28 Beard, M. R. (1915) *Women's work in municipalities*, New York and London: D. Appleton and Company, p v.

29 Beard, *Women's work*, p 48. Unfortunately, Beard wasn't very good at giving her sources. See Scott, A. F. (1993) *Natural allies: Women's associations in American history*, Urbana and Chicago, IL: University of Illinois Press.

30 http://www.bankinginvestment.net/article/581846007/ada-celeste-sweet-strength-in-extraordinary-circumstances/.

31 Batlan, F. (2008) 'The Ladies' Health Protective Association: law, lawyers and urban cause lawyering', *Akron Law Review*, 41 (3): 701–31, pp 707–10.

32 Thomson, E. P. (1897) 'What women have done for the public health', *Forum*, 24 (September): 46–55; Scribner, Mrs J. H. (1898) 'The relation between Woman's Health Protective Associations and the public health', *American Public Health Association Public Health Papers and Reports*, pp 413–21.

33 Batlan, 'The Ladies' Health Protective Association'.

34 Rynbrandt, L. J. (1999) *Caroline Bartlett Crane and progressive reform: Social housekeeping as sociology*, New York and London: Garland Publishing, Inc, p 65.

35 Addams, J. (2005, first published 1907) *Newer ideals of peace: The moral substitutes for war*, New York: Anza Publishing, pp 111–12.

36 Addams, J. (1902) *Democracy and social ethics*, New York: The Macmillan Company, p 99.

37 Addams, J. (1961, first published 1910) *Twenty years at Hull-House*, New York: Signet Books, p 203.

38 Platt, H. L. (2000) 'Jane Addams and the ward boss revisited: class, politics, and public health in Chicago, 1890–1930', *Environmental History*, 5 (2): 194–222, p 196.

39 Rynbrandt, L. J. (1997) 'The "ladies of the club" and Caroline Bartlett Crane: affiliation and alienation in progressive social reform', *Gender and Society*, 11 (2): 200–14, p 201.

40 Rynbrandt, L. J. (2000) 'My life with Caroline Bartlett Crane', *Michigan Sociological Review*, 14: 75–82; see also Rynbrandt, *Caroline Bartlett Crane and progressive reform*.

41 *Annual Report*, 1891, in the Caroline Bartlett Crane Collection, Western Michigan University Archives and Regional History Collections, Kalamazoo, Michigan, cited in Rynbrandt, L. J. (2004) 'Caroline Bartlett Crane and municipal sanitation: applied sociology in the Progressive Era', *Journal of Applied Sociology/Sociological Practice*, 21 (1/6 (1)): 84–94, p 88.

42 La Follette, Mrs R. M. (1911) 'Thought for today', *Washington Post*, 26 October.

43 Weisberger, B. A. (1994) *The La Follettes of Wisconsin: Love and politics in progressive America*, Madison, WI: University of Wisconsin Press.

44 Crane, C. B. (1907) 'How women would sweep our streets', *Los Angeles Times*, 7 May.

[45] On Waring, see Melosi, M. V. (1973) '"Out of sight, out of mind": the environment and disposal of municipal refuse, 1860–1920', *The Historian*, 35 (4): 621–40.

[46] Rynbrandt, 'Caroline Bartlett Crane and municipal sanitation'.

[47] Rynbrandt, *Caroline Bartlett Crane*, p 65, 77.

[48] Shaw, G. B. (Suthers, R. B. (ed, revised edition 1938, first published 1905) *Mind your own business: The case for municipal housekeeping*, London: the Fabian Society and George Allen & Unwin, p 22.

[49] Rodgers, D. T. (1998) *Atlantic crossings: Social politics in a progressive age*, Cambridge, MA and London: The Belknap Press of Harvard University Press, p 42.

[50] Melosi, *Garbage in the cities*, p 23.

[51] Taylor, G. (2015) *Ada Salter: Pioneer of ethical socialism*, London: Lawrence & Wishart Ltd.

[52] Kelley, F. K. (1898) 'Hull House', *The New England Magazine*, July, p 550.

[53] Brockway, F. (1949) *Bermondsey story: The life of Alfred Salter*, London: George Allen & Unwin Ltd.

[54] Taylor, *Ada Salter*, 'London woman mayor refuses to don antique official robe', *New York Tribune*, 24 December 1922.

[55] 'Municipal dreams: the beautification of Bermondsey: "fresh air and fun"', https://municipaldreams.wordpress.com/2013/04/23/the-beautification-of-bermondsey-fresh-air-and-fun/. The number of trees planted is variously cited as seven, nine and ten thousand.

[56] Brockway, *Bermondsey story*, p 88.

[57] (Anon., 1908) *How to become a lady sanitary inspector by a lady inspector*, London: The Scientific Press, p 15.

[58] See Hollis, P. (1987) *Ladies elect: Women in English local government, 1865–1914*, Oxford: Clarendon Press.

[59] King, S. (2006) *Women, welfare and local politics, 1880–1920*, Brighton: Sussex University Press, p 26.

[60] http://uudb.org/articles/charlottemasaryk.html.

[61] Unterberger, B. M. (1974) 'The arrest of Alice Masaryk', *Slavic Review*, 33 (1): 91–106, p 98; Skilling, H. G. (2001) 'Mother and daughter: Charlotte and Alice Masaryk', *Prague: Gender Studies*, p 82.

[62] Masaryk, A. (1904) 'The Bohemians in Chicago', *Charities and the Commons*, 13: 206–10.

[63] Mitchell, *Mary McDowell*, p 181.

[64] Mitchell, *Mary McDowell*, p 98; see Unterberger, 'The arrest of Alice Masaryk'.

[65] Mitchell, *Mary McDowell*, p 77.

[66] Charles Crane was a Chicago industrialist. There were strong Crane–Masaryk family connections: Crane's son Richard was the first United States Ambassador to the Czech Republic; his daughter Frances married Jan Masaryk when he was Czech Ambassador to the UK; and Crane's son John was for several years President Masaryk's English secretary (Mitchell, *Mary McDowell*, p 43).

67 '40,000 in appeal for U.S. to save woman in prison', *Chicago Herald*, 25 April 1916.

68 'Women leaders seeking aid for Alice Masaryk', *Chicago Daily Tribune*, 26 April 1916.

69 Berglund, B. R. (2011) '"We stand on the threshold of a new age": Alice Masaryková, the Czechoslovak Red Cross, and the building of a new Europe', in Sharp, I. and Stibbe, M. (eds) *Aftermaths of war: Women's movements and female activists, 1918–1923*, Leiden and Boston, MA: Brill, pp 355–74, p 367.

70 Crawford, R. (1921) 'Pathfinding in Prague', *The Survey*, 46 (11): 327–32.

71 Hill, *Mary McDowell*, p ix. No websites relating to the two orders mention McDowell as a recipient.

72 Kubickova, N. (2001) 'Historical portraits of important European leaders in social work. Alice Masaryk (1879–1966), Czechoslovakia', *European Journal of Social Work*, 4 (3): 303–11.

73 Sivulka, J. (1999) 'From domestic to municipal housekeeper: the influence of the sanitary reform movement on changing women's roles in America, 1860–1920', *Journal of American Culture*, 22 (4): 1–7.

74 Gugliotta, A. (2000) 'Class, gender, and coal smoke: gender ideology and environmental injustice in Pittsburgh, 1868–1914', *Environmental History*, 5 (2): 165–93.

75 Flanagan, M. A. (1990) 'Gender and urban political reform: the City Club and the Woman's City Club of Chicago in the Progressive Era', *The American Historical Review*, 95 (4): 1032–50; Pellow, D. N. (2004) 'The politics of illegal dumping: an environmental justice framework', *Qualitative Sociology*, 27 (4): 511–25; Schulte, T. K. (2009) 'Citizen experts', *Frontiers*, 30 (3): 1–29.

76 Oakley, A. (1974) *The sociology of housework*, London: Martin Robertson, and Oakley, A. (1974) *Housewife*, London: Allen Lane.

77 Hobhouse, E. (1911) 'Dust-women', *The Economic Journal*, 10 (39): 411–20, pp 412, 411.

Chapter Five

1 https://en.wikipedia.org/wiki/Lake_Placid,_New_York.

2 See Stage, S. (1997) 'Home economics: what's in a name?' in Stage, S. and Vincenti, V. B. (eds) *Rethinking home economics: Women and the history of a profession*, Ithaca, NY and London: Cornell University Press, pp 1–14.

3 Barnett, H. O. W. (1885) *The making of the home*, London: Cassell & Co.

4 Plunkett, H. (1885) *Women, plumbers and doctors: Household sanitation*, New York: D. Appleton and Company.

5 Atkinson, M. (1910) 'The economic relations of the household', in Ravenhill, A. and Schiff, C. J. (eds) *Household administration, its place in the higher education of women*, London: Grant Richards Ltd, pp 121–206, 123, 125.

6 Richards, E. H. (1899) *The cost of living as modified by sanitary science*, New York: John Wiley & Sons, p 26.

[7] Ravenhill, A. (1917) 'The scope of home economics and its subject matter in universities and colleges', *The Journal of Home Economics*, 9 (9): 393–404, p 395.

[8] (1904) *Report of the Inter-departmental Committee on the Physical Deterioration of the Population*, London: HMSO; Newman, G. (1906) *Infant mortality: A social problem*, London: Methuen.

[9] Davin, A. (1978) 'Imperialism and motherhood', *History Workshop Journal*, 5: 9–65.

[10] Talbot, M. (1896) 'Sanitation and sociology', *American Journal of Sociology*, 2 (1): 74–81.

[11] Ravenhill, A. (1951) *The memoirs of an educational pioneer*, Toronto and Vancouver: J. M. Dent and Sons Ltd, p 121.

[12] Blakestad, N. I. (1994) 'King's College of Household and Social Science and the household science movement in English higher education c. 1908–1939', University of Oxford, DPhil thesis, p 101.

[13] Ravenhill, *Memoirs*, p 68.

[14] https://en.wikipedia.org/wiki/Chulalongkorn. King Rama V visited Europe in 1897 and 1907 and was interested in plumbing systems, which may throw some light on his connection with Alice Ravenhill.

[15] Ravenhill, *Memoirs*, p 111.

[16] Ravenhill, *Memoirs*, p 121.

[17] Much of the literature on Ellen Richards refers to her as Ellen Swallow Richards, but she seems herself to have used the name Ellen H. (Henrietta) Richards.

[18] Ravenhill, *Memoirs*, p 113.

[19] Swallow, P. C. (2014) *The remarkable life and career of Ellen Swallow Richards*, Hoboken, NJ: John Wiley & Sons, pp 25–8.

[20] Swallow, *The remarkable life*, p 41.

[21] Richards, *The cost of living*, p 115.

[22] Ravenhill, A. (1913) *The art of right living*, Bulletin No. 9, Department of Agriculture, Victoria, British Columbia.

[23] Richards, E. H. (1904) *The art of right living*, Boston, MA: Whitcomb & Barrows.

[24] Ravenhill, A. (1898) *The housing of the people: VI, our water supply*, Manchester: Women's Co-operative Guild, p 11.

[25] Elliott, S. M. (1907) *Household bacteriology*, Chicago, IL: American School of Home Economics.

[26] Richards, *The cost of living*, p 106.

[27] Ravenhill, 'The scope of home economics', p 400.

[28] Frederick, C. (1919) *Household engineering: Scientific management in the home*, Chicago, IL: American School of Home Economics.

[29] Richards, E. H. (1905) *The cost of shelter*, New York: John Wiley & Sons, pp 33–4.

[30] Swallow, *The remarkable life*, p 57.

[31] Swallow, *The remarkable life*, p 37.

[32] Collins, N. (2002) 'Domestic sciences at Bradley Polytechnic Institute and the University of Chicago', *Journal of the Illinois State Historical Society*, 95 (3): 275–99, p 295.

[33] Richards, E. H. (1910) *Euthenics, the science of controllable environment: A plea for better living conditions as a first step toward higher human efficiency*, Boston, MA: Whitcomb & Barrows, p vii.

[34] Clarke, R. (1973) *Ellen Swallow: The woman who founded ecology*, Chicago, IL: Follet Publishing Company; Richardson, B. (2000) 'Ellen Swallow Richards: advocate for "oekology", euthenics and women's leadership in using science to control the environment', *Michigan Sociological Review*, 14: 94–114.

[35] For examples of the argument that women domestic scientists wanted to keep women at home, see Ehrenreich, B. and English, D. (1979) *For her own good: 150 years of the experts' advice to women*, London: Pluto Press; Hardyment, C. (1988) *From mangle to microwave: The mechanization of household work*, Cambridge: Polity Press.

[36] Richards, *Euthenics*, p 142.

[37] Richards, *Euthenics*, p 161.

[38] Stam, D. C. (1989) 'Melvil and Annie Dewey and the communitarian ideal', *Libraries & Culture*, 24 (2): 125–43, p 131.

[39] Wiegand, W. A. (1996) *Irrepressible reformer: A biography of Melvil Dewey*, Chicago, IL: American Library Association, pp 251–2.

[40] See Fields, A. M. and Connell, T. H. (2004) 'Classification and the definition of a discipline: the Dewey Decimal Classification and home economics', *Libraries & Culture*, 39 (3): 245–59.

[41] Lawrence, M. A. (1907) *Special report on the teaching of cookery to public elementary school children in England and Wales*, London: HMSO, p 2.

[42] See Caine, B. (1988) *Destined to be wives: The sisters of Beatrice Webb*, Oxford: Oxford University Press.

[43] Blakestad, *King's College of Household and Social Science*, pp 98–9; see Caine, *Destined to be wives*, pp 171–3.

[44] Pillow, M. E. (1890s) Lectures, notes and related syllabuses, National Health Society, Domestic and personal hygiene, Pillow Papers, The Women's Library, British Library of Political and Economic Science, 7/MEP/1/2.

[45] Tomes, N. (1997) 'Spreading the germ theory: sanitary science and home economics 1880–1930', in Stage, S. and Vincenti, V. B. (eds) *Rethinking home economics*, pp 34–54, 45.

[46] Pillow, M. E. (1891) Interview in *Woman's Herald*, 28 March (127, vol. 111): 353–4, p 353. Pillow Papers, The Women's Library, British Library of Political and Economic Science, 7/MEP/2/3.

[47] Lawrence, *Special report*, cited in Blakestad, *King's College of Household and Social Science*, p 95.

[48] Haynes, J. R. (2006) 'Sanitary ladies and friendly visitors: Women public health officers in London 1890–1930', PhD thesis, Institute of Education, University of London, p 208.

[49] Ravenhill, A. (1907) 'Home economics in England', *Ninth Annual Conference on Home Economics*, Washington, DC: American Home Economics Association, pp 17–22.

[50] Oakeley, H. D. (1939) *My adventures in education*, London: Williams and Norgate, Ltd, p 143.

[51] Howarth, J. (2004) 'Oakeley, Hilda Diana (1867–1950)', *Oxford Dictionary of National Biography*, Oxford: Oxford University Press.

[52] Oakeley, *My adventures*, pp 116–19.

[53] A contribution (like so many of those mentioned in this book) which has been 'unjustly omitted' from its disciplinary history; see Thomas, E. (2015) 'Hilda Oakeley on idealism, history and the real past', *British Journal for the History of Philosophy*, 23 (5): 933–53, p 951.

[54] Meyer, A. and Black, C. (1909) *Makers of our clothes*, London: Duckworth & Co.

[55] Atkinson, M. (1914) *The economic foundations of the women's movement*, Fabian Tract no 175, London: The Fabian Society, p 18.

[56] Gardiner, B. 'A history of the Biology Department, Queen Elizabeth College 1912–1985', http://www.qeca.org.uk/History_of_QEC_Biology_Department_V1.0.pdf.

[57] Blakestad, *King's College of Household and Social Science*, p 39.

[58] Blakestad, *King's College of Household and Social Science*, p 40.

[59] Ishbel MacDonald had to give up the course early in order to act as her father's hostess in 10 Downing Street.

[60] Stewart, J. (2013) *Child guidance in Britain, 1918–55*, London: Pickering & Chatto.

[61] Blakestad, *King's College of Household and Social Science*, p 182.

[62] The zenith of KCHSS's success was the inter-war period. After 1953, social science was removed from the degree, which attracted only half a dozen students a year, and the College was renamed Queen Elizabeth College; the household course disappeared altogether in 1967.

[63] Richards, E. R. and Talbot, M. (1898) *Home sanitation: A manual for housekeepers*, Boston, MA: Whitcomb and Barrow, pp 55–6.

[64] 'Art in housekeeping: theory and practice at the University of Chicago', *Chicago Daily Tribune*, 9 June 1894.

[65] Marion Talbot Papers, Special Collections Research Center, University of Chicago Library, Box 7, 7: 2.

[66] Talbot, M. (1936) *More than lore: Reminiscences of Marion Talbot*, Chicago, IL: University of Chicago Press, p 99.

[67] Talbot, M. and Breckinridge, S. P. (1912) *The modern household*, Boston, MA: Whitcomb and Barrows, p 8.

[68] Ravenhill, *Memoirs*, p 140.

[69] Berlage, N. K. (1998) 'The establishment of an applied social science: home economists, science, and reform at Cornell University, 1870–1930', in Silverberg, H. (ed) *Gender and American social science*, Princeton, NJ: Princeton University Press, pp 185–231, p 194.

[70] Campbell, H. S. (1882) *The problem of the poor. A record of quiet work in unquiet places*, New York: Fords, Howard & Hulbert; Campbell, H. S. (1886) *Mrs Herndon's income*, Boston, MA: Roberts Bros; Campbell, H. S. (1886) *Miss Melinda's opportunity*, Boston, MA: Roberts Bros.

[71] Campbell, H. S. (1897) *Household economics*, New York and London: G. P. Putnam's Sons, pp xiii, 3, 229.

[72] Collins, J. (2009) 'Beyond the domestic sphere? A home science education at the University of New Zealand, 1911–1936', *Journal of Educational Administration and History*, 41 (2): 115–30; Collins, J. (2008) 'Glorified housekeepers or pioneering professionals? The professional lives of home science graduates from the University of New Zealand', *History of Education Review*, 37 (2): 40–51; Fitzgerald, T. and Collins, J. (2011) *Historical portraits of women home scientists at the University of New Zealand 1911–1947*, Amherst, MA: Cambria Press.

[73] Blakestad, *King's College of Household and Social Science*, p 162; see Manthorpe, C. (1986) 'Science or domestic science? The struggle to define an appropriate science education for girls in early twentieth-century England', *History of Education*, 15 (3): 195–213. The counter-attack was led by a Cambridge science lecturer called Ida Freund, who maintained that the King's College course was academically unsound and subversive.

[74] 'Organization and first meeting of American Home Economics Association', address by Ellen Richards, *The Journal of Home Economics*, 1 (1): 22–26, p 25.

[75] Richards, E. H. (1911) *Conservation by sanitation*, New York: John Wiley & Sons, p vi.

Chapter Six

[1] http://www.scaruffi.com/politics/massacre.html.

[2] Catt, C. C. (1931) 'Man made wars', *Pax*, 6, cited in Rupp, L. J. (1997) 'Sexuality and politics in the early twentieth century: the case of the international women's movement', *Feminist Studies*, 23 (3): 577–605, p 589.

[3] British Committee of the Women's International Congress (1915) *Towards permanent peace. A record of the Women's International Congress held at The Hague, April 28th–May 1st 1915*. London: British Committee of the Women's International Congress, p 4.

[4] Cooper, S. E. (2002) 'Peace as a human right: the invasion of women into the world of high international politics', *Journal of Women's History*, 14 (2): 9–25, p 14.

[5] Davy, J. A. (2001) 'Pacifist thought and gender ideology in the political biographies of women peace activists in Germany, 1899–1970: introduction', *Journal of Women's History*, 13 (3): 34–45. See also Brown, H. (2003) *The truest form of patriotism: Pacifist feminism in Britain, 1870–1902*, Manchester: Manchester University Press; Rappaport, H. (2002) 'The origins of women's peace campaigning', *History Today*, 52 (3): 28–30; Bussey, G. and Tims, M. (1980) *Pioneers for peace: The Women's International League for Peace and Freedom, 1915–1965*, London: the WILPF, British Section; Cooper, S. E.

(1980) 'European peace advocates and the Great War: prevention, protest, resignation and resistance', *Peace & Change*, 40 (2): 216–25.

6   Bell, A. O. (ed) (1977) *The diary of Virginia Woolf, Vol 1, 1915–1919*, New York and London: Harcourt Brace Jovanovich, 23 January 1915, p 26.

7   Cited in Randall, M. M. (1964) *Improper Bostonian: Emily Greene Balch*, New York: Twayne Publishers Inc., p 346.

8   Bremer, F. (1855) (trans. M. Howitt) *Hertha, or a soul's history: A sketch from real life*, London: A. Hall, Virtue & Co.

9   Bremer, F. (1854) 'Invitation to a peace alliance', *The Times*, 14 August, p 5.

10   Götz, N. (2010) '"Matts Mattson Paavola knows Elihu Burritt": a transnational perspective on nineteenth-century peace activism in Northern Europe', *Peace & Change*, 35 (2): 191–221.

11   Beales, A. C. F. (1931) *The history of peace*, London: G. Bell & Sons Ltd, p 98. See also Götz, '"Matts Mattson Paavola knows Elihu Burritt"'.

12   Bremer, F. (1853) (trans. M. Howitt) *The homes of the new world: Impressions of America*, London: A. Hall, Virtue & Co.

13   Bremer, *The homes of the new world*, Letter VIII; Salenius, S. (2013) 'The "emancipated ladies" of America in the travel writing of Fredrika Bremer and Alexandra Gripenberg', *Journal of International Women's Studies*, 14 (1): 113–31.

14   The legal changes meant that from 1858 women could petition the Courthouse rather than the Royal Court to be released from this wardship at 25; from 1863, all women were considered to reach their legal majority at this age.

15   Anderson, B. S. (2000) *Joyous greetings: The first international women's movement, 1830–1860*, Oxford: Oxford University Press.

16   Bremer, F. (1860–62) *Life in the old world* (6 vols), Philadelphia, PA: T.B. Peterson and Brothers.

17   Information on Maude Royden is taken from Fletcher, S. (1989) *Maude Royden: A life*, Oxford: Basil Blackwell; Maude Royden's papers in The Women's Library at the British Library of Political and Economic Science; Morgan, S. (2013) 'A "feminist conspiracy": Maude Royden, women's ministry and the British press, 1916–1921', *Women's History Review*, 22 (5): 777–800; Falby, A. (2010) 'Maude Royden's sacramental theology of sex and love', *Anglican and Episcopal History*, 79 (2): 124–43; Falby, A. (2004) 'Maude Royden's Guildhouse: a nexus of religious change in Britain between the wars', *Historical Papers, Canadian Society of Church History*, pp 165–73. The references to Royden as 'the greatest woman in England' and 'the world famous woman preacher' come from Fletcher, *Maude Royden*, pp 1 and 200; Royden as 'a modern Joan of Arc' from Fey, H. (1937) 'Maude Royden comes to America', *The Christian Century*, 13 January: 45–7, p 47.

18   http://www.statemaster.com/encyclopedia/South-Luffenham.

19   Fletcher, *Maude Royden*, p 53.

20   Royden, M. [Mrs. Hudson Shaw] (1948) *A threefold cord*, New York: The Macmillan Company.

21 There was no law in Britain governing adoption until 1926. Other well-known single women adopted babies, including Christabel Pankhurst, Emmeline Pankhurst and Elizabeth Robins. Elizabeth Blackwell and Frances Power Cobbe are examples among earlier feminists.

22 Royden, A. M. (1922) *Political Christianity*, London: G. P. Putnam's Sons, p 10.

23 Royden, A. M. [Mrs Hudson Shaw] (1947, first published 1921) *Sex and commonsense*, London: Hurst & Blackett Ltd, p 26.

24 Cited in Fletcher, *Maude Royden*, pp 101–2.

25 Cited in Fletcher, *Maude Royden*, p 156.

26 Royden, M. (1928) (untitled), *The Guildhouse Monthly*, pp 120–3.

27 'Miss Dobson' (1928) 'Maude Royden's world tour', *The Guildhouse Monthly*, p 123.

28 Tinkler, P. and Warsh, C. K. (2008) 'Feminine modernity in interwar Britain and North America: corsets, cars and cigarettes', *Journal of Women's History*, 20 (3): 113–43.

29 'PRIVATE MEMORANDUM on the approximate number of Women who would be Enfranchised by various Amendments to the Reform Bill, and their advantages and disadvantages', Catherine Marshall Papers, Cumbria Archive Centre, Carlisle, D/MAR/3/33.

30 Lord R. Cecil to M. Fawcett, 5 August 1914, cited in Kay, H. (2012) 'Chrystal Macmillan: from Edinburgh woman to global citizen', *Deportate, Esuli, Profughe*, 18–19: 125–52, p 134.

31 Royden, A. M. (1915) 'War and the women's movement', in Buxton, C. R. (ed) *Towards a lasting settlement*, The Women's Library, British Library of Political and Economic Science, Royden Papers, 7AMR/2/30.

32 Royden, A. M. (1916) *The great adventure: The way to peace*, London: Headley Brothers, p 12. Royden Papers, The Women's Library, British Library of Political and Economic Science, 7AMR/1/80 Box FL379.

33 Wilson, F. (1976) 'Dame Kathleen Courtney', Unpublished MS, Kathleen Courtney Papers, Lady Margaret Hall, Oxford, MMP/3/2/1, p 26.

34 'President's opening address', cited in Rupp, L. J. (1997) *Worlds of women: The making of an international women's movement*, Princeton, NJ: Princeton University Press, p 121.

35 D'Itri, P. W. (1999) *Cross currents in the international women's movement, 1848–1948*, Bowling Green, OH: Bowling Green State University Popular Press, p 27.

36 Addams, J. (1930) *The second twenty years at Hull-House*, New York: The Macmillan Company, pp 80–1.

37 Addams, *The second twenty years*, p 85.

38 Wenger, B. S. (1990) 'Radical politics in a reactionary age: the unmaking of Rosika Schwimmer 1914–1930', *Journal of Women's History*, 2 (2): 66–99, p 66.

39 There is no full-length biography in English of Rosika Schwimmer. Information in this chapter is taken from Wiltsher, A. (1985) *Most dangerous women: Feminist peace campaigners of the Great War*, London: Pandora;

International Committee for World Peace Prize Award (1937) *Rosika Schwimmer: World patriot: A biographical sketch*; Wenger, 'Radical politics'; Mcfadden, M. H. (2011) 'Borders, boundaries, and the necessity of reflexivity: international women activists, Rosika Schwimmer (1877–1948), and the shadow narrative', *Women's History Review*, 20 (4): 533–42.

40   Van Voris, J. (1987) *Carrie Chapman Catt: A public life*, New York: The Feminist Press, p 105.
41   Lloyd George, D. (1933) *War Memoirs Vol 1*, London: Ivor Nicholson & Watson, p 53.
42   Wiltsher, *Most dangerous women*, p 228.
43   Oldfield, S. (2003) 'Mary Sheepshanks edits an international suffrage monthly in wartime: *Jus Suffragii* 1914–9', *Women's History Review*, 12 (1): 119–31.
44   *Jus Suffragii*, 13 September 1914, p 1.
45   Bean, M. J. W. (2005) *Julia Grace Wales: Canada's hidden heroine and the quest for peace 1914–1918*, Ottawa: Borealis Press.
46   Cited in Bean, *Julia Grace Wales*, p 49.
47   Patterson, D. S. (1971) 'Woodrow Wilson and the mediation movement, 1914–17', *The Historian*, 33 (4): 535–56, p 537.
48   Patterson, D. S. (2008) *The search for negotiated peace: Women's activism and citizen diplomacy in World War I*, London: Routledge, p 38.
49   Wenger, 'Radical politics', p 70.
50   A. Jacobs to R. Schwimmer, 10 February 1904, cited in Rupp, *Worlds of women*, p 183.
51   Pethick-Lawrence, E. (1914) 'Union of women for constructive peace', *The Survey*, 33, 5 December, p 230.
52   Cited in Randall, *Improper Bostonian*, pp 149–50.
53   Lloyd's sister Augusta subsequently married Florence Kelley's son Nicholas.
54   C. C. Catt to J. Addams, 14 December 1914, cited in Schott, L. (1985) 'The Woman's Peace Party and the moral basis for women's pacifism', *Frontiers*, 8 (2): 18–24, p 18.
55   Addams, J. (1922) *Peace and bread in time of war*, New York: The Macmillan Company, pp 61–2.
56   Mead, L. A. (1915) 'The Woman's Peace Party', *The Advocate of Peace (1894–1920)* (World Affairs Institute), 77 (2): 35–6, 36.
57   Jacobs, A. (1996, first published in Dutch 1924) *Memories: My life as an international leader in health, suffrage and peace*, New York: The Feminist Press, pp 81–2.
58   Cited in Patterson, *The search for negotiated peace*, p 53.
59   '"Now I dare to do it". An interview with Dr Aletta Jacobs', in Cook, B. W. (ed) (1978) *Crystal Eastman: On women and revolution*, Oxford: Oxford University Press, pp 237–41, p 240.
60   Colby, V. (2003) *Vernon Lee: A literary biography*, Charlottesville, VA and London: University of Virginia Press, p 320.

[61] Lee, V. (1915) *The ballet of the nations*, London: Chatto and Windus; Lee, V. (1920) *Satan the waster: A philosophic war trilogy with notes and introduction*, London: John Lane.

[62] Sieberg, H. and Zorn, C. (eds) (2014) *The Anglo-German correspondence of Vernon Lee and Irena Forbes-Mosse during World War I*, Lewiston, New York and Lampeter, Wales: The Edwin-Mellen Press, p 220.

[63] Oldfield, S. (1994) 'England's Cassandras in World War One', in Oldfield, S. (ed) *This working-day world*, London: Taylor & Francis, pp 89–100, p 90.

[64] Sharp, E. (1915) 'The congress and the press', in British Committee, *Towards permanent peace*, pp 20–1, 20.

[65] Patterson, *The search for negotiated peace*, p 52.

[66] Mulley, C. (2009) *The woman who saved the children: A biography of Eglantyne Jebb, founder of Save the Children*, Oxford: Oneworld Publications, p 227, and Sklar, K. K., Schüler, A. and Strasser, S. (eds) (1998) *Social justice feminists in the United States and Germany: A dialogue in documents, 1885–1933*, New York: Cornell University Press, p 246, both get the names confused.

[67] This story is told by various authors, see, for example, Patterson, *The search for negotiated peace*, pp 73–4; Wiltsher, *Most dangerous women*, p 84; Oldfield, 'England's Cassandras', pp 89–90.

[68] H. S. Walker, Lieutenant Colonel, Chief Permit Officer Downing Street to C. Marshall, 16 April 1915, Catherine Marshall Papers, Cumbria Archive Centre, Carlisle, D/MAR/4/76.

[69] 'List of British women desiring to attend the congress', in British Committee, *Towards permanent peace*, pp 13–14.

[70] Fletcher, *Maude Royden*, p 123.

[71] Fletcher, *Maude Royden*, p 124.

[72] C. C. Catt to A. Jacobs, 15 December 1914, cited in Rupp, *Worlds of women*, p 27.

[73] A. Jacobs to M. R. Smith, 22 April 1915, in Sicherman, B. (ed) (1984) *Alice Hamilton: A life in letters*, Cambridge, MA: Harvard University Press, pp 185–6.

[74] Bean, *Julia Grace Wales*, pp 63–5.

[75] Randall, *Improper Bostonian*, pp 146–7.

[76] Balch, E. G. (2003, first published 1915) 'Journey and impressions', in Addams, J., Balch, E. G. and Hamilton, A., *Women at The Hague: The International Congress of Women and its results*, Urbana and Chicago, IL: Chicago University Press, pp 8–9.

[77] Balch, 'Journey and impressions', p 6.

[78] Balch, 'Journey and impressions', p 9.

[79] Addams et al., *Women at The Hague*, pp 72–3.

[80] Appendix 3, 'Resolutions adopted by the International Congress of Women at The Hague May 1, 1915', in Addams et al., *Women at The Hague*, pp 72–7, p 76.

[81] A. Hamilton to M. R. Smith, 5 May 1915, cited in Sicherman, *Alice Hamilton*, p 190.

Notes

82 A. Hamilton to L. deKoven Bowen, 16 May 1915, cited in Sicherman, *Alice Hamilton*, p 192.
83 Wiltsher, *Most dangerous women*, p 112.
84 Addams, *Peace and bread*, p 11.
85 Addams, J. (2003, first published 1915) 'The revolt against war', in Addams, J. et al., *Women at The Hague*, pp 27–38, p 28.
86 Hamilton, A. (1943) *Exploring the dangerous trades: The autobiography of Alice Hamilton, M.D.*, Boston, MA: Little, Brown and Company, p 173.
87 Addams, 'Factors in continuing the war', p 45.
88 A. Jacobs to J. Addams, 15 September 1915, Papers Aletta Henriëtte Jacobs, Collection IAV, Atria, Institute on Gender Equality and Women's History, Amsterdam.
89 Kraft, B. S. (1978) *The peace ship*, New York: Macmillan Publishing, p 94.
90 Kraft, *The peace ship*, p 86.
91 Balch, E. G. (1916) 'International colonial administration', reprinted in Randall, M. M. (ed) *Beyond nationalism: The social thought of Emily Greene Balch*, New York: Twayne Publishers.
92 Robson, S. (2007) *The First World War*, Harlow: Pearson Education Limited, p 103.
93 Swanwick, H. M. (1915) *Women and war*, London: The Union of Democratic Control, p 3.
94 Ashworth, L. M. (2011) 'Feminism, war and the prospects for peace: Helena Swanwick (1864–1939) and the lost feminists of inter-war international relations', *International Feminist Journal of Politics*, 13 (1): 25–43, p 29.
95 Swanwick, H. M. (1935) *I have been young*, London: Victor Gollancz, p 318.
96 F. Kelley to M. R. Smith, 22 May 1919, reprinted in Sklar, K. K. and Palmer, B. W. (eds) (2009) *The selected letters of Florence Kelley, 1868–1931*, Urbana, IL: University of Illinois Press, pp 238–9.
97 Wiltsher, *Most dangerous women*, p 209.
98 Williams, E. (1919) 'A visit to Vienna', in *WILPF Towards peace and freedom: The Women's International Congress, Zürich, May 12th–17th, 1919*, pp 10–11, 10.
99 Oldfield, S. (1984) *Spinsters of this parish: The life and times of F. M. Mayor and Mary Sheepshanks*, London: Virago, p 181.
100 Randall, *Improper Bostonian*, p 261.
101 Storr, K. (2010) *Excluded from the record: Women refugees and relief, 1914–1929*, Bern: Peter Lang.
102 WILPF, *Towards peace and freedom*, pp 6–7.
103 Cited in Oldfield, 'England's Cassandras', p 98.
104 Kuhlman, E. (2008) *Reconstructing patriarchy after the Great War: Women, gender, and postwar reconciliation between nations*, Houndmills, Basingstoke: Palgrave Macmillan, p 5.
105 Swanwick, *I have been young*, pp 320–1.
106 Sharer, W. B. (2001) 'The persuasive work of organizational names: The Women's International League for Peace and Freedom and the struggle for collective identification', *Rhetoric Review*, 20 (3/4): 234–50, p 237.

107 Randall, *Improper Bostonian*, p 256.
108 Cited in Johnston, A. M. (2014) 'The disappearance of Emily G. Balch, social scientist', *The Journal of the Gilded Age and Progressive Era*, 13 (2): 166–99, p 197.
109 Cited in Randall, *Improper Bostonian*, p 372.
110 Cited in Oldfield, 'Mary Sheepshanks edits', p 128.
111 Royden, *Political Christianity*, pp 111–12.
112 Cited in Randall, *Improper Bostonian*, p 385.
113 Salomon, A. (Lees, A. (ed) 2004, first published in German 1983) *Character is destiny: The autobiography of Alice Salomon*, Ann Arbor, MI: University of Michigan Press, p 13.
114 Madeleine Doty, cited in Rupp, *Worlds of women*, p 118.
115 Sharer, 'The persuasive work', p 243.
116 Fletcher, *Maude Royden*, p 176.

Chapter Seven

1 Melman, B. (1996) 'Under the Western historian's eyes: Eileen Power and the early feminist encounter with colonialism', *History Workshop Journal*, 42: 147–68.
2 Berg, M. (1996) *A woman in history: Eileen Power, 1889–1940*, Cambridge: Cambridge University Press, p 153.
3 Marshall, T. H. (1950) *Citizenship and social class, and other essays*, Cambridge: Cambridge University Press (the citizenship essay was first published in 1949). On Marshall's ideas, see Bulmer, M. and Rees, A. M. (eds) (1996) *Citizenship today: The contemporary relevance of T. H. Marshall*, London: UCL Press.
4 Cited in Balme, J. H. (2015) *Agent of peace: Emily Hobhouse and her courageous attempt to end the First World War*, Stroud: The History Press, p 48.
5 Fry, R. (1929) *The life of Emily Hobhouse*, London: Jonathan Cape, p 28.
6 Cited in Balme, J. H. (2012) *To love one's enemies: The work and life of Emily Hobhouse*, Stuttgart: Ibidem-Verlag, p 13.
7 Weber, M. (1999) 'The Boer War remembered', *The Journal of Historical Review*, 18 (3): 14–27.
8 Emily Hobhouse got a question asked about this practice in the House of Commons on 26 February 1901, with the result that it was revised the next day.
9 https://www.geni.com/projects/Anglo-Boere-Oorlog-Boer-War-1899-1902-British-Concentration-Camps/854.
10 Balme, *To love one's enemies*, p 42.
11 Hasian, M. (2003) 'The "hysterical" Emily Hobhouse and Boer War concentration camp controversy', *Western Journal of Communication*, 67 (2): 138–63, p 149; de Reuck, J. (1999) 'Social suffering and the politics of pain: observations on the concentration camps in the Anglo-Boer War 1899–1902', *English in Africa*, 26 (2): 69–88, p 78.

Notes

[12] Hobhouse, E. (1901) *Report to the Committee of the Distress Fund for South African Women and Children, of a visit to the camps of women and children in the Cape and Orange River colonies*, London: The Friars Printing Association, Ltd, p 3.

[13] Hobhouse, *Report to the Committee*, p 4.

[14] Hobhouse, E. (1901) 'Concentration camps', *The Contemporary Review*, 1 July: 528–37, p 530.

[15] Hobhouse, E. (1902) *The brunt of the war and where it fell*, London: Methuen & Co., p xvi.

[16] Hobhouse, E. (1924) *War without glamour: Or, women's war experiences written by themselves*, Bloemfontein: Nasionale Pers Beperk.

[17] Weber, 'The Boer War remembered'.

[18] St John Brodrick to E. Hobhouse, 17 July 1901, cited in Fry, *The life of Emily Hobhouse*, p 156.

[19] Balme, *To love one's enemies*, p 460.

[20] L. D. Streatfeild to H. Deane, 23 December 1901, Lucy Deane Streatfeild Papers, The Women's Library, British Library of Political and Economic Science, 69/2/10.

[21] Jacobs, A. (1996, first published in Dutch 1924) *Memories: My life as an international leader in health, suffrage and peace*, New York: The Feminist Press, p 78.

[22] E. Hobhouse to the Cape Town Commander 27 October 1901, cited in Balme, *To love one's enemies*, p 339.

[23] *The Daily News*, 25 November 1901, cited in Balme, *To love one's enemies*, p 374.

[24] Fisher, J. (1971) *That Miss Hobhouse*, London: Secker & Warburg, p 186.

[25] Cited in Balme, *Agent of peace*, p 29.

[26] Patterson, D. S. (2008) *The search for negotiated peace: Women's activism and citizen diplomacy in World War I*, London: Routledge, p 244.

[27] As a result of Hobhouse's disturbing behaviour, the government promulgated a new Order in Council in November 1916 prohibiting any British subject from going to enemy territory without official permission (Patterson, *The search for negotiated peace*, p 254).

[28] Balme, *Agent of peace*, p 89, pp 90–1.

[29] Balme, *Agent of peace*, p 53.

[30] Balme, *Agent of peace*, p 82.

[31] Salomon, A. (Lees, A. (ed), 2004, first published in German 1983) *Character is destiny: The autobiography of Alice Salomon*, Ann Arbor, MI: The University of Michigan Press, p 140.

[32] Balme, *Agent of peace*, p 94.

[33] Kuhlmann, C. (2003) 'Gender and theory in the history of German social work – Alice Salomon, Herman Nohl and Christian Klumker', in Hering, S. and Waaldijk, B. (eds) *History of social work in Europe (1900–1960)*, Opladen: Leske + Budrich, pp 95–104, p 100.

[34] Salomon, *Character is destiny*, p 52.

[35] Salomon, *Character is destiny*, p 87.

[36] Hegar, R. L. (2008) 'Transatlantic transfers in social work: contributions of three pioneers', *British Journal of Social Work*, 38: 716–33, p 727.

[37] Salomon, *Character is destiny*, p 95.

[38] Salomon, *Character is destiny*, pp 106–7.

[39] Salomon, *Character is destiny*, p 120.

[40] Salomon, *Character is destiny*, p 111.

[41] Salomon, *Character is destiny*, p 228.

[42] See Everard, M. (2016) 'Fateful politics: the itinerary of Rosa Manus, 1933–1942', pp 240–300 in Everard, M. and de Haan, F. (eds) *Rosa Manus (1881–1942)*, Leiden and Boston, MA: Brill.

[43] 'Alice Salomon on American Settlement work', in Sklar, K. K., Schüler, A. and Strasser, S. (eds) (1998) *Social justice feminists in the United States and Germany: A dialogue in documents, 1885–1933*, New York: Cornell University Press, pp 159–67, p 161.

[44] Walker, N. (1915) 'Chicago housing conditions, X: Greeks and Italians in the neighborhood of Hull House', *American Journal of Sociology*, 21 (3): 285–316.

[45] Comstock, A. P. (1912) 'Chicago housing conditions, VI: The problem of the Negro', *American Journal of Sociology*, 18 (2): 241–57, p 248.

[46] Costin, L. B. (1983) *Two sisters for social justice: A biography of Grace and Edith Abbott*, Urbana and Chicago, IL: University of Illinois Press, p 46.

[47] Costin, *Two sisters*.

[48] Abbott, G. (1909) 'The Bulgarians of Chicago', *Charities and the Commons*, 21 (15): 653–60.

[49] Abbott, G. (1909) 'A study of the Greeks in Chicago', *American Journal of Sociology*, 15 (3): 379–93, pp 381, 393.

[50] Costin, *Two sisters*, p 85.

[51] Abbott, G. (1914) *The problem of immigration in Massachusetts. Report of the Massachusetts Commission on immigration*, Boston, MA: Wright & Potter Printing Co.

[52] Abbott, G. (1908) 'The Chicago employment agency and the immigrant worker', *American Journal of Sociology*, 14 (3): 289–305; see Buroker, R. L. (1971) 'From voluntary association to welfare state: The Illinois Immigrants' Protective League, 1908–1926', *The Journal of American History*, 58 (3): 643–60.

[53] Abbott, 'The Chicago employment agency', p 305.

[54] Abbott, G. (1917) *The immigrant and the community*, New York: Century Co., pp 55, 61.

[55] Abbott, *The immigrant*, pp 61–2.

[56] Abbott, *The immigrant*, p 66.

[57] Costin, *Two sisters*; Leppänen, K. (2006) 'International reorganisation and traffic in women', http://www.vethist.idehist.uu.se/lychnos/articles/2006–58.pdf.

[58] Abbott, *The immigrant*, pp 277–8.

[59] Attitudes of individuals and different Settlements varied. See Lissak, R. S. (1989) *Pluralism and progressives: Hull House and the new immigrants,*

1890–1919, Chicago, IL: University of Chicago Press, chapter 3; Bilton, C. (2006) 'Knowing her place: Jane Addams, pragmatism and cultural policy', *International Journal of Cultural Policy,* 12 (2): 135–50.

[60] Bosch, M. (ed) (1990) *Politics and friendship: Letters from the International Women's Suffrage Alliance, 1902–1943,* Columbus, OH: Ohio State University Press, p xiii.

[61] Bosch, *Politics and friendship,* p 15.

[62] Rupp, L. J. (1997) *Worlds of women: The making of an international women's movement,* Princeton, NJ: Princeton University Press, p 73.

[63] Addams, J. (2005, first published 1907) *Newer ideals of peace: The moral substitutes for war,* Chester, NY: Anza Publishing, pp 17–19, 236, 145.

[64] Addams, 'Patriotism and pacifists', cited in Fischer, M. (2010) 'Keywords: what's an advocate to do with the words she's given?' *The Pluralist,* 5 (3): 32–40, p 37.

[65] Duster, A. M. (ed) (1970) *Crusade for justice: The autobiography of Ida B. Wells,* Chicago, IL: University of Chicago Press, p 244.

[66] Duster, *Crusade for justice,* pp 18–9.

[67] *The Memphis Appeal,* 25 December 1884, cited in Duster, *Crusade for justice,* p 19.

[68] 'Lynching' was named after the habit of a white frontier judge called Charles Lynch, who in the late 1700s dispensed with jury trials in favour of instant hanging.

[69] Karcher, C. L. (2006) 'Ida B. Wells and her allies against lynching', *Comparative American Studies,* 3 (2): 131–51, p 140.

[70] Black history biographies, Ida B. Wells-Barnett, http://www.cbn.com/special/blackhistory/bio_idabwells.aspx.

[71] Wells, I. B. (ed) (1893) *The reason why the colored American is not in the World's Columbian Exposition,* Chicago.

[72] Wells-Barnett, I B (1895) *A red record: Tabulated statistics and alleged causes of lynching in the United States,* Chicago, p 8.

[73] Wells-Barnett, *A red record,* p 95.

[74] Wells-Barnett, *A red record,* p 31.

[75] Holton, S. S. (2001) 'Segregation, racism and white women reformers: a transnational analysis, 1840–1912', *Women's History Review,* 10 (1): 5–25, p 12.

[76] Holton, 'Segregation, racism and white women reformers'.

[77] Zackodnik, T. (2005) 'Ida B. Wells and "American atrocities" in Britain', *Women's Studies International Forum,* 28: 259–73.

[78] *London Sun,* cited in Tucker, D. M. (1971) 'Miss Ida B. Wells and Memphis lynching', *Phylon,* 32 (2): 112–22, p 119.

[79] See Lengermann, P. M. and Niebrugge, G. (1998) *The women founders: Sociology and social theory 1830–1930,* Long Grove, IL: Waveland Press, Inc., chapter 5.

[80] Cooper, A. J. (n.d.) 'Autobiographical fragment', in Lemert, C. and Bhan, E. (eds) *The voice of Anna Julia Cooper: Including A Voice from the South and*

other important essays, Lanham, MD: Rowman & Littlefield Publishers, Inc., p 28.

81   Giles, M. S. (2006) 'Dr Anna Julia Cooper, 1858–1964: Teacher, scholar, and timeless womanist', *The Journal of Negro Education*, 75 (4): 621–34, p 623.
82   Bailey, C. (2004) 'Anna Julia Cooper: "Dedicated in the name of my slave mother to the education of colored working people"', *Hypatia*, 19 (2): 56–73.
83   Lemert and Bhan, *The voice of Anna Julia Cooper*, p 107.
84   Lemert and Bhan, *The voice of Anna Julia Cooper*, p 41.
85   Cited in Lengermann and Niebrugge, *The women founders*, p 188. This quotation from Anna Julia Cooper appears in United States passports.
86   Giles, 'Dr Anna Julia Cooper', p 621.
87   Cooper, A. J. and Koschwitz, E. (eds) (1925) *Le pèlerinage de Charlemagne: Publié avec un glossaire*, Paris: A. Lehure.
88   Alridge, D. P. (2007) 'Of Victorianism, civilizationism, and progressivism: the educational ideas of Anna Julia Cooper and W. E. B. DuBois, 1892–1940', *History of Education Quarterly*, 47 (4): 416–46, p 439.
89   Bailey, *Anna Julia Cooper*, p 60.
90   Alridge, 'Of Victorianism', p 427.
91   Schmidt, H. (1995) *The United States occupation of Haiti, 1915–1934*, New Brunswick, NJ: Rutgers University Press.
92   See Plastas, M. (2008) 'A different burden: race and the social thought of Emily Greene Balch', *Peace & Change*, 33 (4): 469–506.
93   Balch, E. G. (ed) (1927) *Occupied Haiti; being the report of a committee of six disinterested Americans representing organizations exclusively American, who, having personally studied conditions in Haiti in 1926, favor the restoration of the independence of the Negro republic*, New York: Writers' Publishing Co., pp 1–2.
94   Balch, *Occupied Haiti*, p 61.
95   Balch, *Occupied Haiti*, pp 115–16.
96   Rees, A. M. (1996) 'T. H. Marshall and the progress of citizenship', in Bulmer, M. and Rees, A. M. (eds) *Citizenship today: The contemporary relevance of T. H. Marshall*, London: UCL Press, pp 1–23.

Chapter Eight

1   Anderson, L. G. (1912) 'Forcible feeding', (letter) *British Medical Journal*, 6 July, p 48.
2   Practice in different prisons varied, but most of the 1,000 or so suffragettes who went to prison were classified as 'Second Division' rather than 'First Division' prisoners. Some were classified as 'Third Division', which meant confinement in cells and hard labour. See Geddes, J. F. (2008) 'Culpable complicity: the medical profession and the forcible feeding of suffragettes, 1909–1914', *Women's History Review*, 17 (1): 79–94.
3   http://spartacus-educational.com/Whunger.htm.
4   Lennon, J. (2009) 'The hunger artist', *Times Literary Supplement*, 22 July; Tinker, H. 'Nonviolence as a political strategy: Gandhi and Western

thinkers', *Journal of the Gandhi Peace Foundation*, New Delhi, India, http://tamilnation.co/ideology/nonviolence.htm.

[5] Purvis, J. (2009) 'Suffragette hunger strikers, 100 years on', *The Guardian*, 6 July.

[6] Adams, K. H. and Keene, M. L. (2008) *Alice Paul and the American suffrage campaign*, Urbana, IL: University of Illinois Press.

[7] Lytton, C. and Warton, J. (1914) *Prisons and prisoners: Some personal experiences*, London: William Heinemann, p 8.

[8] Lytton, *Prisons and prisoners*, p 239.

[9] Lytton, *Prisons and prisoners*, p 270. On the suffragettes' conditions in prison more generally, see Purvis, J. (1995) 'The prison experiences of the suffragettes in Edwardian Britain', *Women's History Review*, 4 (1): 103–33.

[10] Lytton, *Prisons and prisoners*, p 333.

[11] Gilman, C. P. (1911) *The man-made world; Or, our androcentric culture*, New York: Charlton Company, pp 204–5.

[12] Gordon, M. (1922) *Penal discipline*, London: George Routledge & Sons, Ltd, p 1.

[13] Gordon, *Penal discipline*, pp 29, 147.

[14] Gordon, *Penal discipline*, pp 71–2.

[15] Gordon, *Penal discipline*, p 6.

[16] Cited in Cheney, D. (2010) 'Dr Mary Louisa Gordon (1861–1941): a feminist approach in prison', *Feminist Legal Studies*, 18: 115–36, p 125.

[17] Smith, M. F. (2016) 'Virginia Woolf and "the Hermaphrodite": a feminist fan of Orlando and critic of Roger Fry', *English Studies*, 97 (3): 277–97, p 285.

[18] Hood, P. (Gordon, M.) (1907) *A jury of the virtuous*, London: Hurst & Blackett.

[19] Smith, 'Virginia Woolf', p 279.

[20] Gordon, M. (1936) *Chase of the wild goose: The story of Lady Eleanor Butler and Miss Sarah Ponsonby, known as the Ladies of Llangollen*, London: Hogarth Press. On Gordon's relationships with the Jungs, see Smith, 'Virginia Woolf'. A few of Mary Gordon's letters to and from Jung survive in the ETH Zurich University Archives. These are dated between 1928 and 1939 and refer to some crisis in Gordon's life and also to her experiences with mediums in which Jung was interested.

[21] Fitzpatrick, E. (1990) *Endless crusade: Women social scientists and progressive reform*, New York: Oxford University Press, p 56.

[22] On criminological work at Hull-House see Moyer, I. L. (2003) 'Jane Addams: pioneer in criminology', *Women & Criminal Justice*, 14 (2–3): 1–14.

[23] Fitzpatrick, *Endless crusade*, p 92.

[24] Freedman, E. B. (1981) *Their sisters' keepers: Women and prison reform in America, 1830–1930*, Ann Arbor, MI: The University of Michigan Press, p 134.

[25] Davis, K. B. (1913) 'A plan of rational treatment for women offenders', *Journal of the American Institute of Criminal Law and Criminology*, 4 (3): 402–8.

[26] McCarthy, T. C. (1997) *New York City's Suffragist Commissioner: Correction's Katharine Bement Davis*, New York: Department of Correction, http://www.

correctionhistory.org/html/chronicl/kbd/kbdfrpdf.html, p 41. On Davis's criminological work see Deegan, M. J. (2003) 'Katharine Bement Davis (1860–1935): her theory and praxis of feminist pragmatism in criminology', *Women & Criminal Justice*, 14 (2/3): 15–40.

[27] Charles Mansell Moullin was Vice-president of the Men's League for Women's Suffrage, a group of 30 or so men who pledged to use their electoral power to help enfranchise women.

[28] Geddes, J. F. (2009) 'The doctors' dilemma: medical women and the British suffrage movement', *Women's History Review*, 18 (2): 203–18.

[29] Savill, A., Mansell Moullin, C. and Horsley, V. (1912) 'Preliminary report on the forcible feeding of suffrage prisoners', *British Medical Journal*, 31 August, pp 505–8.

[30] Savill, A. (1917) 'X-ray appearances in gas gangrene', *Proceedings of the Royal Society of Medicine*, 10: 4–16, p 4.

[31] Geddes, J. F. (2008) 'Louisa Garrett Anderson (1873–1943), surgeon and suffragette', *Journal of Medical Biography*, 16: 205–14, p 212.

[32] Murray, F. (1920) *Women as army surgeons*, London: Hodder and Stoughton, p 14.

[33] Murray, *Women as army surgeons*, pp 137, 145.

[34] Murray, *Women as army surgeons*, p 100.

[35] Lawrence, M. (1971) *Shadow of swords: A biography of Elsie Inglis*, London: Michael Joseph, p 18.

[36] Geddes, J. F. (2006) 'The women's hospital corps: forgotten surgeons of the First World War', *Journal of Medical Biography*, 14: 109–17, p 110.

[37] Hamilton, C. (1935) *Life errant*, London: J. M. Dent & Sons Ltd.

[38] Martindale, L. (1951) *A woman surgeon*, London: Victor Gollancz, p 167.

[39] Savill, A. (1916) 'Some notes on the X-ray department of the Scottish Women's Hospital, Royaumont, France', *Archives of Radiology and Electrotherapy*, 20 (12): 401–10, p 402.

[40] Weiner, M.-F. (n.d.) 'Frances Ivens (1870–1944): the first woman consultant in Liverpool', http://www.evolve360.co.uk/Data/10/PageLMHS/Bulletin26/weiner.pdf, p 70; Ivens, M. H. (1917) 'The part played by British medical women in the war', *British Medical Journal*, 18 August: 203–8; Weiner, M.-F. (2014) 'The Scottish Women's Hospital at Royaumont, France 1914–1919', *The Journal of the Royal College of Physicians of Edinburgh*, 44: 328–36, p 329.

[41] Brown, K. (2008) *Fighting fit: Health, medicine and war in the twentieth century*, Stroud: History Press, p 73.

[42] Weiner, 'The Scottish Women's Hospital', p 329.

[43] Cited in Inglis, L. (2014) 'The art of medicine: Elsie Inglis, the suffragette physician', *The Lancet*, 384: 1664–5, p 1665. On the official war history's neglect of Inglis, see Weiner, 'The Scottish Women's Hospital', p 333.

[44] See Weiner, 'The Scottish Women's Hospital.' Their work was appreciated much more by other countries: Ivens was awarded various honours by the French, including the highest possible, the Croix de la Légion d'Honneur; six other Royaumont doctors got the Croix de Guerre. Inglis, who went

on to do sterling work in Serbia and Russia, was the first woman to be awarded the Order of the White Eagle (V class) by Crown Prince Alexander of Serbia. Like Emily Hobhouse in South Africa, her Serbian memorials commemorate a woman ignominiously forgotten by her native country.

[45] Murray, *Women as army surgeons*, p 123.

[46] On the Endell Street Hospital's work, see Geddes, J. F. (2007) 'Deeds *and* words in the suffrage military hospital in Endell Street', *Medical History*, 51 (1): 79–98; Leneman, L. (1994) 'Medical women at war, 1914–1918', *Medical History*, 38 (2): 160–77.

[47] Anderson, L. G. and Chambers, H. (1917) 'The treatment of septic wounds with bismuth-idoform-paraffin paste', *The Lancet*, 189 (4879): 331–3.

[48] Sharp, E. (2009, first published 1933) *Unfinished adventure: Selected reminiscences from an Englishwoman's life*, London: Faber and Faber Ltd, p 160.

[49] Sheard, H. (2011) '"They will both go to heaven and have crowns and golden harps": Dr Vera Scantlebury Brown and female leadership in a First World War military hospital', in Davis, F., Musgrove, N. and Smart, J. (eds) *Founders, firsts and feminists: Women leaders in twentieth century Australia*, University of Melbourne: eScholarship Research Centre, pp 90–104.

[50] Bryder, L. (2003) *A voice for mothers: The Plunket Society and infant welfare, 1907–2000*, Auckland, NZ: Auckland University Press, p 44, p 74.

[51] Delamont, S. (2004) 'Martindale, Louisa (1872–1966)', *Oxford Dictionary of National Biography*, Oxford: Oxford University Press.

[52] Loudon, I. (1992) 'Some international features of maternal mortality, 1880–1950', in Fildes, V., Marks, I. and Marland, H. (eds) *Women and children first: International maternal and infant welfare 1870–1945*, London: Routledge, pp 5–28, p 11.

[53] Pankhurst, E. S. (1930) *Save the mothers*, London: Alfred A. Knopf, pp 15, 46.

[54] Campbell, J. (1917) *The Carnegie United Kingdom Trust Report on the physical welfare of mothers and children in England and Wales*, London: Carnegie United Kingdom Trust; Campbell, J. (1924) *Maternal mortality*, London: Ministry of Health Reports on Public Health and Medical Subjects no. 25; Campbell, J. (1927) *The protection of motherhood*, London: Ministry of Health Reports on Public Health and Medical Subjects no 48.

[55] See Jacobs, A. (1996, first published in Dutch 1924) *Memories: My life as an international leader in health, suffrage and peace*, New York: The Feminist Press.

[56] Jacobs, A. (1899) *De vrouw, haar bouw en haar inwendige organen (The woman, her construction and her internal organs)*, Deventer: Kluwer.

[57] Jacobs, *Memories*, p 49.

[58] Jacobs, *Memories*, p 120.

[59] Jacobs, *Memories*, p 101.

[60] Van Voris, J. (1987) *Carrie Chapman Catt: A public life*, New York: The Feminist Press, p 105.

[61] Turner, J. and Johnston, H. (2015) 'Female prisoners, aftercare and release: residential provision and support in late nineteenth-century England', *British Journal of Community Justice*, 13 (3): 35–50.

62 Elston, M. A. (2001) '"Run by women, (mainly) for women": medical women's hospitals in Britain, 1866–1948', *Clio Medica*, 61: 73–107.

63 Barass, P. (1950) *Fifty years in midwifery: The story of Annie McCall M.D. written and arranged by Patricia Barass*, London: Health for All Publishing Co, p 107.

64 Barass, *Fifty years in midwifery*, p 44.

65 Barass, *Fifty years in midwifery*, p 75.

66 'Entry of students 1874 to 1927', Records of Clapham Maternity Hospital, London Metropolitan Archives H72/SM/C/01/03/001.

67 This unfortunately includes my own (*The captured womb: A history of the medical care of pregnant women* (1984, Oxford: Basil Blackwell)).

68 Minute book, Records of Clapham Maternity Hospital, London Metropolitan Archives H24/CM/A/01/001; Loudon, I. (1986) 'Obstetric care, social class, and maternal mortality', *British Medical Journal*, 293: 606–8.

69 Minute book, Records of Clapham Maternity Hospital, London Metropolitan Archives H24/CM/A/01/001.

70 Stockham, A. B. (1889) *Tokology: A book for every women*, Chicago, IL: Alice B. Stockham & Co; Gaskin, I. M. (2011) *Birth matters: A midwife's manifesta*, London: Pinter & Martin. On the Stockham–Tolstoy connection, see Edwards, R. (1993) 'Tolstoy and Alice B. Stockham: the influence of "Tokology" on *The Kreutzer Sonata*', *Tolstoy Studies Journal*, 6: 87–104.

71 Wald, L. (1915) *The house on Henry Street*, New York: Henry Holt and Company, p 4.

72 Wald, *The house on Henry Street*, p 7.

73 Wald, *The house on Henry Street*, p 44.

74 Buhler-Wilkerson, K. (1993) 'Bringing care to the people: Lillian Wald's legacy to public health nursing', *American Journal of Public Health*, 83 (12): 1778–86.

75 Wald, *The house on Henry Street*, p 38.

76 Wald, *The house on Henry Street*, p 52.

77 Feld, M. N. (2008) *Lillian Wald: A biography*, Chapel Hill, NC: University of North Carolina Press; Cook, B. W. (1979) 'Female support networks and political activism: Lillian Wald, Crystal Eastman and Emma Goldman', in Cott, N. and Pleck, E. (eds) *A heritage of her own*, New York: Simon & Schuster, pp 412–44.

78 Cross, C. (1989) 'Introduction', in Cross, C. (ed) *Lillian D. Wald: Progressive activist*, New York: The Feminist Press, pp 1–15.

79 Cross, 'Introduction', p 10.

80 Feld, *Lillian Wald*, p 90.

81 Feld, *Lillian Wald*, pp 142–53.

82 Wald, L. (1909) 'Address to the House Committee hearing on establishing a Federal Children's Bureau', reprinted in Cross, *Lillian D. Wald*, pp 67–71, p 67.

83 Wald, 'Address to the House Committee', pp 68–9.

84 Addams, J. (2004, first published 1935) *My friend, Julia Lathrop*, Urbana and Chicago, IL: University of Illinois Press.

[85] Parker, J. K. and Carpenter, E. M. (1981) 'Julia Lathrop and the Children's Bureau: the emergence of an institution', *Social Service Review*, 55 (1): 60–77.

[86] Abbott, G. (1915) 'The midwife in Chicago', *American Journal of Sociology*, 20 (5): 684–99. Assuming that the bags of all the 182 midwives in the study were examined, this means that 107 were clean.

[87] Westwood, L. (2001) 'A quiet revolution in Brighton: Dr Helen Boyle's pioneering approach to mental health care, 1899–1939', *Social History of Medicine*, 14 (3): 439–57.

[88] Boyle, A. H. (1909) 'Account of an attempt at the early treatment of mental and nervous cases (with special reference to the poor)', *The British Journal of Psychiatry*, 55 (231): 683–92, p 684. Boyle's facility preceded the Maudsley Hospital and the Tavistock Clinic by almost 20 years.

[89] Boyle, 'Account of an attempt', p 684.

[90] Boyle, 'Account of an attempt', p 685; Boyle, A. H. (1914) 'Some observations on early nervous and mental cases, with suggestions as to possible improvement in our methods of dealing with them', *The British Journal of Psychiatry*, 60 (250): 381–98, p 382.

[91] Boyle, 'Some observations', p 384.

[92] Boyle, A. H. (1905) 'Some points in the early treatment of mental and nervous cases (with special reference to the poor)', *The British Journal of Psychiatry*, 51 (215): 676–81, p 680.

[93] Westwood, 'A quiet revolution', p 443.

[94] Boyle, 'Account of an attempt', pp 687–8.

[95] Boyle, 'Account of an attempt', p 688.

[96] *Annual Report for 1917*, Lady Chichester Hospital, The Keep, Brighton 11B/18/1/63/1/1A.

[97] http://www.ourstory.co.uk/newsletters/winter02/illusion.htm.

[98] Martindale, *A woman surgeon*, p 158.

[99] http://radicaltyneside.org/events/dr-ethel-williams.

[100] Murdoch, M. (1915) 'The part to be taken by women in the reconstruction of public health after the war', reprinted in Malleson, H. (1919) *A woman doctor: Mary Murdoch of Hull*, London: Sidgwick and Jackson, Ltd, pp 222–31.

[101] Cited in Martindale, *A woman surgeon*, p 159.

[102] Cohen, S. L. (2004) 'Walker, Jane Harriett (1859–1938)', *Oxford Dictionary of National Biography*, Oxford: Oxford University Press.

[103] Fraser, A. M. (1911) 'Tuberculin dispensaries', *British Journal of Tuberculosis*, 5 (2): 124–6, p 125.

[104] Holton, S. S. (1998) 'Feminism, history and movements of the soul: Christian Science in the life of Alice Clark (1874–1934)', *Australian Feminist Studies*, 13 (28): 281–94.

[105] Oldfield, S. (2004) 'Pye, Edith Mary (1876–1965)', *Oxford Dictionary of National Biography*, Oxford: Oxford University Press.

[106] See Hall, L. A. (1994) 'Chloe, Olivia, Isabel, Letitia, Harriette, Honor, and many more: women in medical and biomedical science 1914–1945', in Oldfield, S. (ed) *This working-day world*, London: Taylor & Francis, pp 192–202.

[107] Brown, V. (2006) *Women's hospitals in Brighton and Hove*, East Sussex: The Hastings Press, p vii.

[108] Cited in Boyd, N. (2014) *Animal rights and public wrongs: A biography of Lizzy Lind-af-Hageby*, US: CreateSpace, p 13.

[109] http://www.dyingtolearn.org/animalUse.html; http://www.peta.org.uk/issues/animals-not-experiment-on/education-training/.

[110] Lind-af-Hageby, L. and Schartau, L. K. (1913, first published 1903) *The shambles of science: Extracts from the diary of two students of physiology*, London: The Animal Defence & Anti-vivisection Society, p 77.

[111] Extract from the original (withdrawn) edition of *The shambles of science*, cited in Boyd, *Animal rights and public wrongs*, p 23.

[112] Mason, P. (1997) *The brown dog affair: The story of a monument that divided a nation*, London: Two Sevens Publishing, pp 17–18.

[113] Cited in Leneman, L. (1997) 'The awakened instinct: vegetarianism and the women's suffrage movement in Britain', *Women's History Review*, 6 (2): 271–87, p 286.

[114] Lansbury, C. (1985) *The old brown dog: Women, workers, and vivisection in Edwardian England*, Madison, WI: University of Wisconsin Press.

[115] Boyd, *Animal rights and public wrongs*, pp 96–7.

[116] Boyd, *Animal rights and public wrongs*, pp 34–5.

[117] Lytton and Warton, *Prisons and prisoners*, pp 12–13.

Chapter Nine

[1] Oliver, T. (ed) (2004, first published 1902 as *Dangerous trades: The historical, social and legal aspects of industrial occupations as affecting health*) *Dangerous trades: History of health and safety at work*, Bristol: Thoemmes Continuum; Squire, R. E., 'Rabbit down', *Dangerous trades: History of health and safety at work*, pp 724–7, p 724; Deane, L. A. R., 'Laundry workers', in Oliver, T. (ed) *Dangerous trades: History of health and safety at work*, Bristol: Thoemmes Continuum, pp 663–72, p 668.

[2] See Harrison, B. (1996) *Not only the 'dangerous trades': Women's work and health in Britain, 1880–1914*, Abingdon: Taylor & Francis.

[3] MacKenzie, D. A. (1977) 'Arthur Black: a forgotten pioneer of mathematical statistics', *Biometrika*, 64 (3): 613–16. Arthur's daughter, who was adopted by Clementina, was Gertrude Speedwell Massingham, a Labour candidate in the 1929 and 1931 elections.

[4] 'Miss Clementina Black: death of social worker and novelist', *Manchester Guardian*, 20 December 1922, p 14.

[5] Black, C. (1922) 'Things I have seen by Clementina Black', *Manchester Guardian*, 20 December, p 14.

[6] Black, C. (1876) 'The troubles of an automaton', *New Quarterly Magazine*, 6: 463–87.

[7] A. Levy to V. Lee, November 1886, cited in Vadillo, A. P. (2005) *Women poets and urban aestheticism*, Houndmills, Basingstoke: Palgrave Macmillan, p 52.

[8] Livesey, R. (2007) 'Socialism in Bloomsbury: Virginia Woolf and the political aesthetics of the 1880s', *The Yearbook of English Studies*, 37 (1): 126–44, p 132.

[9] Auchmuty, R. (1975) 'Spinsters and trade unions in Victorian Britain', *Labour History*, 29: 109–22, p 112.

[10] Reeves, M. P. (1913) *Round about a pound a week*, London: G. Bell and Sons Ltd; Davies, M. L. (1915) *Maternity: Letters from working-women*, London: G. Bell and Sons, Ltd.

[11] Oakeshott, G. M. (1903) 'Artificial flower-making: an account of the trade, and a plea for municipal training', *The Economic Journal*, 13 (49): 123–31.

[12] Robson, J. (2016) *Radical reformers and respectable rebels*, Houndmills, Basingstoke: Palgrave Macmillan.

[13] Black, C. (1907) *Sweated industry and the minimum wage*, London: Duckworth.

[14] Gardiner, A. G. (1907) 'Introduction', in Black, C., *Sweated industry*, pp ix–x.

[15] Anon. (1915) 'Married women's work', *British Medical Journal*, 2866: 828–9, p 829.

[16] Black, C. (1915) 'Introduction', in Black, C. (ed) *Married women's work*, London: G. Bell and Sons Ltd, pp 1–15, p 11.

[17] Black, C. (1892) 'Match-box making at home', *The English Illustrated Magazine*, 104: 625–9, p 625.

[18] Dimand, R. W., Dimand, M. A. and Forget, E. L. (eds) *A biographical dictionary of women economists*, Cheltenham: Edward Elgar, p 46.

[19] Besant, A. (1888) 'White slavery in London', *The Link*, no 21, 23 June; see Satre, L. J. (1982) 'After the match girls' strike: Bryant and May in the 1890s', *Victorian Studies*, 26 (1): 7–31.

[20] Meyer, A. L. and Black, C. (1909) *Makers of our clothes*, London: Duckworth and Co., pp 3, 2.

[21] Meyer and Black, *Makers of our clothes*, p 10.

[22] Meyer and Black, *Makers of our clothes*, p 8.

[23] Murphy, W. A. W. (2008) 'An analytical framework for studying the politics of consumption: the case of the National Consumers' League', *Sociology*, Paper 15, http://collected.jcu.edu/soc-facpub/15.

[24] Black, C. (1906) 'Introduction to tabulated cases', in Women's Industrial Council, *Home industries of women in London: Interim report of an inquiry by the Investigation Committee of the Women's Industrial Council*, London: The Women's Industrial Council, pp 44–50, p 44.

[25] See Strasser, S., McGovern, C. and Judt, M. (1998) *Getting and spending: European and American consumer societies in the twentieth century*, Cambridge: Cambridge University Press.

[26] Nathan, M. (1926) *The story of an epoch-making movement*, London: William Heinemann, p 23.

[27] Nathan, *The story of an epoch-making movement*, p 39.

[28] Kelley, F. (1899) 'Aims and principles of the Consumers' League', *American Journal of Sociology*, 5 (3): 289–304, pp 289–90.

29 Haydn, J. (2014) 'Consumer citizenship and cross-class activism: the case of the National Consumers' League, 1899–1918', *Sociological Forum*, 29 (3): 628–49.

30 Kelley, 'Aims and principles', pp 293–4.

31 The Consumers' League of New York (1922) 'Behind the scenes in a hotel', reprinted in Rothman, D. J. and Rothman, S. M. (eds) (1987) *Women and children first*, New York and London: Garland Publishing Inc.

32 Clark, S. A. and Wyatt, E. F. (1911) *Making both ends meet: The income and outlay of New York working girls*, New York: Macmillan Co., 1911, pp 66, 76.

33 MacLean, A. M. (1899) 'Two weeks in department stores', *American Journal of Sociology*, 4 (6): 721–44, p 734.

34 Chatriot, A., Chessel, M-E. and Hilton, M. (eds) (2006) *The expert consumer: Associations and professionals in consumer society*, Aldershot: Ashgate; see especially Chessel, M-E., 'Consumers' leagues in France: a transatlantic perspective', pp 53–69.

35 Nathan, *The story of an epoch-making movement*, p 89.

36 https://en.wikipedia.org/wiki/Th%C3%A9r%C3%A8se_Bentzon.

37 Nathan, *The story of an epoch-making movement*, p 90.

38 Glage, L. (1981) *Clementina Black: A study in social history and literature*, Heidelberg: Carl Winter – Universitätsverlag, p 67.

39 Black, C. (1918) *A new way of housekeeping*, London: W. Collins Sons & Co Ltd, pp 30–5.

40 Black, *A new way of housekeeping*, p 65.

41 Stetson (Gilman) C. P. (1912) *What Diantha did*, London: T. Fisher Unwin.

42 Black, C. (1894) *The agitator*, London: Bliss, Sands & Co.

43 Sutherland, J. (2011) *Lives of the novelists: A history of fiction in 294 lives*, London: Profile, p 244.

44 Holmes, R. (2014) *Eleanor Marx*, London: Bloomsbury, p 131.

45 'C. T.' (1948) 'C. E. Collet: obituary', *Journal of the Royal Statistical Society*, 111 (3): 252–4, p 252.

46 Collet, C. E. (1936) 'Herbert Somerton Foxwell', *The Economic Journal*, 46 (184): 589–619, p 618.

47 Collet, C. E. (1899) *Report by Miss Collet on the money wages of indoor domestic servants*, London: HMSO.

48 Collet, C. E. 'Diary of a young assistant mistress 1878–1885', typescript, Collet Archives, Modern Records Centre, University of Warwick, MSS. 29/8/2/1–81, p 3.

49 Miller, J. (2003) *Relations*, London: Vintage Books, pp 105, 112.

50 Groenewegen, P. D. (1994) 'A neglected daughter of Adam Smith: Clara Elizabeth Collet (1860–1948)', in Groenewegen, P. D. (ed) *Feminism and political economy in Victorian England*, Aldershot: Edward Elgar, pp 147–73. Collet's destruction of many letters and papers relating to her interaction with Gissing prevents us from knowing much about the nature of the Collet–Gissing relationship. Nonetheless, it was Collet whom Gissing entrusted with his literary estate, and with the care of his sons, duties which she performed very conscientiously for the 45 years during which she

survived his early death. See Mcdonald, D. (2004) *Clara Collet 1860–1948: An educated working woman*, Abingdon: Woburn Press.

51 Like Clementina Black, Clara Collet tried writing fiction to make money, but she wasn't so successful at it. One melodramatic short story called 'Over the way' was published under the name Clover King in 1891; another, called 'Undercurrents', was not published in Collet's lifetime (it is available in Postmus, B. (1995) 'Clara Collet's "Clairvoyance"', *The Gissing Journal*, 31 (4): 1–32).

52 Abbott, E. (1907) 'Employment of women in industries: cigar-making: its history and present tendencies', *Journal of Political Economy*, 15 (1): 1–25; Abbott, E. (1909) 'The manufacture of boots and shoes', *American Journal of Sociology*, 15 (3): 335–60.

53 Collet Archives, Modern Records Centre, University of Warwick, MSS.29/8/1/1–146.

54 Collet Archives, The Women's Library, British Library of Political and Economic Science, E. Abbott to C. Collet, 14 November 1908, 7CCF 13.9.

55 Booth, C. (ed) (1889–91) *Life and labour of the people in London*, London: Williams and Norgate.

56 Collet, C. E. (1889) 'Women's work', in Booth, C. *Life and labour*, First Series, Poverty IV, London: Macmillan, pp 256–327.

57 Collet, C. E. (1898) 'The collection and utilisation of official statistics bearing on the extent and effects of the industrial employment of women', *Journal of the Royal Statistical Society*, 61 (2): 219–70, p 232.

58 Marshall, M. P. (1902) 'Review of educated working women by Clara Collet', *The Economic Journal*, 12 (46): 252–7, p 252.

59 Collet, C. E. (1911) *Women in industry*, London: Women's Printing Society.

60 Abram, A. (1909) *Social England in the fifteenth century*, London: George Routledge and Sons, Ltd; Eckenstein, L. (1896) *Women under monasticism*, Cambridge: Cambridge University Press.

61 Collet, C. E. (1902) 'Mrs. Stetson's economic ideal', in Collet, C. E. (1902) *Educated working women*, London: P. S. King & Son, p 121, p 132.

62 Howsam, L. (1989) 'Sound-minded women: Eliza Orme and the study and practice of law in late-Victorian England', *Atlantis*, 15 (1): 44–55, p 49.

63 Orme, E. (1874) 'Sound-minded women', *The Examiner*, 1 August, pp 820–1.

64 Ravenhill, A. (1951) *The memoirs of an educational pioneer*, Toronto and Vancouver: J. M. Dent and Sons Ltd, pp 78–9.

65 Royal Commission on Labour (1893) *The employment of women. Reports by Miss Orme, Miss Collet, M.A., Miss Abraham and Miss Irwin on the conditions of work in various industries in England, Wales, Scotland and Ireland*, London: Eyre & Spottiswoode; Foley, C. A. (1894) Review of *The employment of women*, *The Economic Journal*, 4 (13): 185–91, p 186.

66 Martindale, H. (1938) *Women servants of the state 1870–1938: A history of women in the civil service*, London: George Allen & Unwin Ltd, p 52.

67 Mcfeely, M. D. (1988) *Lady inspectors: The campaign for a better workplace, 1893–1921*, New York and Oxford: Basil Blackwell, p 42.

68 Martindale, H. (1944) *From one generation to another, 1839–1945: A book of memoirs*, London: George Allen & Unwin Ltd.

69 Lucy Deane Streatfeild Archives, Business diary 1893 September–December, entries for 27 October and 5 November, 69/1/1, The Women's Library, British Library of Political and Economic Science.

70 Wheeldon, C. (2015) '"Pioneers in the corridors of power": Women civil servants at the Board of Trade and the Factory Inspectorate, 1893–1919', PhD thesis, Goldsmiths' College, University of London, p 157.

71 McFeely, *Lady inspectors*, p 82.

72 Squire, R. E. (1927) *Thirty years in the public service*, London: Nisbet & Co Ltd, p 67.

73 McFeely, *Lady inspectors*, p 83.

74 McFeely, *Lady inspectors*, p 51.

75 Squire, *Thirty years*, p 54.

76 http://archiveshub.ac.uk/data/gb1924-matchmakersunion.

77 Squire, *Thirty years*, p 56.

78 Hutchins, B. L. and Harrison, A. (1911) *A history of factory legislation*, London: P. S. King & Son, p 204.

79 Squire, *Thirty years*, p 150.

80 Deane, 'Laundry workers', p 664, 669.

81 Spurgeon, A. (2012) 'The contribution of the Women's Factory Inspectorate (1893–1921) to improvements in women's occupational health and safety', M Phil thesis, University of Worcester, p 72.

82 Spurgeon, 'The contribution of the Women's Factory Inspectorate', p 76.

83 Spurgeon, 'The contribution of the Women's Factory Inspectorate', p 42.

84 Anon. (1898) 'Lead poisoning in the Potteries', *British Medical Journal*, 23 July: 245–6.

85 Anderson, A. M. (1922) *Women in the factory*, London: John Murray, p 107.

86 Spurgeon, 'The contribution of the Women's Factory Inspectorate', p 62.

87 Wheeldon, *Pioneers*, p 145.

88 Holdsworth, C. (1997) 'Women's work and family health: evidence from the Staffordshire Potteries, 1890–1920', *Continuity and Change*, 12 (1): 103–28.

89 Wheeldon, *Pioneers*, pp 237–8.

90 Anderson, *Women in the factory*, p 139.

91 Squire, *Thirty years*, p 26.

92 Spurgeon, *The contribution of the Women's Factory Inspectorate*, p 86.

93 See, for example, Jones, H. (1988) 'Women health workers: the case of the first Women Factory Inspectors in Britain', *Society for the Social History of Medicine*, 1 (2): 165–81; Long, V. (2011) 'Industrial homes, domestic factories: the convergence of public and private space in interwar Britain', *Journal of British Studies*, 50 (2): 434–64; see also the discussion in Harrison, *Not only the 'dangerous trades'*.

94 Buchert, L. (2004) 'Kerstin Hesselgren (1872–1964)', *Prospects: Quarterly Review of Comparative Education*, 34 (1): 127–36, p 127.

95 See Wisselgren, P. (2016) 'Women as public intellectuals: Kerstin Hesselgren and Alva Myrdal', in Fleck, C., Hess, A. and Lyon, E. S. (eds) *Intellectuals and*

their publics: Perspectives from the social sciences, London: Routledge, pp 225–41 and p 229.

96 Cited in Buchert, 'Kerstin Hesselgren', p 133.

97 Buchert, 'Kerstin Hesselgren', p 133.

98 Eastman, C. (1910) *Work-accidents and the law*, The Pittsburgh Survey, New York: Charities Publications Committee, p 226.

99 Anderson, M. (1996) 'Does the evidence support the argument? Margaret Byington's cost of living survey of Homestead', in Greenwald, M. W. and Anderson, M. (eds) *Pittsburgh surveyed: Social science and social reform in the early twentieth century*, Pittsburgh, PA: University of Pittsburgh Press, pp 106–23; Byington, M. F. (1910) *The homestead: The households of a mill town*, New York: Charities Publication Committee.

100 See Sass, R. (1999) 'The unwritten story of women's role in the birth of occupational health and safety legislation', *International Journal of Health Services*, 29 (91): 109–45.

101 Hamilton, A. (1943) *Exploring the dangerous trades: The autobiography of Alice Hamilton, M.D.*, Boston, MA: Little, Brown and Company, p 114.

102 Hamilton, *Exploring the dangerous trades*, p 32, p 46.

103 Hamilton, *Exploring the dangerous trades*, p 101.

104 Hamilton, *Exploring the dangerous trades*, pp 99–100.

105 Sicherman, *Alice Hamilton*, p 2.

106 Sicherman, *Alice Hamilton*, p 169.

107 Hamilton, *Exploring the dangerous trades*, p 124.

108 Hamilton, *Exploring the dangerous trades*, p 7.

109 Hamilton, *Exploring the dangerous trades*, p 125.

110 Sicherman, *Alice Hamilton*, p 166.

111 Hamilton, *Exploring the dangerous trades*, p 158.

112 Sicherman, *Alice Hamilton*, p 201, p 203.

113 Hamilton, *Exploring the dangerous trades*, p 287.

114 Martindale, *From one generation to another*, pp 34–5.

115 Bondfield, M. (1948) *A life's work*, London: Hutchinson & Co. Ltd.

116 Bondfield, M. G. (1904) 'The effects on health of women's employment in shops', *Journal of the Royal Sanitary Institute*, 25 (3): 738–45, p 741.

117 Whitelaw, L. (1990) *The life and rebellious times of Cicely Hamilton*, London: The Women's Press, p 39.

118 Bondfield, *A life's work*, p 110.

119 Bondfield, *A life's work*, p 120.

120 Williamson, P. (2004) 'Bondfield, Margaret Grace (1873–1953)', *Oxford Dictionary of National Biography*, Oxford: Oxford University Press.

121 Bondfield, *A life's work*, p 51.

122 Bondfield, *A life's work*, p 55. Bondfield refers to 'Fraulein Soloman', whom I take to be Alice Salomon.

123 Hamilton, M. A. (1924) *Margaret Bondfield*, London: Leonard Parsons, p 12.

124 Bondfield, *A life's work*, p 47.

125 Bondfield, *A life's work*, p 339.

Chapter Ten

[1] Hamilton, C. (1909) *Marriage as a trade*, New York: Moffat, Yard & Company, p 53, 65.

[2] Cited in Allen, J. A. (2009) *The feminism of Charlotte Perkins Gilman: Sexualities, histories, progressivism*, Chicago, IL: University of Chicago Press, p 136.

[3] Gilman, C. P. (1998, first published 1898) *Women and economics*, Mineola, NY: Dover Publications, Inc., pp 90, 132.

[4] See Schreiner, O. (1911) *Woman and labour*, London: T. Fisher Unwin, 'Introduction', pp 11–30.

[5] Hamilton, C. (1935) *Life errant*, London: J. M. Dent & Sons Ltd, p 32.

[6] Hamilton, C. M. (1910) *A pageant of great women*, London: The Suffrage Shop.

[7] See Cameron, R. (2009) 'From *Great Women* to *Top Girls*: pageants of sisterhood in British feminist theater', *Comparative Drama*, 43 (2): 143–66, p 145.

[8] Cockin, K. (2005) 'Cicely Hamilton's warriors: dramatic reinventions of militancy in the British women's suffrage movement', *Women's History Review*, 14 (3–4): 527–42, pp 532–4.

[9] DuBois, E. C. (1997) *Harriot Stanton Blatch and the winning of woman suffrage*, New York and London: Yale University Press, pp 48, 65.

[10] Macmillan, C. (1931) *The nationality of married women*, London: Nationality of Married Women Pass the Bill Committee, p 7.

[11] Macmillan, *The nationality of married women*, p 19.

[12] Breckinridge, S. B. (1931) *Marriage and the civic rights of women: Separate domicile and independent citizenship*, Chicago, IL: University of Chicago Press.

[13] Crawford, E. (2001) *The women's suffrage movement: A reference guide 1866–1928*, London and New York: Routledge, p 651.

[14] Hamilton, *Life errant*, p 92.

[15] Sharp, E. (1933) *Unfinished adventure: Selected reminiscences from an Englishwoman's life*, London: Faber & Faber, pp 164–7.

[16] Martin, A. (1913) *The mother and social reform*, London: National Union of Women's Suffrage Societies, p 21.

[17] See Koven, S. (2004) *Slumming: Sexual and social politics in Victorian London*, Princeton, NJ and Oxford: Princeton University Press, p 201.

[18] Whitelaw, L. (1990) *The life and rebellious times of Cicely Hamilton*, London: The Women's Press, p 212; Crawford, *The women's suffrage movement*, p 266.

[19] Linda Gordon's research into welfare reform activists in the US between 1890 and 1935 found that a third of the women were in long-term couple relationships with other women; Gordon, L. (1992) 'Social insurance and public assistance: the influence of gender in welfare thought in the United States, 1890–1935', *The American Historical Review*, 97 (1): 19–54.

[20] Hamilton, *Marriage as a trade*, pp 221–2.

[21] The classic histories are Faderman, L. (1981) *Surpassing the love of men: Romantic friendship and love between women from the Renaissance to the present*, New York: Morrow; Faderman, L. (1991) *Odd girls and twilight lovers: A history*

of lesbian love in twentieth century America, New York: Columbia University Press.

22 Scudder, V. D. (1937) *On journey*, London: J. M. Dent and Sons, p 4.

23 See Franzen, T. (1996) *Spinsters and lesbians: Independent womanhood in the United States*, New York and London: New York University Press, p 108; see also Vicinus, M. (1985) *Independent women: Work and community for single women: 1850–1920*, London: Virago.

24 Fredriksen-Goldsen, K. I., Lindhorst, T., Kemp, S. P. and Walters, K. L. (2009) '"My ever dear": social work's "lesbian" foremothers – a call for scholarship', *Affilia: Journal of Women and Social Work*, 24 (3): 325–36, p 329.

25 Fredriksen-Golden et al., '"My ever dear"'; on Addams and Rozet Smith see Elshtain, J. B. (2002) *Jane Addams and the dream of American democracy: A life*, New York: Basic Books; Polikoff, B. G. (1999) *With one bold act: The story of Jane Addams*, Chicago, IL: Boswell Books.

26 A. Jacobs to J. Addams, 12 June 1923, cited in Rupp, L. J. (1997) *Worlds of women: The making of an international women's movement*, Princeton, NJ: Princeton University Press, p 98.

27 On Edith Abbott and Sophonisba Breckinridge, see Costin, L. B. (1983) *Two sisters for social justice: A biography of Grace and Edith Abbott*, Urbana and Chicago, IL: University of Illinois Press; see also Fitzpatrick, E. (1990) *Endless crusade: Women social scientists and progressive reform*, New York: Oxford University Press. On Julia Lathrop and Florence Kelley, see Muncy, R. (1991) *Creating a female dominion in American reform 1890–1935*, New York: Oxford University Press.

28 Rupp, *Worlds of women*, p 99.

29 http://sueyounghistories.com/archives/2008/02/19/2162/.

30 Fredriksen-Golden et al., '"My ever dear"', p 331.

31 Schwartz, J., Peiss, K. and Simmons, C. (1989) '"We were a band of willful women": the Heterodoxy Club of Greenwich Village', in Peiss, K. and Simmons, C. (eds) *Passion and power: Sexuality in history*, Philadelphia, PA: Temple University Press, pp 118–37, 136.

32 Waitt, A. (1988) 'Katherine Anthony: feminist biographer with the "warmth of an advocate"', *Frontiers: A Journal of Women's Studies*, 10 (1): 72–7, 73.

33 Dedication in Scudder, *On journey*.

34 Bates, K. L. (1922) *Yellow clover; a book of remembrance*, New York: E. P. Dutton & Company; see Leopold, E. (2006) '"My soul is among lions": Katharine Lee Bates' account of the illness and death of Katharine Coman', *Legacy*, 23 (1): 60–73.

35 Palmieri, P. A. (1983) '"Here was fellowship": a social portrait of academic women at Wellesley College, 1895–1920', *History of Education Quarterly*, 23 (2): 195–214, p 206.

36 Allen, J. M. (2013) *Passionate commitments: The lives of Anna Rochester and Grace Hutchins*, Albany, NY: State University of New York Press, p 69.

37 Feld, M. N. (2008) *Lillian Wald: A biography*, Chapel Hill, NC: The University of North Carolina Press, p 35; Cross, C. (ed) (1989) *Lillian D. Wald: Progressive activist*, New York: The Feminist Press, pp 9–10.

38 Rathbone, E. F. (1938) *War can be averted*, London: Victor Gollancz Ltd.
39 Pedersen, S. (2004) 'Rathbone, Eleanor Florence (1872–1946)', *Oxford Dictionary of National Biography*, Oxford: Oxford University Press; Pedersen, S. (2004) *Eleanor Rathbone and the politics of conscience*, New Haven, CT and London: Yale University Press.
40 Bondfield, M. (1948) *A life's work*, London: Hutchinson & Co. Ltd, p 75.
41 Boyd, N. (2014) *Animal rights and public wrongs: A biography of Lizzy Lind-af-hageby*, US: CreateSpace.
42 Jensen, M. M. (2004) 'Roper, Esther Gertrude (1868–1938)', *Oxford Dictionary of National Biography*, Oxford: Oxford University Press.
43 Oldfield, S. (1984) *Spinsters of this parish: The life and times of F. M. Mayor and Mary Sheepshanks*, London: Virago, p 195.
44 Mulley, C. (2009) *The woman who saved the children: A biography of Eglantyne Jebb, founder of Save the Children*, Oxford: Oneworld Publications, pp 100, 116, 124, 130, 132.
45 Jennings, R. (2007) *A lesbian history of Britain*, Oxford: Greenwood World Publishing, p 101.
46 Dyhouse, C. (2006) *Students: A gendered history*, Abingdon: Routledge, p 71.
47 http://www.brightonourstory.co.uk/newsletters/winter02/illusion.htm.
48 Davis, A. E. L. (2004) 'Hardcastle, Frances (1866–1941)', *Oxford Dictionary of National Biography*, Oxford: Oxford University Press.
49 Martindale, L. (1951) *A woman surgeon*, London: Victor Gollancz, p 228.
50 Pye, E. M. (ed) (1956) *War and its aftermath. Letters from Hilda Clark*, London: Friends Book House, p 5.
51 Pye, *War and its aftermath*, H. Clark to E. Pye, 21 September 1938, p 117.
52 Collette, C. (1989) *For labour and for women: The Women's Labour League, 1906–1916*, Manchester: Manchester University Press.
53 Dyhouse, C. (1998) 'Driving ambitions: women in pursuit of a medical education, 1890–1939', *Women's History Review*, 7 (3): 321–43.
54 Youngran, J. (2004) 'Murrell, Christine Mary (1874–1933)', *Oxford Dictionary of National Biography*, Oxford: Oxford University Press.
55 Morrell, C. (1997) 'Octavia Hill and women's networks in housing', in Digby, A. and Stewart, J. (eds) *Gender, health and welfare*, London: Routledge, pp 91–121.
56 Morrell, 'Octavia Hill', p 109.
57 Hamer, E. (1996) *Britannia's glory: A history of twentieth-century lesbians*, London: Cassell, p 56; Kisby, A. (2014) 'Vera "Jack" Holme: cross-dressing actress, suffragette and chauffeur', *Women's History Review*, 23 (1): 120–36, p 127.
58 Kisby, 'Vera "Jack" Holme'.
59 http://www.new.llangollen.org.uk/history/georgian-llangollen/item/41-monument-to-mary-carryl-the-ladies-of-llangollen/41-monument-to-mary-carryl-the-ladies-of-llangollen.html; Gordon, M. (1936) *Chase of the wild goose: The story of Lady Eleanor Butler and Miss Sarah Ponsonby, known as the Ladies of Llangollen*, London: Hogarth Press. See Smith, M. F. (2016)

Notes

'Virginia Woolf and "the Hermaphrodite": a feminist fan of Orlando and critic of Roger Fry', *English Studies*, 97 (3): 277–97, p 281.

60 Fisher, J. (1971) *That Miss Hobhouse*, London: Secker & Warburg, p 33; Balme, J. H. (2015) *Agent of peace: Emily Hobhouse and her courageous attempt to end the First World War*, Stroud: The History Press, p 108.

61 Mattis, A. (2010) '"Vulgar strangers in the home": Charlotte Perkins Gilman and modern servitude', *Women's Studies*, 39: 283–303.

62 Bell, F. E. E. (1907) *At the works: A study of a manufacturing town*, London: Edward Arnold.

63 Bell, F. and Robins, E. (1893) *Alan's wife: A dramatic study in three scenes*, London: Henry & Co.

64 Kelly, K. E. (2004) '*Alan's wife*: mother love and theatrical sociability in London of the 1890s', *Modernism/modernity*, 11 (3) 539–60.

65 Gates, J. E. (1994) *Elizabeth Robins, 1862–1952*, Tuscaloosa, AL and London: The University of Alabama Press.

66 Wiley, C. (1990) 'Staging infanticide: the refusal of representation in Elizabeth Robins' *Alan's wife*', *Theatre Journal*, 42 (4): 432–46, p 437.

67 John, A.V. (2007) *Elizabeth Robins: Staging a life*, Stroud: Tempus Publishing Limited, p 123.

68 Garland, H. and Garland, M. (1997) 'Helene Lange', in *The Oxford Companion to German Literature*, Oxford: Oxford University Press.

69 Rupp, L. J. (1997) 'Sexuality and politics in the early twentieth century: the case of the international women's movement', *Feminist Studies*, 23 (3): 577–605, p 582.

70 Rupp, 'Sexuality and politics', p 583.

71 Oldfield, *Spinsters of this parish*, pp 154–5.

72 Twellmann, M. (ed) (1972) *Erlebtes-Erschautes. Deutsche Frauen kämpfen für Freiheit, Recht und Frieden 1850–1940* (*Living and perceiving. German women fight for freedom, justice and peace*), Meisenheim am Glan, Germany: Anton Hain Verlag; see Duelli-Klein, R. (1982) 'Accounts of "first wave" feminism in Germany by German feminists', *Women's Studies International Forum*, 5 (6): 691–6.

73 Stoehr, I. (1991) 'Housework and motherhood: debates and politics in the women's movement in Imperial Germany and the Weimar Republic', in Bock, G. and Thane, P. (eds) *Maternity and gender policies: Women and the rise of the European welfare states, 1880s–1950*, London and New York: Routledge, pp 213–22.

74 Braker, R. (2001) 'Helene Stöcker's pacifism in the Weimar Republic: between ideal and reality', *Journal of Women's History*, 13 (3): 70–97.

75 Allen, A.T. (1985) 'Mothers of the new generation: Adele Schreiber, Helene Stöcker, and the evolution of a German idea of motherhood, 1900–1914', *SIGNS*, 10 (3): 418–38; Hackett, A. (1984) 'Helene Stöcker: left wing intellectual and sex reformer', in Bridenthal, R., Grossman, A. and Kaplan, M. (eds) *When biology became destiny: Women in Weimar and Nazi Germany*, New York: Monthly Review Press, pp 109–30.

[76] Volcansek, M. L. and DeWitt, L. (1996) 'Helene Stöcker', in Salokar, R. M. and Volcansek, M. L. (eds) *Women in law: A bio-bibliographical sourcebook*, Westport, CT: Greenwood Press, pp 299–303, p 300.

[77] Anthony, K. (1916) *Feminism in Germany and Scandinavia*, London: Constable & Company Ltd, p 88.

[78] Key, E. K. S. (1909) *The century of the child*, New York: Putnam.

[79] Allen, A. T. (1991) *Feminism and motherhood in Germany, 1800–1914*, New Brunswick, NJ: Rutgers University Press, p 139. Although Marianne Weber wrote widely on the law, marriage and women's situation, it's a telling comment on her reputation that only her biography of her husband has been translated into English. See Lengermann, P. M. and Niebrugge, G. (1998) *The women founders: Sociology and social theory 1830–1930*, Long Grove, IL: Waveland Press, Inc., chapter 6.

[80] Scaff, L. A. (1998) 'The "cool objectivity of sociation": Max Weber and Marianne Weber in America', *History of the Human Sciences*, 11 (2): 61–82, 43, 45.

[81] Weber, M. (1912) 'Authority and autonomy in marriage', in *Selections from Marianne Weber's reflections on women and women's issues*, trans. Kirchen, E., cited in Lengermann and Niebrugge, *The women founders*, p 212; Weber, Max (1930, trans. T. Parsons) *The Protestant ethic and the spirit of capitalism*, London: George Allen & Unwin Ltd.

[82] Cited in Roth, G. (1988) 'Marianne Weber and her circle: Introduction', in Weber, M., trans. and ed. Zohn, H. (1988, first published in German 1926) *Max Weber: A biography*, New Brunswick, NJ and London: Transaction Publishers, pp xv–lxi, xl; see also Adair-Toteff, C. (2011) 'The famous Weber', *Contemporary Sociology*, 40 (6): 675–7.

[83] Linklater, A. (1980) *An unhusbanded life: Charlotte Despard, suffragette, socialist and Sinn Feiner*, London: Hutchinson, p 172.

[84] Linklater, *An unhusbanded life*, pp 99–100.

[85] Mulvihill, M. (1989) *Charlotte Despard: A biography*, London: Pandora, p 2.

[86] Linklater, *An unhusbanded life*, p 108.

[87] Mulvihill, *Charlotte Despard*, p 86.

[88] Liddington, J. and Crawford, E. (2011) '"Women do not count, neither shall they be counted": suffrage, citizenship and the battle for the 1911 Census', *History Workshop Journal*, 71 (1): 98–127.

[89] Linklater, *An unhusbanded life*, p 170.

[90] Cousins, J. and Cousins, M. (1950) *We two together*, Madras: Ganesh, p 170.

[91] Anthony, *Feminism in Germany and Scandinavia*, p 60.

[92] Lane, A. J. (ed) (1981) *The Charlotte Perkins Gilman Reader*, London: The Women's Press, p 205.

[93] Gilman, C. P. (2002, Hill, M. R. and Deegan, M. J. (eds) first published 1915), *The dress of women: A critical introduction to the symbolism and sociology of clothing*, Westport, CT: Greenwood Press, p 31.

[94] Dyhouse, C. (1998) 'Driving ambitions: women in pursuit of a medical education, 1890–1939', *Women's History Review*, 7 (3): 321–43, pp 331, 336.

95 Cockin, K. (2004) 'Craig, Edith Ailsa Geraldine (1869–1947)', *Oxford Dictionary of National Biography*, Oxford: Oxford University Press.

96 Bell, A. O. (ed) *The diary of Virginia Woolf, vol. 2 1920–1924*, New York and London: Harcourt Brace Jovanovich, 30 March 1922, p 174.

97 Cited in Glendinning, V. (1983) *Vita: The life of Vita Sackville-West*, London: Weidenfeld and Nicolson, pp 250–1.

98 Troubridge, U.V. (1961) *The life and death of Radclyffe Hall*, London: Hammond.

99 Bell, A. O. (ed) (1982) *The diary of Virginia Woolf, vol. 4 1931–1935*, New York and London: Harcourt Brace Jovanovich, 16 March 1931, p 13, and 4 February 1931, p 9.

100 http://www.findagrave.com/memorial/184/carrie-chapman-catt.

101 Royden, M. (1948) *A threefold cord*, New York: The Macmillan Company, p 15.

102 M. Royden to K. Courtney, 10 May 1905, 22 December 1900 and 5 April 1900, Maude Royden Papers, Lady Margaret Hall, Oxford, MMP/3/1/1.

103 C. C. Catt to A. Jacobs, 26 February 1913, Papers Carrie Chapman Catt, Collection IAV, Atria, Institute on Gender Equality and Women's History, Amsterdam.

104 A. Jacobs to C. C. Catt, 23 October 1928 and 28 May 1929, Papers Carrie Chapman Catt, Collection IAV, Atria, Institute on Gender Equality and Women's History, Amsterdam.

105 Cited in Faderman, *Odd girls and twilight lovers*, p 26.

106 Cross, *Lillian D. Wald*, p 8.

107 Whitelaw, *Cicely Hamilton*, pp 113–14.

108 Hill, M. A. (ed) (1995) *A journey from within: The love letters of Charlotte Perkins Gilman, 1897–1900*, Lewisburg, PA: Bucknell University Press, p 246.

109 See Vicinus, M. (2004) *Intimate friends: Women who loved women, 1778–1928*, Chicago, IL and London: University of Chicago Press.

110 Wilson, F. (1976) *Dame Kathleen Courtney*, Kathleen Courtney Papers, Lady Margaret Hall, Oxford, MMP/3/2/1, p 18.

111 Davis, A. F. (1973) *American heroine: The life and legend of Jane Addams*, New York: Oxford University Press, p 306.

112 Davis, K. B. (1929) *Factors in the sex life of twenty-two hundred women*, New York: Harper & Brothers; see Francis, M. (1996) '"For this girl was my grand passion" … Reinterpreting the first large scale survey of women's sexuality in America (1929)', *Canadian Woman Studies/Cahiers de la Femme*, 16 (2): 36–41.

113 Davis, *Factors in the sex life*, Appendix II 'A comparison of the questionnaire with the personal-interview method in research involving matters of sex'. For a more modern discussion of this issue, see Oakley, A., Rajan, L. and Robertson, P. (1990) 'A comparison of different sources of information on pregnancy and childbirth', *Journal of Biosocial Science*, 22: 477–87.

114 Bartley, P. (2002) *Emmeline Pankhurst*, London: Routledge, p 195; http://1914–1918.invisionzone.com/forums/.index.php?/topic/102079-dr-mary-louisa-gordon/.

[115] Women's Labour League (1912) *The needs of little children: Report of a conference on the care of babies and young children*, London: Women's Labour League.

[116] Ravenhill, A. (1909) 'Some results of an investigation into hours of sleep among children in the elementary schools of England', *Child Study*, (1): 116–22.

[117] Gilman, C. P. (2003, first published 1900) *Concerning children*, Walnut Creek, CA: AltaMira Press, pp 119–20.

[118] Gilman, C. P. (1903) *The home: Its work and influence*, New York: McClure, Phillips & Co., p 71.

[119] Gilman, *Concerning children*, p 67.

[120] Cited in Mahood, L. (2009) *Feminism and voluntary action: Eglantyne Jebb and Save the Children, 1876–1928*, Houndmills, Basingtoke: Palgrave Macmillan, p 1.

[121] Mulley, *The woman who saved the children*, p 213.

[122] Keynes, J. M. (1919) *The economic consequences of the peace*, London: Macmillan & Co; Mulley, *The woman who saved the children*, p 225.

[123] Muckle, J. (1990) 'Saving the Russian children: materials in the Archive of the Save the Children Fund relating to Eastern Europe in 1920–33', *The Slavonic and East European Review*, 68 (3): 507–11.

[124] Mulley, *The woman who saved the children*, p 301.

[125] Mulley, *The woman who saved the children*, p 313.

[126] Mulley, *The woman who saved the children*, pp 303, 274.

[127] Lind-af-Hageby (1924) *Be peacemakers: An appeal to women of the twentieth century to remove the causes of war*, London: The A. K. Press, pp 45–6.

[128] Kay, H. (2012) 'Chrystal Macmillan: from Edinburgh woman to global citizen', *Deportate, Esuli, Profughe* (18–19): 125–52, p 132.

[129] Addams, J., Balch, E. G. and Hamilton, A. (2003, first published 1915) *Women at The Hague: The International Congress of Women and its results*, Urbana and Chicago, IL: Chicago University Press, Appendix 3, p 76.

[130] WILPF (1919) *Towards peace and freedom: The women's international congress. Zürich. May 12th–17th*, London: British section of the WILPF.

[131] Minutes of the Conference at The Hague December 7th to 10th 1922, p 268, WILPF Papers, The Women's Library, British Library of Political and Economic Science, WILPF/4/7.

[132] Howlett, C. F. (2009) 'American School Peace League and the first peace studies curriculum', *Encyclopedia of peace education*, Teachers' College, Columbia University http://www/tc.edu/centers/epe.

[133] http://publicdomainreview.org/2012/01/11/selma-lagerlof-surface-and-depth/; Ulvros, E. H. (2001) *Sophie Elkan: Hennes liv och vänskapen med Selma Lägerlof*, Lund, Sweden: Historiska Media.

[134] Harris, I. M. (1988) *Peace education*, London: McFarland, p 105.

[135] Zeiger, S. (2000) 'Teaching peace: lessons from a peace studies curriculum of the Progressive Era', *Peace & Change*, 25 (1) 53–70, pp 56–61.

[136] Mead, L. A. (1912) *Swords and ploughshares or The supplanting of the system of war by the system of law*, New York: G. P. Putnam's Sons, pp 155–7.

[137] Howlett, C. F. (2009) 'Lucia Ames Mead: publicist for peace education in the United States', *Encyclopedia of peace education*, Teachers' College, Columbia University http://www/tc.edu/centers/epe.

[138] Clapperton, J. H. (1885) *Scientific meliorism and the evolution of happiness*, London: Kegan Paul, Trench & Co.

[139] den Otter, S. M. (2004) 'Clapperton, Jane Hume (1832–1914)', *Oxford Dictionary of National Biography*, Oxford: Oxford University Press.

[140] Clapperton, *Scientific meliorism*, p 279.

[141] Clapperton, J. H. (1894, first published 1888) *Margaret Dunmore; Or, a socialist home*, London: Swan Sonnenschein & Co; for a discussion see Parkins, W. (2011) 'Domesticating socialism and the senses in Jane Hume Clapperton's *Margaret Dunmore; Or, a socialist home*', *Victoriographies*, 1 (2): 261–86; Suksang, D. (1992) 'Equal partnership: Jane Hume Clapperton's evolutionist-socialist utopia', *Utopian studies*, 3 (1): 95–107.

[142] Creedon, A. (2006) *'Only a woman': Henrietta Barnett, social reformer and founder of Hampstead Garden Suburb*, Chichester: Phillimore & Co Ltd, p 154.

[143] Barnett, H. (1930) *Matters that matter*, London: John Murray, 'The garden suburb, address on "Problems of reconstruction" delivered at the Summer School held at the Institute in the Hampstead Garden Suburb, August, 1917', p 135, original emphasis.

[144] Barnett, *Matters that matter*, 'The ethics of housing', December 1925, p 127.

[145] 'Humane slaughter of animals for England', *The Spectator*, 27 October 1928, p 17.

[146] Creedon, *'Only a woman'*, p 141.

[147] Sanderson Furniss, A. D. and Phillips, M. (1920) *The working woman's house*, London: The Swarthmore Press.

[148] Sanderson Furniss and Phillips, *The working woman's house*, p 57.

[149] Cowman, K. (2015) '"From the housewife's point of view": female citizenship and the gendered domestic interior in post-First World War Britain, 1918–1928', *English Historical Review*, 130 (543): 352–83.

[150] Holton, S. S. (1994) '"To educate women into rebellion": Elizabeth Cady Stanton and the creation of a transatlantic network of radical suffragists', *The American Historical Review*, 99 (4): 1112–36, p 1118.

[151] DuBois, E. (1986) 'Spanning two centuries: the autobiography of Nora Stanton Barney', *History Workshop Journal*, 22 (1): 131–52, p 139.

[152] Barney, N. S. (1944) *World peace through a people's parliament: A second house in world government*, Committee to Win World Peace in a People's Parliament; Barney, N. S. (1946) *Women as human beings*, published privately by the author.

[153] Walpole, B. (2015) 'ASCE recognizes Stanton Blatch Barney; pioneering civil engineer, suffragist', *ASCE News*, 28 August, http://news.asce.org/asce-recognizes-stanton-blatch-barney-pioneering-civil-engineer-suffragist/.

Chapter Eleven

1 https://www.ssa.gov/history/perkins5.html.
2 Pasachoff, N. (1999) *Frances Perkins: Champion of the New Deal*, New York and Oxford: Oxford University Press, p 15.
3 http://francesperkinscenter.org/life-new/.
4 Burnier, D. (2008) 'Erased history: Frances Perkins and the emergence of care-centred public administration', *Administration & Society*, 40 (4): 403–22.
5 Perkins, F. (1934) *People at work*, New York: The John Day Company, p 286.
6 http://francesperkinscenter.org/life-new/.
7 Downey, K. (2009) *The woman behind the New Deal: The life of Frances Perkins, FDR's Secretary of Labor and his moral conscience*, New York: Doubleday.
8 Seeber, F. M. (1990) 'Eleanor Roosevelt and women in the New Deal: a network of friends', *Presidential Studies Quarterly*, 20 (4): 707–17.
9 Torres, C. (2016) 'Women's network behind Frances Perkins' appointment', *Revista de Estudios Norteamericanos*, 19: 151–66, p 161.
10 Seeber, 'Eleanor Roosevelt and women', p 709.
11 Roosevelt, E. (1937) *This is my story*, New York: Harper & Row; Webb, B. (1979, first published 1926) *My apprenticeship*, Cambridge: Cambridge University Press, pp 321–2; Steel, D. A. 'Souvestre, Marie Claire (1835–1905)', *Oxford Dictionary of National Biography*, Oxford: Oxford University Press. Dorothy Strachey Bussy's famous novel *Olivia* (1949, London: The Hogarth Press) was an anonymously published account of a lesbian relationship between a student and a teacher, based on Strachey's time in Souvestre's schools.
12 Streitmatter, R. (ed) (1998) *'Empty without you': The intimate letters of Eleanor Roosevelt and Lorena Hickok*, New York: The Free Press.
13 Ware, S. (1987) *Partner and I: Molly Dewson, feminism, and New Deal politics*, New Haven, CT and London: Yale University Press, p xv.
14 Streitmatter, 'Empty without you'.
15 http://firstladieslibrary.org/biographies/firstladies.aspx?biography.
16 Roosevelt, Mrs F. D. (1933) *It's up to the women*, New York: Frederick A. Stokes Company.
17 Roosevelt, E. (1949) *This I remember*, New York: Harper & Bros, p 7.
18 Daniels, D. G. (1996) 'Theodore Roosevelt and gender roles', *Presidential Studies Quarterly*, 26 (3): 648–65, p 655. The result was a nineteen-volume report (United States Congress (1911) *Report on the condition of women and child wage earners in the United States*, Washington, DC: Government Printing Office).
19 Press, J. (2009) 'Frances Kellor, Americanization, and the quest for participatory democracy', PhD thesis, New York University.
20 Cited in Gustafson, M. (1997) 'Partisan women in the Progressive Era: the struggle for inclusion in American political parties', *Journal of Women's History*, 9 (2): 8–30, p 17.
21 Testi, S. (1995) 'The gender of reform politics: Theodore Roosevelt and the culture of masculinity', *The Journal of American History*, 81 (4): 1909–33.

22 See Thane, P. (1996) *Foundations of the welfare state*, London and New York: Longman, p 283.

23 Chambon, A., Johnstone, M. and Köngeter, S. (2015) 'The circulation of knowledge and practices across national borders in the early twentieth century: a focus on social reform organisations', *European Journal of Social Work*, 18 (4): 495–510. See also Stewart, J. (2014) 'Healthcare systems in Britain and Ireland in the nineteenth and twentieth centuries: the national, international and sub-national contexts', in Lucey, D. S. and Crossman, V. (eds) *Healthcare in Ireland and Britain from 1850: Voluntary, regional and comparative perspectives*, London: Institute of Historical Research, pp 61–78.

24 Gerth, H. and Wright Mills, C. (trans. and eds) (1947) *From Max Weber: Essays in sociology*, London: Kegan Paul, Trench, Trubner & Co Ltd, p 78.

25 Skocpol, T. (1992) *Protecting soldiers and mothers: The political origins of social policy in the United States*, Cambridge, MA and London: The Belknap Press of Harvard University Press; Sarvasy, W. (1997) 'Social citizenship from a feminist perspective', *Hypatia*, 12 (4): 54–73; Gordon, L. (ed) (1990) *Women, the state and welfare*, Madison, WI: University of Wisconsin Press.

26 Sarvasy, W. (1992) 'Beyond the difference versus equality policy debate: postsuffrage feminism, citizenship, and the quest for a feminist welfare state', *SIGNS*, 17 (2): 329–62, p 354.

27 Modern welfare regimes all to some extent subscribe to this male breadwinner model, although there are differences in the way they accommodate women both as unpaid carers and as paid workers. See Lewis, J. (1992) 'Gender and the development of welfare regimes', *Journal of European Social Policy*, 2 (3): 159–73.

28 Nutley, S., Davies, H. and Walter, I. (2002) *Evidence based policy and practice: Cross sector lessons from the UK*, London: ESRC UK Centre for Evidence Based Policy and Practice.

29 Kellor, K. (1914) 'A new spirit in party organization', *The North American Review*, 199 (703): 879–92, pp 884, 883, 880.

30 *The Progressive National Service, a Department of the Progressive Party: What it is, what it does, what it means to you* [n.d.] p 6.

31 Press, 'Frances Kellor'.

32 Daniels, 'Theodore Roosevelt', p 661.

33 Bederman, G. (1995) *Manliness and civilization: A cultural history of gender and race in the United States, 1880–1917*, Chicago, IL and London: University of Chicago Press.

34 Kellor, F. A. (1948) *American arbitration: Its history, functions and achievements*, New York: Harper & Bros; see Partridge, S. K. (2012) 'Frances Kellor and the American Arbitration Association', *Dispute Resolution Journal*, February/April: 17–21.

35 Rupp, L. J. (1997) *Worlds of women: The making of an international women's movement*, Princeton, NJ: Princeton University Press; Sharp, I. and Stibbe, M. (2017) 'Women's international activism during the interwar period, 1919–1939', *Women's History Review*, 26 (2): 163–72.

36 Report of the Third Congress of the Women's International League for Peace and Freedom (1921) Vienna, 10-17 July, p 86.

37 Sklar, K. K, Schüler, A. and Strasser, S. (eds) (1998) *Social justice feminists in the United States and Germany: A dialogue in documents, 1885–1933*, New York: Cornell University Press, p 341.

38 Letter from R. Schwimmer to L. M. Lloyd, 14 October 1930, cited in Mcfadden, M. H. (2011) 'Borders, boundaries, and the necessity of reflexivity: international women activists, Rosika Schwimmer (1877–1948), and the shadow narrative', *Women's History Review*, 20 (4): 533–42, p 538.

39 Wernitznig, D. (2015) "'It is a strange thing not to belong to any country, as is my case now". Fascism, refugees, statelessness, and Rosika Schwimmer (1877–1948)', *Deportate, Esuli, Profughe*, 27: 102–8, p 103.

40 See Bussey, G. and Tims, M. (1980) *Pioneers for peace: Women's International League for Peace and Freedom 1915–1965*, London: WILPF.

41 M. Royden to the Duke of Edinburgh, 14 May 1956, copy to Mrs Pandit, Royden Papers, The Women's Library, British Library of Political and Economic Science, 7AMR/1/12/2.

42 Crease, M. R. S. (1998) *Ladies in the laboratory: American and British women in science, 1800–1900*, Lanham, MD and London: The Scarecrow Press Inc., p 142.

43 Ravenhill, A. (1938) *The native tribes of British Columbia*, Victoria, BC: C. F. Banfield; Ravenhill, A. (1944) *A corner stone of Canadian culture: An outline of the arts and crafts of the Indian tribes of British Columbia*, Victoria, BC: British Columbia Provincial Museum.

44 See Wan, L. (2013) 'A nation of artists: Alice Ravenhill and the BC Society for the Furtherance of British Columbia Indian Arts and Crafts', *BC Studies*, 178: 51–70.

45 Innes, S. (2004) 'Atkinson, Mabel (1876–1958)', *Oxford Dictionary of National Biography*, Oxford: Oxford University Press.

46 Vietzen, S. (2010) 'Beyond school: some developments in higher education in Durban in the 1920s and the influence of Mabel Palmer', *Natalia*, 14: 48–58.

47 Jensen, K. (2017) 'War, transnationalism and medical women's activism: the Medical Women's International Association and the Women's Foundation for Health in the aftermath of the First World War', *Women's History Review*, 26 (2): 213–28.

48 Blanchard, P. (1919) 'Impressions of the psychological sessions of the International Conference of Women Physicians', *The Pedagogical Seminary*, 26 (4): 391–8, p 393.

49 Anon. (1920) *Proceedings of the International Conference of Women Physicians*, New York: The Women's Press, 6 vols.

50 von Oertzen, C. (2014) *Science, gender, and internationalism: Women's academic networks, 1917–1955*, New York: Palgrave Macmillan.

51 von Oertzen, *Science, gender and internationalism*, p 27.

52 http://www.columbia.edu/cu/alumni/Magazine/Summer2001/Gildersleeve.html.

53 Carlson, B. (2007) 'The IRI and its Swedish connection (International Industrial Relations Institute)', *American Studies in Scandinavia*, 39 (1): 13–32, p 14.

54 van Kleeck, M. (1919) 'The task of working women in the international working women's movement', cited in Oldenziel, R. (2000) 'Gender and scientific management: women and the history of the International Institute of Industrial Relations, 1922–1926', *Journal of Management History*, 6 (7): 323–42.

55 van Kleeck, M. (1934) 'Our illusions regarding government', *The Compass*, 15 (9): 10–12, p 11.

56 Casebeer, K. M. (1994) 'Unemployment insurance: American social wage labor organization and legal ideology', *Boston College Law Review*, 35 (2): 295–9.

57 Jordan, J. M. (1994) *Machine-age ideology: Social engineering and American liberalism, 1911–1939*, Chapel Hill, NC and London: The University of North Carolina Press, p 193.

58 Alchon, G. (1998) 'The "self-applauding sincerity" of overarching theory, biography as ethical practice and the case of Mary van Kleeck', in Silverberg, H. (ed) *Engendering social science: The formative years*, Princeton, NJ: Princeton University Press, pp 293–325, p 309.

59 Selmi, P. and Hunter, R. (2001) 'Beyond the rank and file movement: Mary van Kleeck and social work radicalism in the Great Depression, 1931–1942', *Journal of Sociology and Social Welfare*, 28 (?): 75–100.

60 Carlson, 'The IRI and its Swedish connection'.

61 Alchon, G. (1991) 'Mary van Kleeck and social-economic planning', *Journal of Policy History*, 3 (1): 1–23.

62 See Delegard, K. M. (2012) *Battling Miss Bolshevik: The origins of female conservatism in the United States*, Philadelphia, PA: University of Pennsylvania Press, chapter 5. This rumour apparently stemmed from a Children's Bureau publication on maternity benefit systems referring to the most comprehensive study of maternity benefits and insurance done anywhere to date by Mme A. Kollantai.

63 Nielsen, K. E. (2001) *Un-American womanhood: Antiradicalism, antifeminism, and the first red scare*, Columbus, OH: Ohio State University Press, p 83.

64 Catt, C. C. (1927) 'An open letter to the D. A. R.', *The Woman Citizen*, 10–12: 41–2.

65 Daughters of the American Revolution (1927) 'Doubtful speakers', The records of the WILPF, U.S. Section, Swarthmore College Peace Collection, reel 42, #826–8.

66 Sharp, I. (2013) 'Feminist peace activism 1915 and 2010: are we nearly there yet?' *Peace & Change*, 38 (2): 155–80, p 162.

67 Wenger, B. S. (1990) 'Radical politics in a reactionary age: The unmaking of Rosika Schwimmer, 1914–1930', *Journal of Women's History*, 2 (2): 66–99.

68 Wernitznig, D. (2017) 'Out of her time? Rosika Schwimmer's transnational activism after the First World War', *Women's History Review*, 26 (2): 262–79.

69 Pastor, P. (1974) 'The diplomatic fiasco of the modern world's first woman ambassador, Róza Bédy-Schwimmer', *East European Quarterly*, VIII (3): 273–82, p 278.

70 Hazard, H. B. (1929) 'Supreme Court holds Madam Schwimmer, pacifist, ineligible to naturalization', *The American Journal of International Law*, 23 (3): 626–32, p 629.

71 Wenger, 'Radical politics', p 88.

72 Lloyd, L. M. and Schwimmer, R. (1942) *Chaos, war, or a new world order: What we must do to establish the all-inclusive, non-military, democratic federation of nations*, Chicago, IL: Campaign for World Government.

73 Schwimmer was nominated for the Nobel Peace Prize in 1948 but she died that year, and the Committee found no suitable living candidate for the award.

Chapter Twelve

1 Spender, D. (1982) *Women of ideas, and what men have done to them*, London: Routledge & Kegan Paul, p 15.

2 Sharp, I. (2013) 'Feminist peace activism 1915 and 2010: are we nearly there yet?' *Peace & Change*, 38 (2): 155–80, pp 172–4.

3 The more refined modern version of this manoeuvre is the term 'social maternalism', which deftly reconfines women intellectuals and activists to the home.

4 Rowbotham, S. (2011) *Dreamers of a new day: Women who invented the twentieth century*, London: Verso.

5 Westhoff, L. M. (2009) 'Gender and the exclusionary politics of social knowledge: men and women in the civic federation of Chicago', *Women's History Review*, 18 (1): 23–44; Leppänen, K. (2005) *Rethinking civilization in a European context*, Göteborg, Sweden: Acta Universitatis Gothoburgensis.

6 Burdett, C. (2011) 'Is empathy the end of sentimentality?' *Journal of Victorian Culture*, 16 (2): 259–74.

7 Morgan, B. (2012) 'Critical empathy: Vernon Lee's aesthetics and origins of close reading', *Victorian Studies*, 55 (1): 31–56, p 37.

8 Burdett, 'Is empathy the end of sentimentality?' p 268.

9 Beer, G. (1997) 'The dissidence of Vernon Lee: Satan the Waster and the will to believe', in Raitt, S. and Tate, T. (eds) *Women's fiction and the Great War*, Oxford: Clarendon Press, pp 107–31, p 107.

10 Follett, M. P. (1918) *The new state: Group organization, the solution for popular government*, New York: Longman, Green and Company. See Tonn, J. C. (2003) *Mary Parker Follett: Creating democracy, transforming management*, New Haven, CT and London: Yale University Press.

11 Phillips, J. R. (2010) 'Scholarship and public service: the life and work of Mary Parker Follett', *Public Voices*, 11 (2): 47–69.

12 Follett, *The new state*, p 194.

13 Follett, *The new state*, p 346.

Notes

[14] Feldheim, M. A. (2004) 'Mary Parker Follet: lost and found – again, and again, and again', *International Journal of Organizational Theory and Behavior*, 6 (4): 341–62.

[15] https://www.thoughtco.com/mary-parker-follett-biography-3528601.

[16] https://www.thoughtco.com/mary-parker-follett-biography-3528601.

[17] The study of network history is sadly managing to repeat the theme of omitting the women. Daniel Rodgers' *Atlantic crossings: Social politics in a progressive age* (1998, Cambridge, MA and London: The Belknap Press of Harvard University Press) says virtually nothing about the women; his index entry for 'Women' says 'see under social maternalism'. Thomas Adam's *Buying respectability: Philanthropy and urban society in transnational perspective, 1840s to 1930s* (2009, Bloomington, IN: Indiana University Press) has no reference to Jane Addams; the women reformers appear in a chapter entitled 'Beautiful ladies'.

[18] Cited in Diner, S. J. (1977) 'Scholarship in the quest for social welfare: a fifty-year history of the Social Service Review', *Social Service Review*, 51: 1–66, p 11.

[19] Coghlan, C. L. (2005) '"Please don't think of me as a sociologist": Sophonisba Breckinridge and the early Chicago School', *The American Sociologist*, 36 (1): 3–22.

[20] Harvey, L. (1987) *Myths of the Chicago School*, Farnborough: Avebury, p 31.

[21] Deegan, M. J. (1990) *Jane Addams and the men of the Chicago School, 1892–1918*, New Brunswick, NJ: Transaction Books, p 154.

[22] Deegan, M. J. (1997) 'The Chicago men and the sociology of women', in Plummer, K. (ed) *The Chicago School: Critical assessments*, Vol 1, London: Routledge, pp 198–230.

[23] Deegan, M. J. (1997) 'Hull-House maps and papers: the birth of Chicago sociology', in Plummer, K. (ed) *The Chicago School: Critical assessments*, Vol 11, London: Routledge, pp 5–19; see Shaw, I. (2009) 'Rereading the Jack-Roller: hidden histories in sociology and social work', *Qualitative Inquiry*, 15 (7): 1241–64.

[24] Delamont, S. (1992) 'Old fogies and intellectual women: an episode in academic history', *Women's History Review*, 1 (1): 39–61.

[25] Delamont, 'Old fogies', p 46. See McDonald, L. (1994) *The women founders of the social sciences*, Ottawa, Canada: Carleton University Press.

[26] Bulmer, M. (1996) 'The survey movement and sociological methodology', in Greenwald, M. W. and Anderson, M. (eds) *Pittsburgh surveyed: Social science and social reform in the early twentieth century*, Pittsburgh, PA: University of Pittsburgh Press, pp 15–34, p 22.

[27] Hamilton, C. (2013, first published 1922) *Theodore Savage*, Boston, MA, and Brooklyn, NY: HiLoBooks; republished 1928 as *Lest ye die: A story from the past or of the future*, London: Jonathan Cape.

[28] Cockburn, C. (2007) *From where we stand: War, women's activism and feminist analysis*, London: Zed Books, p 7.

[29] Forsås-Scott, H. (1996) 'The revolution that never was: the example of Elin Wägner', *The European Legacy*, 1 (3): 914–19, p 916.

[30] Cited in Leppänen, *Rethinking civilization*, p 55.

[31] Leppänen, *Rethinking civilization*, p 57.

[32] A copy of Askanasy's unfinished book is in The Women's Library at the British Library of Political and Economic Science (7AHA FL643).

[33] Barnett, H. (1930) 'The Toynbee Halls of America', in Barnett, H. (ed) *Matters that matter*, London: John Murray, p 32.

[34] Smyth, E. (1933) *Female pipings in Eden*, London: Peter Davies Limited, p 194.

Index

Page numbers in italic type denote photographs.